Mysteries of the Mind

Great Mysteries

Mysteries of the Mind

by Colin Wilson and Stuart Holroyd

Aldus Books London

Editorial Consultants:
COLIN WILSON
DR. CHRISTOPHER EVANS

Series Coordinator:	John Mason
Design Director:	Günter Radtke
Picture Editor:	Peter Cook
Editors:	Kit Coppard Eleanor Van Zandt
Copy Editor:	Mitzi Bales
Research:	Marian Pullen Sarah Waters
General Consultant:	Beppie Harrison

New Enlarged Edition
SBN: 490 004245

Printed and bound in Yugoslavia by
Mladinska Knjiga, Ljubljana

Introduction

The human mind tantalizes us with its mysteries. Science teaches us that our world functions according to natural laws, immutable and unchanging. Yet in ordinary experience there are coincidences and unexplained happenings which seem to challenge this orthodox position. Some happen at moments of crisis—at the point of death or severe danger—when mind seems to speak directly to mind, often across vast distances. Others happen in the everyday world, as when you think of a friend and the telephone rings, and there is his voice, as if you had actually summoned him. Or a dream turns out to foreshadow an actual event. What can we make of these mysterious events, when our minds appear to have ranged far beyond the bodies which (we are taught) so rigidly encase them?

Even more extraordinary are the men and women of strange powers. They can be traced all through history. In some societies they are treated as honored wise ones; in our rational, Western world they are more often met with curiosity, suspicion, and fear.

What can we learn about ourselves from these people of wild talents? Is there a scientific way to measure their abilities? Is the world of our minds far stranger than we can begin to guess? The evidence is enigmatic and intriguing.

Contents

Chapter 1 Wild Talents

In our rational, scientific world, do people exist who are capable of mysterious feats? What do we know, for all our science, of the energies within our minds? There are many well-authenticated accounts of strange happenings we cannot explain by the natural laws which we believe govern our universe. Are these stories then fakes, or is it possible that there is a dimension of existence which we have not yet recognized? There seems to be evidence that telepathy is possible, that mind can speak directly to mind. Poltergeist activity apparently indicates that mind can act directly on matter. What can we learn from these strange abilities?

Few of us would flatly deny that the universe is a stranger place than the generally accepted natural laws can account for. Most of the time we choose not to think about it. When we discover that some people appear to have strange powers, powers that apparently enable them to ignore the normal physical laws that contain the rest of us, we prefer not to think about that either because we have no easy explanation. It makes life more complicated, and it is a subtle threat to our own sense of safety in a known world. When we do think about it we hunt for the trick, the deception, the proof that everything is as we would like it to be so that we can return, safely, to not thinking about it. But these wild talents tug at our sleeves, whisper in our ears. Throughout all recorded history people have been fascinated and have felt threatened by these unexplained abilities. In our recent history we have conducted complicated tests and formulated sophisticated explanations—and then a young Israeli comes along and stops clocks and bends spoons: trivial accomplishments in themselves, but how do we explain them? Then we find we have started to think about strange powers and extraordinary events.

I met the young Israeli wonder worker Uri Geller one morning in the summer of 1974 in the office of a London business tycoon. The meeting had been arranged with a view to my working on a film about Geller's life. A secretary showed me into the inner office. Uri, a good looking but seemingly quite

Opposite: the Israeli psychic Uri Geller. His hotly disputed control of matter by the power of his mind alone has made him the focus of a great deal of controversy and much scientific speculation.

An Experiment in Telepathy

One of Geller's favorite methods of demonstrating his mind-reading power is to reproduce a simple drawing which has just been done and then hidden from his sight, usually inside a sealed envelope. Above: an experimenter, isolated from Geller in an adjoining room, makes a rough sketch of a chair.

ordinary young man, appeared to be a little nervous or preoccupied. We chatted briefly, after which the three of us went to lunch at a nearby restaurant. We sat at a table in the corner, the woman and I side by side and Uri opposite us with his back to the room. When we had ordered, he offered to try to demonstrate his powers, but said, "I don't know if it will work. Sometimes it doesn't."

We began with an experiment in *telepathy* (the transmission of thoughts by means other than the five senses). Uri handed me one of the restaurant cards on the table and, turning away from me, asked me to make a drawing on its blank side. I made a sketch of a creature I had invented some time ago to amuse my children. It took only a few seconds, as I had drawn it many times before. I glanced at Uri as I did it. He was staring out across the restaurant, and he could not have watched me without being seen to do so by the secretary beside me. When I had finished, he asked me to cover the drawing with my hand. Then he turned back to the table and took another of the cards. He asked me to concentrate hard and to try to transmit the thought of what I had sketched. A minute went by with no result. Uri shook his head. "It seems very complicated; is it a kind of amoeba?" Slowly and hesitantly he began to draw the creature's right ear—the spot where I always begin the drawing. "You've got it," I said. "Go on!" He completed the drawing quickly. I had carefully redrawn the picture in my mind as I tried to transmit it—which probably accounts for the identical starting point.

Uri then demonstrated other powers. He caused a restaurant spoon to bend by stroking it gently. He made the hands of my watch turn back two hours and the date go forward two days by stroking a coin placed over its face, explaining afterward that he derives power from metal. He had a little trouble trying to break my American Automobile Association key. Ideally, he said, the key should have more personal associations. However, he placed it against a metal radiator, and after a few seconds said, "It's starting to go." The key snapped in two.

Finally, he tried to transmit a picture to me by telepathy. I attempted to make my mind receptive, but no image came into it. Feeling rather embarrassed, I just drew the first thing that came into my head: a check mark. Uri showed me the piece of paper he was holding away from me. It contained a mirror image of the symbol I had drawn. It could be significant in this connection that Uri is left-handed.

After I left Uri Geller I immediately began to sift my impressions. Only the day before, a highly skeptical scientist had warned me to watch carefully for conjuring tricks, especially as Uri had earlier been a stage conjuror. I had to admit that most of the things he had done could have been tricks. For instance, snapping the key with his fingers, and altering the hands and date on my watch with the winder would have been well within the ability of a skillful conjuror. But how could he have faked the drawing of what I had drawn? And if that feat was due to genuine telepathic powers, the other demonstrations could also be genuine.

A couple of months after this Ted Bastin, a quantum physicist,

Left: the sketch has been hidden in two sealed envelopes, one inside the other. After he has rejoined Geller, the experimenter holds the envelopes in his hand, and Geller rests his hand on top. Concentrating intently, Geller starts to draw with his other hand.

Above: comparing the two drawings. Geller has succeeded in sketching a chair very similar to the one that the experimenter had drawn.

Left: the blob-like doodle that the author of this book drew, and Geller's reproduction of it, apparently by telepathy. The author's drawing is on the right.

Mind over Metal

and I appeared on a television discussion show about supernormal powers—a subject about which Ted is distinctly skeptical. When I mentioned Uri Geller, however, Ted told me he had conducted extensive tests and was convinced that Uri was genuine. A few days later Ted rang me up to announce that Uri had just performed a most spectacular feat in his laboratory. He had dematerialized half a crystal that had been sealed in a metal container. Bastin said that there was no way in which Uri could have touched the crystal.

Assuming that Uri Geller possesses extraordinary powers, where do they come from? I think the answer must be from his subconscious mind. In recent years psychologists have come to the conclusion that *poltergeists* (ghosts or spirits that make noises or fling objects) originate in the subconscious minds of teenagers who have been seriously disturbed by the problems of adolescence. On the other hand, some investigators believe that poltergeists have a separate existence—that is, that they are real ghosts—but that they have to borrow energy from disturbed adolescents before they can become active. Whatever the truth of the matter, it seems probable that the subconscious mind provides the energy that causes heavy objects to rise and fly across a room or doors to open and bang shut. If this is so, it is reasonable to assume that the energy which causes spoons to bend and broken watches to tick originates in Uri Geller's highly active subconscious mind.

If these strange powers exist in some hidden depths of the mind, what are they doing there? Are they common to all of us, and are they available to anyone who knows how to use them? We may find part of the answer in an experience of John G. Bennett, the foremost living disciple of the remarkable Russian mystic Georgei Gurdjieff.

In 1923 Bennett was at Gurdjieff's Institute for the Harmonious Development of Man at the Prieuré in a suburb of Paris. For some days Bennett had been suffering from almost constant diarrhea, and each morning he felt weaker and found it harder to get up. One morning he woke up shaking with fever, and decided to stay in bed. But in the instant of making this

Right: the snapped handle of a spoon apparently bent by Geller. Skeptics suggest he is only a gifted conjuror who can deftly substitute a previously bent spoon (or fork, or key, or nail, or whatever) for the object he started the demonstration with. It is particularly hard for any observer to keep precise track of where things are at a given moment because Geller works best in what has been described as "rampant confusion"—moving back and forth from one experiment to another, sometimes failing, and then abruptly producing a success.

decision, he found himself getting out of bed and dressing. It felt, he said, as if he was being "held together by a superior Will that was not my own." After a morning's work, he felt too ill to eat lunch. Nonetheless, he joined a dancing class in the afternoon. Gurdjieff's dances involved movements of great complexity, requiring tremendous concentration and physical coordination. As the exercises continued Bennett felt an immense lassitude descend on him. It became agony even to move, but he forced himself to go on. Gurdjieff introduced new exercises which were so complex that the other students began to drop out one by one. Bennett, however, felt Gurdjieff's eyes on him as if commanding him to go on, even if it killed him.

"Suddenly, I was filled with an influx of immense power. My body seemed to have turned into light. I could not feel its presence in the usual ways. There was no effort, no weariness, not even any sense of weight. . . ." When the lesson was over he

Above: the power of mind over metal? Geller and the results of one of his demonstrations.

Above: J. G. Bennett in 1960. He was a disciple of Georgei Gurdjieff and attended the master's institute.

Below: the lime tree grove at the Prieuré, where Gurdjieff set up his institute. It was under these trees that Bennett, while practicing the group exercises, experienced a sudden and great "influx of an immense power."

decided to test the power that had entered his body. He took a spade and began to dig at a rate that would normally have exhausted him in two minutes. In spite of the summer heat, he continued digging for over an hour.

Later Bennett went for a walk toward a nearby forest where he met Gurdjieff. Without preliminaries, Gurdjieff began to talk about energies. "There is a certain energy," he said, "that is necessary for work on oneself . . . we can call it the Higher Emotional Energy. . . . There are some people in the world, but they are very rare, who are connected to the Great Reservoir or Accumulator of this energy. . . ." Gurdjieff implied that he was one of those who can tap the Great Reservoir and permit others to borrow its energy.

Bennett continued his walk in the forest, still filled with a tremendous sense of power. He recalled that Peter Ouspensky, another Russian mystic and associate of Gurdjieff's, had once said that if we wish to prove how little control we have over our emotions, we have only to try to be astonished at will. Bennett said to himself: "I will be astonished." Instantly he felt overwhelmed with amazement. "Each tree was so uniquely itself that I felt that I could walk in the forest forever and never cease from wonderment. Then the thought of 'fear' came to me. At once I was shaking with terror. Unknown horrors were menacing me on every side. I thought of 'joy,' and I felt that my heart would burst from rapture. The word 'love' came to me, and I was pervaded with such fine shades of tenderness and compassion that I saw that I had not the remotest idea of the depth and range of love. Love was everywhere and in everything. It was infinitely adaptable to every shade of need. After a time it became too much for me; it seemed that if I plunged any more deeply into the mystery of love, I would cease to exist. I wanted to be free from this power to feel whatever I chose, and at once it left me."

What is this strange power that Gurdjieff was able to evoke in his disciples? It is not as mysterious as it sounds. We are all familiar with its commonest form, which we call "second wind." In most energetic sports, such as long distance running, we force ourselves beyond the normal point of exhaustion. Then sometimes, quite suddenly, we feel a resurge of energy that enables us to continue for longer than usual. On rare occasions we can even force ourselves to continue until we get our third wind. The American philosopher and psychologist William James wrote about this in his essay "The Energies of Man."

"Everyone is familiar with the phenomenon of feeling more or less alive on different days. Everyone knows on any given day that there are energies slumbering in him which the incitements of that day do not call forth, but which he might display if these were greater. Most of us feel as if a sort of cloud weighed upon us, keeping us below our highest notch of clearness in discernment, sureness in reasoning, or firmness in deciding. Compared with what we ought to be, we are only half awake. Our fires are damped, our drafts are checked. We are making use of only a small part of our possible mental and physical resources."

"Stating the thing broadly, the human individual thus lives

unusually far within his limits; he possesses powers of various sorts which he habitually fails to use. He energizes below his *maximum*, and he behaves below his *optimum*."

In other words, for everyday purposes human beings have certain predetermined limits. It is like the thermostat on a central heating system. When the temperature rises above a certain point it automatically switches off the heating. When our tiredness reaches a certain limit, we also switch off automatically, and allow ourselves to sink into a passive state. But if some crisis arises, we refuse to allow ourselves to remain passive. We become alert and suddenly, as our thermostat readjusts itself, we discover we have become fully alive again.

The implication seems to be that each of us contains a vast reservoir of energy. William James also asks what it is that gives a Leonardo or a Beethoven his creative energy. His answer is excitement, determination, a sense of purpose. He adds: "We live subject to arrest by degrees of fatigue which we have come only from habit to obey. Most of us may learn to push the barrier further off, and to live in perfect comfort on much higher levels of power."

This was the aim of Gurdjieff's work. He forced his students to keep pushing the barriers farther and farther back. One of his followers, Fritz Peters, has described how Gurdjieff gave him the task of mowing the lawns at the Prieuré. At first the work took Peters several days. Gradually Gurdjieff accustomed him to doing more and more in a day until finally Peters could mow all the lawns, which consisted of several acres, in one day. What Gurdjieff called his "dervish dances" were also designed to break the chain of habit. Try rubbing your stomach with one hand while patting yourself on the head with the other, or tapping the toes of one foot on the floor while rubbing the other foot back and forth like a pendulum. Most people find such movements difficult. Yet Gurdjieff trained his students to do something different with feet, arms, and head at the same time. He would also suddenly order them to break off whatever they were doing, and to freeze in some complicated attitude.

As Gurdjieff recognized, even exercises as difficult as these can become a habit. Fritz Peters tells a story which reveals that Gurdjieff himself could forget how to establish contact with his own reservoir of energy. At the end of World War II Peters, then a soldier and suffering from battle fatigue and nervous strain, called on Gurdjieff at his Paris apartment. Gurdjieff was busy and asked Peters to wait for him in another room. After a minute or two alone, Peters felt so miserable and desperate that he interrupted Gurdjieff again. Gurdjieff instantly saw the seriousness of the situation, and set his work aside. As he sat with Gurdjieff, Peters experienced a sudden trickle of power flowing into him like a spring. It slowly increased until all his tiredness had vanished. But Gurdjieff himself now looked completely exhausted. Peters had no doubt that Gurdjieff had somehow given him his own energy. A crowd of people then arrived at the house, and Gurdjieff dragged himself away to entertain them. Five minutes later he returned to the kitchen radiating vitality, and remarked to Peters that the experience had been good for both of them. In

"Higher Levels of Power"

Below: Georgei Gurdjieff, modern cult figure whose system of mental and physical exercises was designed to awaken the latent powers he felt exist in us all.

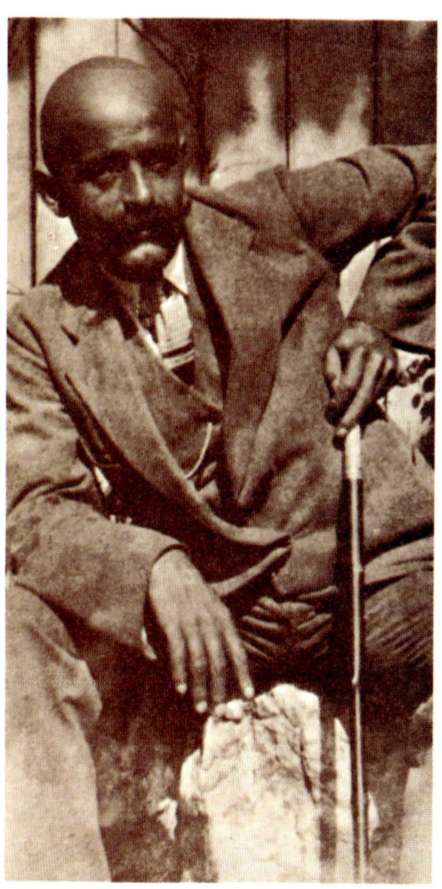

Above: one of Gurdjieff's dances, the Dervish Dance, performed here by Olgivanna Lloyd Wright, Mme. Galoumian and Jeanne de Salzmann. Gurdjieff's dances were designed not only for control of the body, but—by their complicated and demanding patterns—also needed unbroken mental concentration. Thus the ritual movements were meant to act on all aspects of the student's body and mind.
Below: Olgivanna Lloyd Wright, widow of the architect Frank Lloyd Wright, carries on his work through the Taliesin Fellowship. Mrs. Wright, a follower of Gurdjieff's for a time, has incorporated aspects of the Prieuré regime into the life of the community in California. They include hard manual work by all members whether students or staff, the importance of music, and the absolute authority of the leader.

other words, the effort of revitalizing Peters had awakened Gurdjieff to a recognition that he had lost touch with his own "source of power, meaning, and purpose." He promptly re-established contact, and recharged his own batteries.

There is nothing mystical or occult about this. We all have within us a robot, akin to the automatic pilot in an airplane, whose task is to simplify our lives by handling a series of routines. Learning to type or speak French or drive a car requires considerable effort and concentration, but once we have mastered it, our robot takes over and does it far more quickly and efficiently than we could do it consciously. The trouble is, the robot can become so efficient that it takes over most of our life. We begin to live like a robot. We automatically drink our martini, eat our dinner, watch TV. It takes a holiday or some sudden crisis to jar us out of this automatic living, to allow our real selves to take over from the robot.

There can be no doubt that Gurdjieff helped Bennett overcome his fatigue, just as he helped Peters. But at a certain point, Bennett's own inner dynamo took over and he wrested control from his robot. He was suddenly dazzled by vistas of possible feeling. For, like our bodies, our feelings are also controlled by the robot. We seldom experience new feeling. For the most part, we play the same old phonograph record over and over again—a record that, except in times of crisis, is full of bland harmonies. What Bennett had realized was that he could experience new intensities of feeling every day; that he could experience a compelling feeling for every tree and every blade of grass.

Our minds contain a vast unused library of "phonograph records." And not just our minds. The world around us is full of an infinite number of interesting things that the robot has been trained to ignore. This is perhaps the most important insight that arises from Bennett's description of his experience: ". . . I was pervaded with such shades of tenderness and compassion that *I saw that I had not the remotest idea of the depth and range of love*." We accept the universe around us as stable and normal, just as a child who knew nothing about water might accept the surface of a pond as a glittering mirror, unaware that there are green depths below, teeming with innumerable forms of life. How many other things is this true of? How much mystery and complexity and reality is hidden from us by ignorance and habit?

Human beings live within arbitrary limits. Not only do we have an arbitrary idea of our powers and capabilities, but we also have an arbitrary idea of the complexity and interestingness of the world around us. Habit has confined human beings in a thoroughly stale universe.

A word of caution should be offered, however. Why should Bennett get tired of the power to see and feel more widely than ever before? Why does he say: "I wanted to be free from this power to feel whatever I chose . . ."? The reason is that these arbitrary limits to our powers are also safety limits. Our habits, which can become so oppressive, are also intended to protect us. Bennett could have achieved many of the same effects of power and perception by taking a psychedelic drug such as mescalin or LSD. These also destroy the robot and disconnect our habit mechanisms so that the world appears new and strange. Psychedelic drugs also release the capacity to feel whatever we choose—the thought of love can produce a tidal wave of love.

On the other hand, a negative thought produces equally powerful results. One man who had taken LSD under medical supervision described how the thought of death produced the hallucination that peoples' faces had become grinning skulls, and the air seemed thick with the smell of earth and decaying flesh. Some people who have had bad trips have become permanently unbalanced mentally. The power of the mind can be highly dangerous, and meddling with it simply for kicks is as irresponsible as allowing a child to drive a high-powered car. Bennett realized that it would be wiser to learn to extend the range of his consciousness step by step, and to consolidate each step before moving on rather than to take a sudden leap into powers that were beyond his understanding and almost

Carrying on the Master's Work

Below: a group portrait of the Fellowship at Taliesin West, designed by Frank Lloyd Wright. Mrs. Wright is at the far right. Taliesin is a residential architectural firm and school founded by the world-famous architect.

The mysterious power that some individuals seem to possess over animals—apparently communicating directly with them and compelling obedience by the sheer force of personality—has fascinated men throughout the centuries.
Below: a traditional form of animal control—a lion tamer. His power over a dangerous animal could possibly be telepathic.

certainly beyond his ability to control.

Once we know the world is not as dull and ordinary as it may seem, we have taken a major step toward doing something about it. The real objection to habit is that it makes us lazy, paralyzing the will. Once we realize that our robot is insulating us against much that is rich and rewarding in the world around us, we can begin to organize the will to resist the power of habit.

While we know enough about second wind to understand Bennett's experience, it is altogether more difficult to grasp how Gurdjieff could have projected energy into Bennett and Peters. What is the nature of this energy? The following may throw some light on it.

In 1919 Bernard Kajinsky, a Russian electrical engineer, was awakened in the night by a ringing sound like that of a spoon hitting glass. The next day he learned that his closest friend had died of typhus. When he called on his friend's mother, he discovered that she had been about to give him a dose of medicine at the moment he died. Kajinsky, suddenly excited, asked her to show him exactly what she had done. She took a silver spoon and dropped it into a tumbler. It made the same ringing sound that had startled him awake.

Kajinsky was a scientist with no interest in telepathy or extrasensory perception. But he had no doubt that his friend had thought of him at the moment of death, and that the sound of the spoon striking glass had somehow been conveyed to him. He thereafter made an exhaustive study of telepathy and reached the conclusion that "the human nervous system is capable of reacting to stimuli whose source is not yet known."

Kajinsky's work came to the attention of a famous Russian animal trainer, Vladimir Durov, who was convinced that his animals could read his mind. Durov began to conduct experiments in association with Vladimir Bekhterev, a distinguished neurologist. Under Bekhterev's supervision, Durov gave complicated telepathic orders to his animals. Usually the animals would carry them out. For example, Bekhterev wrote instructions on a sheet of paper and handed it to Durov. Durov looked into the eyes of his German shepherd dog Mars for several seconds without speaking. Mars went into the next room, looked on three tables and, finding what Bekhterev had asked for on the third—a telephone directory—carried it to Durov in his mouth.

Many animal lovers have noticed that their pets seem to possess some telepathic power. Edward Campbell, a British newspaper editor who studied this question, tells an interesting story about a German animal trainer, Hans Brick. Brick's favorite lion was a man eater named Habibi, and Brick's bond with the lion was a strange one. It was tacitly agreed between them that the lion—which was savage and unbroken—was entitled to kill Brick if it could find a moment when his attention lapsed. While Brick maintained his full attention the lion never attacked him. But on several occasions when his attention had wavered, an attack came instantly. Brick insisted it was his own fault. "I know the rules; so does he," he said.

During World War II Brick was interned in England for a while, and Habibi was looked after by a zoo. When Brick was

Animal Telepathy

Left: Dr. Robert Morris of the Psychical Research Foundation in North Carolina conducting a test of ESP in animals. In this test, a person just outside the room tries to influence which squares the cat will move to. Dr. Morris feels that there is considerable evidence for believing that animals have psi powers. "Results with animals are at least as positive and consistent as human results," he says.

The Power of Psi

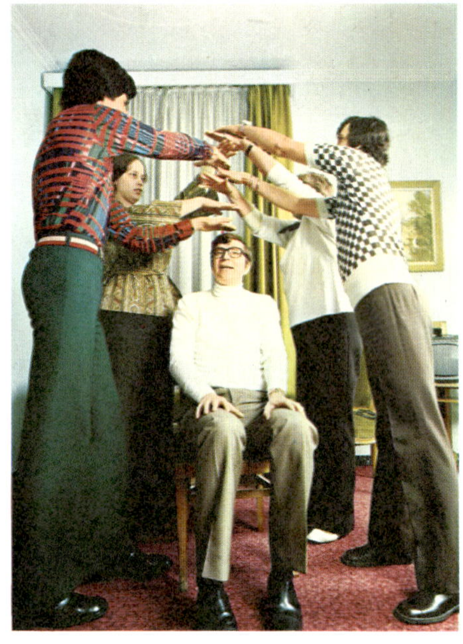

Above: Geller and his friends try to lift the author into the air, using only their fingertips. They begin by trying to lift him that way, and of course fail. Then they stack their hands above his head, so that no person has his own two hands placed together.

released, a British film company asked him to supervise some wild animal sequences in a film using Habibi. A problem arose because the owner of the zoo wanted payment for having tended Habibi, and Brick could not afford the fee. According to Campbell, at six o'clock on Sunday morning Brick walked into the zoo, went to Habibi's cage on an upper floor, released the lion, and looped a whip loosely around his neck. Brick then made a mental pact with the animal: Habibi was not to attack him while they were making their escape from the zoo.

The animals in other cages were in an uproar as the lion walked out. Rabbits and peacocks were ranging freely about the floor, but Habibi made no attempt to attack them. Brick walked to the door, Habibi following. They went down a flight of stairs and into the street. The lion walked quietly behind Brick and entered a traveling cage that he had parked in the next street. In effect, Brick had told the lion telepathically: "These are special circumstances. You want to get out; I want to get you out. No tricks . . ." And the lion had kept to his side of the bargain.

So far we have been speaking of telepathy which, most investigators agree, seems to depend on some form of waves. They are generally known as *Psi* waves (Psi is a Greek letter used in parapsychology for psychic ability or phenomenon.) At present we have no idea of the nature of such waves. We might compare Psi waves with radio waves. But radio waves can be used only to communicate, whereas when Gurdjieff used Psi power on Bonnett and Peters he seems to have been doing much more than merely communicating.

In 1940, not long before the invasion of the USSR, Joseph Stalin ordered an investigation into the powers of a psychic named Wolf Messing, who appears to have possessed Psi powers to an extraordinary degree. Messing described these experiments in a Soviet science magazine. His first test was to walk into a bank, present the cashier with a note, and will him to hand over 100,000 rubles in cash. Two official witnesses went with Messing when he did this. They saw the cashier take packets of banknotes out of the safe and hand them over. Messing put them in a briefcase and left. Then, with the two witnesses he reentered the bank, and handed back the money and the note—which was in fact a sheet of blank paper. The clerk looked at it, suddenly realized what he had done—and collapsed with a heart attack.

The stories about Brick and Messing may make one conclude that Gurdjieff simply used his Psi powers to suggest certain feelings to Fritz Peters. But it is difficult to see why, in that case, the effort should have exhausted Gurdjieff—and even more difficult to see how Peters could have been so genuinely reinvigorated. For the moment, it may be best to acknowledge that we do not even begin to understand the possibilities of Psi, and leave it at that.

Psi powers are not as rare as we might suppose. In fact, there are a number of simple experiments that anyone can do to verify that they are more than merely autosuggestion. The simplest test requires four or five people. One of the group, the subject, stands in the center of the room with the others around him.

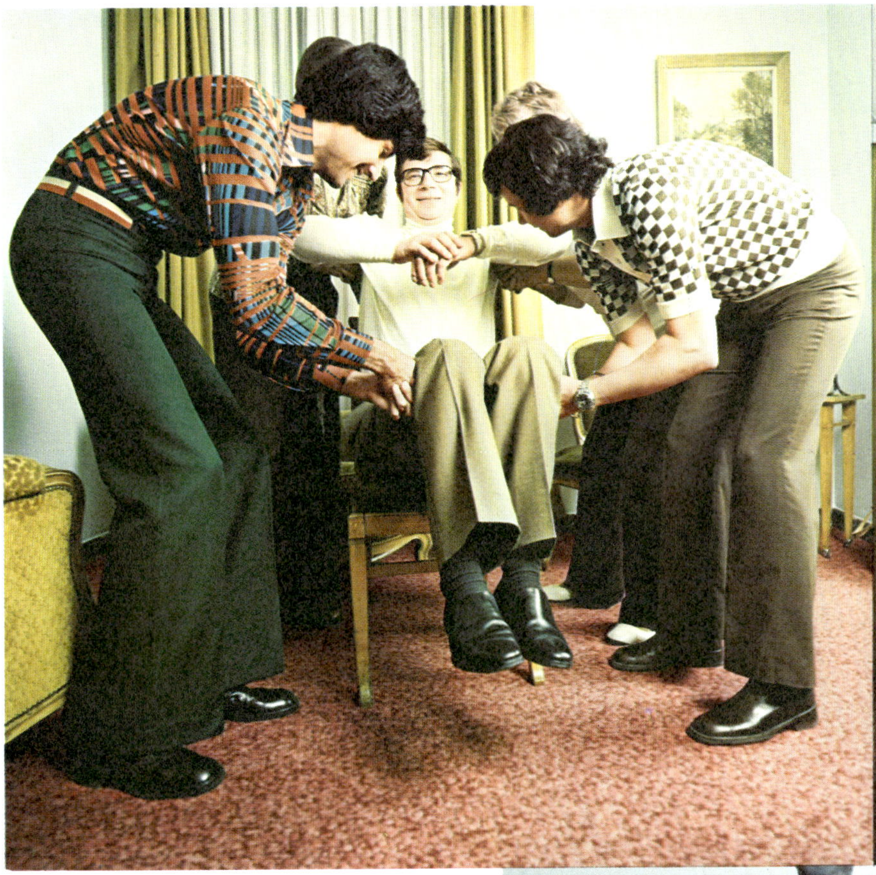

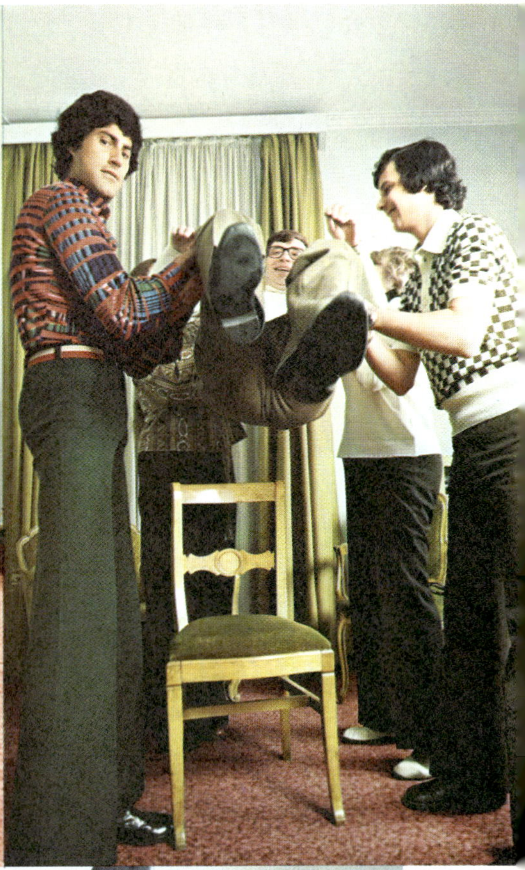

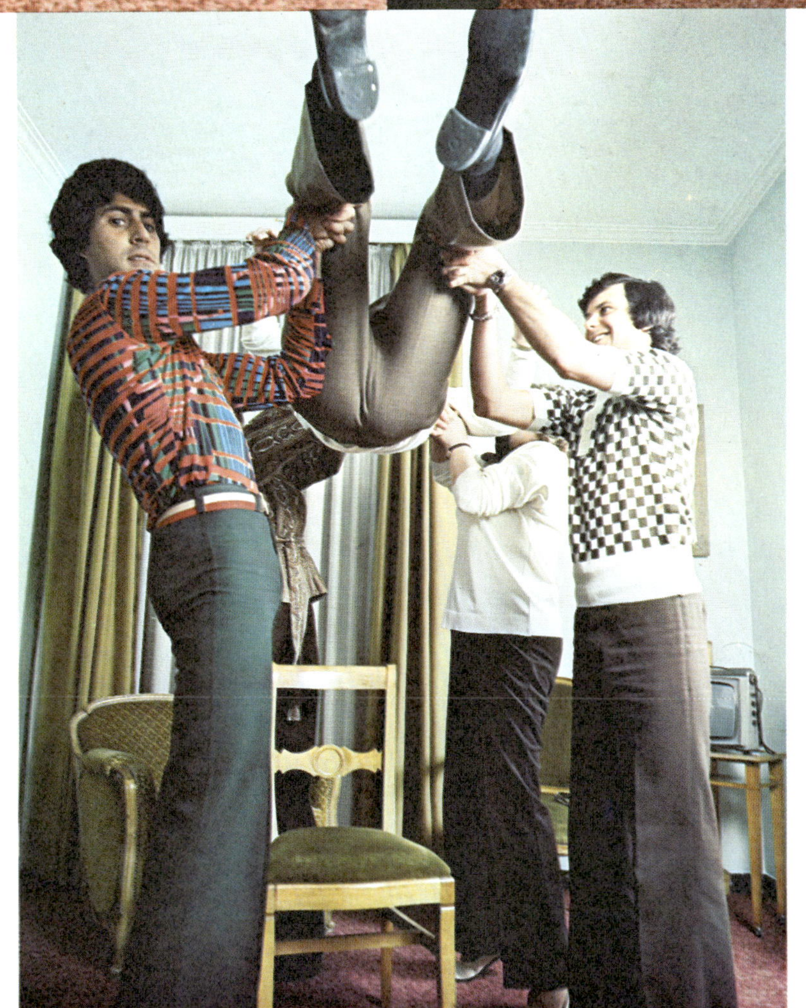

Above: on a command from Geller, everyone replaces their index fingers under Wilson's arms and knees.

Above right: immediately the author begins to rise in the air.

Right: Wilson sails up and away.

Mind over Matter

The subject closes his eyes tightly, and the others place their fingers gently against his chest, shoulders, and back making sure not to exert pressure. The aim of the experiment is to make the subject sway in a particular direction, which the others can decide upon by movement of the eyes or a nod of the head. They concentrate hard on willing the subject to sway in the chosen direction. He usually feels a force pulling him in the chosen direction, as if he were a compass needle and someone had brought a magnet close to him. It usually takes only a few seconds, depending on the suggestibility of the subject.

The second experiment, which also takes five people, is lifting a seated person using only index fingers. It is familiar to most schoolchildren. The chosen subject sits in a chair, and the the other four attempt to lift him by placing a finger under his armpits and knees. It is, of course, impossible. Then the four place their hands, one on top of the other, on the head of the seated person. No person should have his own two hands next to each other. All concentrate hard for about 20 seconds. Then they quickly remove their hands from the head, place their index fingers under the subject's knees and armpits—and the seated person is lifted effortlessly into the air. The glib explanation of this is that the hands piled on the subject's head operate as a kind of Psi accumulator. The interesting question is why and how they do so—and at present we have no answer.

The third experiment can be performed with a sheet of paper about two inches square. Fold it from corner to corner, from top to bottom, and from side to side. By pinching the corner folds, it can now be turned into a kind of paper dart, its point at the intersection of the fold lines. Take a needle and stick it blunt end first into a cork. Balance the paper dart on the needle point so that it looks like a partly opened umbrella. Making sure that you do not breathe on it, try to will it to rotate about the needle point.

Below: Robert Leftwich, modern British dowser or water diviner who uses a divining rod to practice his old art, also claims that he can disperse clouds simply by mental effort.

The first time I attempted this, nothing happened—which is what I expected. However, I kept the dart by my typewriter, and every now and then I tried to make it turn, cupping my hands around it. Eventually I stopped trying to make it move by sheer will power, and imagined that it was moving. Immediately, it began to rotate. I thought for a moment that this was due to the heat from my hands, so I tried stopping it. It stopped. Then I made it turn in the opposite direction. Once I had acquired the trick, I found it easy to make it rotate in either direction, even without my hands cupped around it.

The original paper model for this experiment was sent to me by Robert Leftwich, a water diviner who also claimed to be able to dispel clouds by concentrating on them. Although I later met Leftwich, I never saw him dispersing clouds. However, a well-authenticated experiment in cloud dispersal was filmed by a British television program in June 1956 on Hampstead Heath in London. This kind of Psi power is known as *telekinesis* (making objects or bodies move without visible force). Many experiments on this subject have been carried out by Soviet researchers.

It seems possible, then, that thought can exert some form of pressure quite distinct from powers of telepathic suggestion.

This in turn suggests that stories of the power of blessings and curses may have a foundation in fact. If Gurdjieff could make Peters feel better, he could also, presumably, have made him feel worse. Ira Levin's novel *Rosemary's Baby* has an episode in which a black magic group wills a man to death. If thought pressure is a reality, such telekinetic homicide may be possible. Donald Omand, a Church of England clergyman who has performed many exorcisms, believes that if a group of people determinedly brood on someone they dislike, they can inflict psychic damage. Directing mental forces may be as harmful as physical assault.

Gurdjieff tells this story about a station master in a small Russian town. Early every morning as he rang the bell announcing the arrival of the mail train, the station master would also shout curses. Asked why he did this, he explained that whenever he rang the bell, people all over the town woke up and invoked curses on his head. In order to fend these off, he redirected the malevolence back against the townspeople.

By the beginning of the 20th century scientists knew a great deal about the nature of light waves. One of the things they thought they knew was that light is an imponderable, that if it consisted of waves of radiation it could have no weight, and would exert no pressure. Einstein's Theory of Relativity predicted that, on the contrary, light particles have weight and should be subject to gravitation. During the 1918 eclipse of the sun he was proved spectacularly right. Measurements showed that the light rays actually bent as they passed through the sun's gravitational field. Nowadays, scientists design spaceships with "light sails" to exploit the pressure exerted by light waves.

Orthodox science has yet to accept the idea of thought pressure, and decrees that thought is supposed to be an imponderable. There are many scientists who, in the face of much evidence, decline to accept the reality of telepathy. Nevertheless, evidence has continued to accumulate until the point has now come when the only way to deny telepathy is to ignore the facts or to refuse to examine them closely. The only way to explain many of these facts is to assume that thought, like light, can exert its own kind of pressure.

A final question: if we are higher up the evolutionary ladder than other animals, why is it that Brick's lions, like many dogs and other pets, seem to possess more highly developed telepathic powers than we? The answer may be that we have allowed just as powerful faculties in us to fall into disuse. In our most primitive form our capacities may have been as highly developed as those of other animals—more highly developed, probably, or we might not have survived against predators. As we developed tools, the use of fire, and other techniques, we had less and less need for such innate powers. We needed reason and conscious awareness rather than instinct and subconscious awareness.

Humankind seems always to have been more interested in power than in inner awareness. This desire for power is the scarlet thread we shall find running through the history of men of strange powers.

Above: a demonstration of a cloud dispersal by Dr. Rolf Alexander in Ontario in September 1954. The cloud he was concentrating on has been circled. It is shown in this sequence of photography at various intervals of time — and at various stages of dispersal.

Chapter 2 The Will to Power

History reveals that some have learned to control the mysterious powers of their minds. The impulse to wield power over fellow human beings seems to be a universal one, and perhaps no power is so tempting as the ability to control the thoughts and actions of others. Old Testament prophets arranging duels with pagan gods; Simon Magus challenging St. Peter; and the half-legendary figure of the medieval magician Faust are examples of men using their psychic powers to influence others—if with widely differing motives. The great magicians appear to share common traits: egoism, and the need to impress.

In the mid-1930s a young American psychologist named Abraham Maslow spent most of his vacation in the monkey house of New York's Bronx Zoo. The thing that impressed him most about the animals' behavior was that they all seemed to be sex maniacs. Every minute of the day, males were mounting females, males were mounting other males, females were mounting other females. It looked like a simian Sodom and Gomorrah. Maslow's first conclusion was that this behavior was proof of Sigmund Freud's view that sex is the most important of all animal urges. It was only much later that another solution dawned on him: the animals were demonstrating dominance behavior.

Zoologists have grasped the full importance of the concept of dominance only in recent years. Farmers, however, have known about it for centuries. In the farmyard, the most dominant chicken can peck all the others; the second most dominant can peck all except the most dominant, and so on down to the weakest, who has no other to peck and may be pecked by all the others. The same pecking order can be seen everywhere in nature, among jackdaws, baboons, wolves, rats, mice, and other animals that live in groups.

What about human beings? Civilization has made us appear to be less obsessed with dominance, but anyone who has worked in a large office or factory knows this is untrue. The pecking order and the concern with status are still there, even if they are partly hidden by conventions of social behavior. In primi-

Opposite: the irresistible, sinister power of hypnotic eyes compells attention from the casual passerby—in this case fulfilling its purpose as an advertising poster for a dramatic film performance.

The Mysterious Power of Magic

Opposite: feats of magic in the Old Testament were generally done by men of God as grand gestures to prove the superior power of the Jewish God, Jehovah, to the non-Jewish world. This painting shows the miracle performed by the High Priest Aaron who, at a meeting with the Egyptian Pharaoh to demand freedom for the Israelites, turned his staff into a snake.

tive societies the dominance hierarchy is absolutely clear, for it is part of the social structure. The ruler seems to wield a mysterious, almost divine power that is seldom if ever challenged. The young men submit themselves to all kinds of painful tests to establish their right to a place in the dominance hierarchy.

Our primitive ancestors knew all about the pecking order and the will to power, but when people began to live in cities, the old carefully graduated social structure gave way to the disorganized scramble for status. Nowadays, we refer to such a scramble as the "rat race," but this is unfair to the rats. Of all creatures, none is so obsessed by the will to power as man. From what we know of magicians, it seems likely that magic developed as an instrument of this will to power.

It seems certain that primitive man was familiar with what we have called "thought pressure." Palaeolithic cave paintings, some of them 20,000 years old, show tribal *shamans* (magician-priest-doctor) performing magical operations to aid the hunters. The anthropologist Ivar Lissner has described how modern shamans still perform these operations. The shaman makes a drawing or clay model of an animal that is to be hunted. Then, by means of spells, he summons it to a certain place. The following day the hunters go to that place—and find the animal there. In his book *Patterns of Islands* Sir Arthur Grimble describes the ceremony of "calling the porpoises," which he witnessed in the Gilbert Islands. The shaman fell asleep in his hut, and entered a trancelike state in which he invited the porpoises to a feast. When he awoke, he rushed out of the hut. All of the villagers ran into the sea, and stood there armed with clubs. Shoals of seemingly hypnotized porpoises then swam gently into shore, where they were dragged onto the beach and killed by the villagers.

Modern man finds it impossible to understand how this magic works, but it is obviously only one step away from Messing's Psi power over the bank clerk that enabled him to rob a bank unarmed. Primitive man also used magic against other human beings. We are not sure precisely when this began to happen, but we are reasonably certain that it did happen because at a certain point in history, some of our distant ancestors suddenly stopped making models and drawings of other men. Why? Because they realized that if magic was potent against deer and bison, it could be effective against people. The mind power that could lure animals to their destruction could also destroy human beings. So anybody who made a drawing or model of a person immediately became suspect. This suspicion still applies among many primitive people today. They generally refuse to be photographed in the belief that the camera is capable of stealing the soul.

Slowly, over the course of many thousands of years, the tribal shaman evolved into the modern sorcerer. That is, he ceased to be what is called a white witch—a benevolent and helpful worker of magic—and became more interested in obtaining power for himself. We can see this transformation beginning in the Old Testament prophets such as Moses, Joshua, Elijah, and Daniel. It is true that they are men of God,

A Duel of Minds

and that their power apparently comes from God. But it is significant how often they are engaged in magical contests in which they demonstrate their power at the expense of competing magicians. Aaron throws down his rod in front of the Pharaoh and it turns into a snake. The rival Egyptian magicians do the same thing and their rods also become snakes. But Aaron's snake eats up all the other snakes. Elijah challenges 450 priests of Baal to a test of magic in which they are to call on their god to light the fire under a sacrificial bullock. Their god fails them. Elijah, with great dramatic flair, tells his people to drench his bullock and firewood with water three times. Then he calls upon Jehovah. The God of the Jews sends down a fire that consumes the bullock, the wood, and the water. After this, Elijah orders the people to kill all the priests of Baal. The will to power swaggers through the whole story.

The desire to dominate, to assert themselves, to humiliate or destroy those who oppose them is something that can be observed again and again in the lives of the great magicians. Moreover, the magical contest—the battle with a rival—is a standard feature of the lives of the magicians. In the 1st century A.D. the Greek magician Apollonius of Tyana engaged in a contest with a rival named Euphrates. Simon Magus, the magician of Samaria referred to in the Acts of the Apostles, was supposed to have been challenged by St. Peter. The legend is

Below: the fall of Simon Magus as visualized by a 15th-century Italian artist, Benozzo Gozzoli. St. Peter's prayers succeed in vanquishing the demons who, according to the legend, were supporting Simon Magus in the air. On the throne is the Roman emperor Nero, before whom the contest was supposed to have been staged.

Above: the power of men like Simon Magus may simply be that of hypnosis, and the strength of will over others. In these photographs from a French journal of 1891, the reactions of a 23-year-old mental patient when under hypnosis are shown. They show her complete lack of resistance to the suggestions of the hypnotist.

that Simon conjured up huge black hounds that rushed at Peter. The apostle held out a loaf of holy bread, and the hounds vanished into thin air. In one version of the legend, Simon then rose into the air, hovered for a moment, and flew through a window. Peter fell to his knees and prayed, whereupon Simon plummeted to the ground. He died from his injuries in this fall.

There can be no doubt that many such stories are pure invention. Others, however, are too detailed—and too widely reported—to be wholly invented. The interesting question is: What genuine powers did men such as Simon Magus possess? The account of him given in the Acts of the Apostles is, understandably, belittling. Describing himself as "some great one," Simon angered St. Peter by offering him money in exchange for the gift of the Holy Spirit. Christian documents are inclined to regard Simon as a charlatan. He claimed to be able to make himself invisible, change himself into an animal, and walk unharmed through fire. The Christians said that all this was achieved by bewitching the senses of the onlookers. Modern writers have taken this to mean that he used some form of hypnosis. For example, legend says that when Simon went to Rome, Nero ordered him to be decapitated by one of his officers. Simon, however, bewitched the officer into decapitating a ram instead. When he reappeared with his head still on his shoulders, Nero was so impressed by his powers that he made Simon his court magician.

But was Simon's means of control over the officer ordinary hypnosis or was it the kind of Psi power exercised by Wolf Messing on the bank clerk? The latter is altogether more likely, because hypnosis takes the cooperation of the person about to be hypnotized. It is unlikely that Simon was able to make himself invisible or turn himself into an animal. But he certainly seemed to have command of the power of thought pressure, just as some people are born with a green thumb.

At this point, it is time to raise the question of how such a power could work. Let us look more closely at some of the recorded examples.

The poet W. B. Yeats was a member of the Order of the Golden Dawn, one of the first and best known occult societies of

The Power of Hypnosis

Right: Svengali, the sinister character in a 19th-century novel, hypnotized a beautiful young artist's model into doing all he bid. His name became a synonym for evildoers who gain sway over others for their own purposes.

Below: Strindberg, the Swedish playwright and novelist, believed himself to have special psychic powers, which he exercised when he wanted to avoid an unwanted meeting with someone.

late 19th century England. In his autobiography Yeats describes an incident that occurred on a walk taken by one of the other Golden Dawn members and MacGregor Mathers, one of the order's founders. "Look at those sheep," said Mathers. "I am going to imagine myself a ram." The sheep immediately began to run after him.

Mathers could also use his strange powers on people, just as the Swedish playwright August Strindberg believed he himself could. Once when Strindberg was eating alone in a restaurant, he recognized two friends among some drunk people at another table. To his dismay, one of them began to approach him. Strindberg fixed his eyes on the man. At this, the friend looked bewildered and returned to his table apparently convinced that Strindberg was a stranger.

Strindberg once attempted to practice black magic, and he believed that his later suffering and bad luck was a result of this dabbling with evil forces. It was when he was separated from his second wife. He wanted desperately to bring about a reconciliation, and had to think of a way of seeing her. He decided to use his telepathic powers to make his daughter just sick enough to require a visit from him. Using a photograph of the girl, he tried to bring about her illness. When the two children of his first marriage got sick a short time later, he felt that he was responsible, and that his use of the evil eye had misfired. Strindberg dates his misfortunes from then on.

One of the most celebrated German criminal cases of 1936 concerned a hypnotist named Franz Walter, who liked to pose as a doctor. One day, boarding a train to Heidelberg, he entered a carriage occupied by a young woman. Walter talked to her, and discovered she was on her way to see a doctor about stomach pains. Walter sympathized, told her he was a doctor, and invited her to have coffee with him. She felt frightened and wanted to refuse, but when Walter took her hand, she found she could not. She later recalled that "it seemed to me as if I no longer had a will of my own." Walter had somehow hypnotized her without her consent. Later, when he wrote to her ordering her to come to him in another town, she felt strangely giddy, and immediately went to him.

Under hypnosis, she was raped by Walter, who then ordered her to become a prostitute and to give him her earnings. When she later married, he hypnotized her into making several attempts on her husband's life. The husband eventually reported her behavior to the police, and a police doctor, Ludwig Mayer, recognized some of the symptoms of hypnotism. He managed to dehypnotize her and unlock her memories of her ordeals, which Walter had ordered her to forget. Walter was tried, found guilty, and sentenced to 10 years in prison.

There is a link between these examples. Mathers' ability to attract the sheep is an example of the kind of telepathy that can exist between humans and animals. But Mathers was deceiving the sheep in the same sort of way that Wolf Messing deceived the bank clerk. Telepathy can be used for a kind of hypnosis or suggestion. In the case of Strindberg and his drunk friend, the playwright projected the suggestion: "I am not Strindberg" so that

Imprisoned by a Spell

Trilby O'Ferral in George du Maurier's 1894 novel *Trilby* was an artist's model working in Paris. Though her background was disreputable, her heart was of pure gold. Disappointed in love, she fell into the hands of Svengali, an unscrupulous Hungarian musician with strange powers.

Hypnotized by Svengali, she became a great singer: tall, elegant, with a divine voice that moved audiences to tears. When the man she truly loved saw her at a concert, he was heartbroken that she did not recognize him. Svengali, however, did recognize the young man and, in a spasm of hatred, died of a heart attack. Trilby was instantly released from the spell, with no memory of her triumphs or the ruthless training Svengali had given.

But Trilby began to fade away. Slowly she became thinner and more feeble. One day she saw a photograph of Svengali. As Trilby stared into the "big black eyes full of stern command," her smile became fixed, and she began to sing, "holy, heavenly sweetness." As she stopped singing Trilby fell back against the pillows and, whispering "Svengali, Svengali, Svengali," died.

Left: a hypnotist as a social attraction in the 1850s, when the phenomenon fascinated the general public. The ladies are swept up into an ecstatic rapture, seeing only what the hypnotist suggests.

The Legend of Faust

Above: Faust and Mephistopheles, the Devil, from a book of 1608. The legend of the man who sold his soul to the Devil for power—and who then became a great magician as a result—is one of the most durable of all stories about black magic. The legendary Faust has been the subject of many novels, plays, and operas since the mid-16th century.

Below: one of the legendary magical feats of Faust. This story is first recorded in 1589. Taking a tour of Leipzig with some students, Faust jeers at workmen trying to get a huge barrel of wine out of a cellar. The owner offers the contents to whomever can get the barrel out. Faust goes in, mounts the barrel as if it were a horse, and rides it out. The owner has to keep his promise, and Faust and his young friends share the wine.

the friend turned and walked away. In the Walter case, Dr. Mayer established that the hypnotist had hypnotized the young woman against her will. There can be no doubt that Walter immediately recognized her as a good hypnotic subject. It is also clear from Mayer's book on the case that Walter was driven by a "will to power." A coarse, rather stupid man, he pretended he was a qualified doctor, and many incidents in the case reveal the pleasure he took in his power over his victim. The interesting point in this case is that Walter did not hypnotize his victim by the usual means—for example, by getting her to focus her eyes on a swinging pendulum—but he did it instantaneously by some kind of suggestion. There was some natural form of sympathy between the two, although it seems akin to the sympathy between a snake and a hypnotized rabbit.

When we look more closely at these cases, we find another interesting link. Mathers was a strange mixture of charlatan and genuine scholar. He liked to pose as a Scottish laird of distinguished ancestry while, in fact, he was the son of a clerk and was born in London. He was a quarrelsome man, intensely jealous of his status as head of the Order of the Golden Dawn. He was also driven by a restless will to power. Strindberg had a paranoid egoism that is evident in much of his work. According to the police doctor, Franz Walter also was an egoist driven by the craving to be admired. Mathers, Strindberg, and Walter all lacked a stable background to their lives. It would be scarcely an exaggeration to describe them as homeless wanderers. In all three we see the basic characteristics of the magician: the desire for fame, the will to power, a natural talent for using thought pressure to dominate others.

After Simon Magus, the most famous magician in European history is Faust, also known as Dr. Faustus. The Faust legend has maintained its potency for almost five centuries, and has inspired at least three great works of literature—Christopher Marlowe's *Dr. Faustus* (1604), Goethe's *Faust* (1808 and 1832), and Thomas Mann's *Doctor Faustus* (1947)—as well as many musical works. From all these, the picture that emerges of Faust is of a brilliant, proud, restless man who longs to share the secrets of the gods. But these characteristics have evolved over the centuries, and as we go backward in time we come closer to the truth about the person who called himself Faust. Thomas Mann's Faust is a great musician; Goethe's Faust is a restless scholar, chafing against the frustration of being merely human; Marlowe's Faustus is a scholar who has been led into temptation by the lust for power. The book on which all these were based is Johann Spies' *Historia von D. Johann Faustus*, which appeared in Berlin in 1587. Its hero is little more than a magical confidence trickster. Significantly, his chief gift is hypnosis—although, of course, the author does not use that word.

In a typical episode in the Spies book, Faust goes to a Jew and offers to leave behind his arm or leg as security for a loan. The Jew accepts, and Faust appears to saw off his leg. Embarrassed and disgusted by this, the Jew later throws the leg into a river—whereupon Faust appears and demands his leg back. The Jew is forced to pay him heavy compensation. In another anecdote, Faust asks a wagoner with a load of hay how much hay he will allow him to eat for a few pence. The wagoner says jokingly: "As much as you like." When Faust has eaten half the wagonload, the wagoner repents his generosity and offers Faust a gold piece on condition he leaves the rest undevoured. When he reaches home the wagoner discovers that his load is intact, "for the delusion which the doctor had raised was vanished."

Even the Faust of this original book is described as "a scholar and a gentleman." He is said to have been the son of honest German peasants, born near Weimar in 1491, but brought up by a well-to-do uncle in Wittenberg. This uncle sent him to university. Faust's "strong powers of mind" soon distinguish him, and his friends urge him to enter the Church. But Faust has greater ambitions. He begins to dabble in sorcery. He studies Chaldean, Greek, and Arabic. He takes his degree of Doctor of Divinity, and also a medical degree. In due course, he becomes a famous doctor. It is intellectual brilliance that is his downfall, "the boldness of his profane enquiries"—a quality that later generations would consider a virtue, and for which even Spies has a sneaking admiration. Faust wishes to become a great magician, and this is why he invokes the Devil. Having entered into his pact with the Devil, Faust is corrupted by the Prince of Darkness, who proceeds to fill him with greed and lust for power.

At this point, it is worth quoting the *Historia* on a subject that has some bearing on the lives of magicians. "It used to be an old saying that the magician, charm he ever so wisely for a year together, was never a sixpence richer for all his efforts." This belief that unusual powers cannot be used for financial gain is fundamental and persistent. And there seems to be some truth in it. None of the great magicians from Simon Magus to MacGregor Mathers has died rich, and most of them have died paupers. The few who have succeeded in living comfortably—Emanuel Swedenborg and Gurdjieff, for example—made their money in

Faust the Fraud

When the Devil tempted Faust to make a pact with him, he promised riches as well as power. But, according to one of the early tales about Faust, the Devil did not live up to his word. Being not a penny richer, and in financial straits, Faust reproached the Devil. However, he was told that, as a magician, he could now solve his money problem.

Faust therefore went to a Jewish moneylender in the town and borrowed some money. When at a later time the moneylender wanted his money back, with the interest due, Faust said that he had none. Instead, Faust offered to cut off his leg and give it as further security, redeeming the limb on paying off the loan.

The moneylender accepted the arrangement. Faust appeared to cut off his leg, and gave it over. Later the moneylender decided that he had no use for the leg, and that Faust would not be able to replace it, so he threw it into the river.

Three days later Faust summoned the moneylender to settle the account and redeem his leg. When the man confessed what he had done, Faust demanded his leg back immediately. The unfortunate moneylender, afraid of trouble, gave Faust more money instead of collecting from him.

"The Demi-God of Heidelberg"

Right: Faust raising the Devil, from an English book on Faust published in 1830. Three hundred years after the real Faust had lived, the figure of the magician who made a pact with the Devil still had a strong grip on the popular imagination.

Opposite: Goethe's Faust. In his version, Faust is a serious aging scholar. Mephistopheles tempts him by giving him a vision of the most beautiful woman in the world, and offering him a potion which will return his youth and vigor so that he will be able to win her love. Faust drinks: and not only is his soul lost, but the innocent young girl who comes to love him is also lost. Below: a 1974 performance of a well-known play about Faust. This is a scene from The Royal Shakespeare Company's production of *Dr. Faustus* by Christopher Marlowe. With at Ian McKellen in the title role, the play was adapted and directed by John Barton and designed by Michael Annals. Here Faustus is shown with Mephistopheles, played by Emrys James.

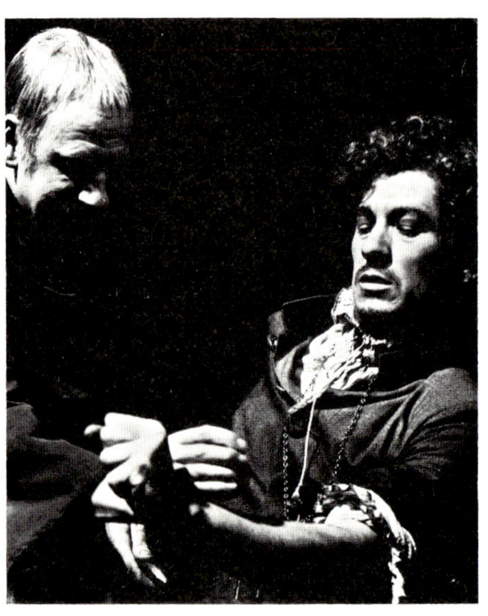

other ways than through their dabbling in magic.

When we pass from the Faust legends to the obscure original, as described by some of his contemporaries, we encounter exactly the sort of person that this investigation has led us to expect: a coarse, vulgar, boastful man, with some natural talent and an overmastering desire for fame. We don't know if he was named Georg Sabellicus or Johannes, but he was often called Faustus Junior. The first we hear of him is in 1507 when, through the good offices of a nobleman, he obtained a post as a teacher in a boys' school in Kreuznach near Frankfurt. Apparently he was a homosexual, for he proceeded to seduce some of his pupils, "indulging in the most dastardly kind of lewdness." When found out, he fled. In 1509, Johannes Faust was given a degree in theology in Heidelberg, some 40 miles from Kreuznach. In 1513, the canon of St. Mary's church in Gotha in what is now East Germany, recorded that he had heard Georg Faust, known as "the demigod of Heidelberg," boasting and talking nonsense in an inn in nearby Erfurt.

The alchemist Trithemius recalls a meeting with Faustus Junior as early as 1507, and dismisses him as a fool, a boaster, and a charlatan. In the few other references we have he is casting horoscopes, making prophecies, or being driven from town to town by his unsavory reputation as a sodomite and *necromancer* (one who foretells the future by communicating with the dead). From Johanne Wier, an acquaintance of Faust who wrote about him, we learn that Faust was wont to boast about "his friend the Devil"—which may have been nothing more than a typical piece of bombast. A story of Faust's malicious humor recorded by Wier describes how Faust, when a prisoner in the castle of Baron Hermann of Batenburg, offered to show the nobleman's chaplain how to remove his beard without a razor, in exchange for a bottle of wine. The chaplain was to rub his beard with the "magic formula" arsenic. The gullible chaplain did this. His beard fell out, just as Faust had prophesied—but it took most of

Pact With the Devil

Below: a scene from a novel about Faust by Friedrich M. von Klinger, whose book appeared in 1791. Here Angélique is a young girl, as good as she was beautiful, whom Faust vowed he would possess. The Devil aided him by turning himself into an old man with a peepshow, showing moral scenes. Angélique gave the poor man alms, and then felt an irresistible urge to look at the wonders of the box. The moral scenes changed slowly and imperceptibly to amorous scenes in which Faust was always shown as the most seductive cavalier, performing the most magnificent deeds to win a shadow resembling herself. At last the Devil showed her some very scandalous pictures. The poor girl fled to her bedroom where Faust awaited her. She fell into his arms and, as the story says, "the scoundrel profited."

the chaplain's skin with it. Wier also tells us that Faust was a drunken wanderer who spent much of his time in low taverns, impressing the locals with conjuring tricks. Other contemporary chroniclers describe him as a liar and a "low juggler."

We do not know when Faust died—it was probably in the 1540s—but we do know how his legendary fame began. A Swiss Protestant clergyman, Johanne Gast, once dined with Faust, and was unfavorably impressed by him—perhaps because of Faust's hints at his pact with the Devil. At all events Gast later spoke of Faust in one of his sermons, declaring that he had been strangled by the Devil, and that his corpse had persisted in lying on its face, although it had been turned on its back five times. This story had the right touch of horror to appeal to the imaginations of his congregation. Soon other stories grew up. One told how the Devil had twisted Faust's head around completely so that it looked down his back. Another recounted how, toward the end of his life, Faust began to hope that he might escape the Devil's clutches—but the trembling of the house at night warned him that the end was near.

The 16th century was an age of religious persecution, a time when a man could be executed on the mere suspicion that he did not believe in the Trinity. The very idea of a man selling his soul to the Devil was enough to make Faust's contemporaries turn pale. Little wonder, then, that Spies' *Historia* became one of the most popular works of its time. Phillip Melancthon, a follower of Luther, also preached about Faust. He gilded the lily somewhat with a story that Faust had defeated and eaten a rival magician in Vienna. Luther also has two slighting references to Faust in his *Table Talk*, from which it is clear that he regarded Faust as a common charlatan rather a demonic wonder worker. The only powers that some of Faust's educated contemporaries were willing to grant him were the gifts of casting accurate horoscopes and of foretelling the future. In 1535, for instance, Faust correctly predicted that the Bishop of Munster would recapture the city, and in 1540 he foretold the defeat of the European armies in Venezuela.

Legend has made Faust the most famous figure in the history of necromancy. But when we peer through the legendary mist, what do we find? Most of the more sensational stories about the man as told by people who knew him, tell of feats that have been more or less duplicated by other men of strange powers down the ages. It is difficult to decide whether this helps to support or to discredit Faust's credentials as a magician. When we try to sift fact from legend, it becomes clear that Faust knew something about hypnosis. It may be that he also knew how to conjure poltergeists. The priest Gast claimed that when Faust was angered by the poor hospitality offered to him by some monks, he sent a poltergeist to trouble them. Apparently the rattling spirit created such a furore that the monks had to abandon their monastery. Accounts made it plain that Faust was stupid, boastful, and malicious. The same is true of many men of strange powers. As we shall see, Faust's restless egoism, his desire to impress, his need to bend nature to his will are characteristic of many of the best-known magicians from Simon Magus onward. Magicians are not comfortable people to know.

Below: the temptations of Faust from von Klinger's novel. The Devil offers him worldly wealth and power— symbolized here by the crown, the jewels, and the bishop's miter—and lovely women.

Above: von Klinger's Devil, whom he called Leviathan, finally returns to his true and monstrous form and seizes Faust, who makes a magnificent speech of defiance. Leviathan gives a mocking laugh that shakes the world, then tears Faust's body into pieces, scornfully throws the limbs away, and carries his soul off to hell.

Chapter 3 Wonderworkers

Are there such things as miracles? Many of the strange phenomena viewed so suspiciously in the West are accepted calmly in the East: yoga is full of wonders, and the mystical exercises of Zen Buddhism are designed to integrate mental and physical powers for perfection of action. Also, the stories of Christian saints are full of miraculous happenings, unexplainable by the laws of nature. Swedenborg, scientist and mystic, had amazingly vivid visions of heaven and hell—and then astounded the skeptical with casual feats of clairvoyance in very ordinary matters. Different as they are, the evidence seems to indicate that these wonder-workers do have qualities in common.

When Louis Jacolliot, an eminent French lawyer and later a chief justice, went to India in the early 1860s, he was a free-thinker with a profound skepticism about religion. However, when his servant announced one morning that a fakir (Hindu holy man) wished to see him, his curiosity got the better of him and he decided to see the man. Jacolliot opened the conversation by saying that he had heard that fakirs possess the power to move objects without touching them—a power that is now called psychokinesis. The fakir—a thin bony little man—replied that he himself possessed no such power, but that spirits lent him their aid. The Frenchman asked if he might see a demonstration of these powers. The Hindu said that he would demonstrate and requested seven flowerpots filled with earth, seven thin wooden rods each a yard long, and seven large leaves from any tree in the garden.

The wooden rods were stuck in the flowerpots so that they were upright. Then a hole was made in the center of each leaf, and the leaves were impaled on each rod so that they fell down and covered the flowerpots. The fakir stood up, joined his hands above his head, and intoned a Hindu prayer. After that he seemed to go into a state of ecstasy, his hands outstretched toward the flowerpots. Suddenly, Jacolliot felt a breeze on his face. During the next 10 minutes, it blew several times. Slowly and gently the leaves began to rise up the wooden rods, then to float downward again. Jacolliot went closer to see if the Hindu could somehow

Opposite: the wise men of the East, with strange power over the material world—like this Muslim Sufi gliding across a river on his prayer mat—have attracted curious Westerners for hundreds of years.

"The Force of I"

be causing them to move by a trick. But the leaves continued to rise and fall undisturbed as Jacolliot passed between them and the fakir. For the remainder of that morning Jacolliot tried different tests to discover if the fakir used trickery. He arranged the flowerpots and rods himself in case of collusion between his servant and the fakir. He had the rods fixed into holes bored in a plank. It made no difference; the leaves still rose and fell as before.

Finally, the fakir asked Jacolliot if he would like to ask a question of the spirits. In doing so, Jacolliot used an alphabet of brass letters with which he printed his name in his books. Thinking of a dead friend, he began to take letters out of their bag one by one. When he pulled out the letter "A," the leaves moved. He returned the letter to the bag and repeated the process. This time the leaves moved when he pulled out the letter "L." By this process the leaves slowly spelled out the message: "Albain Brunier died at Bourg-en-Bresse January 3, 1856." This was the friend Jacolliot had been thinking of.

Jacolliot concluded that the Hindu had simply read his mind. He thought of a way to test this suspicion and tried it with the fakir next day. As he held the bag containing the letters, he concentrated on changing the name to "Halbin Pruniet." The leaves spelled out "Halbin Pruniet" instead of "Albain Brunier;" but no amount of concentration could change the date of Brunier's death, or the name of the city in which he died.

Jacolliot had experiences in psychokinesis with other fakirs, one of whom was able to hold down a small table so firmly that Jacolliot's attempts to move it only tore off one of its folding leaves. The same fakir dropped a papaw seed into a pot filled with damp earth, went into a trance for two hours, and caused the seed to sprout into an eight-inch-tall plant. Jacolliot's most startling experience was when a fakir named Covindasamy caused a phosphorescent cloud to form in the air. After a moment, white hands appeared in the cloud. One of them held Jacolliot's hand for a moment. At his request, it plucked a flower from a bowl and dropped it at his feet. Next, the fakir conjured up the shade of an old Brahmin priest. When Jacolliot asked it whether it was once alive on earth, the word "Am" (yes) appeared on its breast in glowing letters as if written with phosphorus. Finally, the fakir materialized another shade that moved around the room playing a flute. When the apparition vanished, it left the flute on the ground. It was a flute that Jacolliot had borrowed from a rajah and that he had had in his locked house.

What is so impressive about these stories is that Jacolliot does not write as an occultist. The book in which they appear is a sober study of Hinduism, and these stories of his experiments are added almost as an afterthought. He is merely interested in recording inexplicable events to which he attaches no undue importance. Not being concerned with psychical research, which in the 1860s had not yet attracted much attention, he does not attempt to classify the phenomena as the products of extrasensory perception, telepathy, or psychokinesis. He puts it that, "What we call spirit force is called by the Hindus *artahancarasya* or the force of I." It seems clear that he is referring to what we have called Psi power. The fakirs themselves believe that all such

Opposite: Indian sadhus, or holy men, in a procession going to bathe at the holy junction of the Ganges and Yamuna rivers, during a ceremony that takes place only every six years. These sadhus spend their lives seeking ways to gain access to the powers they believe exist at the innermost core of their being, where the human soul is identical with God.

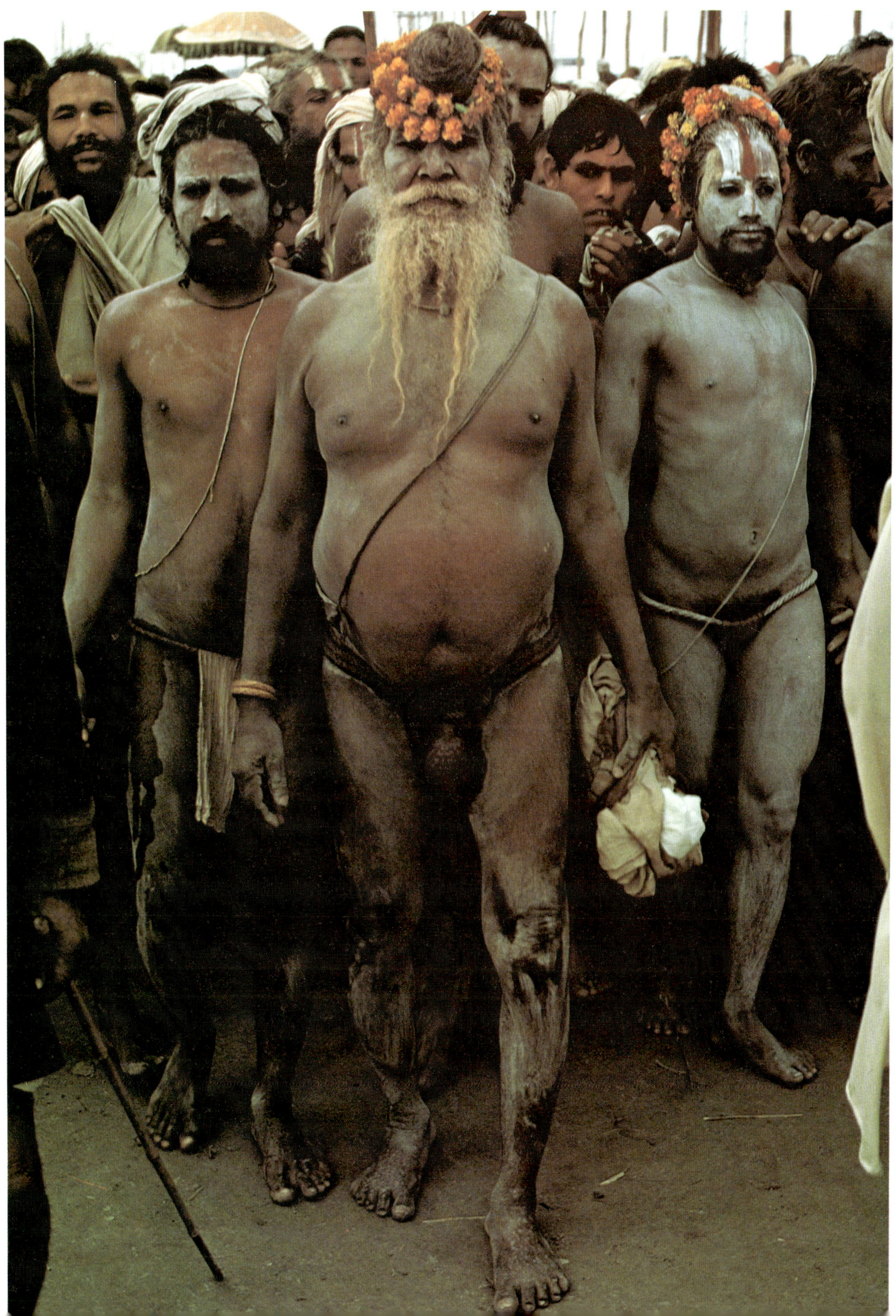

In Zen archery, or kyudo, each movement has its own importance, and the entire performance, from moving into position with the bow to watching the arrow fly to the target, is ideally an expression of the archer's perfect mental serenity. When the center of the target is hit, it is taken to be proof of his mastery of himself. Hitting the target, therefore, is secondary: the attitude of mental calm is the main purpose of such archery. Each step, as shown here, has its own name, and there are precise instructions for mastering every aspect so that the whole exercise flows with grace and simplicity.

Stepping into place and setting the torso in the right position, then breathing deeply.

Setting the bow in place. It is held in the left hand.

Lifting up the bow. This is done in two stages with pauses.

Drawing the bow. The correct shooting position is attained.

Taking aim. The archer concentrates on the right form.

phenomena spring from the same source—the spirits. The fact that Jacolliot actually saw entities that appeared to be spirits suggests that this idea cannot be wholly dismissed.

Most Hindus find nothing strange about such marvels. The ancient Hindu scriptures—the Vedic hymns, the *Upanishads*, the *Bhagavad Gita*—all teach that the human soul, the Atman, is identical with the godhead, Brahman. Thus, if one could penetrate through all a man's outer layers to the very depth of his being, one would find Brahman. Stripped of its religious essence, this echoes the central conviction of occult philosophers: the deeper we penetrate our innermost being, the closer we approach the strange powers that all men possess, but that few can tap or consciously use.

The science of yoga, which is basically a system of meditation, is intended to enable man to gain control over his body and emotions, and to move inward toward the "source of power, meaning, and purpose." A yogi assumes one of the traditional yoga postures, withdraws deep into himself, concentrates his gaze, and attempts to still his mind. The aim is total inner serenity. In attempting yoga, many westerners make the mistake of simply suspending the mind, as if sitting in church. Consequently they find it difficult to prevent it from wandering. The more experienced practitioner soon realizes that, although the posture suggests absolute rest, the mind is actually in gear, concentrating with a certain earnestness as if engaged in some difficult and dangerous operation. In the imagery of the Buddhist scriptures, the mind is like a pond, and the aim is to still the pond until it becomes a perfect mirror reflecting the moon, man's basic divinity. Great importance is attached to *prana* (breathing) because the breath is identified with life, or the

Secrets of Zen

Above: The archer lets fly at the target, watches the arrow, and listens to the string twang till it stops.

spirit.

Eugen Herrigel, a German professor who taught in Japan for many years, determined to attempt to master the secrets of Zen, the peculiarly Japanese form of Buddhism. A central aim of Zen studies is the total integration of one's mental and physical powers. One of Herrigel's spiritual exercises directed toward this end was learning how to draw an archer's bow correctly. He watched his Zen master draw the bow without effort and release the arrow casually. It flew to the center of the target. When Herrigel tried it, he found it almost impossible even to draw the string of the massive bow.

After a long period of frustration, Herrigel was told by the Zen master that he was not breathing correctly. "Press your breath down gently after breathing in so that the abdominal wall is tightly stretched, and hold it there for a while. Then breathe out as slowly and evenly as possible and, after a short pause, draw a quick breath of air again—out and in continually in a rhythm that will gradually settle itself. If it is done properly, you will feel the shooting becoming easier every day. For through this breathing you will not only discover the source of all spiritual strength, but will also cause this source to flow more abundantly, and to pour more easily through your limbs the more relaxed you are." It took Herrigel a year to succeed in drawing the bow with this perfect ease. Then came another long struggle, this time to release the arrow without a jerk, "as if the bow string had cut through the thumb that held it."

What Herrigel had to learn so painfully was to use his whole being, his subconscious as well as his conscious mind, in drawing and releasing the bow. Once this was learned, he had also learned the basic secret of Zen. This union of every part of one's self also

Mystical Traditions of the Hindu Fakirs

enables men and women to begin to grasp the perfect truth about Being. For Zen Buddhism holds that our central problem is that we have become too self-conscious, or rather, that we have developed what the novelist D. H. Lawrence called "head consciousness."

We are all familiar with the sensation of doing some simple physical activity badly because we are thinking about it. For instance, if we are aware of someone staring at the way we walk, we begin to walk awkwardly. If something makes us self-conscious about our accent, we begin to trip over words. According to the mystical tradition, this awkwardness has reached deep into human consciousness so that most of our powers are tied in a knot and unable to find expression. To some extent, relaxation can help to release these powers. For example, the fashionable cult of Transcendental Meditation is basically a kind of self-hypnosis that brings deep relaxation, leading to the release of hidden powers. We are out of tune with ourselves. We oppose ourselves like clumsy adolescents tripping over our own feet. All spiritual disciplines aim at removing this self-division. But, as Zen recognizes, the basic problem is how to arouse our "true will."

All the mystical traditions, Western as well as Eastern, recognize that the awakening of the true will can occur in a single flash. That is why the Zen master may sometimes kick his disciple violently. In one of the Zen stories, the disciple is awakened to a state of total enlightenment by such a kick. Similarly, there is a story told of the 19th-century Hindu saint Ramakrishna. When he was a young priest, Ramakrishna became deeply depressed because he seemed unable either to escape from the boredom of everyday existence or to catch a glimpse of Brahman. One day in despair he seized a sword, and was about to plunge it into himself. Suddenly the Divine Mother revealed herself to him. Ramakrishna was filled with a vision of an endless sea of vitality and self-knowledge, and with such deep ecstasy that he became unconscious. Undoubtedly the threat of death aroused his true will—showed him, as it were, the trick of parting the curtain of everyday existence that obstructs our view of reality.

Above: the fakir Sri Ramakrishna.

According to Ramakrishna, such powers as Jacolliot's fakir exhibited are merely the first consequences of this deeper knowledge of reality, and are utterly without value. Again and again he insists on the triviality of the feats that are traditionally ascribed to yogis and fakirs—for example, walking on water, moving objects without touching them, and climbing a rope that hangs unsupported in the air. The yogi who wants to do such things, says Ramakrishna, is at a rudimentary level of spiritual progress. The yogi who has tasted *samadhi*—the moment of absolute union with Brahman, the moment in which he realizes that his own soul is Brahman—cares only to strive for continual union. The conjuring tricks he regards with contempt.

Yet these examples of strange powers, called conjuring tricks by Ramakrishna, are a vital part of the Hindu tradition. One of the most extraordinary spiritual autobiographies of this century is Paramhansa Yogananda's *Autobiography of a Yogi*, to which the eminent orientalist W. Y. Evans-Wentz wrote an introduction that vouched for its authenticity. The book breathes the essential spirit of the Hindu religion, yet it is so full of tales of miracles that the skeptical westerner's first reaction is to dismiss it as a pack of lies. At the age of eight, Yogananda was dangerously ill with cholera. He was told by his mother to bow mentally, being too weak to move physically, to a picture of a great yogi on the wall of his room. As he did so, the room seemed to glow with light, and his fever disappeared. Shortly after this, he quarreled with his sister about some ointment she was using to cure a boil. He told her that the following day her boil would be twice as large, and that he would have a boil on his forearm. Both things turned out as he said, and his sister accused him of being a sorcerer.

From this point on the stories become ever more incredible. Yogananda tells of visiting a yogi named Pranabananda. The yogi told him that a certain friend of his was on his way. At exactly the moment foretold, the friend arrived. Yogananda asked him how he had come to be there. The friend explained that Pranabananda had approached him in the street, and told him that Yogananda was waiting in his room. Then the yogi had vanished into the crowd. What baffled Yogananda and his friend was that Pranabananda had been with Yogananda

Below: like the pious biographies of saints of Christianity, the holy writings of Hinduism are full of miracles. Here a poor Brahmin, a friend of Krishna, the incarnation of the god Vishnu, is urged by his wife to ask Krishna's help. After much arguing, he sets out with only a handful of rice as an offering. Krishna greets him graciously, and the Brahmin is too ashamed to ask for aid. Returning home, he finds that his hovel has been transformed into a golden palace.

throughout the previous hour. It seems, then, that Pranabananda had been able to project his astral body—the spiritual second body.

In another chapter of his autobiography Yogananda describes visiting the "perfume saint," a yogi able to induce the smell of any perfume. At Yogananda's request, the yogi caused a scentless flower to smell of jasmine. When Yogananda arrived home, his sister was also able to smell the scent of jasmine on the flower, thus allaying any suspicion that the yogi had managed merely to suggest the perfume to Yogananda.

Some of the most incredible of Yogananda's stories are about Babaji, the 19th-century "Yogi-Christ." One tells of how he allowed a disciple to hurl himself from a high crag, and then resurrected him. Another recounts how he materialized an immense golden palace in the Himalayas. Yogananda tells these stories at second hand, and it may be that he intended them to be accepted as myths or parables rather than as literal truth. But the stories he tells of his own *guru* (religious teacher or spiritual adviser) Sri Yukteswar, are almost as astonishing. Yukteswar also appears simultaneously in two places, Calcutta and Serampore. One day when his disciples are about to attend a festival in stifling heat, Yukteswar assures them that a cooling umbrella of cloud will be sent to help them. As he said, the sky clouds over and a gentle rain falls during the festival. However, Yukteswar did not claim to have conjured up the rain himself.

The climax of Yogananda's book is the description of the death and resurrection of Yukteswar. He predicted the time of

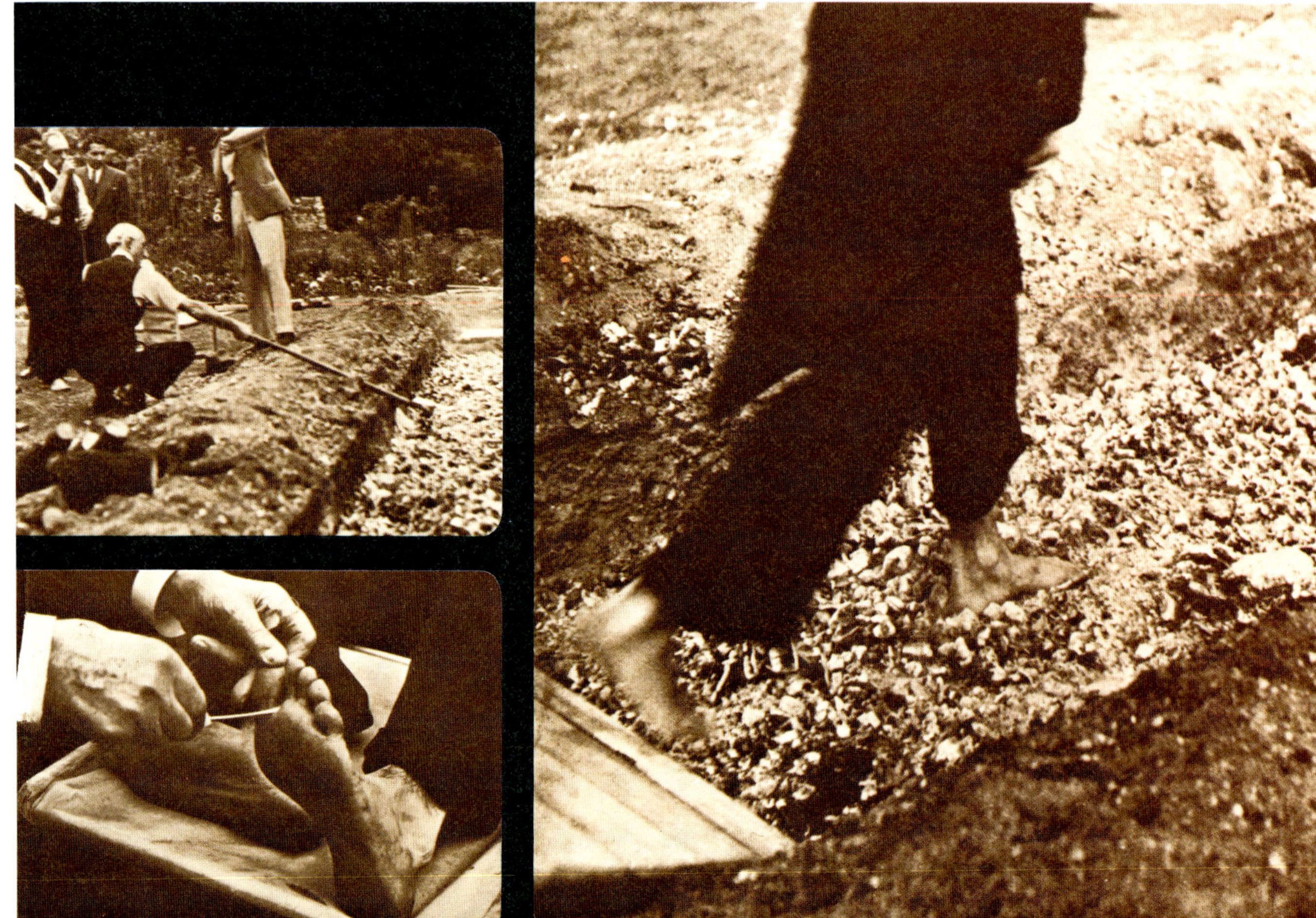

Below: an attempt in 1935 to scientifically assess the well-known yoga feat, the fire walk. A young Indian named Kuda Bux agreed to perform the fire walk for a group of scientists from the University of London Council for Psychical Investigation. An 11-foot trench was filled nine inches deep with red-hot embers, with a temperature of 430°C (806°F) at the surface. Swabs were taken of Bux's feet just before the walk and proved they were unprotected. He stepped into the pit and took a total of four steps. He was reported to have walked steadily and deliberately but quickly, the entire walk lasting just over four seconds. When his feet were examined after the walk, there was no sign of injury. An Englishman attempted to duplicate the walk, but jumped out after two steps; his feet blistered badly.

Walking on Fire

his death, and died exactly when he had foretold. After his death, he appeared to Yogananda in a hotel room in Bombay, and Yogananda insists that he was there in the flesh. Before vanishing, Yukteswar explained to his disciple at length that his task was now to serve as a savior on an astral plane, or another dimension of the world.

It is possible, of course, to dismiss the whole of Yogananda's book as the invention of a religious crank. But before doing so, it is well to bear in mind that most of the strange powers described in it have been observed and vouched for many times in the records of the reputable Society for Psychical Research. Moreover, we know that many yogis and fakirs have remarkable control over their bodies. Some have survived after being buried alive for some time—a feat that is beyond the understanding of most of us. Until we have a more systematic knowledge of the possibilities of higher states of consciousness, it may be as well to keep an open mind.

How, for example, do we account for the apparently ghastly self-mutilations of the Moslem holy men called the dervishes? Gurdjieff's disciple John G. Bennett has described a Moslem dervish ceremony that he witnessed twice in Istanbul. The dervishes knelt on the floor, swaying as they chanted the name of Allah. At a certain point of intense emotion, they began to drive spikes and skewers through their cheeks and arms. One old man lay down on the ground and placed a sharp sword, edge downward, across his stomach. Another man stepped onto the sword, balancing himself by holding the hands of two men on

Above: St. Joseph of Copertino flying in a religious rapture. This picture was published in a book in 1735. St. Joseph was even said to have lifted others into the air with him in his ecstasies.

either side. When the man stepped down, the old dervish raised the sword from his body and revealed that it had not even made a mark. Bennett examined the sword after the ceremony. It was as sharp as a razor and bore no trace of blood.

The Western temperament is more given to intellectual speculation and is less mystical than the Eastern—which partly explains why the technological advances of the West have been so much greater than those of the East. All the same, the West has produced many great mystics who believe that certain kinds of truth are reached not through logical reasoning or the experiences of the senses, but through some kind of spiritual intuition. The father of Western mysticism was the Greek philosopher Plato, who lived in the 5th century B.C. In his *Symposium*, Plato writes about the teachings of his mentor Socrates. The older philosopher explains how the lover begins by desiring attractive bodies, then learns to admire beautiful souls, and ends by loving the beauty of the universe itself. This, says he, is the true aim of all love.

Socrates' insistence on the love of the impersonal has remained the central theme of Western mysticism ever since. The Greek philosopher Plotinus, who taught in Rome in the 3rd century A.D., described the aim of the mystic as "the flight of the Alone to the Alone." Later, Christian mystics often used words such as "darkness" and "emptiness" to describe the God of the true mystic. In the Middle Ages, when alchemy began to fascinate those of a philosophical turn of mind, mysticism and magic became oddly mixed up together. The alchemist sought the Philosopher's Stone, a substance believed capable of turning base metals into gold, and the elixir of everlasting life. The mystic sought union with God. For many thinkers, the two kinds of search became identical.

One of the most remarkable of these mystical alchemists was the German shoemaker Jakob Boehme, born in Gorlitz, Silesia—now part of East Germany. At the age of 25 in 1600 Boehme had his first experience of mystical insight. He found himself staring at a pewter dish whose polished surface reflected the sunlight. Gazing into it, Boehme found himself drifting into a kind of ecstasy. He had the sensation of being able to see into the heart of all nature. He walked out to the fields, and it seemed to him that the trees and grass were transparent, and lit by a kind of flame from within.

How can we explain such mystical ecstasies? They seem to be due to the release of a flood of emotional energy—a flood so powerful that it overwhelms the senses. Many people have experienced something of the kind—perhaps when listening to music or looking at magnificent scenery—so we are inclined to dismiss such experiences as mere emotion. But we fail to understand the possibilities of mere emotion. Boehme's mystical intensities carried him into a realm in which he seemed to see into the heart of the universe. He wrote of a later ecstasy that "the Gate was opened to me, so that in a quarter of an hour I knew more than if I had been many years at a university." He tried to express this insight in a number of strange works. His first book caused him a great deal of trouble: the local clergyman denounced him as a false prophet, and the magistrates ordered him to stop writing. Fortunately he ignored them, and he produced a number of strange and difficult masterpieces full of the language of the alchemists, attempting to describe the soul's relation to God. Although he died in relative obscurity, his fame afterward spread all over Europe. He influenced another great visionary, the English poet and painter William Blake, whose work vibrates with the same feeling of strange hidden realities lying behind the curtain of the everyday world.

The state of ecstasy can produce remarkable effects. There is reliable evidence that it caused a devoutly religious monk to rise into the air and fly. Giuseppe Desa was born at Apulia, Italy, in 1603. He was feeble and sickly as a child. At the age of 22 he joined the Franciscan order, and soon became well known for his prayers and fasting. One day after Mass, he suddenly rose into the air, floated above the congregation, and hovered over the altar. The candle flames did not burn him. From this time on Father Joseph as he was now known, often levitated and flew considerable distances. Many eminent contemporaries witnessed this strange feat, including the great German philosopher Leibniz. There are so many apparently reliable records of his flights that it seems probable they were not faked. Significantly, when a hostile and envious superior started to bully and humiliate him, Father Joseph ceased to fly. He recovered his spirits, however, and afterward flew through the air and embraced the statue of the virgin above the altar. A century after his death, he was canonized as St. Joseph of Copertino.

Science cannot explain levitation, although there are thousands of well-authenticated cases on record, particularly from India. But then, neither can science explain how John G. Bennett, seriously weakened after a three-day attack of dysentery, could dig furiously for an hour without collapsing. We know little about the powers of the mind because in most of us they are undeveloped. If we lived in a world in which there was only the moon and no sun, no one would believe that light could cause sunburn or make forests burst into flames. We know the universe only to the extent of our as yet feeble attempts to perceive and measure it, and the results are often absurd and contradictory.

One of the most eminent Protestant mystics was also a distinguished scientist and engineer. Emanuel Swedenborg was born in Stockholm in 1688 and began his career as a mathematician. He also studied watchmaking, carpentry, and music. Later he became Assessor of the Swedish board of mines, and demonstrated his engineering skill when he transported five ships overland for 15 miles during his country's war with Denmark.

In 1744 when he was 56, Swedenborg had an overpowering dream in which a roaring wind flung him on his face. Then Jesus appeared and spoke the words: "Well then, do it!" From this time onward, Swedenborg began to go into ecstatic trances and to see visions. His books contain vivid descriptions of journeys he claimed to have made through heaven and hell under the guidance of angelic spirits.

One's first reaction to this is to conclude that Swedenborg must have gone mad. But people who met him and expected to find a lunatic were surprised by his sanity and good humor.

Remarkable Feats of Ecstasy

Below: Emanuel Swedenborg, the Swedish mystic. Although his visions did not begin until he was in his fifties, he writes about himself that "from my fourth to my tenth year I was constantly engaged in thought upon God."

Above: Jean-Marie-Baptiste Vianney, the curé of Ars, was a parish priest who spent his life fighting the temptation to retire to the solitude of a monastery. He was such a perceptive confessor that the faithful flocked from all over France to seek his counsel. He said little, but what he said was always precisely to the point—so much so that many thought he was able to look into their minds.

Moreover, his powers of clairvoyance were witnessed by many. One night when about to sit down to dinner in Gothenburg, he suddenly turned pale and announced that a great fire had just broken out in Stockholm 250 miles away. It was threatening his own house, he said. For the next two hours he was in a state of agitation. Then he said with relief: "Thank heavens, the fire is under control. It had almost reached my doorstep." The next day he wrote a detailed description of the fire to the governor of Gothenburg, and the day after that, a letter arrived confirming to the last detail all that Swedenborg had said.

One day when Swedenborg was at the royal court, the queen asked him perhaps mockingly if he had seen her deceased brother on his visits to heaven. Swedenborg replied gravely that he had not. The queen then remarked that, if Swedenborg met him, perhaps he would give him her greeting. The next time Swedenborg came to court, he told the queen that he had seen her brother and had given him her message. The brother, he said, sent his apologies for not having answered her last letter to him before he died, but he would now do so through Swedenborg. The scientist then repeated her brother's reply to various points in her letter. The queen was dumbfounded as she declared "No one but God knows this secret."

About this time the Dutch ambassador to the Swedish court died. When his widow afterward received an invoice for a silver tea service, she was convinced that her husband had paid for it shortly before his death. But she could not find the receipt. She asked Swedenborg for help. A few days later as she sat with friends, Swedenborg told her: "Your husband says the receipt is in the bureau upstairs." "Impossible," said the widow, "I have searched it." Swedenborg said that there was a secret drawer, which he described. The widow went to the bureau, found the secret drawer, and opened it. The receipt was inside.

Many of Swedenborg's contemporaries believed that these remarkable demonstrations proved that his visions of heaven and hell must be true. We should be more cautious. One of his books contains a description of Mars and its inhabitants that is wholly nonsensical in the light of our present knowledge of the planet. We can only conclude that if Swedenborg had visions—as he almost certainly did—then some of them were false ones.

Of the more modern European wonder workers, perhaps the most interesting is Jean-Marie-Baptiste Vianney, the curé (parish priest) of Ars. In 1818 at the age of 34, Vianney was appointed to the parish of Ars near Lyon. He was a simple man, not particularly intelligent, and generally narrow-minded. Yet his piety and reported understanding of the human soul soon spread his reputation far afield. He had mystical visions, although he would say little about them—and many seriously ill people who came to see him were cured. His most famous miracle took place during a year of famine when there were only a few cupfuls of wheat left in the village granary. Vianney prayed all night. The next morning when a girl tried to enter the granary, she found the door blocked. Forcing it open, she found the place full of grain—enough to feed most of the parish for months.

This story was not investigated by an independent observer, and one hardly needs to be a skeptic to be suspicious of it. But, even allowing for the credulity of the more devoted members of his flock, Vianney seems to have possessed special powers, particularly of telepathy. As his fame spread, people came from far and wide to attend services at his church.

Powerful religious feelings sometimes seem able to release deep and hidden forces in the human soul. But it is important to realize that many of these powers are little more than by-products of our inner evolution. What is impressive about all the mystics, from Boehme to Yogananda, is not the wonders or visions. It is the sense they all share that the everyday world conceals some tremendous reality that all are capable of seeing if they can discover how to look. We feel something of this kind in the paintings and poetry of William Blake. We feel it in Vincent Van Gogh's evocative painting *Starry Night*, which the artist painted with candles tied around his hat so that he could see the canvas in the dark. Works such as these suggest something of the ecstatic intensity experienced by Boehme when he found himself looking "into the heart of nature," or by Ramakrishna when he was overwhelmed by the vision of the Divine Mother. They give us a glimpse of the source of power, meaning, and purpose that lies deep inside all human beings.

A Hidden Source of Mental Power

Below: Vincent Van Gogh's *The Starry Night*. (Collection, The Museum of Modern Art, New York, acquired through the Lillie P. Bliss Bequest). The stars swirling across the mysterious, radiant sky glow like so many mystic suns.

Chapter 4
Magicians and Mystics

Do the rituals of magic really hold the key that unlocks secret powers? What has happened to the men who have claimed success in the strange and mysterious world of spells and symbols? Cornelius Agrippa, living in the 16th century, believed he could summon spirits, and his enemies feared it was true. Paracelsus, the arrogant physician, was gifted with a magical prowess in healing—and died from a fall while in a drunken stupor. Franz Anton Mesmer healed wealthy invalids in Paris, apparently by summoning powers within the patients that neither he nor they realized they possessed. Is magic a mystery even to the magician?

It was a windy, chilly evening in March, 1865, and most of the inhabitants of the French village of Solliés-Farliede were indoors. A limping man approached the cottage of a workman and knocked on the door. The girl who opened it shrank back when she saw the unkempt stranger, whose beard was as tangled as a bird's nest. The man pointed to his mouth, then to his ears, and shook his head, indicating that he was deaf-mute. The girl's father came to the door and, after the kindly fashion of country people, invited the tramp in for a meal. The girl, Josephine, kept house for her father. The only other occupant of the small country cottage was Josephine's 15-year-old brother.

From the first moment, Josephine felt terrified of the ugly stranger. His manners were eccentric and uncouth. Instead of filling his glass with wine, he poured in a little at a time, putting the bottle down several times. He made the sign of the cross over his glass before drinking, as if afraid the Devil was in it. After the meal, the girl's father questioned the man by means of pencil and paper. They learned that his name was Timotheus Castellan, that he had been a cork cutter, and that he had had to abandon the trade after an injury to his hand. Now, he said, he traveled around the country making a living as a healer and water diviner. Curious neighbors came in to see the magician, and all were impressed. That night, the tramp slept in a haystack. Josephine lay on her bed, fully dressed, her mind full of foreboding.

The next day her father and brother went off to work, and

Opposite: Franz Anton Mesmer treating a patient. Mesmer, the Austrian doctor who discovered the kind of suggestion first known as "mesmerism," from his name, and now called hypnotism. He used the power of suggestion to rouse a patient's subconscious to throw off symptoms of disease. Mesmer himself thought that his cures came about through his use of magnets, which rearranged the patient's "vital fluids" flowing like the tides through the body.

Above: an early practitioner of the strange art of hypnotism, in the traditional pose that has since become a hallmark of the stage hypnotist capturing his subject.

Castellan went with them. Shortly afterward, however, he returned to the cottage. Josephine let him in, and went about her housework. Several neighbors called in at the cottage, having heard about the wonder worker, and brought him presents of food. One of them saw Castellan making strange signs in the air behind Josephine's back.

At lunchtime, the two ate together. Suddenly, Castellan stretched out his hand, pointing two fingers at Josephine. She immediately became unconscious. When she woke up, Castellan was sprinkling water on her face. Then he picked her up, carried her into the bedroom, and raped her. Although she was fully conscious, she was unable to move. At one point a neighbor knocked on the door and called her name, but she found herself unable to reply.

Later that afternoon Castellan left the cottage, and beckoned to her. In a state of confusion she followed him. Neighbors asked her where she was going, but though she answered, her words were unintelligible.

That night the couple stayed at a farmhouse and slept together. The next day they persuaded a farmer at the nearby village of La Cappelude to give them a bed. The farmer and his household were baffled by Josephine's behavior. Sometimes she seemed like an infatuated newlywed, kissing and caressing the ugly deaf-mute; then suddenly she would turn away, as if nauseated. During the evening she managed to talk to a girl who lived nearby and asked her if she could stay with her overnight. Castellan overheard their conversation, however, and ordered Josephine to remain with him. He made a sign with his hand. She collapsed in his arms and remained in a trance for an hour.

Two days later the distraught girl succeeded in giving Castellan the slip. She approached a group of men and asked them to take her home. A search for the tramp began immediately, but it turned out later that soon after the girl's escape he had been arrested for vagrancy. Two doctors examined Josephine and pronounced that the tramp had deprived the girl of her will by "magnetism" (hypnosis). A court sentenced him to 12 years' hard labor.

What are we to make of this sinister beggar? He was undoubtedly a confidence man and a liar. Josephine declared that she had escaped while he was in conversation with a band of hunters; evidently he could speak and hear normally. It seems clear that Castellan's intention in hypnotizing Josephine was not only to obtain a mistress, but also to get a companion whose attractions would persuade country people to provide him with meals and a bed. Yet his powers were certainly genuine. He was a water diviner, healer, and hypnotist of remarkable ability. He was, in short, both a genuine magician and a charlatan—a mixture we have already found in Simon Magus and Faust, and will encounter again and again in the history of magic.

The Castellan case, which is well documented, underlines something we should not forget: that magical powers are not confined to a few famous names in history. In every age there are thousands of such men and women, and their powers are

The Black Magicians

of many kinds. Timotheus Castellan evidently recognized Josephine as an easy hypnotic subject as soon as he saw her—just as Franz Walter earmarked his victim on the train. What is more interesting is that Josephine undoubtedly recognized Castellan as a man who might gain power over her. Moreover, if the evidence of the neighbor is to be believed, Castellan did not hypnotize Josephine by the usual methods. He made passes in the air when her back was turned. This suggests that he was exercising some form of thought pressure.

It is a curious fact that the careers of most magicians seem to follow a definite pattern: a spectacular rise to power or fame, followed by a long slow downfall. Timotheus Castellan's downfall obviously began when he mesmerised Josephine. We do not know enough of the historical Faust to know when his career took the downward plunge; but the fact that we know nothing about his later years or his death suggests that his fame evaporated before he was 40 years old.

Faust and Castellan had another interesting thing in common: both were black magicians. This term may seem quaint in our scientific age, but it is less absurd than it sounds. The black magician is, quite simply, a man who wants power for himself, for self-aggrandizement. He wants to be able to vent his spite on enemies, and to satisfy all his desires. Black magicians are usually defined as those who have made a pact with the Devil, but this is not necessarily the case. A magician may summon the Devil or one of his demons and remain a white magician so long as his purpose is benevolent. On the other hand, a magician may have no interest in the Devil or may even deny his existence, but if his intentions are malicious and self-centered, he is a black magician.

Faust was not the most celebrated magician of his age. He had two remarkable contemporaries, Cornelius Agrippa and Paracelsus, whose fame greatly and deservedly surpassed his own, and who were undoubtedly white magicians. Agrippa and Paracelsus were both students of that strange mystical system of knowledge called the Cabala, whose purpose is to show the fallen man his way back to Paradise and the godhead. The two works that contain the essence of cabalistic teaching—the *Sefer Yetsirah*, Book of Creation, and the *Zohar*, Book of Splendor—are of such profound importance in the history of magic that we must say a few words about them here.

The Book of Creation dates from the 2nd century A.D. The Book of Splendor appeared in an Aramaic manuscript written by a student named Moses de Léon in the late 13th century. It is, however, a tradition that the teachings of both books date from the beginning of human history, when angels taught Adam the secret of how to recover his lost bliss. Cabalists think of man as a being who is tied up and enveloped in a complicated straitjacket—like Houdini before one of his celebrated escapes—and whose problem is to discover how to untie all the knots. Most men do not even realize that they are tied up. The cabalist not only knows it: he knows also that man's highest state is total freedom.

According to the Cabala, when Adam sinned he fell from a state of union with God. He fell down through 10 lower states

ALGA S TNA
ALGAR
INRI

of consciousness into a state of amnesia, in which he totally forgot his divine origin, his true identity. Man's task, therefore, is to clamber back until he once more attains his highest state. The journey is long and hard. It is not simply a matter of climbing, like Jack clambering up the beanstalk, because the "beanstalk" passes through 10 different "realms." But even that image is too simple: the beanstalk does not pass straight upward, like a fireman's pole, but wanders from side to side.

The image of the beanstalk is apt because the Cabala is essentially the study of a sacred tree—the Tree of Life. At the top of the tree is God the Creator, who is called Kether (the crown). The nine other branches of the tree are wisdom, beauty, power, understanding, love, endurance, majesty, foundation, and kingdom. These are known collectively as the Sefiroth—emanations, or potencies, and it is they that constitute the realms through which the beanstalk passes. There is a further complication. The traditional picture of the Tree of Life looks rather like a diagram of a chemical molecule, in which the atoms are connected to each other by lines. These lines correspond to the 22 paths of the Cabala that connect the realms.

The Tree of Life no longer grows on earth. How, then, does the aspirant set about climbing it? There are three main ways. First, one may explore the realms on the astral plane. Another way to explore the realms of the Cabala is through inner vision—that is, by achieving a semitrancelike or visionary state in which the realms appear before the inner eye. A third way is the obvious one: study of the Cabala itself. It is, however, perhaps the most difficult way of all, because its revelations of man's consciousness and destiny are not spoken of directly, but lie hidden in an enormously complex system of symbols.

The realms of the Sefiroth, however, are not themselves symbols. According to the Cabala, they are real worlds. For instance, if the wandering astral body finds itself in a realm containing doves and spotted leopards, a land bursting with an almost overwhelming glory of life, it is almost certainly in the realm of Netshah, or Venus—symbol of endurance and victory.

The doctrines of the Cabala were probably far above the head of a charlatan such as Faust. But Cornelius Agrippa and Paracelsus were not charlatans. They regarded themselves as scientists and philosophers, and they were far more intelligent than Faust. Yet both of them were flawed by the defects we have come to realize are characteristic of so many magicians: a craving to be admired, and a crude will to power. When these ambitions are frustrated, even men of genuine powers will often misuse their powers like a charlatan.

Like Faust, Cornelius Agrippa became the subject of many remarkable legends. What was the truth behind such incredible tales? Cornelius Agrippa—whose real name was Heinrich Cornelis—was born in Cologne in 1486. His parents were sufficiently well-off to send him to the recently founded university of Cologne, where he proved to be a brilliant scholar. It was an exciting time for young intellectuals. Gutenberg had invented the printing press some 50 years before Agrippa was born, and the printed book had created the same kind of

The Mysterious Tree of Life

Opposite: an etching by Rembrandt of a scholar in his study gazing at a strange vision in which there is a magic disk covered with mystic symbols from the Cabala. Many great scholars of the period were as fascinated by the secret knowledge of the Cabala as by the more widely known medieval sciences of alchemy and astrology.

Below: the Tree of Life of the Cabala. The center circle at the top represents God the Creator. Each of the other circles are ways in which God manifests himself, and through which the soul returning to God must pass.

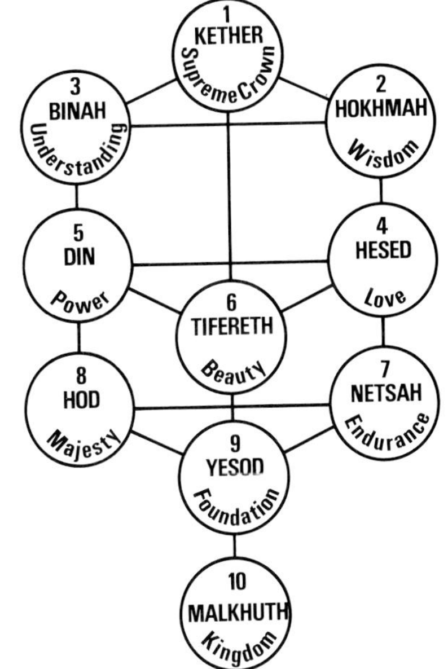

The Strange World of Cornelius Agrippa

revolution as radio and television were to do five centuries later. Agrippa read everything he could lay his hands on. One day he discovered the Cabala, and it at once appealed to something deep within him. A magician was made.

At the age of 20 Agrippa became a court secretary to the Holy Roman Emperor, and a distinguished career seemed assured for him. But Agrippa was a divided man. Part of him, as we have said, craved celebrity and power; but he loathed the world of diplomacy and courtly intrigue by which such success could be achieved. By now he was also obsessed by the ultimate other world of the Cabala.

At about this time, he attended the University of Paris where he studied mysticism and philosophy. There he met a Spaniard named Gerona, who had recently been forced to flee from his estate in Catalonia after a peasants' revolt. Agrippa offered to help him, sensing that if their mission succeeded, Gerona's gratitude might enable Agrippa to settle in Spain and devote his life to study of the Cabala. They went to Catalonia, and Agrippa devised a brilliant plan that enabled them to capture a stronghold from the revels. But they were later besieged, Agrippa was forced to flee, and Gerona was captured and probably murdered. The episode was typical of the bad luck that was to pursue Agrippa for the rest of his life.

He returned to his job as court secretary, but he felt so frustrated that he left after a few months and began wandering around Europe. Within a year or two he had acquired a reputation as a black magician, and it was to cause him a great deal of trouble. In 1509 he taught in Dôle, France under the patronage of Queen Margaret of Austria. The local monks became jealous of this patronage, however, and plotted against him. When one of them preached against him in the presence of the queen, Agrippa decided it was time to move on. In 1515 he was knighted on a battlefield in Italy, and became Cornelius Agrippa von Nettesheim—a name taken from that of a small village near Cologne.

He was granted a pension by King Francis I of France, but this was revoked when Agrippa refused to cast horoscopes for the king's mother. Agrippa was later made official historian by Queen Margaret, but was unwise enough to publish a work in which he attempted to demonstrate that all knowledge is useless. This so enraged his academic colleagues that he lost his job. Soon he was imprisoned for debt. Agrippa certainly lacked tact, for after this he again made the mistake of speaking his mind about Queen Margaret, for which he was thrown into prison and tortured. His health broken, he died in 1535 at the age of 49. Legend says that, as he lay on his deathbed, he cursed his wasted life and the black arts that had seduced him. Whereupon his black dog rushed out of the house and threw itself into a river—clearly proving thereby that it was a demon in disguise.

These biographical snippets, however richly spiced with legends, hardly add up to a man of strange powers. The certainty that Agrippa was indeed a magician, however, lies in the three volumes of his treatise *The Occult Philosophy*, which is regarded as one of the great magical texts. The book makes it

Below: Heinrich Cornelius, better known as Agrippa. A German scholar of the Renaissance period, he showed interest in a wide range of subjects, including magic. He was accused of using black arts.

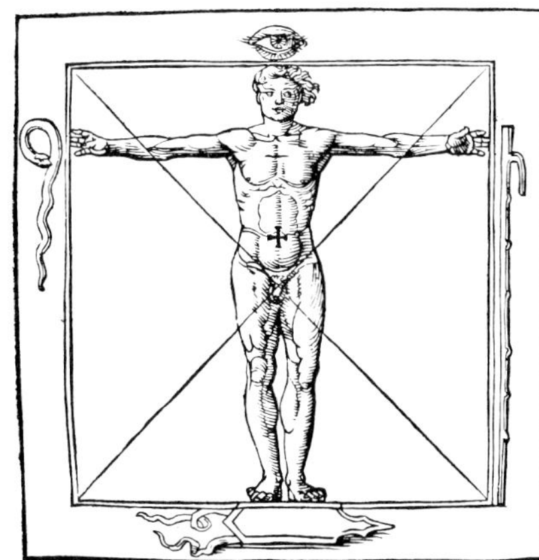
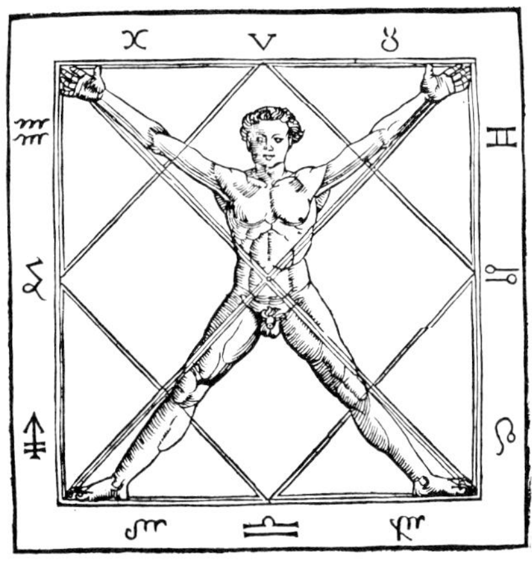

Left: an illustration in Agrippa's 16th-century book on the occult showing the human as a miniature copy, or microcosm, of the universe, or macrocosm. The theory of the human being as a tiny replica of the universe has always been an important tenet of magic.

clear that Agrippa knew all about thought pressure. Magic, he insists, is a faculty that springs from the power of the mind and imagination. There are mysterious relations between the human body and the universe, and between the earth on which we live and higher spiritual worlds. Thus, he argued, a stone can teach us about the nature of the stars. Agrippa believed that all nature is bound together by a kind of vast spider's web. Most human beings never learn to use their innate magical powers because they believe that they are cut off from the rest of nature. The magician, on the contrary, knows that his thought, if properly directed, can set the web vibrating and cause effects in far distant places.

Agrippa wrote his extraordinary masterwork when he was only 23 years old. It shows that, even at this early age, his study of the Cabala had given him some profound insights. Because he was always in danger of being burned as a black magician, he was careful to insist in his book that his knowledge is of a kind that any serious student can acquire from study of the great philosophers and mystics. But he also admits that he has successfully practiced divination and foretelling the future. For example, he describes two methods by which he claims to have detected the identity of thieves. One method is to pivot a sieve on forceps held between the index fingers of two students. The sieve will begin to swing like a pendulum when the name of the guilty person is mentioned. Similarly, if the sieve is pivoted so that it can be made to spin, it will stop spinning when the thief's name is spoken.

Agrippa insists that the success of these and other magical techniques are due to spirits—similar, presumably, to the spirits that help fakirs to perform their wonders. The overwhelming impression that emerges from the book is that Agrippa was a sensitive—born with the gifts of precognition, telepathy, and the ability to influence events by using the power of his mind. His belief that mind is more powerful than matter runs like a thread through the book. *The Occult Philosophy* is the work of a young man—full of vitality and brilliance—and of a dreamer who peered into a world that few of us have the gift to see.

The case of Paracelsus is even more tantalizing than that of Agrippa. His writings prove him to have been a more remark-

The Ill-fated Magician's Apprentice

Once, the stories go, a student of the magician Agrippa managed to get into his master's study when the magician was away. The student found Agrippa's book of spells and started reading it. There was a knock on the door; but the student, engrossed in his reading, ignored it. The knock sounded again loudly. Then the door flew open and a demon leaped in. Demanding to know why it had been summoned, the evil fiend caught the terrified student by the throat and strangled him. Not long afterward Agrippa returned. Horrified by what might happen if a dead body—especially that of one of his students—were discovered in his house, Agrippa ordered the demon to restore the student to life long enough to be seen in the busy marketplace.

The demon did as Agrippa bid. The student, apparently alive and in good health, left Agrippa's house and walked through town. After a little while he dropped dead. The townspeople were at first convinced that the unfortunate youth's death was completely natural. But when the body was examined closely, the telltale marks of the strangler's fingers were clear on his throat. Agrippa fled town to avoid scandal.

The Power of Words

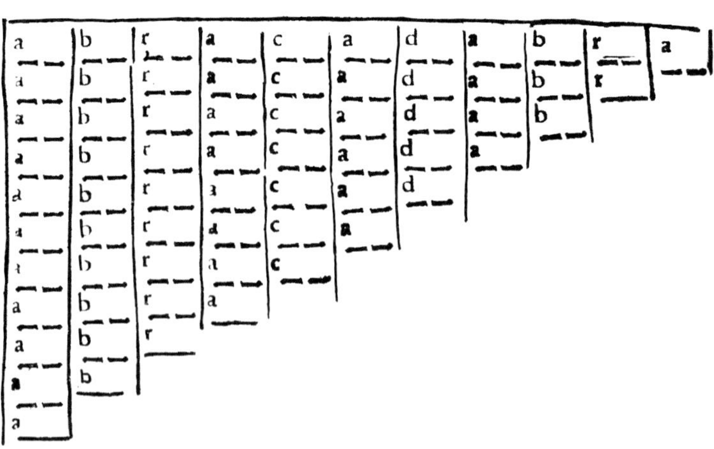

Right: "abracadabra" is a magic word often used in ordinary talk. Agrippa says that the word will cure all kinds of fever if it is written out in this form and hung around the sick person's neck. During the terrible plague of 1665 in England, it was said that many tried to ward off disease with "certain words or figures, as particularly the word Abracadabra."

able man—a great scientist as well as a magician. But, again, seeking the truth about him is like groping about in a fog, so obscured is his life with myth and legend.

He was born as Theophrastus Bombastus von Hohenheim in 1493, the son of an impoverished Swiss nobleman who had become a doctor. He studied medicine in Basel and completed his education at universities in Italy and Germany. His gifts as a physician were immediately apparent, and a series of remarkable cures soon earned him a formidable reputation. In 1524, when he was only 29 years old, he was appointed professor of medicine at Basel University. In nine years he had become one of the great names in medicine in Europe.

It was at this point that his career, so rich in both achievement and promise, was undermined by the same kind of character defects that brought ruin to Agrippa, and that seem to be hallmarks of so many magicians. He was vainglorious. He chose the pseudonym "Paracelsus" because it implied that he was greater than Celsus, the famous physician of ancient Rome. He was a heavy drinker, and was prey to sudden violent tempers. One of his first acts as professor at Basel University was to order his students to hold a public burning of the books of Avicenna, Galen, and other famous doctors of the past. This enraged his colleagues, who condemned him as an exhibitionist and a charlatan. When they plotted against him, Paracelsus compounded his unpopularity by calling them names—like many paranoid people he had a powerful gift for invective. For a while his reputation held his enemies at bay and when he cured the publisher Frobenius of an infected leg that other doctors had decided to amputate, it seemed that he had become invulnerable to attack. Soon after this, however, a patient declined to pay his bill and Paracelsus took him to court. Owing to the plots of his enemies, he lost the case, whereupon he rained such violent abuse on the heads of the judges that a warrant was issued for his arrest. He was forced to flee Basel—and his long soul-destroying downfall had begun.

For the remainder of his life Paracelsus wandered all over Europe as an itinerant doctor, writing book after book of which few were published in his lifetime, and pouring scorn and invective on his enemies. Fourteen years of wandering and disappointment wore him out. In 1541, when he was 48 years

Below: Agrippa as the bogeyman disciplinarian of naughty boys, from the English version of a famous 19th-century German picture book for children *Struwwelpeter*. Three boys are jeering at a black man, and the great sorcerer first sternly rebukes them. When they ignore him, he seizes them and dips them, wriggling, into his magic inkstand. When they emerge, they have been made as black as crows.

Right: Theophrastus Bombast von Hohenheim, the physician who took for himself the name Paracelsus. He chose this name because *para* means beyond in Greek, and it so indicated that he was greater than Celsus, the greatest Roman Doctor.

Above: one of the illustrations from Paracelsus' complicated work *Prognosticatio*, emphasizing the futility of man's own efforts, and the necessity of humility under the powerful hand of God. For Paracelsus, theology was an essential part of medicine because a doctor should also treat the soul.

old, he was invited by the Prince Palatine to settle at his seat in Salzburg. At last he might have found contentment in a quiet life of study. But he continued to drink too much, and six months later he rolled down a hill in a drunken stupor, and died of his injuries.

Then, ironically, his books began to be published, and they spread his fame over Europe once more. They have a range and boldness of imagination that is reminiscent of Leonardo da Vinci's notebooks. Paracelsus immediately became a kind of patron saint of occultism—a position he maintains even today, with his writings being studied by a new generation of occultists.

As with Agrippa, it is difficult to discover four centuries later what genuine powers lay behind the many legends of Paracelsus's magical prowess. One thing is clear: most of the stories concern remarkable cures, and this suggests that he was primarily gifted with seemingly magical powers of healing. For example, we are told that he cured an innkeeper's daughter who since birth had been paralyzed from the waist down. The medicine he gave her was probably saltpeter in teaspoonfulls of wine. This would obviously have had no effect, but it seems that the hypnotic force of his personality and his natural healing power brought about a cure. We are also again confronted by the paradox of the split personality: a man who was bad-tempered, thin-skinned, and boastful, yet who could be taken over by some strange power that rose from his subconscious depths and made him a great healer.

Charlatans-with Genuine Powers?

So we reach the odd conclusion that the contemporaries of Agrippa and Paracelsus were probably right when they called them charlatans—but that, at the same time, both men possessed genuine powers. It would be another four centuries before the great Swiss psychologist Carl Jung attempted to explain these powers scientifically in terms of that vast reservoir of energy known as the subconscious mind.

In the 16th century it was still dangerous for a man of knowledge to gain a reputation as a wizard or sorcerer. The witch hunting craze was spreading across Europe, and many people were being burned for being in league with the Devil. This no doubt explains why we know so little of the lives of the alchemists who followed in the footsteps of Agrippa and Paracelsus. That remarkable 16th-century French physician and prophet Nostradamus took care to hide his visions in verse of such obscurity that even nowadays we cannot be certain what most of them mean.

The tide turned in the 17th and 18th centuries—the age of scientists such as Newton, Huygens, and Harvey—and the seeker after forbidden knowledge once again became respectable, at least in Protestant countries. Sir Isaac Newton—one of the greatest names in science and philosophy—spent as much time in his alchemical laboratory as at his telescope.

In 1734 was born one of those remarkable pioneers to whom the modern world owes much, but to whom it pays little attention: Franz Anton Mesmer. He was the discoverer of what came to be called mesmerism and later hypnotism. Mesmer, whose parents were Swiss, studied medicine at the University of Vienna, and wrote his doctoral thesis on the

Above: an illustration for a medical work by Paracelsus, which shows the doctor treating one of his patients. Paracelsus said that since man contains all the elements, and needs them for the curing of his illnesses, a good physician must understand all physical sciences plus alchemy.

Above: a portrait of Franz Mesmer, the first man to employ hypnotism.
As the fame of Mesmer's work spread across Europe, so did the derision of people who could not or would not try to understand what the doctor was doing. The cartoonists had a field day.

influence of the planets on human health. He was 40 years of age when he stumbled on the discovery that was to make him famous—and infamous. A wealthy English lady who was passing through Vienna was suffering from stomach cramps, and she called on a Jesuit acquaintance of Mesmer's, to ask if he could lend her some magnets. She was convinced that magnets relieved her stomach pains. When Mesmer heard of this he was intrigued, for it seemed to complement his own theory that there was some kind of vital fluid in the body that flowed like the tides, producing health or sickness. If these tides existed, might it not be possible to influence their movements by magnets?

Mesmer tried using magnets on his own patients—and they seemed to work. Shortly afterward, while Mesmer was bleeding a patient—the standard cure for most ailments in those days—he observed that the bleeding increased when he came closer, and decreased when he moved away. This must mean, he thought, that he himself was a kind of magnet. Mesmer coined the term "animal magnetism" to describe his strange power, and he demonstrated its value when curing a nobleman who was suffering from spasms. For six days Mesmer had moved his powerful magnets over the patient's body to no effect. Then, on the sixth day, as the patient choked with asthma, Mesmer took hold of his foot. The spasm abated.

It looked as though Mesmer had gotten the measure of the patient's vital fluids at last. News of his cure spread all over

Right: "The Magnetism: Mesmer," a painting of about 1784.

Vienna, and made him one of the most celebrated doctors in Austria. He began to experiment with "magnetized water"—vats of water filled with iron filings into which metal rods were fixed. Patients grasped the rods—or one patient held onto a rod while other sufferers held his other hand. Music was played during the treatment, and eventually the patients went into a trance or had convulsions. They were cured by the dozen.

Then came a temporary setback. Mesmer failed to cure a blind girl—understandably so inasmuch as her blindness was due to a detached retina. A scandal arose, however, and he had to leave Vienna. He moved to Paris, and immediately achieved even greater success. His healing sessions began to look like orgies. The patients—men and women together—were lightly clad to help the animal magnetism flow more easily from one patient to the next. As they massaged one another or pressed their thighs together, according to Mesmer's prescribed method, many of them were convinced they could feel the health-giving effect.

The instrument of Mesmer's downfall was the same as that of Paracelsus: envious fellow doctors who denounced him as a charlatan. As with Paracelsus too, Mesmer's arbitrary and autocratic behavior as much as his natural talents was the cause. When a commission of doctor's declared that his cures were due merely to suggestion rather than to magnetism, Mesmer left France in disgrace. He retired to a villa near Constance in southwestern Germany where he spent his

Mesmer and the Forces of Magnetism

Below: "The effects of animal magnetism." The girl is overcome by animals responding to incredible, invisible magnetism.

Two Men of Mystery

Below: Jacques Casanova, the adventurer, was apparently possessed of occult talents. His name has become a synonym for seducer.

remaining days in peace. The doctors were right that Mesmer cured by suggestion, of course. What they failed to realize was that Mesmer's cures proved that the power of suggestion is a greater force than anyone had suspected. If the subconscious mind can be convinced by suggestion, it can bring about extraordinary cures. This point was underlined a few years later when one of Mesmer's disciples, the Marquis of Puysegur, was trying to "magnetize" a shepherd boy by stroking his head and, to his astonishment, induced a deep trancelike sleep. He had stumbled on hypnotism. Even today, after almost two centuries, we know little more about the underlying mechanism of hypnotism than did Puysegur. Once more we confront the strange paradox: that a man can be completely self-deceived about the nature of his powers and nevertheless be a genuine magician.

Nowhere is this more apparent than in the case of the man whose name has become synonymous with seduction: Jacques Casanova, the adventurer and confidence trickster who flourished in the second half of the 18th century. Not only was Casanova an accomplished faith healer (he cured an ailing Venetian senator by means of suggestion), but he was also remarkably successful at fortune telling by means of cards and other oracles. Indeed, the accuracy of his predictions sometimes alarmed Casanova himself. For instance, he told one girl that she would go to Paris and become the king's mistress—and that is exactly what happened. Casanova believed that he somehow conjured up real spirits when he was muttering his bogus incantations. What seems more likely is that he possessed the same occult faculty as Paracelsus or Faust to some degree.

Casanova met, and immediately disliked, another charlatan who acquired a reputation as a great magician: the man who called himself the "Count of Saint-Germain." When Saint-Germain arrived in Vienna in the mid-1740s he seemed to be about 30 years old—a man of powerful and dominant personality, with the typical magician's streak of boastfulness and desire to astonish. In Vienna he was befriended by members of the nobility, and was brought to Paris by the Marshal de Belle-Isle. By 1758 he had become a close friend of Louis XV and his mistress Madame de Pompadour.

Part of Saint-Germain's attraction was his reputation as a man of mystery. No one seemed to have any idea of where or when he was born. But his knowledge of history seemed to be enormous, and occasionally he said things that suggested he knew far more about certain events in the remote past than any mere student possibly could know. In short, he implied that he had actually witnessed them in person. He would learnedly discourse on the priesthood of Egypt in a way that suggested he had studied in ancient Thebes or Heliopolis. Another puzzle was that he was never seen to eat, although it is now known that he had a special diet. He explained that he lived on some elixir of which only he knew the formula. He was a student of alchemy, and claimed to have discovered the secret of the Philosopher's Stone. What is certain is that he had learned a great deal about metallurgy and chemistry.

Saint-Germain continued to fascinate students of occultism.

Many of them believe he is alive today—possibly in Tibet. The unromantic truth is that he died in his mid-70s in 1784, suffering from rheumatism and morbid depression. Accounts of people who met him indicate that, far from being a man of mystery and an enigma, he struck many intelligent people as a fool, charlatan, boaster, and swindler.

If Saint-Germain seems to have been fundamentally a confidence man, the same cannot be said of his famous contemporary Count Alessandro di Cagliostro. That he was a fraud there can be little doubt, but that he also possessed highly developed occult faculties is fairly certain. His enemies said that Cagliostro's real name was Giuseppe Balsamo, and that he had been a confidence trickster in his native Italy. As a schoolboy he was exuberant and ungovernable, and ran away from seminary school several times. In his teens he became a wanderer, like many talented and penniless young men, and lived by his wits. But he was also an avid student of alchemy, astrology, and

Above: the Count of Saint-Germain, who admitted this name was false, was and remains one of history's figures of mystery. All accounts agree that he was a charming and knowledgeable man, but no one ever knew where he came from before he arrived in Vienna and from there made his way to the French court.

Left: an illustration from Saint-Germain's manuscript *La Tres Sainte Trinosophie* (The Most Holy Threefold Wisom). It shows a mystic initiation. The woman is Isis. The man to be initiated is naked—as he came into the world and as he will now be born again. Stripped of all clothing, rank, and power, he may bring to the temple nothing that he owns, but only that which he himself is. The objects on the table are three of the Tarot card suits, symbols of water, fire, and air.

Right: the Count Alessandro di Cagliostro, who was born of Italian peasant parentage. He was quick and clever and early appreciated that a man from far places enjoyed great prestige, and that most people will believe any story told with assurance.

Far right: Cagliostro's beautiful wife, who assisted him in frauds. Born Lorenza, she became known to Paris society as Seraphinia Felichiani Comtesse de Cagliostro.

ritual magic, and he soon had a wide, if not very coherent, knowledge of occultism.

At the age of 26 in 1769 Cagliostro fell in love with Lorenza, the beautiful 14-year-old daughter of a coppersmith. They married, and for many years she was his partner in adventure and fraud, her beauty being one of their greatest assets. When Casanova met them in the south of France the year after their marriage as they were returning from a pilgrimage to Santiago de Compostella in Spain, they appeared to be people of means, traveling in style and distributing alms to the poor. In Paris, the couple came under the protection of a nobleman, who then seduced Lorenza and tried to make her leave her husband. Cagliostro had her thrown into jail, but later reunited with her and took her to England.

In London he joined the Freemasons. Soon, however, he founded his own masonic order, infusing its ceremonies with occult rituals purportedly based on ancient Egyptian practices that Cagliostro claimed he had discovered in an Egyptian manuscript on a bookstall. Cagliostro was undoubtedly convinced that his Egyptian masonry was the product of divine inspiration. It was certainly the turning point in his fortunes. From London he journeyed to Venice, Berlin, Nuremberg, and Leipzig. In each city, he visited the masonic lodge, made speeches on his Egyptian rite, and initiated members. His argument seems to have been that the Egyptian rite was as different from, and as superior to, established freemasonry as New Testament Christianity is from Old Testament Judaism. He was feted and admired, and became a rich man.

Cagliostro came to Strasbourg in 1780, and soon became the most talked about man in town. Although he was wealthy, he lived modestly in a room above a tobacco shop. His cures became legendary. He was often able to heal the sick simply by the laying on of hands. On one occasion he successfully delivered a baby after midwives had given up the mother for dead.

It was in Strasbourg that he met the man who was to bring about his downfall: Cardinal de Rohan. He was a churchman who longed for royal favor, but who unfortunately was disliked by Queen Marie Antoinette. Cagliostro deeply impressed Rohan, who spoke of his luminous and hypnotic eyes with almost religious fervor.

The cardinal's downfall occurred in 1785 in the famous Affair of the Diamond Necklace. A pretty swindler who called herself the Countess de la Motte Valois became Rohan's mistress, and persuaded him that the queen wanted him to secretly buy a diamond necklace worth $300,000. In fact, the queen knew nothing of it, and the money raised by the cardinal went straight into the countess's pocket. When the jewelers finally approached the queen for a long overdue installment on the money, the whole affair came to light. The countess was tried and publicly flogged. Rohan and Cagliostro were also tried and, although they were acquitted, the scandal damaged both of them irreparably. In addition, the months that Cagliostro spent in jail before trial broke his nerve—and his luck.

Cagliostro went to London after leaving prison. There he accurately predicted the nature and date of the French Revolution and of the fall of the Bastille. Then he traveled around Europe, often hounded by the police. Finally, he made the extraordinary error of going to Rome to propagate his Egyptian freemasonry under the nose of the Pope. He was arrested and thrown into the papal prison in the Castel Sant'Angelo, and was later transferred to the even worse prison of San Leo. Eight years after his arrest in 1787, French soldiers captured San Leo prison and searched for Cagliostro, intending to treat him as a revolutionary hero. In fact, he had been dead for several years—though exactly when and how he died is still unknown.

Of all the great magician-mystics, Cagliostro is the most tragic. One of his enemies said of him that he possessed "a demonic power that paralyzes the will." But in retrospect he seems less a demon than a fallen angel. The one magician-mystic who certainly had—and used—a paralytic power of will over others was Rasputin, the sinister, enigmatic Russian monk. His is an extraordinary story.

Count Cagliostro - Con-man Supreme

Left: an English cartoon shows Cagliostro at a masonic lodge in London, where he came after his release from the Bastille in 1786. An English brother mason performed a satirical sketch of "a visiting quack." Cagliostro, just to the left of the table, took offense and walked out. The cartoonist has Cagliostro saying as he shows his displeasure, "Per Dio Santo! Son Scoperto!" ("Dear God, I am found out!")

The Enigmatic Russian Monk

On January 1, 1917, the temperature in the Russian city of Petrograd—now Leningrad—was sub-zero. From a bridge over the frozen Neva River a few spectators watched a group of policemen who stood around a hole in the ice. A diver emerged, grasping the end of a rope that disappeared into the dark water beneath him. When he was out, the policemen heaved on the rope. A body broke the surface and slid onto the ice. The corpse was a bearded man in his late 40s; his face was battered and swollen. He had been bound with ropes, but before dying he had managed to free one hand, which was raised to his chest as if making the sign of the cross. He was wearing only one boot; the other was in the hands of a police inspector who stood nearby. It was this boot, found by a boy, that had led police to the spot.

Grigori Rasputin, who had been murdered three days before, was one of the most notorious figures in Petrograd. Now that he was dead, he would become a legend all over the world—a symbol of evil, cunning, and lust. If ever you see a magazine story titled "Rasputin, the Mad Monk," you can be sure it will be full of lurid details of how Rasputin spent his days in drunken carousing, his nights in sexual debauchery; how he deceived the czar and czarina into thinking he was a miracle worker; how he was the evil genius who brought about the Russian Revolution and the downfall of the Romanov dynasty. It is all untrue. Yet it makes such a good story that there is little chance that Rasputin will ever receive justice. The truth about him is that he really was a miracle worker and a man of strange powers. He was certainly no saint—very few magicians are—and tales of his heavy drinking and sexual prowess are undoubtedly based on fact. But he was no diabolical schemer.

Rasputin was born in the village of Pokrovskoe in 1870. His father was a fairly well-to-do peasant. As a young man, Rasputin had a reputation for wildness until he visited a monastery and spent four months there in prayer and meditation. For the remainder of his life, he was obsessed by religion. He married at 19 and became a prosperous carter. Then the call came again; he left his family and took to the road as a kind of wandering monk. When eventually he returned, he was a changed man, exuding an extraordinarily powerful magnetism. The young people of his village were fascinated by him. He converted one room in his house into a church, and it was always full. The local priest became envious of his following, however, and Rasputin was forced to leave home again.

Rasputin had always possessed the gift of second sight. One day during his childhood this gift had revealed to him the identity of a peasant who had stolen a horse and hidden it in a barn. Now, on his second round of travels, he also began to develop extraordinary healing powers. He would kneel by the beds of the sick and pray; then he would lay his hands on them, and cure many of them. When he came to what is now Leningrad, probably late in 1903, he already had a reputation as a wonder worker. Soon he was accepted in aristocratic society in spite of his rough peasant manners.

Opposite: Rasputin, the Russian mystic and faith healer, pictured as he was when his hypnotic power was first recognized in Russia. Rasputin became a power in the royal court through successful treatment of the czar's sick child, and his success aroused both violent hatred and equally passionate devotion.

Rasputin–the Mystic and Healer

It was in 1907 that he suddenly became the power behind the throne. Three years before, Czarina Alexandra had given birth to a longed-for heir to the throne, Prince Alexei. But it was soon apparent that Alexei had inherited hemophilia, a disease that prevents the blood from clotting, and from which a victim may bleed to death even with a small cut. At the age of three, the prince fell and bruised himself so severely that an internal hemorrhage developed. He lay in a fever for days, and doctors despaired of his life. Then the czarina recalled the man of god she had met two years earlier, and sent for Rasputin. As soon as he came in he said calmly: "Do not worry the child. He will be all right." He laid his hand on the boy's forehead, sat down on the edge of the bed, and began to talk to him in a quiet voice. Then he knelt and prayed. In a few minutes the boy was in a deep and peaceful sleep, and the crisis was over.

Henceforward the czarina felt a powerful emotional dependence on Rasputin—a dependence nourished by the thinly veiled hostility with which Alexandra, a German, was treated at court. Rasputin's homely strength brought her a feeling of security. The czar also began to confide in Rasputin, who became a man of influence at court. Nicholas II was a poor ruler, not so much cruel as weak, and too indecisive to stem the rising tide of social discontent. His opponents began to believe that Rasputin was responsible for some of the czar's reactionary policies, and a host of powerful enemies began to gather. On several occasions the czar had to give way to the pressure and order Rasputin to leave the city. On one such occasion, the young prince fell and hurt himself again. For several days he tossed in agony, until he seemed too weak to survive. The czarina dispatched a telegram to Rasputin, and he telegraphed back: "The illness is not as dangerous as it seems." From the moment it was received, the prince began to recover.

World War I brought political revolution and military catastrophe to Russia. Its outbreak was marked by a strange coincidence: Rasputin was stabbed by a madwoman at precisely the same moment as the Archduke Franz Ferdinand was shot at Sarajevo. Rasputin hated war, and might have been able to dissuade the czar from leading Russia into the conflict. But he was in bed recovering from his stab wound when the moment of decision came.

Rasputin's end was planned by conspirators in the last days of 1916. He was lured to a cellar by Prince Felix Yussupov, a man he trusted. After feeding him poisoned cakes, Yussupov shot him in the back; then Rasputin was beaten with an iron bar. Such was his immense vitality that he was still alive when the murderers dropped him through the hole in the ice into the Neva. Among his papers was found a strange testament addressed to the czar. It stated that he had a strong feeling he would die by violence before January 1, 1917, and that if he were killed by peasants, the czar would reign for many years to come; but, if he were killed by aristocrats—as he was—then "none of your children or relations will remain alive for more than two years." He was right. The czar and his family were all murdered in July 1918 an amazing example, among many, of Rasputin's gift of precognition.

Left: a caricature of the rumored orgies at the court, in the style of an icon, or holy picture. The nude figure dancing with Rasputin greatly resembles the czarina.

Below: Rasputin recovering from the first attempt on his life.

SIC
OMNIA
ORATORIUM
FELIX CUI
A CONSILIUS
NE·LOQUA
RIS DE DEO
ABSQ·LV·
MINE·
HOC HOC AGEN TIBUS
NOBIS. ADERIT IPSI DEUS.
DISCE BENE MORI
Admai
Saday Eloy Agla Tetragramate

Chapter 5 Magic at Work

Perhaps it is easy to dismiss the accounts of strange powers among medieval men—it was long ago, and the historians were uncritical—but how can we explain the bizarre events in the lives of magicians who lived nearer to our own time? Is it possible that the Roman god Mercury could be summoned up in 20th-century Paris? And what about the extraordinary Madame Blavatsky, who dealt in wonders, only some of which can be explained away by trickery and fraud? The evidence is mixed, but the tales are fascinating . . . and there seems to be no easy answer for a rational, scientific explanation.

It was 11:30 at night on December 31, 1913, and the room in Paris was filled with the smell of incense. The room was lit by a flame that burned on an altar. Laid out beside this were a chain, a scourge, a dagger, a jar of oil, a loaf of bread, and a flask of wine. The dark robed man who stood before the altar was Aleister Crowley, an English practitioner of magic who liked to refer to himself as the Beast 666 from Revelations. The naked man beside him was his disciple Victor Neuberg. Crowley began to intone:

Hail! Asi! Hail, Hoor-Apep! Let
The Silence speech beget . . .

As he chanted, Crowley rang a bell twice.

As he chanted the words of the ritual, he seized the scourge and whipped Neuberg's bare buttocks. Then he took the dagger and scratched a cross on Neuberg's chest above the heart, and bound the chain about Neuberg's forehead:

The scourge, the dagger, and the chain
Cleanse body, breast, and brain!

This strange ritual continued until the clock sounded midnight—New Year's Day of 1914. Then the priest and his neophyte began to chant in Latin. Suddenly the shape of a naked boy seemed to form in the air in front of them. He was surrounded by thousands of golden wands, which glowed with a clear light. Around each wand two live serpents seemed to be writhing. This was the caduceus, the wand traditionally

Opposite: a magician invoking an angel before his magic altar, with demons clustering around the edge of the mystic circle that preserves him from harm.

The Strange Power of Ritual Magic

Below: Victor Neuberg, who took part with Aleister Crowley in a series of magical exercises in January, 1914, that have come to be known as the Paris Working.

associated with Mercury, the messenger of the Gods. It indicated that Crowley had succeeded in invoking Mercury—the Roman equivalent of the older Greek god Hermes, traditional founder of magic arts.

To the skeptic, the whole thing sounds absurd, and the vision seems to be some kind of hallucination induced with the help of the incense and the orgiastic flogging. We cannot say if this is so with any certainty. What we can say is that the ceremony Crowley was performing was not some wild invention of his inflamed imagination. It was a traditional magic ceremony of a kind that had been performed thousands of times in the temples of the ancient world. It was no surprise to Crowley that he saw Mercury and his caduceus. He expected to see Mercury, just as a chemist expects to see blue litmus paper turn red when he dips it in acid.

But how is it possible for a modern Westerner to take magic seriously? Is it not a primitive superstition—or, at best, an early form of crude science? No magician would agree. According to Crowley and most other practicing magicians, magic is quite simply the science of "causing changes to occur in conformity with will." This view was put forward by the French magician Eliphas Lévi, of whom Crowley believed himself to be a reincarnation. According to Lévi, magic is based on human will power which is a force "as real as steam or the galvanic current." In short, both Lévi and Crowley believed that magic is the directed use of the power that we have labeled thought pressure. Steam is lighter than air, yet it can drive an engine. Electricity is invisible, yet it can light a whole city. The will is intangible and invisible, yet magicians believe that, if properly directed, it can change the world.

We might expect ritual magic to be something that changes from age to age according to the temperament of individual magicians and the cultures to which they belong. To a minor extent this is true. Yet perhaps the most surprising thing about magic is that the way people have regarded it and the manner in which it has been used have altered little in thousands of years. Anyone who reads about the magic of the ancient Chaldeans or Chinese, or about the modern gypsies or dervishes, soon discovers that certain basic ideas and methods occur again and again. If magic is purely wishful thinking and nonsense, it has managed to be remarkably consistent wishful thinking and nonsense.

The god Hermes Trismegistus whom Crowley invoked was identical with Thoth, an important god of the ancient Egyptians. Magicians of ancient Alexandria in Egypt declared that Thoth was not a god, but a king who had reigned for more than 3000 years and had written various books on religion and magic. This king was known in Greek as Hermes Trismegistus, Thrice-Greatest Hermes. According to legend, he was buried in the great pyramid of Giza, and when his body was uncovered he was found to be holding an emerald tablet that contained an inscription beginning: "As above, so below." This has two meanings, one religious and one magical. Its religious meaning is that God is identical with the soul—a belief that is one of the central tenets of Hinduism. The magical meaning is that a

Left: Crowley in 1911 at his altar in special dress and with the equipment for his rituals.

man is a small model of the universe. Man is the *microcosm* (from Greek words meaning little world), and the universe is the *macrocosm* (great world). Man and the universe are connected by thousands of fine threads—a doctrine later elaborated by Paracelsus. You might say that man is an organ of the universe, just as the heart is an organ of the body. That is why students of magic believe that astrology, which claims that celestial bodies influence human affairs, can predict future events.

Like the Cabala, the many works attributed to Hermes

Below: a caricatured self-portrait by Crowley. He dramatized himself as the Great Beast, and made his motto "Do What Thou Wilt."

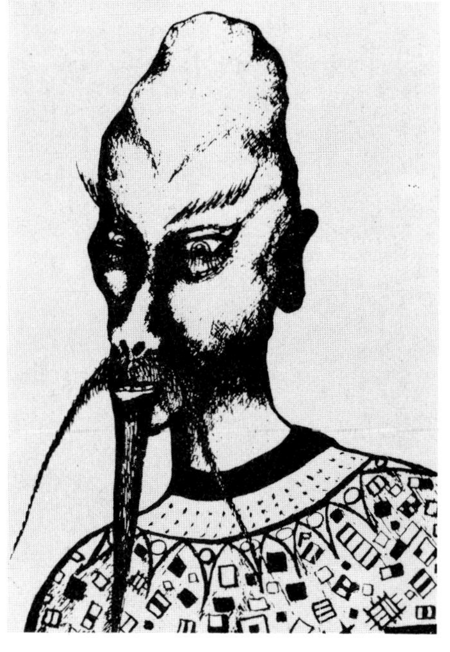

Trismegistus—which in fact were probably written in Alexandria between 300 B.C. and A.D. 300—were a source of inspiration to many great thinkers of the Middle Ages and after. They were studied not only by mystics such as Albertus Magnus, the 13th-century Christian bishop who taught St. Thomas Aquinas, but also by Agrippa and Paracelsus. We have already argued that the success of most magicians is due to their possession of strange powers. The question we must now ask is this: Can certain rituals, such as those enacted by Crowley, confer magical powers? For evidence let us look at the careers of three of the most celebrated occultists of the last four centuries.

Below: Hermes Trismegistus appears in this 15th-century mosaic pavement in central Italy. Hermes Trismegistus is said by some to be the Egyptian god Thoth in the form of an earthly king. As this king, Hermes Trismegistus reigned in peace for 3226 years.

Magic-an Ancient Religion Revived

Dr. John Dee, the most highly regarded magician of Shakespeare's time, is almost unique among magicians in that he possessed practically no occult powers. Perhaps this is why he managed to avoid the usual magician's destiny of spectacular success and tragic downfall.

He was born in 1527, the son of a minor official in the court of King Henry VIII. From childhood on he was an avid reader, and when he went to Cambridge University at the age of 15, he allowed himself only four hours' sleep a night. After Cambridge he went to the University of Louvain in Belgium, where Agrippa had also studied. When Dee read Agrippa's *Occult Philosophy*, he knew that he had stumbled on his life's work—the pursuit of magical knowledge. At the age of 23 he gave a series of free lectures on geometry in Rheims, France, and was so popular that he was offered a professorship. But he preferred to return to England to pursue his occult studies.

When Elizabeth I came to the throne in 1558, she asked Dee to cast a suitable date for her coronation. Dee did so, and from this time on he enjoyed royal protection. Even so, as one suspected of magical practices, he still had to behave with extreme caution. Moreover, Queen Elizabeth was notoriously stingy: her patronage did nothing to improve Dee's finances, and he remained poor all his life. Dee married a lady-in-waiting who bore him eight children. He lived quietly and studied astrology, crystal gazing, and alchemy.

The aim of crystal gazing is to induce a semitrancelike state in which the subconscious mind projects future events as images in the crystal. Dee was too much of an intellectual to be good at this. He realized that what he needed was a working partner with natural occult faculties, especially in scrying. In 1582 he met Edward Kelley, a young Irishman who claimed to have second sight. Kelley was undoubtedly a crook—he had had both his ears cut off for forgery—but it seems equally certain that he did possess second sight, and that he was also a medium. Dee's wife took an immediate dislike to the Irishman, but when Kelley went into a trance and began to get in touch with spirits, Dee was so delighted that he overruled his wife's objections.

How did Dee and Kelley go about summoning the spirits? One famous print shows them in a graveyard practicing necromancy. From what we know of the pious Dee, however, it seems unlikely that he went in for this sort of thing. We can learn more from his *Spiritual Diaries*. It is clear that he went into training before endeavoring to summon the spirits. He abstained for three days from sexual intercourse, overeating, and the consumption of alcohol, and he took care to shave his beard and cut his nails. Then began a two-week period of magical invocations in Latin and Hebrew beginning at dawn and continuing until noon, then beginning again at sunset and continuing until midnight. Kelley, meanwhile, gazed intently into the crystal ball. At the end of 14 days, Kelley would begin to see angels and demons in the crystal. Later, these spirits would walk about the room. Dee, however, does not seem to have seen the spirits, but he recorded lengthy dialogues he had with them.

Below: a statuette of the Egyptian god Thoth from the Ptolemaic period, about 323 to 30 B.C. He was worshiped as a moon-god and inventor of hieroglyphics. He was a magician who had known "these formulas which commanded all the forces of nature and subdued the very gods themselves."

Edward Kelley the Natural Medium

Mohammed

Apollonius of Tyana

Edward Kelley

Roger Bacon

Paracelsus

John Dee

Portraits from the frontispiece of a book about John Dee, royal magician to Queen Elizabeth I. Published 50 years after his death, it was a disparaging book based on Dee's personal diaries. It succeeded in damaging his reputation.

One's instant response to this is the conviction that Kelley made Dee believe that nonexistent spirits had manifested themselves. The trouble with this view is that the conversations, which came via the mouth of Kelley, were often so crammed with abstruse magical lore that it is almost inconceivable that the illiterate Irishman could have made them up as he went along. Dee, of course, was familiar with the lore, and certain of the demons quoted chunks of Agrippa's *Occult Philosophy*. This makes it possible that Dee transmitted them telepathically to Kelley. The likeliest explanation, however, is that Kelley was a natural medium.

Count Adalbert Laski, a servant of Henry III of France, was so impressed by these seances of Dee and Kelley that he invited them to visit the king of Germany. Dee and his family, and Kelley and his wife spent four years traveling around Europe as guests of various kings and noblemen, and their performances were sensationally successful.

Kelley was a difficult man, given to sudden tantrums and to fits of boredom and depression; but in spite of their ups and downs, he and Dee continued to work together for many years. They finally separated while they were still on their travels in Europe. Kelley achieved some success on his own as an alchemist and scryer, but eventually he died in prison. Dee returned to England in 1589 and lived for another 19 years, hoping in vain that the spirits would lead him to a crock of gold. Today his reputation among occultists is secure, for he was the first magician on record to make use of spirit communication. He was 200 years before his time; but in spite of his lack of worldly success, he remains one of the great names in the history of magic.

In 1801 there appeared in London a work called *The Magus, or Celestial Intelligencer* by Francis Barrett. It was supposed to be "a complete system of occult philosophy." Nowadays it is not highly regarded by students and adepts of the magic arts, because many of the rituals it details are garbled and inaccurate. Nevertheless, it was an important work for it was almost the first attempt at a serious description of magical practices since Agrippa's *Occult Philosophy* nearly three centuries earlier. After Agrippa's time, fear of persecution had driven the magicians underground for 200 years.

The Age of Reason, as thinkers and writers of mid-18th-century Europe called their period, had made magic superfluous—or at least unfashionable. But the tide soon turned again. All over western Europe novels such as Horace Walpole's *The Castle of Otranto* began to appear, in which high adventure and crimes of passion were mixed with supernatural events. Of course, most readers did not really believe in the supernatural trappings of such stories—but their enormous popularity shows that ghosts, magic, and the paranormal continued to fascinate. At the end of *The Magus*, Barrett printed an advertisement asking for students to help him found a "magic circle," and an active group was established at Cambridge.

Nine years after publication of *The Magus*, there was born

A Prophecy From the Grave

Guy Fawkes was one of the conspirators in the Gunpowder Plot of November 5, 1605, to blow up the English Houses of Parliament. He has since grown into a folktale figure for English children, and the anniversary of the unsuccessful political plot is now a day for fun with fireworks and bonfires. But few know that Guy Fawkes and the scholar-magician John Dee, astrologer to Queen Elizabeth I, are linked in a curious tale.

The story says that Fawkes came upon Dee and his assistant Edward Kelley in a graveyard as they were carrying a body away. They were taking it to a chamber where they were going to raise it from the dead in order to ask questions of it. Fawkes offered to pay for the opportunity of questioning the corpse himself, hoping to find out about the fate of the conspiracy in which he was engaged. Dee angrily refused payment, but agreed to allow him to put his question.

When the half-decayed body rose eerily, Fawkes asked "Will the end be successful?"

The corpse, lit only by a glimmering blue light, replied, "The end will be death."

And for Guy Fawkes it was. He was caught and executed as a traitor after the plot failed.

Res
RAPHAEL
Rael

in Paris a remarkable man who, more than any other, was responsible for the great magical revival that swept across Europe in the 19th century: Alphonse-Louis Constant, better known as Eliphas Lévi. The son of a poor shoemaker, Lévi was a dreamy, sickly, highly intelligent and imaginative child with powerful religious inclinations. At the age of 12 in 1822, he decided he was destined for the Church. He had a craving to belong to some spiritual order, some great organization, that would enable him to devote his life to the truths of the spirit. His teacher at the seminary of Saint Nicholas du Chardonnet was Abbot Frere-Colonna, a remarkable idealist who believed that man was slowly ascending toward God, and that a great age of the Holy Spirit was at hand. The abbot had studied Mesmer's doctrines, and believed that they were inspired by the Devil. He devoted some time to denouncing them in class, but succeeded only in awakening young Lévi's interest in such forbidden matters. When the abbot was dismissed through the intrigues of jealous colleagues, Lévi's disillusion with the Church began.

Lévi still hungered for a faith, however. He became a sub-deacon, and one of his chief tasks was teaching catechism to the young girls. One day a poor woman begged him to prepare her daughter for first communion, and Lévi's initial feelings of protectiveness developed into a wild infatuation for the girl. Nothing came of it, but the experience convinced him that he was not intended for the priesthood. When he turned away from his vocation, his mother committed suicide.

After 14 years in a seminary, Lévi found the world a hard place to adjust to. He still wanted to be a believer, and dreamed of Frere-Colonna's spiritual rebirth of mankind. So, although he began to write for radical newspapers—and spent time in prison on sedition charges as a result—his search for a faith continued. He discovered the writings of Swedenborg, and then the Cabala with its doctrine that man can overcome original sin and rise toward the godhead. Honoré de Balzac's mystical novel *Louis Lambert* was also a vital influence. Lévi studied that strange fortune-telling deck of cards known as the Tarot, and linked its 22 cards of the Major Arcana with the 22 paths of the Cabala. Lévi came to certain important conclusions about magic. The first was that the will is a far greater power than we realize, and that magic is learning how to use this power. The second was that all space is permeated with a medium that Lévi called astral light, which can take the impression of thoughts and feelings, and is the medium through which thoughts are conveyed in telepathy. Third, he believed deeply in the microcosm-macrocosm doctrine enshrined in Hermes Trismegistus's inscription, "As above, so below."

Lévi was in his 40s when his *Dogma and Ritual of High Magic* was published in 1856, and it established a reputation that was consolidated four years later by his *History of Magic*. In the first book he describes one of the most curious incidents of his life. On a visit to London, he records, he was asked to try to raise the spirit of the ancient Greek magician Apollonius of Tyana. After a month of preparation and fasting, Lévi spent

Raising the Spirits of the Dead

Opposite: Edward Kelley, John Dee's disreputable assistant, shown raising a ghost with an assistant of his own. The ghost they called up was said to have buried a large amount of money in life and, reportedly, "satisfied their wicked desires and inquiries."

Below: detail from a portrait of John Dee painted in 1594. Dee managed to avoid persecution as a witch by his connection with the court—it has even been suggested that he may have acted as a spy for the queen's well-developed intelligence network—but his magic never brought him riches, and he died in poverty.

Levi Invokes Apollonius

Below: Eliphas Lévi in 1862, six years after his first magical treatise, *Dogma and Ritual of High Magic*, was published. It is said that he introduced no very original ideas, but that he was the first to see a connection between the Tarot and the Cabala.

12 hours in ritual incantations. At last, the shade of Apollonius appeared in a gray shroud, and telepathically answered questions Lévi put to it about the future of two of his acquaintances. It prophesied the death of both. Lévi's description of the invocation has considerable dramatic quality:

"I kindled two fires with the requisite prepared substances, and began reading the invocations of the 'Ritual' in a voice at first low, but rising by degrees. The smoke spread, the flame caused the objects on which it fell to waver, then it went out, the smoke still floating white and slow about the marble altar. I seemed to feel a quaking of the earth, my ears tingled, my heart beat quickly. I heaped more twigs and perfumes on the chafing dishes, and as the flames again burst up, I beheld distinctly, before the altar, the figure of a man of more than normal size, which dissolved and vanished away. I re-commenced the evocations, and placed myself within a circle which I had drawn previously between the tripod and the altar. Thereupon the mirror which was behind the altar seemed to brighten in its depth, and a wan form was outlined therein, which increased and seemed to approach by degrees. Three times, and with closed eyes, I invoked Apollonius. When I again looked forth there was a man in front of me, wrapped from head to foot in a species of shroud, which seemed more gray than white. He was lean, melancholy, and beardless, and did not altogether correspond to my preconceived notion of Apollonius. I experienced an abnormally cold sensation, and when I endeavored to question the phantom I could not articulate a syllable. I therefore placed my hand upon the sign of the pentagram, and pointed the sword at the figure, commanding it mentally to obey and not alarm me, in virtue of the said sign. The form thereupon became vague, and suddenly disappeared. I directed it to return, and presently felt, as it were, a breath close by me; something touched my hand which was holding the sword, and the arm became immediately benumbed as far as the elbow. I divined that the sword displeased the spirit, and I therefore placed it point downward, close by me, within the circle. The human figure reappeared immediately, but I experienced such an intense weakness in all my limbs, and a swooning sensation came so quickly over me, that I made two steps to sit down, whereupon I fell into profound lethargy, accompanied by dreams, of which I had only a confused recollection when I came to myself. For several subsequent days, the arm remained benumbered and painful."

In spite of these setbacks, Lévi persisted and, according to his own account, was able to consult the spirit on two more occasions on some fine points of cabalism.

Lévi was a widely respected magician for the remainder of his life, and attracted many disciples. That he had occult powers—or that his disciples were convinced he had—is certain. A disciple to whom Lévi had given a prayer to recite before he fell asleep found that the words of the prayer were glowing in the dark, and that Lévi's spirit was standing by his bed. It seems likely that Lévi possessed the power of projecting his astral body.

His books strike the modern reader as wildly imaginative and confused, but they exerted an immense influence on a whole generation of students of the occult. His death in 1875 was mourned by hundreds of occultists in France, Germany, and England, who regarded him as the great master.

In 1831, when Lévi was still studying for the priesthood, there was born in Russia a woman who was to exert an even greater influence than he on 19th-century occultism: Elena Hahn, later Petrovna, but known as Madame Blavatsky. Born into an aristocratic family, she married at 16, left her husband soon after, and began to travel around the world. She was an explosive, charming, delightful personality. For a while she worked as a bareback rider in a circus, and dabbled in many odd interests. She had undoubted mediumistic powers, and throughout her life odd manifestations were apt to occur in her presence: inexplicable rappings, ringing of bells, and movements of

Below: a representation of the occasion on which Eliphas Lévi, influential 19th-century occultist, evoked the ghost of Apollonius of Tyana, an ancient Greek magician.

Left: this drawing by Lévi was the frontispiece of his second volume of *Dogma and Ritual*. It is a symbol connected with the Witches' Sabbath (or sabbat). In Lévi's version the torch of knowledge lies between the horns of a goat's head that expresses sin; the caduseus represents eternal life and the breasts humanity; and the two arms—one male and one female—stand for the occult sciences.

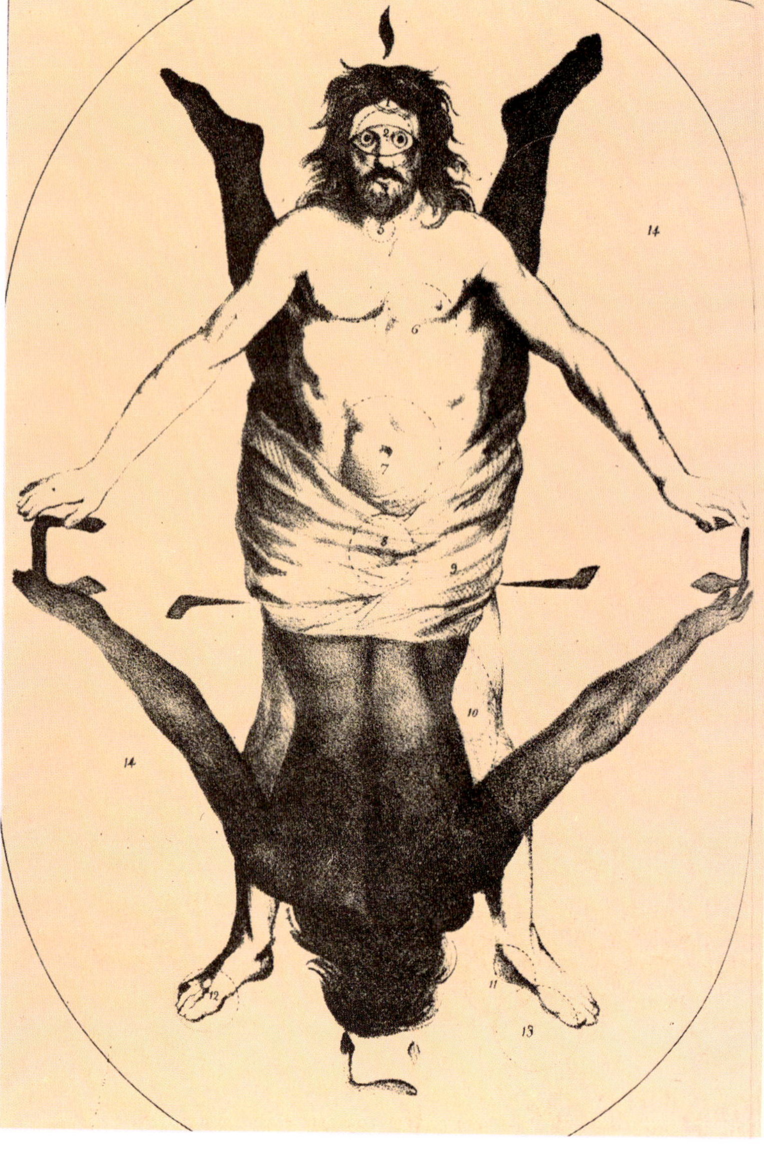

Right: Lévi calls this drawing "the great cabalistic symbol of Zohar." Like many symbolic expressions of the Cabala, the two figures form a six-pointed star as a representation of the mystical number six. Lévi said the Zohar was one of the masterpieces of occultism.

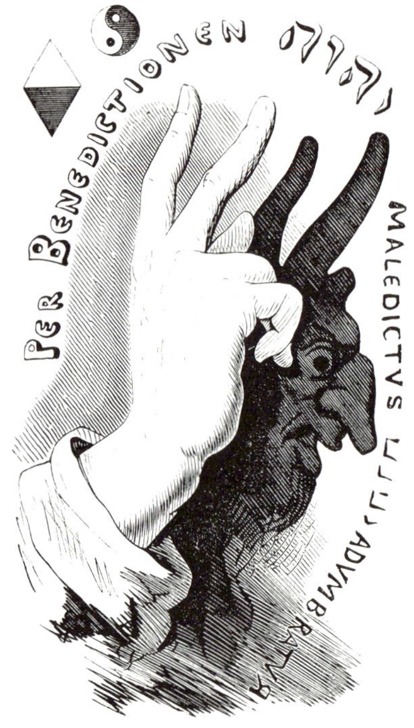

Below: the accursed blessing, as drawn by Lévi. The fingers held in the position for a Christian benediction become a demon in the shadow they throw. This is a symbol of good and evil as two inseparable sides of one coin.

objects. In fact, it seems that she had the power of raising poltergeists. After living carelessly until she was just past 40, and then wondering how to make a living, she decided to turn her occult abilities to account and become a medium.

On going to the United States she met Colonel Olcott, a lawyer and journalist who became her lifelong admirer and tireless publicist. She told Olcott that she was in touch with a certain spiritual Brotherhood of Luxor, presumably priests of ancient Egypt, and he believed her—as he believed everything else she told him. Together they formed the Theosophical Society, a movement for the study of ancient wisdom. For three years it flourished in America. In 1879, as interest seemed to wane, they decided to move to India, which Madame Blavatsky regarded as the fountainhead of spiritual wisdom.

In Bombay, Theosophy was an immediate success. The charismatic personality of Madame Blavatsky fascinated the Hindus even more than it had fascinated the Americans. She claimed that the Secret Masters in Tibet, a group of spiritual initiates, had imparted their wisdom to her. When disciples asked her questions about these matters, paper notes fell from the air. The notes contained detailed replies to the questions and were signed "Koot Hoomi." These notes later became famous as the Mahatma Letters. Koot Hoomi, a semidivine Master, was even seen by some devotees one moonlight night.

In 1884 the bombshell came. A housekeeper with whom Madame Blavatsky had quarreled told a Western journalist that most of the magical effects were merely tricks. The Mahatma Letters were simply dropped through a crack in the ceiling of the room in which the disciples had gathered, and the seven-foot-tall Koot Hoomi was actually a model carried around on someone's shoulders. Examination of a cabinet in which many manifestations had occurred revealed a secret panel. The Society for Psychical Research, which had been investigating her powers, issued a skeptical report.

It might seem that the Blavatsky reputation was irretrievable. Not a bit of it. Madame Blavatsky set sail for London—and soon the Theosophical Society was flourishing again, although it never achieved anything like its earlier success. Once again, accounts of Madame Blavatsky's magical powers began to circulate among occultists. The poet W. B. Yeats, a serious and long-term student of the occult—reported that when he visited Madame Blavatsky, her cuckoo clock made hooting noises at him. A. P. Sinnett, who later became her faithful disciple, complained when he visited her that he had attempted to raise spirits at seances, but could not even get rapping sounds. "Oh, raps are the easiest thing to get," she replied—and raps immediately sounded from all parts of the room.

When Madame Blavatsky died in 1891, six years after the fiasco that drove her out of India, she left behind a host of disciples who firmly believed in the existence of Koot Hoomi and the Tibetan Masters. She also left behind two huge books, *Isis Unveiled* and *The Secret Doctrine*, in which she explains that the earth is destined to evolve through seven "root races," of which we are the fifth. Much of these enormous, bewildering books is taken up with descriptions of the root races.

In retrospect, it seems fairly certain that Madame Blavatsky was a genuine medium of unusual powers. It is more certain that, when her somewhat erratic powers were feeble, she helped them out with trickery—a temptation to which dozens of bona fide mediums and magicians have succumbed. She was in short both a charlatan and a genuine magician, and her hypnotically powerful personality made her one of the most remarkable women of the 19th century.

Madame Blavatsky and the Tibetan Masters

Below: Madame Blavatsky, the Russian-born woman who had an enormous influence on the great 19th-century occult revival.

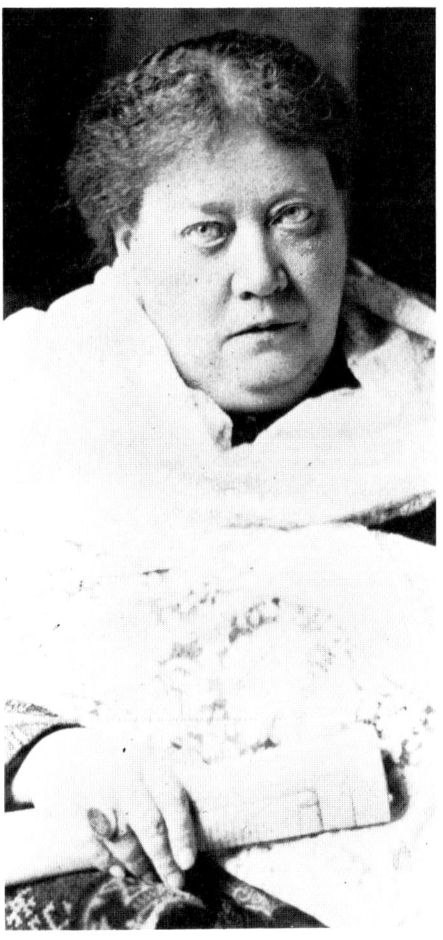

Chapter 6
The Great Magical Revival

What went on in the secret chambers of the Golden Dawn? The meeting place of the magical society was in an ordinary London street, and the members led ordinary lives in the city—but once behind the forbidden door, dressed in vivid magical robes, they were wholly caught up in a deliberate attempt to make contact with the mysterious forces of the universe, and to explore the possibilities of the deepest subconscious levels of the human will. Armed with secret regalia, and following ancient ritual, they set out to contact demons and angels on the astral pathways of the spirit world.

One day in 1885 a middle-aged clergyman named Woodford was passing an idle hour at a secondhand bookstall on Farringdon Street in London. Among the dusty volumes he came upon a bound, handwritten manuscript that was obviously in cipher. Woodford was a student of the occult, and he recognized certain symbols of the Cabala in the text. He bought the manuscript but, after several unsuccessful attempts to decode it, put it aside. Two years later, in the summer of 1887, he sent the manuscript to a friend, Dr. William Wynn Westcott, a coroner who was interested in occultism and freemasonry. Westcott was familiar with the first major work on ciphers, the *Steganographia* by the 15th-century alchemist Abbot Johann Trithemius, and it did not take him long to conclude that the mysterious pages were actually written in Trithemius's code. When deciphered they proved to be five magical rituals for introducing newcomers into a secret society, together with notes on various cabalistic matters.

Concealed among the pages Wescott found a letter in German, which stated that anyone interested in these rituals should contact a certain Fräulein Sprengel at an address in Stuttgart. Westcott lost no time in writing to her. Fräulein Sprengel replied, divulging that she was a member of a German magical order. A correspondence about magic ensued, and eventually Fräulein Sprengel gave Westcott permission to found an English branch of the order, and to use the rituals to initiate members. Accordingly, in 1888, Westcott founded

Opposite: this insignia was worn by members of the Golden Dawn who had advanced to a higher magical level within the Order. The Golden Dawn drew on the sources of ancient wisdom preserved by the Rosicrucians, as the symbolic rose indicates. Much of the other symbolism comes from the Cabala.

The Hermetic Order of the Golden Dawn

Below: Aleister Crowley in special robes for a magical ceremony in the Golden Dawn in 1899, the year after he joined the group.

a society called The Isis-Urania Temple of the Golden Dawn. (Its pretentious title perhaps reflects the influence of Madame Blavatsky, who had arrived in London from India a few months previously.) Two other students of the occult were co-founders: William Woodman, a retired doctor who had studied the Cabala in Hebrew, and Samuel Liddell Mathers, an eccentric scholar of aristocratic leanings. Before long the Golden Dawn had branches in Edinburgh, Weston-super-Mare, and Bradford, and an enthusiastic following of displaced intellectuals and cranks. Its members included the beautiful actress Florence Farr, the poet W. B. Years, and the young and as yet unknown Aleister Crowley.

This, at any rate, is the story of the founding of the Golden Dawn as put about by Westcott and Mathers. In recent years Ellic Howe, the historian of magic, has looked into the matter closely, and has concluded that Fräulein Sprengel never existed. The cipher manuscript was probably genuine, but it came from a collection of occultist Fred Hockley, who died in 1885, and not from a bookstall in Farringdon Street. Westcott, probably with the connivance of Mathers, forged various letters in German purporting to come from Fräulein Sprengel. His aim evidently was to give the society a certain authority rooted in ancient practices. Mathers was later to denounce the Sprengel letters as forgeries, although he must have known about them from the beginning. Westcott seems to have been a Jekyll and Hyde character. Indeed, his split personality was so marked that he wrote in two completely different styles of handwriting. As for Mathers, who was to change his name to MacGregor Mathers and pose as a Scottish aristocrat, he was one of these curious figures who seem to occur so often in the history of magic—a kind of confidence trickster whose aim was not so much to swindle as to gain respect, admiration, and power.

Does all this mean, then, that the Order of the Golden Dawn was nothing more than a combination of chicanery and wishful thinking? By no means. Its members did, beyond question, pursue serious and genuine studies of the magical arts. At this point, then, we must have a closer look at the whole subject of magic and those who practice it.

First of all, we have to admit that common sense insists that magic is bound to be nonsense. How could some semireligious ceremony have the slightest influence on the real world? Clergymen in church may pray for rain, or prosperity, or victory in battle, but they do not expect their prayers to produce a definite effect; they merely hope that God will pay attention. So why should some magic ceremony, not even addressed to God, have the power to influence actual events?

This is, I repeat, the commonsense view, the so-called scientific approach. But every day, thousands of events occur that science refuses to recognize because they appear to flout scientific laws. Dowsing, telepathy, precognition of future events, and specters of the living are only a few examples. And what of those strange, heightened states of consciousness such as the one that John G. Bennett experienced while at Gurdjieff's Institute? Perhaps we cannot really blame scientists for declining to pay too much attention to these things. The aim of science is

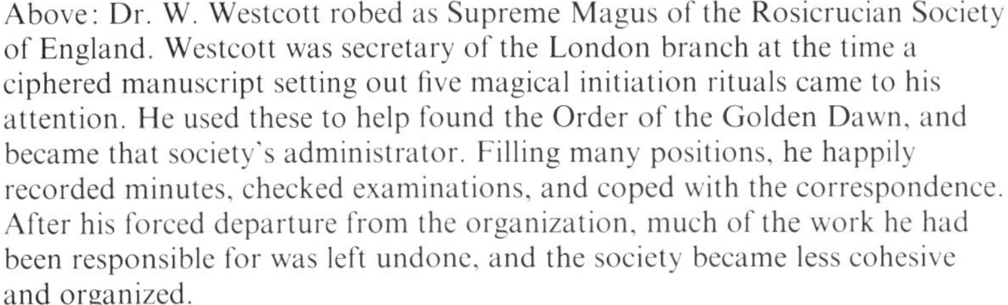

Above: Dr. W. Westcott robed as Supreme Magus of the Rosicrucian Society of England. Westcott was secretary of the London branch at the time a ciphered manuscript setting out five magical initiation rituals came to his attention. He used these to help found the Order of the Golden Dawn, and became that society's administrator. Filling many positions, he happily recorded minutes, checked examinations, and coped with the correspondence. After his forced departure from the organization, much of the work he had been responsible for was left undone, and the society became less cohesive and organized.

Above right: Dr. W. R. Woodman in masonic dress. Woodman became a Golden Dawn Chief through Mathers who was a fellow occultist freemason. Older than the other two, he died before the Golden Dawn had become fully developed.

Right: one of the rare photographs of Samuel Liddell "MacGregor" Mathers. By all accounts, Mathers was the most eccentric of the Golden Dawn founders. Born in England, he took up the habit of wearing full Scots Highland dress after he went to Paris, and called himself Count MacGregor of Glenstrae. He had an imperious temperament and the history of the Order is full of his quarrels. Here he holds the Lotus Wand in a Rite of Isis performed in Paris.

Students of Magic

to describe the universe in terms of natural laws, especially laws that forge unbreakable links between cause and effect—between an occurrence and the forces that make it happen. It is the apparent absence of such a link in magical events that makes scientists skeptical of them. The occultist responds to such skepticism by claiming that scientists refuse, or are unable, to spread their net of inquiry wide enough to encompass strange events. What is beyond dispute is that such events do occur.

When we try to take account of occult events, and to devise some kind of theory that helps to account for them, we discover an interesting thing. Such a theory has already existed for thousands of years. It does not matter whether we call it magic, occultism, shamanism, the Hermetic tradition as based on the works of Hermes Trismegistus. It all amounts to the same thing. Its basic assertion is that there is a far more intimate connection between man and nature than we are inclined to believe. The world is full of unseen forces, and of laws of whose nature we have no inkling. Perhaps there is some strange medium that stretches throughout space—such as Eliphas Lévi's astral light—that transmits these forces as the air transmits sound waves.

How do we make contact with such forces? The answer seems to be that you have to want to with an intense inner compulsion. In his autobiography, the painter Oscar Kokoschka tells of how his mother, who was having tea with his aunt one day in Prague, Czechoslovakia, suddenly leaped to her feet and announced that she must rush home because her youngest son was bleeding. The aunt tried to persuade her that her idea was nonsense, but his mother hurried home—and found that her son had cut his leg with a hatchet while trying to chop down a tree. He would certainly have bled to death if she had arrived any later. This story—and hundreds of others like it equally well attested—indicates that strange powers come into operation where our deepest desires or needs are involved. As we go through our everyday lives, we do not need to exercise much will power; but occasionally, something stirs us to some really deep effort. It is this kind of effort that is likely to produce magical effects. The 20th-century poet Robert Graves has remarked that many young men use a form of unconscious "sorcery" to seduce young women. This is another word for thought pressure.

We could say, then, that organizations such as the Hermetic Order of the Golden Dawn set out to experiment with will power, and to explore the possibilities of reaching deep subconscious levels of the will. Perhaps their magic was a hit-and-miss affair that worked only occasionally; but at least they were trying to learn about the possibilities of the true will.

The magic practiced by the members of the Golden Dawn was based on a number of simple principles. To begin with, they believed that certain basic symbols or ideas have a deep meaning for all human beings. On one occasion, Mathers handed Florence Farr a piece of cardboard with a geometrical symbol on it, and told her to close her eyes and place it against her forehead. She immediately saw in her mind's eye a cliff top above the sea, with gulls shrieking. Mathers had shown her the water

Below: W. B. Yeats, one of the greatest poets of the 20th century, was active one way and another for more than 20 years in the Order. He was initiated in 1890, and was thereafter known by the magical name Daemon est Deus Inversus. This means "the Devil is the reverse side of God." This portrait of Yeats was painted in 1900 by his artist father.

Left: the actress Florence Farr. She was a beautiful woman with a considerable talent for magical ceremonies, and became the head of the London Temple after the resignation of Dr. Westcott.

Ritual Invocation of the God Saturn

The Order of the Golden Dawn was established in London in 1887. It was a secret society whose members, among them famous people, were serious and dedicated. They wanted to establish magic rituals that would open pathways into the world beyond the normal senses. Aleister Crowley, who had been expelled from the Golden Dawn, formed his own order in 1907. Crowley used amended versions of Golden Dawn rituals. It was Crowley's public performance of the Rites of Eleusis in a London auditorium in 1909 that brought him widespread notoriety.

The Rites of Eleusis were a series of seven rituals aimed at invoking the ancient gods. In the ceremonies the will power of the magician was the motivating power, but his will was focused and reinforced by elaborate ritual magic. Crowley presided, Leila Waddell played the violin, and the set rituals were strictly observed. To invoke Saturn, for example, members of the Order recited appropriate prayers around an altar inscribed with symbols dedicated to Saturn. On one occasion the public was shocked when, during the invocation of Saturn, Leila Waddell sat astride Crowley on the altar!

4 9 2
3 5 7
8 I 6

Below: Aleister Crowley when he was 30. This was about the time that he was traveling with his wife in Egypt, and encountered Aiwass, one of the Secret Chiefs, through her as a medium. Aiwass dictated to him the Book of the Law, which became the basis of most of his later teachings.

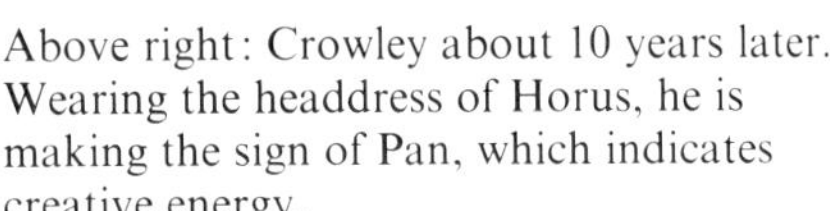

Above right: Crowley about 10 years later. Wearing the headdress of Horus, he is making the sign of Pan, which indicates creative energy.

symbol from the Cabala. There is a close connection between such symbols and the theory of archetypes of the psychologist Carl Jung, who believed that certain symbols are able to strike a chord in the unconscious mind of every human being.

The Golden Dawn taught its students to try to train their imagination, which is the trigger of the will, and gain control over it. One of their exercises was to control likes and dislikes until they could like something they normally hated, and hate something they usually liked. Another exercise was to attempt to see the world through other people's eyes rather than their own—in other words, to completely change their normal point of view. Many modern psychologists would agree that such exercises are valuable and healthy. They are, in fact, similar to exercises practiced in yoga and other meditation disciplines.

The Golden Dawn also made a genuine attempt to draw together all that was best in the ancient magical traditions: Hermeticism, Cabalism, Enochian magic (based on the Apocryphal *Book of Enoch*, which tells of the fall of the Angels and their magic practices), and such magic textbooks as *The Key of Solomon*, *The Magic of Abrahemelin the Mage*, and the *Grimoire of Pope Honorius*.

On the face of it, the Golden Dawn should have been a

wholly beneficial and healthy influence. Unfortunately, too many of its leading figures were driven by the craving that has been the downfall of so many magicians: the will to power, not only over themselves but also over everyone else. Gerald Yorke, a friend of Aleister Crowley, concluded that the story of the Golden Dawn showed that "the majority of those who attempt to tread the occult path of power become the victims of their creative imagination, inflate their egos, and fall." There was a great deal of infighting for the leadership of the Golden Dawn. Dr. Westcott saw himself as the leader, but MacGregor Mathers felt the position should rightly be his. Mathers claimed

Aleister Crowley - the Beast 666

Left: the Stele of Revealing, exhibit number 666 in the Boulak Museum, Cairo. It concerns Ankh-f-n-Khonsu, an ancient Egyptian priest. Crowley, who saw and studied the stele in Cairo, believed he had been Ankh-f-n-Khonsu in one of his previous incarnations.

Below: a self-portrait by Crowley as the Beast 666, the Antichrist of the Apocalypse. His mother had called him this because of his wildness as a child. The device on his skull is the Horus forelock, symbol of solar-phallic power.

Right: Leila Waddell played the violin in Crowley's public Rites of Eleusis, which attracted considerable mocking publicity. As one of Crowley's magical assistants, she has the Mark of the Beast between her breasts.

Above: a sketch Crowley made of a devouring demon. His effect on the people who came into contact with him was like this demon: few escaped from his inner circle with their reason unimpaired.

to be in direct touch with Secret Chiefs, semidivine spirits, who dictated new rituals to him through his wife as a medium. Then there was A. E. Waite, a learned American historian of magic. His interests, however, were more mystical than magical, and he was not a very inspiring person. Finally, there was Aleister Crowley, a remarkable and demonic magician whose career brought ruin to many others as well as himself.

Crowley was the son of a wealthy and puritanical brewer. He was born in Leamington near Stratford-upon-Avon in 1875. His birthplace gave him opportunity to remark with typical bombast and arrogance: "It is a strange coincidence that one small county [Leamington and Stratford are in Warwickshire] should have given England her two greatest poets—for one must not forget Shakespeare." It sounds like a joke, but in fact

Crowley was convinced that he was a great poet. However, though his verse shows considerable talent, he lacked the discipline and sense of language to be even a good poet.

Crowley was a spoiled child who developed an intense dislike of the Plymouth Brethren, the strict religious sect to which his father belonged. He was also obsessed by sex. His first of numerous seductions occurred with a young servant when he was 14 years old. At university he wrote a great deal of poetry, which he published at his own expense. He also developed an incurable desire that lasted all his life to shock respectable people. In his late teens he discovered Mathers' translation of a book called *The Kabbalah Unveiled*, as well as a work by A. E. Waite on ceremonial magic. He quickly established contact with the Golden Dawn.

By the time Crowley entered the Golden Dawn in 1898, the struggle for its control had already been going on for some time. In 1891 Mathers had returned from France to announce that he had met three of the Secret Chiefs in Paris, and had had various magical secrets imparted to him. Dr. Woodman died that year and for the next six years there was a certain amount of tension within the movement. Dr. Westcott resigned from the Order—apparently having been told by his superiors on the London Council that magic was not a suitable occupation for a respectable public official. Mathers spent a great deal of time in Paris working on magical manuscripts at the Bibliothèque Nationale, so the struggle for leadership of the movement continued.

In August 1899 Crowley rented a house in Boleskine, Scotland on the shores of Loch Ness, conferred on himself the title "Laird of Boleskine," donned a kilt, and proceeded to practice the

Crowley's Scarlet Women

Below left: Crowley with Maria Theresa Ferrarri de Miramar, the second woman he married in 1929. This was during the long bleak period when he was struggling to fight off his addiction to heroin. Rose, the first wife whom he had long since abandoned with their child, had died hopelessly insane.

Below: Rose Kelly, first wife of Crowley. It was through her that the flamboyant occultist made contact with Aiwass, although until then she had shown no occult gift.

Right: Crowley and Leah Hirsig, at the Abbey of Thelema, the Sicilian villa in which Crowley tried to establish a new community of his disciples. Leah, whom he usually called the Ape of Thoth, held the office of Scarlet Woman, the Beast's special sexual partner. Their baby Poupée, here in Leah's arms, died shortly afterward.

Below: Crowley taking a pose as the Chinese god of laughter.

magic of Abrahamelin the Mage—a system which, he claimed, he had learned about in the writings of John Dee.

In December 1899, convinced that it was time he moved up to a higher grade in the Golden Dawn, Crowley went to London to demand initiation. This was refused through the efforts of Yeats and various other senior members, who regarded him as an overgrown juvenile delinquent. Crowley therefore went to Paris and persuaded Mathers to perform the necessary rituals.

He also took the opportunity to stir up trouble, convincing Mathers that he had a revolt on his hands. Mathers sent him back to London with instructions to break into the Golden Dawn headquarters, and to put new locks on all the doors. Yeats, Florence Farr, and the other London initiates were enraged.

The legal wrangle that ensued in 1901 broke up the original Golden Dawn 13 years after it had been founded. One group of members, under the leadership of A. E. Waite, managed to continue for another four years, still calling themselves the Golden Dawn. Another group, including Yeats, Florence Farr, and the novelist Arthur Machen, was led until 1905 by Dr. R. W. Felkin, who then founded a magical society called the Stella Matutina, or Morning Star. Finally, in the 1920s, a talented young medium and occultist who called herself Dion Fortune founded the Society of the Inner Light, based on Golden Dawn rituals obtained from Mrs. Mathers—Mathers himself having died in the influenza epidemic of 1918.

The same year of the legal problems the Golden Dawn had received another blow in the form of a sudden spate of unwelcome publicity. It happened when a couple of confidence tricksters who called themselves Mr. and Mrs. Horos were accused of raping a 16-year-old girl. Mrs. Horos had learned that it was supposed to have been Fräulein Sprengel who had given the Golden Dawn its charter. She went to Paris and introduced herself to Mathers as Fräulein Sprengel. Oddly enough, Mathers was taken in—which could argue that he was not at that time aware that Fräulein Sprengel had been invented by Westcott. Mathers soon became suspicious of the couple, whereupon Mrs. Moros and her husband stole some of the rituals of the Golden Dawn and fled to London. There they launched into a career of confidence trickery based on a mixture of spurious occultism, extortion, and sex. When charged with their crimes they claimed to be leaders of the Golden Dawn. As a consequence, many of the most intimate secrets of the order were made public and sensationalized by the press. The publicity, combined with the power struggles within it, sealed the fate of the Golden Dawn.

The Abbey of Thelema

Crowley had decided to get away before the Horos scandal broke. Late in 1900 he had gone to Mexico, where he studied the Cabala, practiced yoga, and—according to his own account—finally became a true magician. When he returned to Paris in 1902 he tried to persuade Mathers to take up yoga. Mathers declined, and their relation became several degrees colder. Eventually it turned into hatred, with Mathers and Crowley pronouncing magical curses on one another. Crowley claimed that his curses were actually responsible for the death of Mathers.

Back in England, Crowley married Rose Kelly, and they traveled to Ceylon and Egypt. They called themselves the Prince and Princess Chioa Khan. In Cairo, Crowley performed various rituals with the intention of invoking the Egyptian god Horus. On April 8, 1904, he received instructions from his wife, who had taken to uttering strange messages while in a trance-like state, to go into a room he had furnished as a temple.

Below: Crowley in Arab dress. His main contribution to the development of magic has been his welding of the Eastern and Western traditions into a single system of thought and ritual.

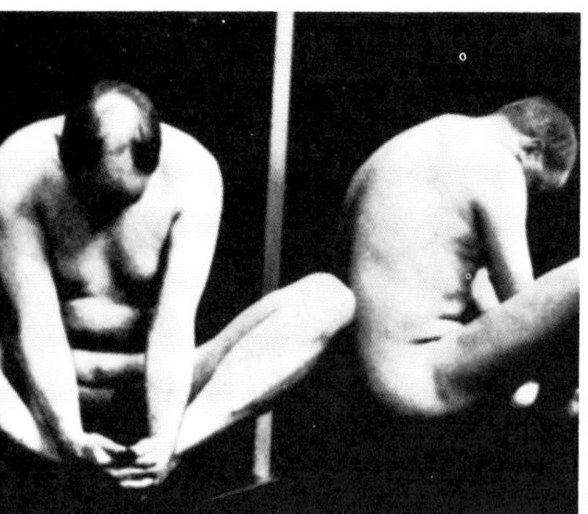
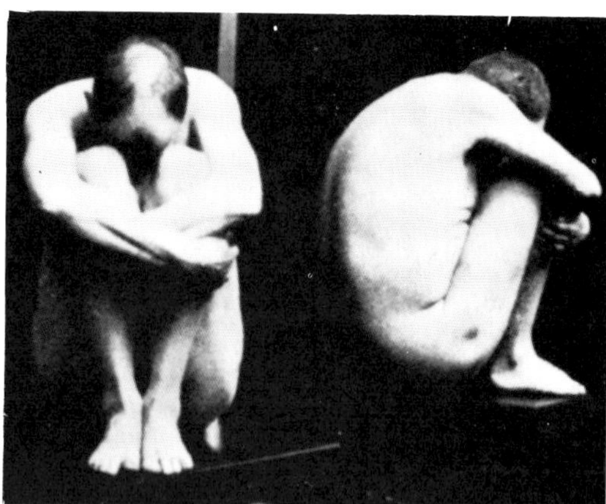
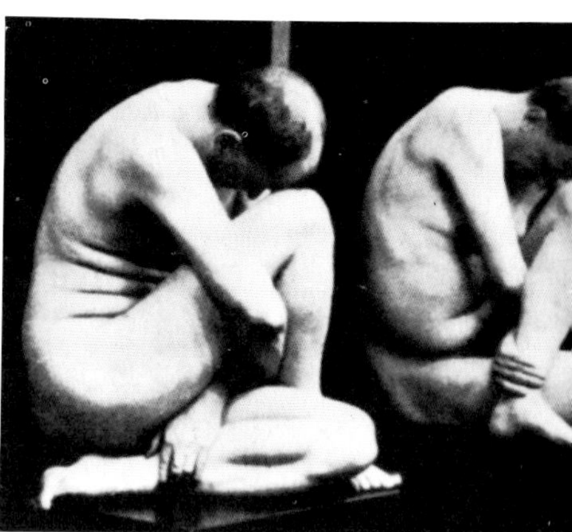

Above: a sequence of pictures of about 1912 in which Crowley demonstrates the yoga technique of breath control known as pranayama. He does the exercises in various of the traditional yoga positions. Yoga breath control—which includes measured inhalation and exhalation as well as breathing with alternate nostrils—is an important part of yoga. It was partly Crowley's great enthusiasm for yoga that cooled his relationship with Mathers.

Suddenly he heard a disembodied voice ordering him to write. What Crowley wrote was an odd document called *The Book of the Law*, which became the cornerstone of his later teaching. He claimed that it was dictated by Aiwass, one of the Secret Chiefs. Its basic teaching was expressed in the phrase: "Do what you will."

In 1905 Crowley went to the Himalayas to attempt the climb of Kanchenjunga, third highest mountain in the world. During the climb he quarreled with the rest of the team and, when they were buried in an avalanche, made no attempt to help them. Several were killed. He deserted his wife and baby in India where the baby died of typhoid. Rose later became an alcoholic, and died insane. In a magazine called *The Equinox* Crowley began to publish the secret rituals of the Golden Dawn. Mathers took him to court for this, but lost his case.

In 1912 Crowley received a communication from another magical organization, the Order of the Temple of the Orient, reproaching him for publishing its secrets. Puzzled by the accusation, Crowley went to see Theodor Reuss, one of the O.T.O.'s leaders. It appeared that the secret in question was something called sex magic. It arose from the system of yoga known as Tantra, which attempts to use the power of sexual energy to fuel the drive toward higher consciousness. The O.T.O. had, it seems, developed its own form of Tantric techniques. Crowley was fascinated, and promptly availed himself of Reuss's permission to set up an English branch of the O.T.O. Magical ritual performed by Crowley often involved sex magic—with his disciple Victor Neuberg it was an act of sodomy. Sex magic remained one of Crowley's central enthusiasms for the rest of his life—though addiction to heroin and cocaine lessened his sex drive in later years.

In the United States during World War I Crowley had an endless series of mistresses, each of whom he liked to call the "Scarlet Woman." He undoubtedly had an exceptional sexual appetite, but it must also be said that he genuinely believed that sex magic heightened his self-awareness, and enabled him to tap increasingly profound levels of consciousness. At all events, during this period Crowley steadily developed a kind of hypnotic power that it is as difficult to account for as it is to describe. William Seabrook, an American writer on the occult, witnessed the use of this power one day when he and Crowley were walking on Fifth Avenue in New York City. Crowley began to follow a complete stranger who was walking along the sidewalk. Crowley followed a few yards behind, keeping in perfect step with him. Suddenly, Crowley allowed his knees to buckle, and dropped momentarily to the ground. At exactly the same moment, the man he was following collapsed in precisely the same manner.

By the early 1920s Crowley, who was suffering from asthma, was almost permanently in debt. A legacy of $12,000 enabled him to move to a small farmhouse in Cefalu, Italy. He called it the Abbey of Thelema, which means "Do what you will," began to practice magic, and invited disciples to join him. He provided apparently limitless quantities of drugs for anyone who wished to use them, and attractive women devotees were expected to help Crowley practice his sex magic. Even with the legacy, however, the money problem remained pressing. Crowley wrote a novel called *Diary of a Drug Fiend* and started his *Confessions*, which he called his hagiography (the biography of a saint). He announced that the earth had now passed beyond Christianity and had entered the new epoch of Crowleyanity. But when one of his disciples died after sacrificing a cat and drinking its blood, the resulting newspaper scandal drove Crowley out of Sicily.

The British press denounced him as "the wickedest man in the world" and, although he loved the publicity, he soon discovered that his notoriety made publishers shy away from his books. He deserted his disciples, one of whom committed suicide, and married again. His second wife, like the first, became insane. Hoping to make money, he sued the English sculptress Nina Hamnett for calling him a black magician. But when witnesses described Crowley's magic, the judge stopped the case, declaring he had never heard such "dreadful, horrible, blasphemous, and abominable stuff."

By the outbreak of World War II Crowley had added alcoholism to his drug addiction even though his daily intake of heroin at that time would have killed a dozen ordinary men. Every now and again he found rich disciples to support him until, inevitably, they lost patience with him. He retired to a rooming house near Hastings in southern England, and died there in December 1947 at the age of 72. John Symonds, a writer who had met him in his last years, later wrote his biography—a hilarious but often disturbing book. Other friends, notably Richard Cammell and Israel Regardie, wrote more sober and admiring accounts of his career. But it was not until the magical revival that began in the mid-1960s that Crowley's reputation began to rise again. Nowadays more than a dozen of his books are in print, and a new generation ardently practices the magic rituals described in them. The Beast has finally achieved the fame he craved. Nonetheless, and fortunately, the great age of Crowleyanity seems as far away as ever.

"The Wickedest Man in the World"

Below: Crowley as an old man at the English seaside boarding house where he died in December 1947.

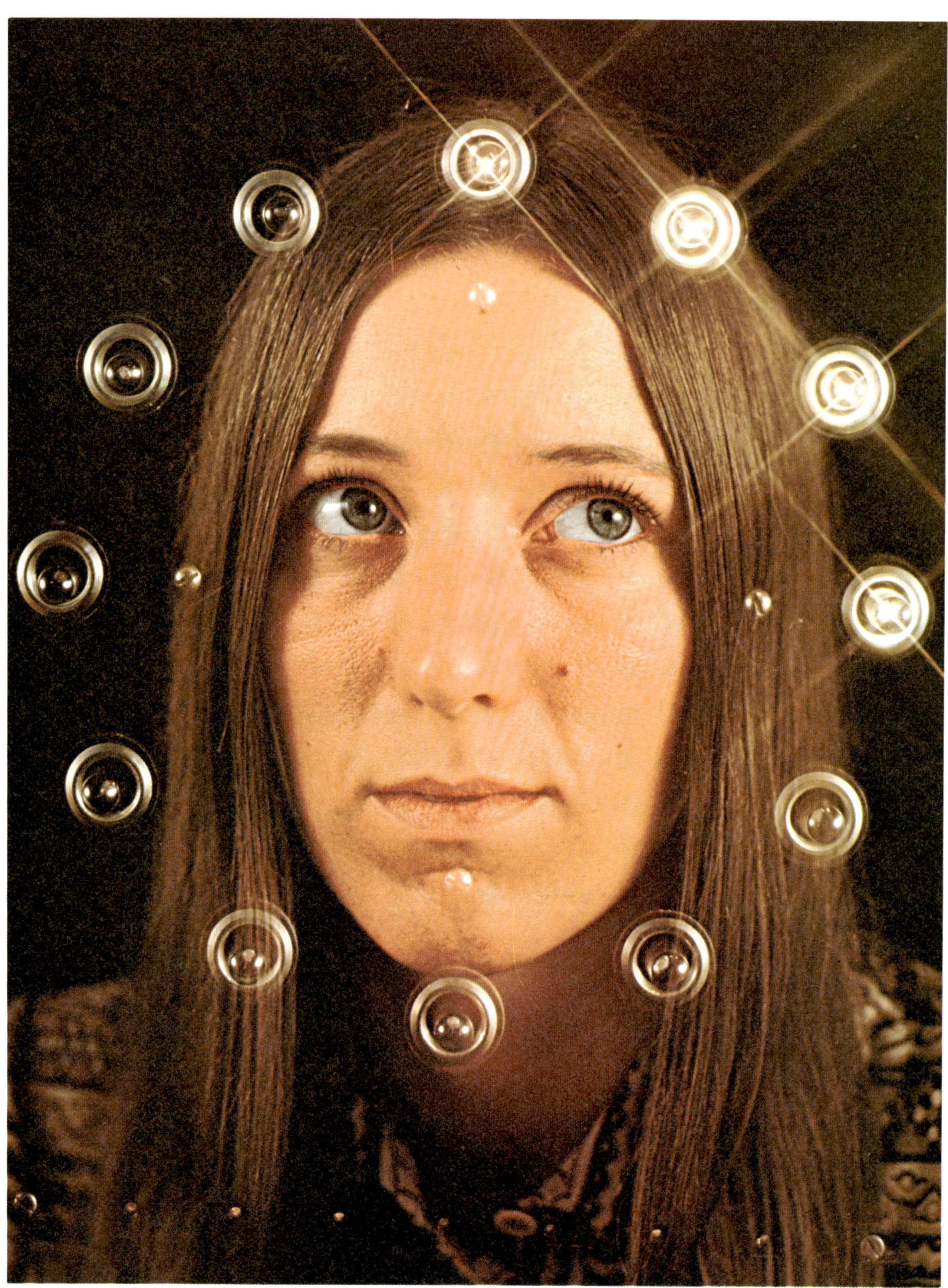

Chapter 7
They Live Among Us

Is it possible to trap the mysterious powers of the mind in the laboratory, to examine and investigate them by means of scientific tests? With the present revival in occult phenomena, more and more scientists are trying to find a method by which many strangely gifted individuals can be accurately and reliably tested. As scientists work to define their powers, some gifted clairvoyants work with police, and many of their successes have been electrifying. Whether these talents lie within the human subconscious, or in contact with spirits or intelligences from some other world, there is clearly much more to discover.

In Paris in the year 1960 there appeared on the bookstalls a volume with the euphonious title *Le Matin de Magiciens* (The Morning of Magicians) by Louis Pauwels and Jacques Bergier. It is a curious hodgepodge of a book, as the authors themselves recognized, for they wrote in the first chapter: "Skip chapters if you want to; begin where you like, and read in any direction; this book is a multiple-use tool, like the knives campers use . . ." To everyone's astonishment the book became a best seller, running through edition after edition in France. Serious critics were irritated and baffled by its success; they pointed out that the book was merely a series of wild speculations on magic, alchemy, telepathy, prophecy, strange cults, the Great Pyramid, Hitler's astrologers, the Cabala, flying saucers, and a thousand other topics. This mass of eccentricity was held together by one simple theme: the world is a stranger and richer place than science is willing to recognize.

It was a message that apparently had wide appeal in France, especially to the young. They were less interested in the book's argument about the narrowness of science than in the imaginative appeal of its magical wonders. Other writers saw that there was money to be made out of the occult. Books on astrology, reincarnation, and visitors from outer space rolled off the presses, and there was no sign of any loss of interest. The craze spread to other countries, notably Germany, England, and the United States. In 1968 a German book called *Remembrance of*

Opposite: a scientific test of precognition. The lights are flashed by a random generator while the girl subject tries to influence the order of flashing. Any successes on her part could only be achieved by her somehow influencing the behavior of the subatomic particles that cause the lights to flash.

The Amazing Gerard Croiset

the Future made a fortune and a name for its author, Erich von Daniken. Translated into English as *Chariots of the Gods?* it sold more copies than any other book except the Bible. Daniken's thesis was that the earth was visited thousands of years ago by spacemen who left signs of their presence in many ancient cultures. Stanley Kubrick's film *2001, A Space Odyssey*, was based on the same idea. It became a kind of cult classic, and its admirers went to see it again and again, just as they might attend a religious ceremony. The great occult boom had arrived.

Curiously enough, a powerful resurgence of interest in the occult has occurred toward the end of every century for the past 400 years. Is this pure chance—or is there, as some people believe, a hidden law that governs such apparently cyclic occult revivals? The question is impossible to answer, but it is clear that we are now in the middle of the most widespread occult revival in history. One of its most significant and encouraging features is that it has captured the interest of a large number of scientists. All over the world universities and other institutions have established laboratories of parapsychology—the scientific investigation of extrasensory perception, clairvoyance, psychokinesis, and other psychic phenomena.

In the Netherlands a famous Institute of Parapsychology was set up at the University of Utrecht, with Professor Willem H. C. Tenhaeff in charge. Tenhaeff has devoted much time to testing the powers of the psychic Gerard Croiset.

Right: W. H. C. Tenhaeff, the Dutch parapsychologist. Tenhaeff has spent much of his time studying the psychological characteristics of psychic sensitives, in particular the Dutchman Gerard Croiset.

Croiset was born in 1909. He was unfortunate in being an unhealthy child, and in having to spend much of his childhood in foster homes. But from an early age he somehow knew about things that were happening in other places. Once when a teacher returned to school after a day's absence, Croiset was able to tell him that he had spent the day in a distant place with a girl who wore a red rose in her dress, and whom he would shortly marry. The teacher was amazed. He had, in fact, taken the day off to see his fiancée, who had worn a red rose.

When he was 25 years old Croiset visited the house of an acquaintance, and picked up a stick lying on a table. Immediately his mind became crowded with images of an automobile accident, and of a body lying on the roadside in a grassy place. The owner of the stick was astonished: it was an accurate description of an incident that frequently occupied his own mind. He told Croiset that he must be clairvoyant. Croiset now began to develop his faculty, and had clear visions of the future—of the Nazi invasion of the Netherlands, and of the loss of the Dutch East Indies to the Japanese, for example.

In recent years Croiset has become internationally known as a psychometrist—a person with the gift of reading the past associations of objects by holding them in his hand. The authenticity of this faculty in Croiset cannot be doubted, for he has been employed on numerous occasions by the Dutch police—and often with remarkable success. In 1949, for instance, Croiset was asked to help in a case of a sex crime. The police had suspects, but were by no means certain which, if any, was guilty. Croiset was handed two wrapped objects. Without opening the first he declared correctly that it was a tobacco

Left: Gerard Croiset explaining a police case in which he had helped to Professor Hans Bender the German parapsychologist. One of the experiments in which Croiset has participated is the "chair test." In this Croiset predicts the characteristics and some previous experiences of the person whom he foretells will occupy a certain chair in a lecture hall at a future date. These tests have shown impressive abilities of precognition by Croiset.

box. He described the house from which it came and the two middle-aged brothers who lived in the house. He went on to give detailed descriptions of the characters of each of the brothers, and he identified them as the rapists. The second package contained a sack. Croiset immediately saw a cow in connection with it and, in fact, it was used as a cow blanket. He described how the two brothers had taken the girl, a mentally retarded child, to a cowshed with hay on the floor, and raped her. After that, the girl had been put into the sack, and the brothers had discussed what to do with her. One wanted to bury her alive, the other to drown her. The brothers quarreled over this, and the girl was allowed to live.

The two men, who had been among the suspects, were tried separately and convicted. Croiset again correctly foretold that one of them would commit suicide within a week or two of conviction. He was also able to tell the police that the brothers had committed other crimes—among them the rape of a Jewish girl in hiding from the Nazis during the war. He was even able to show them the house where this crime had taken place.

Another Dutchman has become even more famous than Gerard Croiset as a psychometrist who occasionally aids the police. He is Pieter van der Hurk, better known as Peter Hurkos. He also has scored some remarkable hits. In 1958 he was asked by the police of Miami, Florida to sit in the cab of a murdered cab driver and give them his impressions of the killer. As he sat there, Hurkos described the murder of the driver in detail. Then

Long-Distance Psychic Detection

Gerard Croiset Junior, son of the world-famous Dutch psychic who has helped police solve many baffling cases, inherited his father's strange powers. He demonstrated this when he assisted in the case of two missing girls in South Carolina—and he did it from thousands of miles away. It all started when the desperate mother of one of the girls, hearing about the Croisets' miraculous ability to locate missing persons, wrote to them in Holland with a plea for help. Croiset Junior replied.

What had happened was that two teenage girls had gone for a walk on Folly Beach near Charleston, South Carolina. They were never seen again. In his reply to the mother, Croiset drew a map of Folly Beach—which he had never seen—including such details as a bus stop and a parked bulldozer. He also wrote a page-and-a-half of comments. The accuracy of the map convinced the skeptical police to take him seriously.

In the letter Croiset said: "The girls will be there [on the beach]; they will be together." The police found the girls where Croiset indicated. And they were together — buried in shallow graves in the sand. They had been murdered.

When movie actress Sharon Tate—pregnant with her first child—and four friends were brutally murdered in her home, the world was appalled at the frightening, mindless savagery of the killers.

Below: police cover the bodies of the victims, found scattered in and around the luxurious house.

he described the killer as tall and thin, with a tattoo on his right arm and a rolling walk like a sailor. His name, Hurkos said, was Smitty, and he had also been responsible for another murder in Miami—that of a man shot to death in his apartment. The police were stunned. There had been such a murder recently but, as far as they knew, it had no connection with the killing of the cab driver. They searched their files and came up with a photograph of an ex-sailor named Charles Smith. Shortly afterward a waitress interviewed by the police recognized the man in the photograph as a drunk sailor who had boasted to her of killing two men. A wanted alert went out for Smith, who was arrested in New Orleans and sent back to Miami. He confessed to the murder of the cab driver and was sentenced to life imprisonment.

Unlike Croiset, Hurkos was not born clairboyant. He acquired his extraordinary gift in the Netherlands during World War II as the result of an accident. Knocked unconscious after a fall from a ladder, he woke up in the hospital with a fractured skull. As he recovered he found to his amazement that he could read people's thoughts, and seemed to know the future. Once when a nurse took his pulse, he told her to be

Peter Hurkos, the Psychic Detective

Below: psychic Peter Hurkos was called in to help reconstruct the crime. Here he studies the room where Sharon Tate died.

The British Dowser Robert Leftwich

careful or she might lose a suitcase belonging to a friend. The nurse had, in fact, just arrived at the hospital by train, and had left a friend's suitcase behind in the dining car. Hurkos told another patient that he ought to be ashamed of himself for selling the gold watch his father had left him when he died. This, too, was true.

His new faculty almost cost Hurkos his life. A patient who had been discharged from the hospital came to shake his hand—and, in that moment of contact, Hurkos knew that the man would shortly be murdered in the street. The victim was involved in resistance against the Nazis. When gossip about Hurkos' prediction reached the Dutch underground movement, it was assumed that Hurkos was a German counterespionage agent and a member was sent to kill him. It took Hurkos some fast talking to convince his would-be assassin that he was not in the pay of the Nazis.

When Hurkos came out of the hospital he found that he was unable to do normal work. He no longer possessed the power of concentration required for everyday tasks. This is significant. It may well be that psychic powers are inherent in all of us, but that we unconsciously suppress them—not because they are of little help to us in everyday circumstances, but because they would actually impede our survival in the modern world. Croiset had become bankrupt as a grocer before he began to use his clairvoyant powers. Likewise, it was only after someone suggested that Hurkos exploit his extraordinary gift on the stage that he made enough money to support himself.

It is also interesting that Croiset was frequently sick as a child, and that Hurkos' gifts emerged only after an accident. This is not to suggest that strange powers are necessarily accompanied by sickness but only that sickness may be one of the factors which releases psychic sensitivity. On the other hand, many healthy people have deliberately cultivated their psychic powers because they needed them. The tiger hunter Jim Corbett, whose *Man Eaters of Kumaon* has become a modern classic, recounts how his life was saved again and again by his "jungle sensitiveness"—his sudden intuitive knowledge that a man-eater was lying in wait for him.

Another psychic whom I myself have met is the British dowser Robert Leftwich. Leftwich was described in a magazine article as a man of tremendous energy. The article had discussed his dowsing abilities, which he had successfully demonstrated on television, and also his power to project his astral body. Leftwich had also explained how he had used his psychic powers as a child at school. When the class was instructed to learn a long poem by heart, Leftwich would memorize only a few lines. The teacher customarily looked around the class and chose someone to recite each successive passage of the poem. When the passage that he had learned was coming up, Leftwich would will the teacher to ask him to recite. He claimed that the trick had always worked.

I was anxious to meet a man who seemed to combine psychic abilities with enormous zest and vitality. I visited him at his home in Sussex, and later he came to my home in Cornwall. His dowsing abilities are undoubtedly remarkable. He demon-

Below: Robert Leftwich, the British dowser using ESP cards for experimentation. Leftwich's dowsing includes locating any kind of subterranean matter: not only water but also pipelines and disused tunnels.

strated the dowsing in the house. I hid a coin under a carpet while he was out of the room. He came in with his divining rod and walked around. The rod bent downward violently as he stood over the coin. He explained that for him dowsing is a matter of tuning in the mind to the specific object. If he had been looking for some other object—a playing card or a matchbox—the rod would have ignored the coin, and dipped over the card or matches. He further explained that the rod could also be made to react over everything except what he was looking for. To demonstrate he walked around the room again, and this time the rod twisted violently in his hands until he stood above the coin; then it became still.

We also did thought transference tests with playing cards. I chose a card from the deck while Leftwich stood on the other side of the room, and tried to transmit its identity to him. His score was exceptionally high. But he is convinced that his powers do not depend just on telepathy, so we tried another test. I shuffled a deck of cards and threw the cards face down on the table. At a certain point he said, "Stop. That's the ace of clubs." He was right. He scored four our of seven on this test.

Leftwich also demonstrated a form of telepathic dowsing. He stood with his back to my wife, and asked her to walk away from him across the garden. We knew where underground waterpipes were located, but he did not. At a certain point,

Above: Leftwich with his divining rod. It dips down over the spot where the specific element he is looking for is buried. According to Leftwich, it is perfectly possible to go dowsing in the rain. Water in the air does not detract from water underground.

Secrets of the Dowser's Art

however, he called "Stop!"She had just crossed an underground waterpipe, and he had located it by using her mind as a transmitter.

The usual explanation of dowsing is that the mind tunes in to some form of electric field. This was the explanation put forward by the philosopher Professor C. E. M. Joad in one of the British Broadcasting Corporation's *Brains Trust* broadcasts of 1946. But, after suggesting that water emits some form of electrical radiation that can be detected by the dowser, Joad went on to admit that he had no idea of the explanation of map dowsing. The map dowser holds a pendulum over a map, and the pendulum begins to swing or vibrate when it is held over the substance he is looking for—water, oil, minerals, or even gold. Joad described how he had witnessed map dowsing in action. A large-scale map, from which all rivers and streams had been carefully removed, was laid out on a table. The map dowser

Right: dowsing through another person. Leftwich, blindfolded, can sense when the woman has crossed the underground water.

went over it with a pendulum, on the end of which was a small bobbin that could spin. The bobbin spun every time the pendulum was suspended over a place where the dowser detected water. At the end of the session, the dowser had located every river, stream, and pond in the area.

Obviously Joad's theory about radiation cannot explain this. Then how can it be explained? Once again, we are driven to return to the hypothesis that the secret lies in our own minds, but not necessarily in the subconscious mind—the Freudian "basement" that is supposed to contain all our most primitive animal impulses. Leftwich, like many other occultists, believes that the answer may lie in a part of the mind which could be called the "superconscious." If the mind can have a subcon-

Above: the resident site engineer demonstrates a sophisticated set of divining rods that a large building contracting firm has considered a worthwhile investment. The small strings contain samples of different materials, such as copper, lead, cast iron, plastic. The user holds the appropriate string in his fingers, and the rods react if they pass over the material. Apparently anyone can use the rods, although some people get a reaction more easily than others. The builders use the rods mainly to locate underground pipes, high-tension voltage lines, and other obstructions on the sites.

Investigating the Wonderworkers

scious basement, might it not also possess a superconscious "attic"?

It was nearly a century ago that respectable scientists such as Sir William Crookes and Sir Oliver Lodge began to take an interest in the paranormal. At that time it looked as if the answers to the questions raised might rest reassuringly within the concepts of life after death, and of a universe of benevolent spirits doing their best to give help and guidance to the living on earth. But since that time every decade has revealed new mysteries, and the problem of finding a single explanation becomes increasingly difficult.

Let us take a look at some of the experiences of Dr. Andrija Puharich, a researcher whom Aldous Huxley described as "one of the most brilliant minds on parapsychology." In 1952 Dr. Puharich investigated the case of Harry Stone, a young Dutch sculptor. In deep trance states Stone spoke ancient Egyptian and wrote hieroglyphics—neither of which he had the slightest knowledge of in his normal state. The messages purported to come from one Ra Ho Tep, an Egyptian of the Fourth Dynasty about 2700 B.C.

In 1963 Puharich heard about José Arigó, a Brazilian healer called the "surgeon of the rusty knife." In April of that year he went to Arigó's town to watch the wonder worker in action. The surgeon proved to be a barrel-chested peasant who thought

Below: the doctor, inventor, and parapsychologist Andrija Puharich with Uri Geller, whom he brought from Israel first to Germany and then to the United States for research at Stanford University.

himself possessed by the spirit of a dead German doctor. Puharich watched Arigó deal with 200 patients in four hours, performing many operations without anaesthetic and at great speed. Arigó removed a tumor from Puharich's own arm in a few seconds. Puharich felt nothing, and the flesh healed in four days without disinfectant or antibiotics. In 1971 Arigó was killed in a car accident. Puharich received the news by telephone, but was unable to confirm it from any of the news agencies. Later that day he discovered that Arigó had been killed that morning, as his caller had said. But when Puharich looked for the phone number of the caller, which he had written on a notepad, it had vanished. Moreover, his secretary who had been with him throughout the day could not recollect him taking the phone call.

This anecdote is recounted in Puharich's most baffling book, *Uri, a Journal of the Mystery of Uri Geller*. Puharich was drawn to Geller by accounts of his feats of mind reading, spoon bending, and his curious power over watches. At his first meeting with Geller, Puharich witnessed some remarkable feats. Geller told a woman to hold a ring in her hand, and placed his left hand over her clenched fist for 30 seconds. At the end of that time the ring was found to be broken into two pieces. Geller also demonstrated his powers of telepathy by performing a reading of the future. He wrote three numbers on a pad and placed it face down on the table. Then he asked Puharich to think of three numbers. Puharich selected the numbers 4, 3 and 2. Uri then turned over the pad—on which was written the figures 4, 3, 2. Geller explained that his experiment did not involve precognition, because he had transmitted the numbers to Puharich. In still other demonstrations of his strange powers, Geller change the time on Puharich's watch as Puharich held it in his own hand, and raised the temperature of a metal thermometer by eight degrees without touching it.

If this were all it would be remarkable enough. But Puharich goes on to make such a startling claim that one's first response is to doubt his sincerity. Briefly he says that Geller is a kind of savior or messiah, controlled by beings from outer space that are hovering a few million miles away in a spaceship called *Spectra*. These beings had apparently visited earth on a number of previous occasions, and had also selected the patriarch Abraham and the Pharaoh Imhotep as avatars, or incarnations of a divine being.

Given the present worldwide interest in the occult, one might expect Puharich's book to have created a sensation and become a best seller. Instead, it was received with a mixture of indifference and hostility. This is not to say that most critics thought Puharich was a liar. Many of them obviously felt that Puharich was sincere but mistaken. Geller has told me that everything in Puharich's book is factually accurate, but that he himself does not necessarily accept the notion that he is a messiah. This raises some fascinating questions, not merely about Geller and Puharich but also about the whole subject of the occult. The fact that a person possesses certain powers proves nothing about the source of those powers. Impressive documentary evidence seems to prove beyond all doubt that the Victorian

Powers From Space?

One day in December 1949, when the boy that would grow up to be the psychic Uri Geller was only three years old, he wandered across the street from the apartment in which he lived with his mother in Tel Aviv, Israel. He crawled through the fence into the magnificent garden of a big house, and wandered in the unaccustomed splendor until the beauty and peace lulled him to sleep.

When he woke he noticed with fascination that a great silent bowl was settling down from the sky. Suddenly between the small boy and the bowl was the shadow of an enormous figure with no arms or legs. A blinding ray came from the place where the face should be. This ray struck the child so forcibly that he toppled over and went into another deep sleep. When he woke the second time, he was cold, it was dusk, and the bowl was gone. He remembered the dazzling light; but instead of being afraid, he felt quiet and peaceful. Uri scampered home and told his mother about his experience. She spanked him for running away, and for making up such stories.

Is it possible, however, that Uri Geller owes his psychic power to the mysterious ray shot he told his mother about?

Opposite: Ted Serios, who became a famous thoughtographer, tries to project a mental image through the lens of a camera held by researcher Dr. Jule Eisenbud.

medium Daniel Dunglass Home was able to wash his face in red hot coals without getting singed, and could cause heavy tables to float through the air. But this does not prove, as he claimed, that his powers came from spirits rather than from his own subconscious mind. Joan of Arc declared that she had been ordered to save France by St. Michael and St. Catherine, and the Church that has sanctified her apparently accepts her claim. But did her voices have any greater reality than those of the beings that visited Geller? In the long history of messianic religious movements, dozens of messiahs have astounded their followers by apparently genuine miracles, such as levitating, healing the sick, and conferring immunity against weapons. But as their promises about the end of the world have proven untrue, we must conclude that most of them were self-deceivers, however authentic their strange powers. Similarly, Puharich's claims regarding Geller's gifts may be true—but this does not prove that Geller is a messiah or that the spaceship *Spectra* exists.

This still leaves us with the basic question: What is the source of energy or power behind these events—and behind so many psychic phenomena? There seem to be two possibilities: what we have called the superconscious, or spirits or celestial intelligences. The problem with the idea of a superconscious is that, while it is easy enough to understand its role in map dowsing or precognition, it is altogether more difficult to understand why it should conceive flying saucers and beings from outer space. Is it possible that the superconscious possesses a sense of humour? Many students of the paranormal would say that this is, indeed, a possibility, to the extent that the activities of the superconscious may be completely freakish and unexplainable.

Consider the curious case of the Abbot Vachère of Mirebeau in France. In 1913 the abbot was regarded as a kindly and conscientious member of the church, well liked by the Pope himself, but without any remarkable talent. He was in his

Below: a view of Rome which Serios tried to reproduce mentally by means of thoughtography during a test by Dr. Eisenbud. He had seen the picture in a book.

Right: one of the images produced by Serios, showing the dome of the Church of Santa Maria di Loreto. Its angle is noticeably not the same as that of the original.

Far right: another image showing Trajan's Column. Again the angle and pattern of shadows varies from that of the target picture.

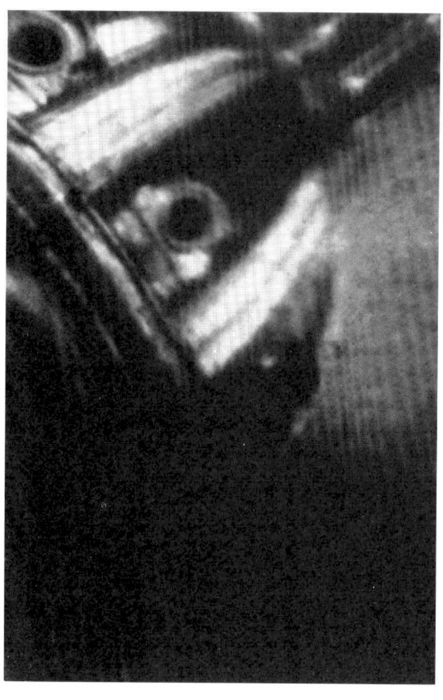

sixtieth year when the first of a series of strange and rather embarrassing events began and drops of reddish moisture began to ooze from the hands and feet of the figure of Jesus in a painting that hung in Vachère's private chapel. Vachère reported the matter to his Bishop who asked to see the picture. It was dispatched to the Bishop, but failed to bleed. When it was returned to its chapel, however, the bleeding started again.

Later, a gang of workmen were building Stations of the Cross

Ted Serios–the Thought Photographer

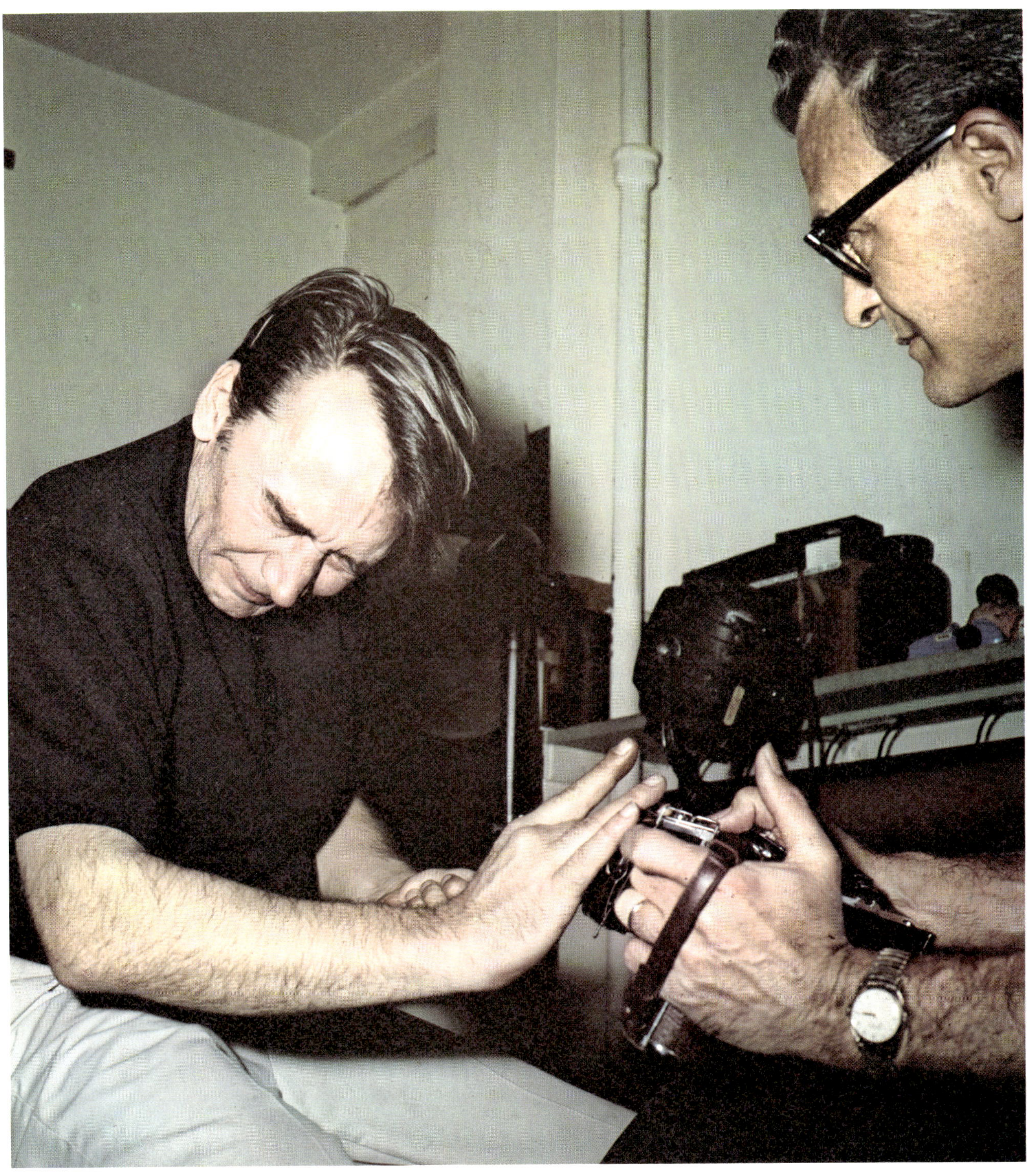

Mind Photography Under Test

Below: in a demonstration of his work for a German television team filming in Denver, Serios began by drawing a sketch of his idea of a primitive man.

near the abbot's home, and Vachère pinned up an ordinary color print of Jesus in their hut. This also began to bleed. The bishop investigated, decided that Vachère was a fraud, and excommunicated the abbot. The bewildered and unhappy Vachère visited his friends at Aix-la-Chapelle; with him in the house, a statue and a picture belonging to his hostess began to bleed.

Many people felt that the bleeding indicated that Abbot Vachère was a saint—or, at least, that he had been selected by God for some special destiny. The Church had no reason to think so, and refused to investigate the phenomena which, however, continued to occur until the abbot died in 1921.

The evidence leaves little doubt that the phenomena were genuine. On the other hand, the Church probably showed common sense in refusing to accept them as evidence of sanctity. Possibly the bleeding statues and pictures were a trick perpetrated by the abbot's superconscious. In any event, like the fakirs' wonders, the phenomena were spiritually worthless.

This story illustrates the fact that most human beings, churchmen as well as scientists, find supernatural phenomena embarrassing and prefer to ignore them. Such phenomena fail to conform to the laws of nature as we know them. Consequently they tend to be regarded as irrelevant freaks rather than as interesting pieces of some as yet unsolved universal jigsaw puzzle.

A similar attitude was shown toward a series of experiments made by Dr. Jule Eisenbud, a psychiatrist and member of the faculty of the University of Colorado Medical School. In 1963 Eisenbud published an article arguing that it is impossible to devise a truly repeatable experiment in the field of paranormal phenomena. A correspondent disagreed and sent him a magazine clipping about a man called Ted Serios. According to the article, Serios could take photographs by means of the mind alone. He would take a polaroid camera in his hands, stare hard into the lens, and somehow produce photographs of recognizable places, of faces or people, or of objects such as cars and buses.

Eisenbud's interest was aroused and he arranged a demonstration. Serios proved to be a bellhop of alcoholic tendencies, who also claimed to have the power of projecting his astral body. But the second claim was unconnected with the ability he demonstrated to Eisenbud. He stared down a small paper tube, which he called his "gismo," toward the camera lens. After a number of failures he succeeded in producing two blurry pictures of a water tower and a hotel. In considerable excitement, Eisenbud immediately got in touch with various scientists and told them what had happened. To his astonishment, they showed only polite interest, and had no wish to see a demonstration. Eisenbud was encountering the reaction we have mentioned above—the embarrassment effect produced by freakish and apparently inexplicable events.

Eisenbud refused to be deterred, however. He continued to test Serios, and some of the resulting "thought photographs" were spectacular. Naturally Eisenbud's first suspicion—like that of everybody else who tested Serios—had been that the

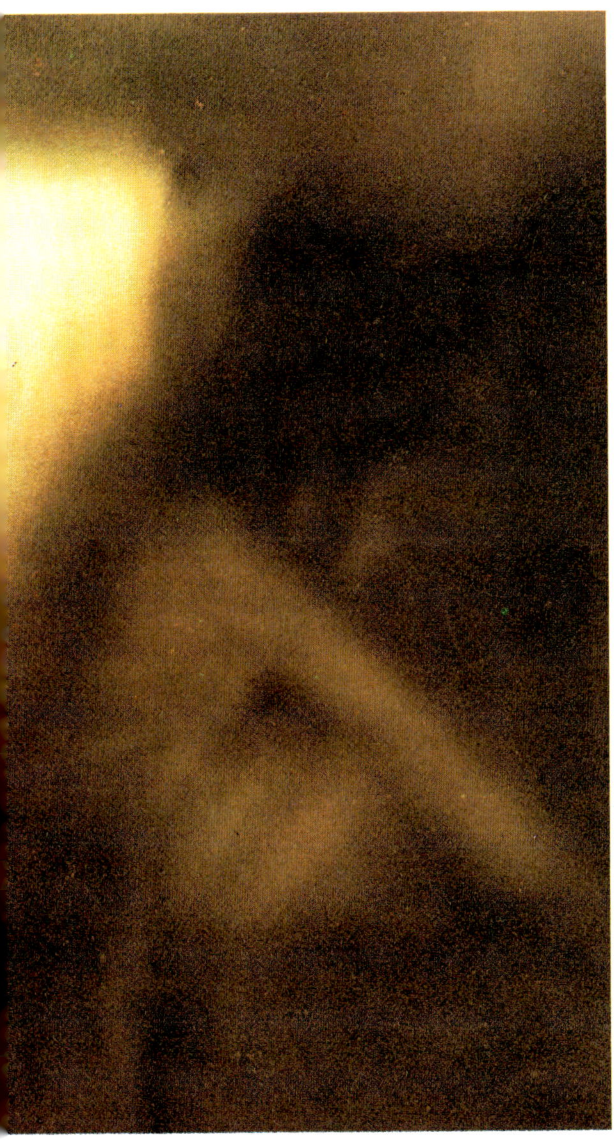

trick lay in the gismo. Serios insisted that the tube of paper merely helped him to concentrate, and close examination of the gismo revealed nothing suspicious. Eisenbud concluded that Serios's powers were genuine, even if they made no sense in terms of any scientific law.

Charles Reynolds and David Eisendrath, two reporters who had watched Serios at work, were convinced he was a fake. They constructed a small device that could be hidden inside the gismo, with a lens at one end and a piece of unexposed film at the other. When this was pointed at the camer, the result was a picture not unlike those that Serios had produced. The account of their invention was printed in *Popular Photography* in 1967, and it gave all the skeptics fresh ammunition. Since then, their article has been cited by people who believe that Serios is a fake, as evidence that he performed his thought photography by sleight of hand. In March, 1974 *Time* magazine ran an article on the occult revival, and included a brief account of Serios and the *Popular Photography* article. *Time* concluded: "Many of

Serios, using a cylinder that he calls a gismo, and which was prepared by the film makers to be sure no devices were added, produced a series of pictures. At first they were totally black, but finally one came up with a crouching man (above left). Later the team noticed the coincidental resemblance of what Serios had photographed to an exhibit of a primitive group in the Field Museum of Natural History located in Chicago (above).

Exploration of "Inner Space"

Serios's followers were shattered. Again, the millennium was deferred."

Now it is certainly possible that Serios is a fraud. But Reynolds and Eisendrath have done nothing to prove the contention. They merely demonstrated that they themselves could construct a gismo fitted with a lens and film. Dr. Eisenbud vainly pointed out that he and other experimenters had examined Serios's gismo for such fraud, and had found none.

My aim here is not to defend Serios—although thought photography is no less extraordinary than paintings that bleed or spoons that bend—but to point out that orthodox science is still a long way from taking a balanced and truly scientific attitude toward paranormal phenomena. There exists a deeply ingrained emotional prejudice that is just as likely to obscure the truth as are the wishful thinking of gullible parapsychologists and the dishonesty of fraudulent psychics.

Finally, if we discard the idea of the superconscious, is it remotely possible that some of these strange forces come from outside man? Might there be other intelligences—either spirits of the dead or creatures from other worlds—that are controlling or influencing the destiny of this planet?

The idea of life outside earth has received support from a number of scientists, but it must be admitted that the evidence is far from convincing. Some scientists have suggested that certain radio signals received from outer space may have been sent by intelligent beings. We also have the curious accounts of people who claim to have been in communication with creatures from flying saucers.

William Paley, a late 18th-century British theologian, used his watch as an argument for the existence of God. He argued that when we open the back and see the works, it is impossible not to recognize that it has been created by an intelligent mind. Therefore when we contemplate the universe, which is far more complex than a watch, how is it possible not to believe that it was created by an intelligent being? The followers of the scientist Charles Darwin were contemptuous of this argument. They insisted that the complexity of the universe—like the complexity of a snow crystal—is due to the operation of natural laws. This argument is not very convincing either, for the complexity of the universe is infinitely greater than that of a snow crystal. Next time you take a walk in the countryside, look at every living thing—trees, flowers, insects, birds, rivers, clouds. Then ask yourself whether you can imagine that they could have been produced by purely mechanical laws.

Intelligences from outer space or the human superconscious mind? Either explanation is possible, and it may be that there is truth in both. But for the human race at this point in history, the most fruitful line of inquiry undoubtedly lies within ourselves. The secret of the powers of shamans, of magicians, of psychics and clairvoyants probably lies in some unexplored part of our inner space. When man invents a spacecraft that will carry him to his own inner moons and planets, he will have discovered the secret that every magician has sought—a secret more fascinating than the Philosopher's Stone or the Elixir of Life.

Opposite: *La Reconnaissance Infinie* (The Infinite Search), a 1933 work by the Belgian surrealist artist René Magritte. The painting seems to call up many of the questions we have about the inexplicability of the universe—and about our place in its mysterious scheme.

£5000
Aunts Legacy
Uncles Legacy
Granpapas Legacy
To the Work house
CLAIRVOYANCE.

Chapter 8
In Search of the Unknown

Are we able to obtain information about the world only through our senses? Or is it possible for mind to transcend the everyday rules and make direct contact with another mind, or even with matter? Scientists trying to come to grips with the increasing evidence that such contact is possible have classified and defined various types of psychic experience—experience which appears to happen to people of all ages and places and stations in life. It is not only the magician who is gifted with mysterious powers: the evidence shows that all humans may have some degree of psychic ability.

It was the custom of Madame D., a Frenchwoman, to take a bath every evening about six o'clock. One evening, shortly after getting into the tub, she began to feel ill. She didn't know that a leak in a gas pipe or an inadequately closed valve had let gas escape into the bathroom. Mme. D. managed to press a call bell located near the tub just before she was overcome by the fumes and slid down into the water. An instant later, her husband rushed into the bathroom, pulled her out of the water, and restored her to consciousness.

After she was able to talk again, her husband asked her if she had experienced a fleeting vision of her past life in minute detail—as drowning people are said to. Mme. D. replied that she had seen a vision, but not the kind one would expect. Instead of seeing her husband and children and events from her past, she had seen the face of a casual acquaintance, Mme. J. "She was near me," said Mme. D., "looking at me sadly. It was impossible in those few moments to remove her from my eyes and thoughts."

The next morning, completely recovered, Mme. D. received word of the death of Mme. J. The woman had been drinking rather heavily on the previous evening, had gone into the bathroom to take a bath, and had drowned in the tub before she could call for help. The time: about six o'clock.

Was it sheer coincidence that at the moment of her near-tragedy Mme. D. should think of a woman she knew only slightly, who at the same time was undergoing a similar ex-

Unusual phenomena have always intrigued and fascinated us.
Dreams that come true, the icy premonition that turns into the tragedy of tomorrow, the eerie sense of having been exactly here, doing exactly this, once before—all these are aspects of a kind of experience that has troubled people's minds and led them to find numerous explanations, ranging from magic to the effects of an overheated imagination.
Opposite: an engraving of 1845 showing six hypnotized people getting a glimpse of their futures.

Experiments in Telepathy

perience? A strictly rational view of this incident (adapted from René Warcollier's *Experiments in Telepathy*) would indicate a "yes" answer. Mme. D. had no way of knowing by normal means that the other woman's life was in danger at that moment. The persistent image of Mme. J. was simply—according to his viewpoint—a peculiar mental association, a trick of the mind with no causal relationship to Mme. J.'s crisis. In other words, a coincidence.

All of us experience odd coincidences at one time or another, even if they're not as dramatic as the vision of Mme. D. We may suddenly for no apparent reason think of a song that was popular perhaps 15 or 20 years ago, switch on the radio, and hear that particular song being played. Or we think of a friend, and a moment later that friend telephones.

Although we are sometimes tempted to think there may be a connection between the two events, most of us don't really believe in such a connection. Our everyday experience tells us that the only way we can get information is through our senses. We cannot know that the radio station is playing the song we thought of until we switch it on and hear it. We cannot know that the friend is dialing our number because we cannot hear or see the friend at that moment. On answering the phone we may say, "I must be psychic, I was just thinking of you!" But we don't seriously believe that our mind can, so to speak, bypass the senses and get information the senses cannot supply.

Increasingly, however, evidence is suggesting that it *is* possible for the mind to transcend the senses. Some of the evidence is startling, such as the experience of Mme. D. Some of it is somewhat unexciting, such as the ability to guess correctly more often than chance would allow which card will turn up next as one goes through the pack. Not all of the evidence is conclusive. But there is enough strong evidence to suggest that occasionally—perhaps frequently—direct mind-to-mind contact does take place. Today there are many scientists who would agree that some kind of mental link existed between Mme. D. and Mme. J. at the moment both were in danger. How such a link is established no one cay say; but that it can be established is one of the more exciting discoveries of modern science.

Not only is mind-to-mind contact possible; but it also seems possible that some minds can get information from inanimate objects without using the senses. This apparently is something that the wife of the American novelist Upton Sinclair was able to do. Back in the 1920s, Mrs. Sinclair discovered that she could reproduce drawings in sealed envelopes, and in his book *Mental Radio* Sinclair tells the story of the discovery. Mrs. Sinclair had experienced a certain amount of pain from illnesses and had learned to exert mental control over this pain. She developed the ability to relax completely, to clear her mind of random thoughts, and to concentrate on a single idea. Her awakening interest in psychic powers developed further when the Sinclairs became acquainted with a young man named Jan, who performed an amazing variety of mental and physical feats including levitation. Mrs. Sinclair established a strong rapport with Jan, and was often able to describe in detail what he was doing at a given moment when he was far away from her. One day she jotted down a dream she had had about him, in which he brought her a little basket of flowers—pink roses and violets. She sketched the outline of the basket and flowers. The next day she received a letter from him. In it, through slits cut in the paper, he had inserted some violets and pink cosmos. The shape that the flowers made on the paper roughly followed the outline of the squat basket she had drawn.

Over the next year or two, Mrs. Sinclair did 290 drawings attempting to copy drawings made by her husband, his secretary, and her own brother-in-law. Some of her successful efforts are shown on pages 128–9. She occasionally wrote comments on her drawings to compensate for her limitations as an artist and to express more precisely the image in her mind's eye. Sometimes she simply wrote what she saw. In an early experiment her brother-in-law, who was in Pasadena some 40 miles away, drew a picture of a fork. At the same agreed-upon-time, Mrs. Sinclair directed her powers of concentration toward his mind, and finally wrote: "See a table fork. Nothing else." In some cases, only part of the original drawing seemed to come through—for Sinclair's drawing of a steamboat she did only the smokestack with smoke coming out of it. Partial successes often resembled the shape of the original drawing—a pocket watch, for example, was seen as a wheel.

Out of the 290 drawings, the Sinclairs counted 65 as successes, 155 as partial successes, and the remaining 70 as failures. Acutely aware that most thoughtful people of his day regarded anything suggesting the occult with a certain amount of contempt, Sinclair went to great pains to stress his and his wife's commitment to a rational view of the world. His socialist friends were critical of this aberration on the part of one of their spokesmen, and one of them wrote a newspaper article entitled "Sinclair Goes Spooky." Sinclair answered their objections with all the eloquence he could command, stating: "I don't like to believe in telepathy, because I don't know what to make of it, and I don't know to what view of the universe it will lead me, and I would a whole lot rather give all my time to my muck-raking job . . . In short, there isn't a thing in the world that leads me to this act, except the conviction which has been forced upon me that telepathy is real, and that loyalty to the nature of the universe makes it necessary for me to say so."

Today, nearly half a century after Sinclair wrote those words, the situation regarding the "spooky" has changed somewhat. If he were writing today, he would not need to be so defensive. Parapsychology—the branch of psychology dealing with telepathy and other psychic abilities—has established itself as a scientific discipline. In 1969 the Parapsychological Association, an international organization of parapsychologists, finally won membership in the American Association for the Advancement of Science. The parapsychologists' bid for membership was championed by the world-renowned anthropologist Margaret Mead. Her plea for their admission to the prestigious scientific body included these words: "The whole history of scientific advance is full of scientists investigating phenomena that the Establishment did not believe were there.

Above: Mary Craig Sinclair. Her telepathic powers inspired her husband, the crusading Socialist writer Upton Sinclair, to become an amateur psychical researcher with her as his subject. Over a period of three years he conducted experiments in which she read the minds of others to draw the same picture they had drawn. Participants in the experiments included her brother-in-law, Sinclair himself, and his secretary. Sinclair classified the many drawings as successes, partial successes, and failures. Success meant that her drawing had "some easily recognized element" of the original, even if it was only the outline. Her success rate was impressive.

The Successes of Mrs. Sinclair

I submit that we vote in favor of this association's work." The final vote was six to one in favor of admission.

The English magazine *New Scientist* found in a poll of its readers a few years ago that 70 percent of the respondents, mainly scientists and technicians, believed in the possibility of extrasensory perception. Of course, to believe in the possibility of something is not the same as believing in the thing itself. Even so, the high percentage suggests that the suspicious, if not hostile, attitude of scientists toward parapsychology is not as prevalent as it was in the past.

Mainstream science has impressive achievements to its credit, technological innovations that were inconceivable a century ago and that have given us undreamed-of control over our environment and the forces of nature. But in spite of all the great changes it has effected in our environment, there are certain aspects of ourselves that mainstream science has not been able to make any sense of, aspects that not only fail to fit into its picture of reality but also actually challenge that picture. As the awareness grows that the human is a threatened species, and that our swift technological advance has disrupted delicate balances in nature that are essential to our survival, more and more people are opening their minds to alternatives to the scientific-rationalist view of the world. Cultures, philosophies, and religions that were formerly regarded as primitive and barbarous are being looked at with new interest. People are asking whether, in traveling so far so fast, we might not have left something behind. Might there not be something

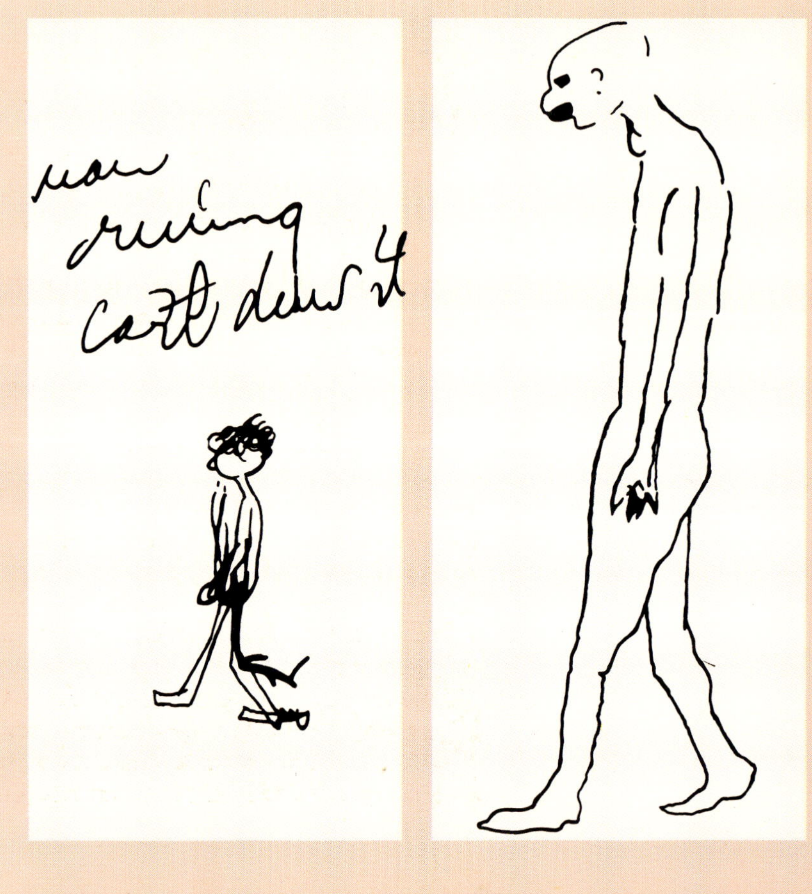

Right: this drawing by Mary Craig Sinclair of a man, labeled "man running can't draw it" bears a great similarity to her husband's man in movement.

useful for us to learn both from neglected areas of the human psyche and from backward or primitive areas of the world?

In 1973 the Parapsychology Foundation of New York sponsored a conference in London on the theme "Parapsychology and Anthropology." The highlight of the conference was a paper entitled "African Apprenticeship" read by an Englishman named Adrian Boshier, who is also a witch doctor.

After years of living among the tribesmen of South Africa, Boshier had become accepted by them as a brother. Finally they invited him to undergo the 12 degrees of initiation that would qualify him as a witch doctor. Boshier's experiences have convinced him that the secrets and magical rites of the *sangomas*, as they call themselves, are not merely superstition. They are, in more colorful guise, the same kinds of phenomena studied in western parapsychology laboratories. The difference is that whereas in the West these phenomena are viewed with suspicion, the tribesmen Boshier knew accepted them as true.

In his paper for the London conference, Boshier gave several examples of the psychic powers of the sangomas. On one occasion he had narrowly escaped being attacked by a leopard while he was exploring an ancient copper mine. Later, on his way back to Johannesburg, he passed through a village in which lived an old woman sangoma whom he knew. He found her sitting in her "hut of the spirits," throwing the bones that she used as aids to divination. She became agitated, for she said she could make no sense of what the bones were telling her. "All I can see is the underworld, the underground," she

Left: Mary Craig Sinclair's reproduction of three circles was exact. Her words written on the drawing show how certain she was. Below left: the likeness of the holly branch's outline to the reindeer's horns makes this drawing count a partial success.

The "African Apprenticeship"

said. Boshier told her about his exploration of the ancient mines, which put her mind at rest. But she warned him, "You must be very careful when you go down there, as the gods of the underworld can be very dangerous. Also, I see you here in my bones next to the leopard. The leopard, too, was in that place, and he does not like people in his home. You must be very careful of this animal—I see you were right next to him."

Tales of the psychic powers of witch doctors have been told by European travelers ever since Africa was opened up to trade and exploration in the 19th century. A typically strange story was told by a hunter and merchant named D. Leslie in a book privately published in Edinburgh in 1875.

Leslie had sent out his local elephant hunters with instructions to meet him on a certain date at a selected spot. They failed to turn up, so he consulted a local witch doctor who demanded to know the number of missing hunters and their names. He then made eight fires, one for each hunter, threw in some roots that produced a sickly smelling smoke, took some medicine, and fell into trance.

After about 10 minutes, he came out of the trance. He raked through the ashes of each of the fires in turn, and told Leslie what had happened to each of his hunters. One had died of fever and his gun was lost, another had been killed by an elephant but his gun had been recovered by another member of the party, a third had killed four elephants and was bringing back their tusks. The survivors, he said, would not be home for three months, and would travel by a different route than that previously chosen. Three months later, Leslie was able to confirm every detail of the witch doctor's account.

Of course, such stories do not prove anything. They are the testimonies of individuals not supported or confirmed by independent investigation, and we know very well that we cannot

Below: a group photograph of the 1973 Conference on Parapsychology and Anthropology held in London. Adrian Boshier, an anthropologist who had been initiated as a witch doctor in South Africa, is the first on the left, back row.

Left: an African diviner of the kind who helpfully accepted Boshier, reading his shells and bones cast on the ground in front of him. The skills of men like these, dismissed by the early European explorers as mere superstition, have since been recognized as being considerably more effective and sophisticated in their psychological element than any explorer ever imagined.

always trust the evidence of our senses or the reliability of our memory. We see and remember what we want to, often for reasons of which we are not aware. It may be argued that man's mind is avid for wonders, mysteries, and sensations, and is uncritical and easily deceived when it comes across them. Marvelous tales told by travelers have enthralled listeners in taverns, at firesides, and around campfires throughout human history. Today, tales that are equally marvelous, sensational, and inexplicable enthrall readers of scientific books as well.

In a New York parapsychology laboratory in 1973 the artist and well-known psychic Ingo Swann underwent a number of tests, carefully observed by scientists and recorded by a television camera. In one test he sat in a chair in the middle of the room and tried to "see" the contents of a cardboard box suspended from the ceiling. No one present knew what was in the box, and the only way to see into it would have been to climb on a ladder. After concentrating for several minutes with his eyes closed, Swann sketched the shapes and identified the colors of the hidden objects. The test was repeated eight times, and each time he scored a hit. Explaining how he did it, Swann said that he went into trance, then felt his spirit float to the ceiling, look into the box, and return to his body. This claim the scientists could neither prove nor disprove, but their electronic equipment did record a noticeable change in his brainwave output before he drew each picture.

A Witch Doctor Takes a Message

Father Trilles, a French missionary, became friends with a celebrated African witch doctor who told him one day that he was going to "a big palaver of all the magicians of this region." The meeting was the next day, but in a place that was four days' walk away. This made Father Trilles skeptical, so the witch doctor invited him to witness his departure.

Testing his friend, the missionary asked him to stop off in a village three days' walk distant and ask another friend to bring him some cartridges. The witch doctor agreed.

That night in his hut the witch doctor smeared a red liquid smelling of garlic all over his body. He chanted and made gestures during the process. Suddenly a large snake descended from the roof and wrapped itself around the witch doctor's body. He fell into a trancelike sleep, his body rigid and his lips flecked with foam. The snake disappeared.

Father Trilles stayed in the hut beside the witch doctor's motionless body all that night. The next morning the magician slowly returned to consciousness. He told his friend about the reunion, and said he had delivered the message.

Three days later Father Trilles' friend arrived with the cartridges.

The Categories of Psychical Phenomena

Below: the psychic Ingo Swann during a series of tests of his out-of-body vision. The experimenter Janet Mitchell is attaching electrodes to his scalp to monitor brain activity. A box containing the various target pictures was suspended about 10 feet over his head.

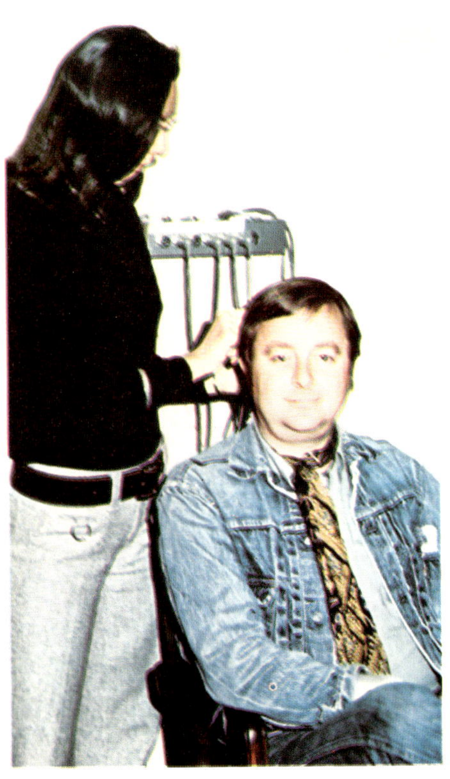

Other people have reported the experience of traveling out of the body, but their accounts—usually involving an illness or other crisis—have little value as evidence. The experiments with Ingo Swann illustrate how in the last few decades the study of the strange and unexplained faculties of the human mind has progressed from the anecdotal stage to the experimental. There are still, however, some critics of parapsychology who reject the experimental evidence and say that delusion, wishful thinking, and outright lying are as rife in the laboratory as in the tavern. Although scientific opinion is more favorable to parapsychology than it was 40 or 50 years ago, the psychic area is still clouded with emotion, distrust, and vagueness, and it is difficult for the layman to make sense of it all.

Parapsychology—or as it is sometimes called, psychical research—includes the study of several phenomena which are often referred to by the umbrella-term "psi" (pronounced "sigh"). These phenomena fall into two groups, mental and physical. The mental phenomena are covered by the term ESP (extrasensory perception), and include telepathy, clairvoyance, psychometry, precognition, and retrocognition. The physical phenomena include psychokinesis or PK (also called telekinesis) in its various forms including teleportation, levitation, and psychic healing; materialization and dematerialization; and out-of-the-body projection.

Telepathy is a word coined by the early psychical researcher F. W. H. Myers to denote the "transmission of thought independently of the recognized channels of sense." In an autobiographical book, *The Infinite Hive*, the English psychical researcher Rosalind Heywood gives a fascinating account of numerous telepathic experiences that occurred in her own life. She recalls an occasion in 1944 during World War II when her husband was due home on his first leave since the Normandy landings. His train from the Channel port of Folkestone was expected at 8 p.m. At 6:30 p.m. Mrs. Heywood lay down for a short rest after a hard day's work. She had been resting for 10 minutes when she got a compulsive urge to phone the station and check the time of the train. She learned that it would arrive an hour earlier than expected. She then got a strong impression that her husband wanted her to meet him at the station and to have a porter ready. She just managed to reach the station and get a porter in time to meet her husband's train. He was delighted at his welcome, and he confirmed that during the journey from Folkestone he had deliberately tried to send her a mental message that the train would be early and he would need help. The telephone booths at Folkestone had had mile-long lines of people waiting for them, he explained, so he had decided to try telepathic communication instead.

Clairvoyance is the ability of a person to receive extrasensory knowledge of a thing or an event that is not known to any other human being at the time. If an experimenter in a parapsychology laboratory shuffles a deck of cards and gives the deck to the subject, and the subject succeeds in guessing the correct order of the cards in the shuffled deck, the feat may be called clairvoyant. Examples of pure clairvoyance are fairly rare, for usually some person—however distant—knows the

Above left: the target pictures used during the Swann tests at the American Society for Psychical Research. Alongside are shown what Swann drew in trying to reproduce the originals by mind reading.

information; and in such cases telepathy, not clairvoyance, is the likelier explanation. For example, the witch doctor who divined the fate of Leslie's hunters may have received the knowledge telepathically from one of the survivors. Similarly, Ingo Swann's discovery of the contents of the box may have been due neither to out-of-the-body projection nor to clairvoyance, but to telepathy with the absent person who placed the items in the box.

Psychometry, or object-reading, is a special kind of clairvoyance in which the subject receives information about a person extrasensorily by handling an object associated with that person. In his book *Supernormal Faculties in Man*, the French parapsychologist Eugène Osty described how the psychic Mme. Morel once traced a missing person. She was

A Wide Range of Paranormal Powers

Right: Rosalind Heywood as both researcher and practitioner has been involved in various psi fields, most notably telepathy. She is a leading figure in psychical research in Britain.

Far right: famous clairvoyant Jeane Dixon with her crystal ball, which she uses for her feats of precognition. She predicted the death of Mahatma Gandhi and foresaw the Kennedy assassination.

given a scarf from his wardrobe, but not told his name. After describing a forest, and giving its approximate location, she focused on the body that she saw lying on the ground there, and said: "He is bald, has a long nose . . . a little white hair above his ears and at the back of his head . . . wearing a long coat . . . soft shirt . . . hands closed . . . I see one finger which has been hurt . . . very old and wrinkled . . . pendant lips . . . Forehead much furrowed, very high and open . . . He is lying on his right side, one leg bent under him. . . ." The search team found the man's body lying where she had said it was, in exactly that position.

Precognition and **retrocognition** are the terms for paranormal knowledge of future and past events respectively. There are many puzzling accounts of precognition on record. In 1956 the American psychic Jeane Dixon wrote in a magazine article: "the 1960 election will be won by a Democrat, but he will be assassinated or die in office." A few weeks before President Kennedy's assassination in Dallas she told a friend who was close to the Kennedys, "The President has just made a decision to go someplace in the South that will be fatal for him. You must get word to him not to make the trip."

Retrocognition is less frequently reported, for it is obviously more difficult to distinguish paranormal knowledge of the past from normal knowledge. The classic case is that of two English women, Miss Moberly and Miss Jourdain. On a visit to the Palace of Versailles on a summer afternoon in 1901, they found (or imagined) themselves thrown back in time to the 18th century, and saw the costumed courtiers and all the paths and buildings as they had been in the days of Marie Antoinette. Fifty years later in 1951 two other Englishwomen visiting Dieppe on the coast of Normandy woke in the middle of the night to sounds of battle. Nothing was visible from their hotel window, but they distinctly heard the sound of gunfire coming from the direction of the beach, tanks rumbling along the roads, and aircraft zooming overhead. Later it was discovered that the occasion was precisely the ninth anniversary of the

1942 Dieppe Raid by Allied Forces, and that the women's account of their experience corresponded exactly with the time schedule of the actual invasion.

Psychokinesis is the movement of objects by mental energy or the power of "mind over matter." A California man recounts how, two nights after his wife's death, he had a strong sensation that she was present in the room, so he said: "If you are here and can hear me, give me a sign." He had no sooner spoken the words than a heavy model chariot with two horses crashed to the floor from a mantelpiece where it had stood for 12 years. Whether the power that moved it came from his wife's spirit, from the man himself, or from a natural cause is arguable, but the accumulated evidence on such phenomena—including clocks stopping or starting for no apparent reason, pictures falling from walls, and vases being hurled across rooms—testifies to the reality of psychokinesis.

Teleportation—less well authenticated than the kinds of phenomena mentioned above—is the ability to move an object from one place to another by psychic means. Andrija Puharich, the scientist who conducted a long series of experiments with Israeli psychic Uri Geller, claims that on one occasion Geller teleported to Israel a camera case that Puharich had left in his home near New York, and that he had said he needed.

Levitation is the ability to rise from the ground or to raise material objects by paranormal means. Tales of levitations by saints or mystics are found in the literature of religions the world over. They are also common in the records of seances with 19th-century mediums. The most famous, controversial, and spectacular case was that performed by the British medium Daniel Dunglas Home, usually referred to as D.D. In front of several distinguished witnesses Home levitated, floated out of a third-story window, and reentered the building through the window of another room.

Psychic healing has a long history and includes some of the miracle cures performed by Christ and many of the Christian saints. Today psychic healing, or faith healing, is practiced not only by members of the clergy in the form of laying-on-of-

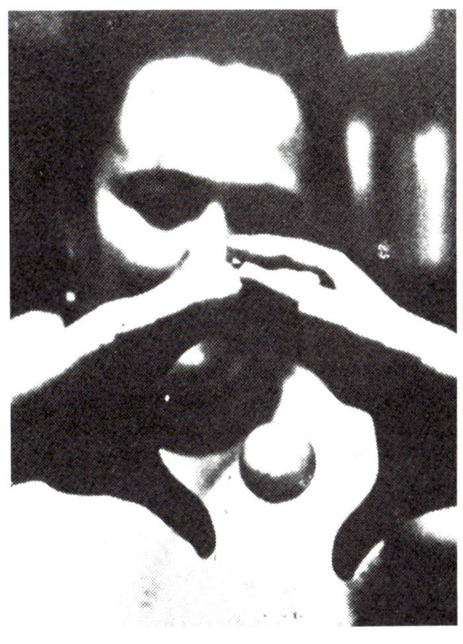

Above: in a Soviet experiment of psychokinesis, a psychic is apparently making a small ball rise up into midair.

Left: the phenomenon of retrocognition, or being thrown back in time, is rare. One famous case, reconstructed in this photograph, involved two Englishwomen who visited the French palace of Versailles in 1901. They found themselves walking in the palace as it was some 200 years before with uniformed gardeners, costumed courtiers, and all the buildings as they had been in the 18th century.

Right: the British medium Colin Evans, apparently successfully levitating during a public seance in London's Conway Hall in 1938.

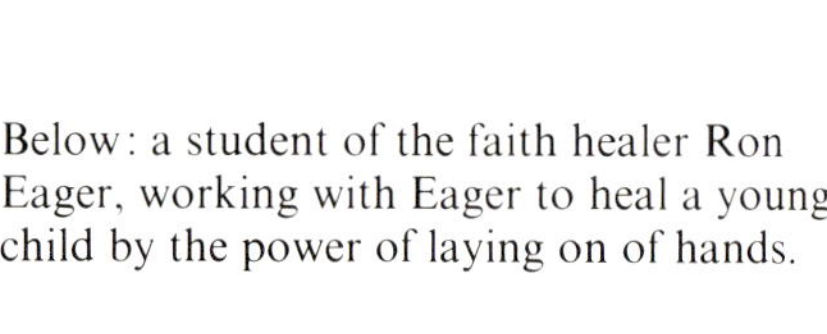

Below: a student of the faith healer Ron Eager, working with Eager to heal a young child by the power of laying on of hands.

hands, but also by people who, without representing any religious viewpoint, seem to be able to will a person to health. A different aspect of the same apparent power has been demonstrated in controlled experiments with plants, in which those plants that had prayers said over them developed into noticeably healthier specimens than the control group over which no prayers were said.

A bizarre variant of psychic healing is psychic surgery. In recent years many Europeans and Americans in terminal stages of illness have been going to the Philippines and Brazil and returning home to tell incredulous friends and doctors how local healers have apparently removed tumors from their bodies simply by massaging and kneading the flesh with their bare hands. Although some observers have been convinced that removal of tissue actually takes place in these treatments, others maintain that the operation is simply a conjuring trick.

Materialization, like psychic surgery, is a highly controversial phenomenon, and most psychical researchers would deny that it actually occurs. As the name implies, it involves the creation of material objects—sometimes living organisms—apparently out of nothing, or out of a substance called ectoplasm that exudes from a medium's body. Dematerialization is the reverse process, the causing of the materialized objects to disappear. One extraordinary story of materialization involved a seal. A zoologist named Mr. Bolton had cared for and prolonged the life of a large seal that had been harpooned, but in spite of his efforts, it had finally died. Ten days after the seal's death Bolton was at a Spiritualist seance when the medium cried out from her cabinet, "Take this great brute away, it is suffocating me." A seal emerged from the cabinet, waddled and flopped across the room, remained beside Bolton for a few moments, then returned to the cabinet and dematerialized. "There is no doubt in my mind," Bolton solemnly told a meeting of the London Spiritualist Alliance, "that it was the identical seal."

Out-of-the-body projection may be involuntary or deliberate. The files of doctors and psychiatrists the world over contain accounts of people who have had the alarming experience of being literally outside themselves and clearly seeing their own bodies objectively at a distance. Deliberate out-of-the-body projection, or astral travel, is a phenomenon well documented in the early records of many cultures.

These, then, are the phenomena, the strange powers and experiences that are collectively known as psi. Records attesting to the reality of psychic phenomena come from all ages and places, and from people of acknowledged intelligence and integrity. Yet argument about psi still rages, for the subject arouses people's hopes, fears, and prejudices. Perhaps more than any other question it sharply separates two distinct human types: those who believe that the universe is governed by rational and discoverable principles and who abhor the supernatural, and those who believe that anything is possible, that man has great powers as yet undeveloped, and that manifestations of the supernatural are glimpses of a superior and more exciting plane of reality than the one on which we normally live. Between the extremes of those who write off psi

Levitation to Materialization

Below: an engraving of 1887 of the medium Florence Cook with her famous materialization, Katie King. Florence Cook was closely studied by Sir William Crookes, an early psychical researcher. He claimed to have authenticated her powers, but there is still considerable speculation about his objectivity.

Above: Ingo Swann in front of his painting *Aft Ship's View of Sagittarius* completed after what he claims was an out-of-body voyage into outer space. Swann apparently trained himself to leave his body at will. He is under conscious control and is fully awake during experiments on the nature of his abilities.

as rubbish and those who are ready to believe anything provided it confounds reason and science, are the majority of people. This majority takes a cautiously open-minded view. They think there must be something in it, are prepared to believe some things but not others, and are intrigued but rather bewildered by the whole subject.

There is one thing that can be said without raising anyone's temperature, however. It is that *psi occurs*. It's not a very exciting statement, but it gives us something to build on if we want to take a clear look at the subject and make some sense of it. Psi is useful not only because it is an umbrella term but also because it is a neutral one. To say that extrasensory perception occurs is more controversial, for it raises the question of how we know that the perceptions are *extra* and not simply a heightened degree of normal sensory perception. Most of the other terms—such as clairvoyance, telepathy, and materialization—have similar pitfalls. To say that psi occurs is simply to

Mind out of Body

say that there are mental and physical events that in the present state of our knowledge cannot be explained.

"Our knowledge" in this context means the knowledge that modern, mainly Western, culture and science are founded on. Psi phenomena can easily be explained as the work of spirits or occult forces associated with gods, demons, or the planets, but to accept such explanations seems to the modern mind a retreat from reason back into the dark ages of superstition. This is the problem. Not only is psi inexplicable in terms acceptable to the modern mind, but it also appears to undermine certain concepts that are absolutely fundamental in our civilization—notably our ideas of time, causality, energy, mind, and matter. This is where attitudes enter the picture. Some people are completely happy with the Western world-view, and with its scientific and technological civilization. Others would like to see it changed for something less materialistic and more spiritual.

In this situation perhaps the first question we should ask is: What is important about psi? If we accept that it occurs, should we go on and ask how, why, and when it occurs, and risk undermining some of our most cherished and useful ideas and attitudes? Or should we consider it a mildly interesting curiosity and aberration?

The possibility that all humans may have some degree of psychic ability is one of the most exciting implications of parapsychology. Perhaps the limitations or boundaries of our minds are not real boundaries at all, but artificial ones of our own making. If these boundaries can be transcended, if psi faculties can be developed and trained, the implications for our society are profound. There is a growing feeling in the Western world today that some fundamental changes are essential if civilization is to survive. Many people believe that psi is important because it points the direction those changes might take. In the words of astronaut Edgar Mitchell, "survival seems to depend more than anything on a transformation of consciousness, an evolution of the mind."

Left: a researcher, Professor A. J. Ellison, attempts to record the out-of-body experience of a hypnotized subject. Professor Ellison measures her electrical skin resistance, and carefully tests the depth of her trance.

The Case of the Sick Colonel

Right: few people have had the strange experience of seeing their own body from outside it. One man who did is a British Army colonel. It happened when he was desperately ill with pneumonia. Through the haze of his illness he heard his doctor say there was nothing more that could be done. The colonel, however, promised himself, "You *shall* get better." He then felt his body getting heavier and heavier, and suddenly discovered he was sitting on top of the cupboard in the corner of the room. He was watching a nurse tending his own unshaven, apparently unconscious body. The colonel was aware of all the small details of the room. He saw the mirror on the dressing table, the frame of the bed, and his inert body under the bedclothes.

The next thing he remembers he was back in his body, and the nurse was holding his hand and murmuring, "The crisis has passed."

During his convalescence he told the nurse what had happened to him, describing the exact motions she had made and the details of the room that had been so clear to him. She suggested that perhaps he had been delirious.

The colonel had a different answer. "I was dead for that time," he said.

Chapter 9 The Beginnings of Psychical Research

Were the mediums of the 19th century able to contact the spirits of the dead? Following the success of the American Fox sisters, the fashion of the seance swept across the United States and Europe as skeptics joined the uncritical enthusiasts in circles around tables in darkened rooms. Three scholars set out to discover if there was any genuine evidence of supernatural phenomena in all the rappings, table-shifting, and materializations. Their methods established a new attitude toward psychic manifestations, and began the modern tradition of scientific analysis. Their reports pose still unanswered questions about communication from mind to mind.

The first recorded psychical researcher was King Croesus of Lydia, who lived in the 6th century B.C. In order to test which of a group of Greek and Egyptian oracles was the most skilled, he sent emissaries to each of them with instructions to ask them at a prearranged time: "What is King Croesus, the son of Alyattes, doing now?" He contrived something theoretically impossible to guess. He cut a lamb and a tortoise into pieces and cooked them together in a brass cauldron. In a brilliant feat of clairvoyance, the oracle at Delphi got the answer right.

Of course, King Croesus wasn't researching in the interests of science. He already believed in the supernatural powers of the oracles, and simply wanted to find out which of them was the best so that he could engage a reliable adviser. He chose well, for in time the clairvoyant and precognitive achievements of the Delphic Oracle became legendary. Her fondness for riddles and ambiguities, however, undermined her usefulness as a royal adviser, as King Croesus found to his cost. When she predicted that one of his campaigns would end in the destruction of a great army he went off to war with buoyant confidence, not dreaming that the doomed army was his own.

So long as people believed in the supernatural as a part of life there was no chance for scientific psychical research to get off the ground. That such a belief was prevalent in Shakespeare's day is obvious from his plays, in which the supernatural is often the pivot of the drama. In *A Midsummer Night's Dream*, for

Literature is rich in tales of psychic experience, and in some cases—like that of Mary Shelley who dreamed the terrifying tale of Frankenstein—it has been the inspiration for literature.
Opposite: Charles Dickens was another noted author who calmly admitted that many of his complicated plots and vivid characters first came to him in dreams.

Above: the three witches in *Macbeth* exemplify Shakespeare's use of psychic material. Curiously, *Macbeth* has come to be known among actors as an unlucky play. The superstition goes that the witches' incantations over their brew are in fact genuine black magic spells.

example, supernatural beings interact with mortals, weaving an intricate web of romantic complications. Shakespeare's audiences accepted the witches in *Macbeth* and the ghost in *Hamlet* at their face value. Modern audiences accept them in the context of the play but regard them as remnants of an age of superstition. A parapsychologist, engaged in studying unusual kinds of perception, might take a different view and ask questions that the Elizabethans could never have conceived. For example, when the witches greet Macbeth as "king hereafter," is this a precognition on their part, or are they picking up telepathically from Macbeth a wish that he would like to see fulfilled? When the ghost of Hamlet's father relates the circumstances of his death, is the whole incident perhaps an hallucinatory glimpse of the past on Hamlet's part? Such questions indicate some of the areas of concern of modern psychical research. It has not demystified the universe, but has focused attention on a different set of mysteries from those that preoccupied earlier ages: the mysteries of the mind.

Two conditions were necessary for the start of scientific psychical research: a society generally skeptical of all things supernatural, and a group of dedicated and intelligent scientists concerned about the limitations of such skepticism. It was not until the mid-19th century that these two conditions were fulfilled. The 18th century was skeptical enough, but it didn't produce the right people. Perhaps this was because reason had so recently been enthroned as a sovereign principle of knowledge. Few intellectuals of the Age of Reason would have risked ridicule by seriously examining the discredited beliefs of their superstitious forebears. When reason as an ideal gave way to romanticism with its emphasis on subjective experience, conditions became more favorable for the development of psychical research.

The poet Shelley, one of the major figures of the romantic age, was a morbid dreamer. In one dream he saw Lord Byron's dead daughter Allegra rise from the Gulf of Spezia, clasp her hands, and smile at him. In another he saw his friends Edward and Jane Williams die horribly in a house flooded by the sea. Not long after these nightmares, Shelley and Edward Williams died together off the coast of Italy, drowned in the Gulf of Spezia.

The great German poet Goethe reported a less ominous precognitive experience in his autobiography. One day he was riding on horseback along a footpath when he saw his own image riding toward him in the opposite direction, dressed in a suit such as he had never worn. He shook himself out of his reverie, and the vision vanished—but eight years later when he was again riding along the same path he suddenly realized that he was wearing exactly the suit that he had formerly dreamed of.

The novelist Charles Dickens also experienced a precognitive vision. He fell asleep in his office one evening and dreamed that he saw a lady in a red shawl standing with her back toward him. He didn't recognize her when she turned around, but she introduced herself as Miss Napier. He could make no sense of it, for he had never heard of any Miss Napier. But the following evening some friends visited him. They brought with them a stranger, a lady wearing a red shawl whom they introduced to him as Miss Napier—the lady of the dream.

In spite of his own psychic experiences and his frequent use of clairvoyant dreams and spirit manifestations in his novels, Dickens was strongly antagonistic to the craze for communication with the spirit world that swept through America and England in the middle of the 19th century. Perhaps when he heard of the "spirit rappings" in Hydesville, New York that launched the Spiritualist movement in 1848, he may have remembered how a great English writer of the previous century had been ridiculed for his interest in a similar phenomenon. In 1762 Dr. Samuel Johnson visited a house in Cock Lane, London where the ghost of a Mrs. Kent was said to be communicating by means of rappings that would occur only in the presence of the 12-year-old daughter of the house, Elizabeth Parsons. The ghost, which soon became famous throughout London, accused Mr. Kent of poisoning his wife. After Dr. Johnson had written a report on the ghost for a magazine, another investigator discovered that the rappings were produced by the girl Elizabeth, whose father was trying to blackmail Kent. Johnson and the other eminent people who had taken an interest in the affair were left looking rather foolish.

The Cock Lane Ghost affair was an inept attempt at an art that became highly skilled and sophisticated in the second half of the 19th century: the fraudulent production of allegedly spiritual phenomena. This was the age of the great physical

Oracles and Soothsayers

Below: a 19th-century view of the Delphic Oracle. A well-documented, classic example of a seer, the Oracle was consulted by many rulers. Her ambiguous utterances were interpreted by attendant priests.

The Cock Lane Ghost Affair

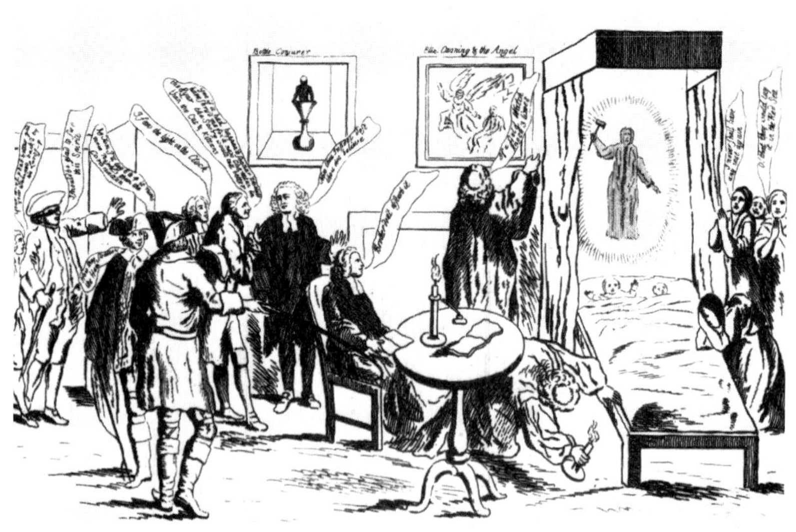

Right: a satirical caricature of 1762 entitled "English Credulity, or the Invisible Ghost," about the strange goings-on that Dr. Johnson wrote about. When the phenomena were found to be a calculated fraud, the reputations of those who had taken part in the business suffered seriously.

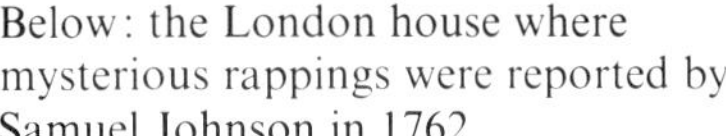

Below: the London house where mysterious rappings were reported by Samuel Johnson in 1762.

mediums, nearly all of whom, with the exception of the greatest of them, D. D. Home, were at one time or another exposed in fraud. With fraudulent mediums producing rappings, spirit photographs, materialized spirit forms (always in semidarkness), automatic writing, and voices from the beyond that conveyed mundane and sentimental messages for a credulous public, it is not surprising that most serious and intelligent people should find the whole psychic business tasteless, tawdry, and repugnant. The characteristic attitude of the intellectuals was well expressed by the philosopher Thomas Henry Huxley in a letter declining an invitation to investigate Spiritualistic phenomena: ". . . supposing the phenoman to be genuine—they do not interest me. If anybody would endow me with the faculty of listening to the chatter of old women and curates in the nearest cathedral town, I should decline the privilege having better things to do. And if the folk in the spiritual world do not talk more wisely and sensibly than their friends report them to do, I put them in the same category. The only good that I can see in a demonstration of the truth of 'Spiritualism' is to furnish an additional argument against suicide. Better live a crossing-sweeper than die and be made to talk twaddle by a 'medium' hired at a guinea a seance."

But there were some highly intellectual and talented men who didn't take Huxley's attitude, who thought that among all the dross there might just be the occasional nugget of solid gold, of significant new knowledge. Among them were Henry Sidgwick, F. W. H. Myers, and Edmund Gurney. These three men, all Fellows of Trinity College, Cambridge, and all sons of clergymen, were the founding fathers of systematic psychical research. Their individual, distinctive talents and personalities complemented each other and meshed together in a way that made them an ideal team for the investigative and theoretical work to which they devoted the greater part of their lives.

That they were the sons of clergymen is significant because undoubtedly a part of their motivation in pursuing psychical research was the hope of finding some grounds for reviving their religious faith, which had been undermined by the prevailing skeptical philosophy of the day. This is made clear by Myers in this famous passage in which he tells how he first broached the subject to Sidgwick: "In a star-light walk which I shall not forget I asked him, almost with trembling, whether he thought that when Tradition, Intuition, Metaphysic, had failed to solve the riddle of the Universe, there was still a chance that from any actual observable phenomena—ghosts, spirits, whatsoever there might be—some valid knowledge might be drawn as to a World Unseen. Already, it seemed, he had thought that this was possible; steadily, though in no sanguine fashion, he indicated some last grounds for hope; and from that night onwards I resolved to pursue this quest, if it might be, at his side."

Sidgwick, who in 1883 became professor of Moral Philosophy

Below: a watercolor showing a spectacular levitation, done in 1783. Even in a rational and scientific period, the belief in the possibility of paranormal behavior—like the floating nightshirted gentleman shown—persisted among many people.

Right: the Fox sisters levitating a table. Although their first communication with the spirits was simply by means of knocks and rappings inside their own house in Hydesville, New York— which had also been experienced by previous tenants—the scope of the phenomena widened when the sisters began to communicate with spirits outside their home.

Below: Daniel Dunglas Home was the greatest physical medium of his time. He produced materializations, psychokinetic effects, bodily elongation, and levitation. He was the only medium of the period never to have been detected in fraud while producing his spectacular effects, in spite of intensive investigation by many eminent psychical researchers.

at Cambridge, possessed as sharp and critical an intellect as any person of his day. Myers' distinction was as a classicist, and he was qualified as a musician and a doctor as well. When Myers, Gurney, Sidgwick, and some other Cambridge and Oxford scholars founded the Society for Psychical Research in 1882, Sidgwick became its President and Gurney its Secretary, a job to which he subsequently devoted all his time and in which he did prodigious work. Myers also worked tirelessly as general organizer of the SPR, lecturing, writing, investigating and collecting material for its publications. Another early member of the SPR was Eleanor Sidgwick, wife of Henry Sidgwick and a prominent psychical investigator. Scientifically trained, she conducted some of the most important research done by the Society and, like her husband, served as its President.

The declared aim of the SPR was to "investigate that large body of debatable phenomena designated by such terms as mesmeric, psychical, and spiritualistic," and to do so "without prejudice or prepossession of any kind, and in the same spirit of exact and unimpassioned enquiry which has enabled Science to solve so many problems, once not less obscure nor less hotly debated." Like most intellectuals of their day, the founders of the SPR shared a belief that science was capable of solving virtually any mystery known to man.

The SPR Begins to Investigate

Though the marvels performed by professional mediums were on the whole to be distrusted, Myers and Gurney became convinced that they must sometimes be genuine. This belief arose as a result of their investigation of William Stainton Moses, a retired clergyman, an Oxford University degree holder, and, in Myers' words, a man of "manifest sanity and probity" who could not for a moment be suspected of fraud.

The records of the psychic effects produced by Stainton Moses are as sensational and as puzzling as those of the better known D. D. Home. Their authenticity is buttressed by the fact that before Moses discovered his own powers he distrusted Spiritualism, and is on record as having said of a book about Home that it was the dreariest twaddle he had ever come across. He began to have second thoughts when through a medium he received a strikingly accurate description of the spirit presence of a friend of his who had died. A few months after this occurrence he had his first experience of levitation. From then on, over a period of nine years, Moses experienced and apparently produced phenomena of the most extraordinary and occasionally alarming nature.

Sergeant Cox, a friend of Moses', wrote an account of a curious happening at his own home in June 1873. He and Moses were in the dining room passing half an hour before going out to a dinner party. Cox was opening letters and Moses was reading *The Times* when suddenly, frequent and loud rapping noises came from the dining table. The table was a large mahogany one that could barely be moved by the strenuous efforts of two men. But it began to sway to and fro, and then it moved several inches across the floor. Cox, a keen psychical researcher, realized that this was an invaluable opportunity to conduct some experiments.

Below: a German drawing of a seance of the 1920s. These sessions, generally held with a medium, were conducted in dim light or total darkness to create what was said to be a suitable atmosphere for spirits. It also provided a suitable atmosphere for sleight-of-hand and other fraud.

The Sidgwicks - Dedicated to Research

Below: Henry Sidgwick, a founder and president of the Society for Psychical Research. Among his investigations were those of Eusapia Palladino, the remarkable and notorious Italian medium, and Leonore Piper.

At his suggestion he and Moses stood two feet away from the table on opposite sides and held their hands about eight inches above it. After they had been waiting about a minute, the table rocked violently, moved seven inches along the floor, and tilted first toward one man and then toward the other. Finally Moses held his hands four inches above the end of the table and asked that it rise and touch his hand three times, which it promptly did.

What is notable in this account is that the noises and movements began unexpectedly, and were almost certainly not deliberately produced by Moses. The same is true of all the other strange things that happened to and around him. Once he found himself suddenly levitated, thrown down on his back on the table, then lifted up again and deposited on the sofa, all of which happened without his being in any way hurt. Frequently small objects from different parts of the house appeared over Moses' head and fell on the table in front of him, having apparently passed through walls or closed doors. When Moses held a seance his sitters could expect to be caressed by breezes heavy with perfumes, entertained by a variety of musical sounds—although there were no instruments in the room, and illuminated by psychic lights emanating from the floor. Materializations of hands and weaving columns of light that suggested human forms would appear in the room. An evening with Stainton Moses couldn't have been dull, and the wonders must have been enhanced by the thought that such a solemn and august gentleman—free of any financial motive—would be unlikely to stoop to the low dodges of many a professional medium's elaborately rigged seance room.

Moses claimed that the remarkable physical phenomena that occurred in his presence were produced by spirits to prove the authenticity of messages that they were communicating to the world through him by means of automatic writing. He published these spirit communications in 1883 as *Spirit Teachings*, a book that became the bible of Spiritualism.

Though Myers had no doubts about the integrity of Moses, he was skeptical about the alleged spirit intelligences and thought that there might be some other explanation for both the automatic writing and the physical phenomena. Unfortunately, by the time the Society for Psychical Research was formed, Moses' psychic powers had declined. He could not be studied under the controlled conditions that the Society sought to bring to all its investigations.

Though psychical phenomena were generally accepted at the time—by those who believed them—as proof of the existence of spirits, and therefore of the reality of survival after death, the founders of the SPR were well aware that this was really only an hypothesis. However much they may have personally longed to have their religious doubts allayed and to establish some definite proof of personal survival, they tried not to let this longing introduce a bias into their systematic investigative work. This work mainly involved conducting experiments in telepathy and clairvoyance, and collecting anecdotal evidence of these phenomena.

A public appeal for evidence got a substantial response and deluged Gurney and Myers with work. One of the respondents was a Manchester clergyman named Creery who had for some time been conducting experiments in telepathy with his five daughters. The Creerys became the first subjects of systematic and controlled research into telepathy conducted by the SPR.

The Creery family reproduced their successes before an investigating committee of the SPR under strictly controlled conditions. However, it was later discovered that the girls had cheated in some less tightly controlled experiments, and Myers and Gurney had to discount the impressive evidence for telepathy gathered in their own work with the Creerys.

In 1883, the year following the Creery experiments, Liverpool businessman Malcolm Guthrie discovered that some of his employees had been experimenting with thought-transference in their spare time, and had obtained remarkable results in transmitting simple drawings. His interest was aroused, so he and a friend, James Birchall, conducted their own experiments with two of the employees, Miss Relph and Miss Edwards, who were said to have shown exceptional ability. These experiments were so successful that they informed the SPR. Edmund Gurney went to Liverpool to supervise some tests himself.

The procedure varied slightly. Normally, the person chosen to do the drawing would do so in another room. The *percipient*—that is, the person who sees in a paranormal way—would be blindfolded and would sit opposite the agent, who would hold the drawing in such a way that the percipient could not have seen it even without the blindfold. The agent would stare intently at the drawing and concentrate on it until the percipient said she was ready to attempt to reproduce it, and her blindfold was removed. The period of concentration might last from half a minute to two or three minutes.

Many of the attempts were failures. In other cases parts of the diagram would be inverted, or transformed in some other way. A vertical line flanked by two circles was interpreted as a pair of scissors. The number of partial or complete successes was strikingly high, many times higher than could be attributed to chance. In one series of trials, reproduced on page 155, all six attempts were either wholly or partially successful.

The Professor of Physics at Liverpool University at this time was young Oliver Lodge, later knighted for his discoveries in the fields of electricity and radio. He heard about the Guthrie experiments and supervised a new series of tests with the young women, introducing some variations of his own and bringing to the work the care and thoroughness that distinguished his work as a research physicist. In one of his variations he had two agents concentrating on different shapes, a square and a cross. The subject, who was used to receiving telepathic transmission from one agent only and didn't know that two were being used in this case, was at first confused but finally drew a cross within a square. The plausible inference seemed to be that the subject had received both messages and assumed, consciously or subconsciously, that they formed a single image.

In addition to their experimental work, the indefatigable Gurney and Myers investigated numerous reported cases of spontaneous telepathic and clairvoyant experiences. Advertisements in *The Times* and other periodicals brought the reports flooding in. In 1883 they wrote 10,000 letters between them, and

Below: Eleanor Sidgwick, Henry Sidgwick's wife and a president of the Society for Psychical Research in her own right. She was skeptical of the survival hypothesis—the Spiritualist dogma that the individual spirit continues to exist after death—for much of her life, but was greatly impressed by the cross-correspondences, a series of messages given to mediums who were working independently, and which only made sense when the separate messages were combined.

"Phantasms of the Living"

conducted hundreds of interviews. To help with the work they enlisted an Oxford scholar, Frank Podmore, whose skepticism and thoroughness in investigation were an invaluable contribution.

As they sifted and analyzed the many reports, the researchers noticed that the largest single category was of what they called "crisis apparitions." In these cases, a person had experienced a vivid, often very realistic, hallucination of another person at a moment later found to coincide with a moment of crisis in that other person's life. The crisis was usually the person's death, or serious injury or illness. In some cases the hallucination was auditory rather than visual: the person's voice would be heard at the time of his crisis.

After three years of research, Gurney, Myers, and Podmore published their evidence for telepathy, both spontaneous and experimental, in the form of a large book entitled *Phantasms of the Living*. This book, the first major work published by the SPR, contained reports of 702 cases of spontaneous psychic experiences, each of them supported by the testimony of more than one person. A summary of a few of these cases will illustrate the kind of material *Phantasms* contains.

A naval commander recalled an occurrence when he was 13 years old. He had nearly drowned when a boat attempting to land in rough sea on an island near Java was capsized. On coming to the surface after being repeatedly submerged, he called for his mother, which amused the men who rescued him. When he returned home some months later he told his family about his narrow escape including how, while he was in the water, he had had a distinct vision of his mother and sisters sitting at home and of his mother sewing something white. They immediately recalled an occasion when they were all sitting just as he said and all had heard a repeated agonized cry of "Mother!" The experience had deeply troubled his mother, who had noted the date and time of it in a diary the next day. Allowing for the longitudinal difference in time between England and Java, the time they heard the cry was found to correspond exactly with the time of the boy's narrow escape.

Another case, involving an actual drowning, occurred in upstate New York in 1867. A little three-year-old girl was playing dolls one winter afternoon in a room where her father, mother, and aunt were also sitting. Suddenly she ran up to her aunt and exclaimed, "Auntie, Davie is drowned!" Davie was the child's cousin, a boy of nine, of whom she was very fond. He and his older brother lived about 25 miles away, and the little girl had not seen them for several months.

The adults had to ask the child to repeat herself twice before they understood what she was saying. Thinking the child didn't know the meaning of what she said, but wishing to avoid a morbid topic of conversation, the mother changed the subject. She did, however, make a note of the time: 4 p.m. A few hours later, the family received a telegram from the boys' father saying: "My little boys, Darius and Davie, were drowned at four o'clock today while skating at Kenks' Lake."

A local newspaper clipping obtained by the SPR researchers confirmed the date and approximate time of the accident.

Below: table rapping became the first popular method of spirit communication, with hundreds of domestic seances like this one.

Left: Colin Brookes-Smith sets up electronic apparatus to try to determine if the "lift" of a levitating table comes from below or above—the medium's knee perhaps if from below. His first results indicate it is from above.

Below: an experiment by two skeptical science writers and two mediums to levitate a table. The table never did leave the floor, but it tilted and rocked itself so vigorously that people had to move out of its way.

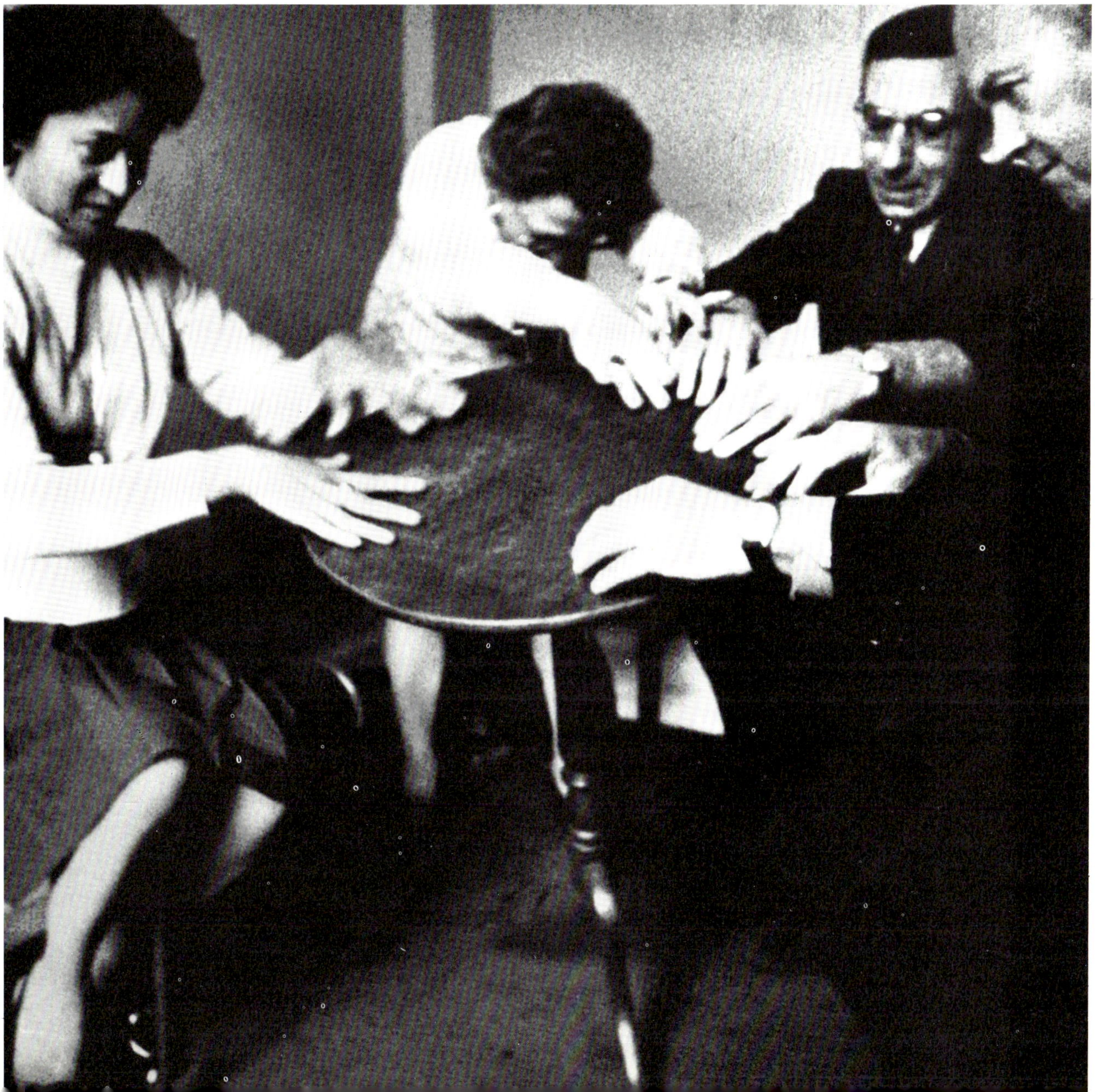

The Guthrie Experiments

A case that has been discussed and argued about ever since it was first published in *Phantasms of the Living* is the famous "Verity case." It is remarkable partly because it is well documented with supporting letters, and also because it contains elements of telepathy, clairvoyance, and possibly out-of-the body projection.

S. H. Beard, a young man who was known and trusted by the officers of the SPR, gave Gurney an account of attempts he made to project himself in spirit into the presence of his fiancée, Miss L. S. Verity. "On a certain Sunday evening," he wrote, "having been reading of the great power which the human will is capable of exercising, I determined with the whole force of my being that I would be present in spirit in the front bedroom on the second floor of a house situated at 22 Hogarth Road, Kensington, in which slept two ladies of my acquaintance . . . The time at which I determined I would be there was one o'clock in the morning, and I also had a strong intention of making my presence perceptible."

A few days later, when he visited Miss Verity, she told him that at 1 a.m. on the night in question she had suddenly awakened and seen him distinctly, standing beside her bed. When he moved toward her she had screamed, awakening her young sister in the next bed, who also saw the apparition. After the figure had vanished Miss Verity called another sister from an adjoining room, and both girls described their vision of Beard, what he was wearing, and where he stood, in exactly the same terms. Gurney subsequently met all three girls, obtained signed statements from them, and carefully cross-examined them. He had no doubt that their testimony was truthful.

Beard tried the trick again about a year later when the Veritys were living in a house in Kew, another part of London. On this particular night his fiancée was sharing a bedroom with a married sister, who had only met Beard once at a ball two years before. It was this sister who saw the apparition of Beard when he projected himself into the bedroom. She wrote in her statement that she had not yet gone to sleep when she saw the door open

Right: psychologist Edmund Gurney. He took part in the experiments conducted by the businessman Malcolm Guthrie, and was one of the most brilliant and respected of the early investigators. His death remains a puzzle in the history of psychical research, for in the middle of one project he committed suicide.

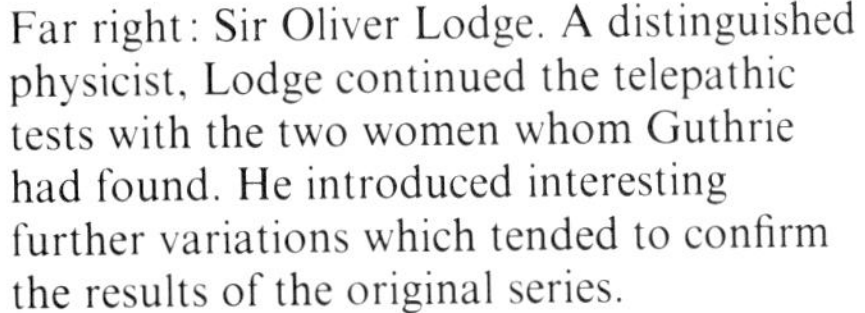

Far right: Sir Oliver Lodge. A distinguished physicist, Lodge continued the telepathic tests with the two women whom Guthrie had found. He introduced interesting further variations which tended to confirm the results of the original series.

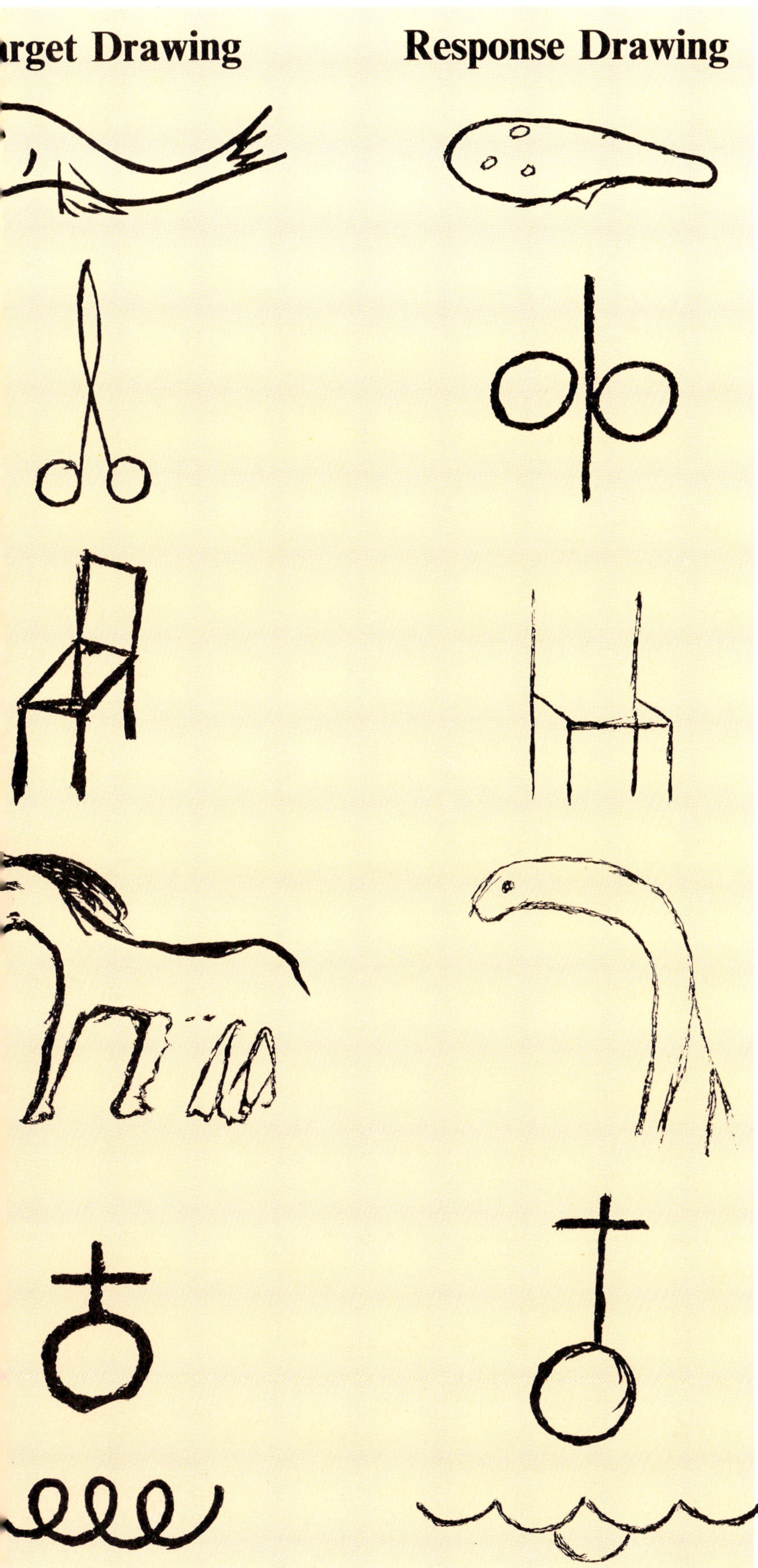

Left: examples of the most successful results from the Guthrie series of experiments with thought transference during October and November 1883. There were about 150 trials altogether. The agents, all of them psychical researchers, would look at a drawing and afterward attempt to transfer the image mentally to the two blindfolded receivers, Miss Relph and Miss Edwards. They would remove the blindfold when they felt themselves ready, and would attempt to reproduce the drawing.

The Founder of Psychic Research

Below: writer and teacher F. W. H. Myers. More than any other, Myers can probably be called the founder of psychical research. He made his resolve to study the possibility of communication with spirits of the dead after a starlight walk with Henry Sidgwick in 1869, and devoted the rest of his lifetime to dedicated research and careful reporting.

and Beard enter the room. She said he came to her bedside and first took her hair in his hand, then took her hand in his and looked intently at the palm. Miss Verity was asleep at the time, and the married sister didn't wake her up and tell her about it until the apparition had gone. What the fiancée thought of this apparent fickleness on the part of the spirit of her intended is not on record.

Beard visited the sisters in Kew the following day. They were astonished when, after they had given him an account of the odd happening of the previous night, he produced from his pocket a paper on which he had written an account of his intentions and his effort to project his image. He had not known that the sister would be visiting them when he conceived the idea.

Gurney again investigated and found the case well corroborated. Intrigued, he asked Beard to send him a note the next time he intended to attempt to project himself. Beard did so. However, he didn't see Miss Verity for two weeks after this attempt. When he did see her, she told him that she had distinctly seen him in her room at midnight on a certain date, and that he had stroked her hair. Beard couldn't remember whether the date she gave coincided with his attempt. But Gurney had Beard's letter stating his intention to appear that evening at a certain time, and by comparing this with Miss Verity's signed statement, he found that both the date and the time coincided. Coincidence of time is most important in such experiments, and in spontaneous apparitions as well. A time gap between the agent's effort to send the image and the seeing of the image by the percipient will tend to suggest that the apparition is a subjective hallucination by the percipient, weakening the case for its being telepathic.

In his discussion of the Verity case in *Phantasms of the Living*, Gurney noted a significant difference between such evidence for telepathy and the evidence obtained from controlled experiments. In the experimental situation the agent is thinking about the image or word or idea he is trying to project, and if the experiment is successful, the percipient receives an impression that is more or less a copy of the impression in the agent's mind. In the case of a willed apparition, such as the Beard experiments, the minds of agent and percipient are occupied in different ways. The agent is not so much thinking of his own image as mentally reaching out toward the percipient, trying to imagine where that person is at the moment, perhaps concentrating on their relationship. "It is thus probable," writes Gurney, "that the percipient's aspect has formed a larger part of the agent's whole idea than his own; yet it is *his* aspect, and nothing else, that is telepathically perceived." The same is true for crisis apparitions, even though the agent may not be consciously trying to project his image.

From this observation Gurney went on to draw a conclusion about the nature of the telepathic process. "As long as the impression in the percipient's mind is merely a reproduction of that in the agent's mind, it is possible to conceive some sort of physical basis for the fact of the transference." He cited several examples from physics, such as the way a permanent magnet brought into a room will magnetize any iron in that room, or the way an electric current in one wire will induce a current in a neighboring wire. As long as the information transmitted telepathically was essentially the same at either end—sending and receiving—it might be assumed to travel via some as yet undiscovered physical medium. But when the percipient saw something *different* from what the agent was thinking—for example, the image of the agent himself—a physical basis for telepathy seemed unlikely.

Another argument against a physical basis for telepathy was that all known physical forces were known to become weaker as they travel over great distances. This is not the case with telepathy. A telepathic message or apparition can be sent as easily across a continent as across a street. Recently, however, scientists have discovered that when certain metals are cooled to the temperature of liquid helium they will conduct an electric current with no loss due to resistance or the distance involved. The existence of these so-called "superconductors" has reintroduced the possibility that some physical force may be at work in cases of telepathy. Yet the nature of this force remains as much a mystery as when Gurney first discussed the problem nearly a hundred years ago.

Some of the peculiarities of telepathic transmission emerged in a series of more than 750 experiments performed between 1910 and 1924 by Professor Gilbert Murray of Oxford University. A small group of family and friends took part in the experiments. While Professor Murray was out of the room, one of them—usually the person chosen as agent—would choose some image or incident for him to guess. The subject announced would then be written down exactly by the participant taking notes. Murray would reenter the room, take the hand of the agent, and try to determine the subject chosen, while the note-taker recorded his efforts. The subjects were a colorful mixture of incidents from literature and history, sometimes including people known to the participants. Here is a typical example, with Murray's daughter, Mrs. Arnold Toynbee, as agent:

Mrs. Toynbee: "I'll think of Rupert [Brooke] meeting Natasha in *War and Peace*. Running in a yellow dress—running through a wood."

Professor Murray: "Well, I thought when I came into the room it was about Rupert. Yes, it's fantastic. He's meeting somebody out of a book. He's meeting Natasha in *War and Peace*. I don't know what he is saying—perhaps 'Will you run away with me?'."

Mrs T.: "Can you get the scene?"

Professor M.: "No, I can't get it."

Great care was taken to insure that Professor Murray was out of earshot of the group. However, the possibility that hyperaesthesia (in this case a sharpening of the hearing faculty) could influence the results was considered by the experimenters. Murray himself noticed that while he was concentrating his attention on the experiment he became acutely sensitive to noises, and that perhaps he was subconsciously receiving aural stimuli from this group. On the few occasions when the subject was not spoken aloud within the group, Murray failed to identify it. Most of these failures, however, occurred during a run of

Saved by ESP!

Among the cases in the records of the Society for Psychical Research is the story of a distinguished Italian engineer. He wrote that one June, studying hard for his examinations, he had fallen into a deep deep sleep during which he apparently knocked over his kerosene lamp. Instead of going out, it gave off a dense smoke that filled the room. He gradually became aware that the thinking part of him had become entirely separate from his sleeping physical body. His independent mind recognized that to save his life he should pick up the fallen lamp and open the window. But he could not make his physical body wake up and respond in any way.

Then he thought of his mother, asleep in the next room, and he saw her clearly through the wall. He saw her hurriedly get up, go to the window, and throw it open as if carrying out the thought in his mind. He also saw her leave her room and come into his. She came to his body and touched it, and at her touch he was able to rejoin his physical body. He woke up with dry throat, throbbing temples, and a choking feeling.

Later his mother verified that she had opened the window before coming in to him—exactly as he had seen it through a solid wall.

failures in which the subject was usually spoken, so it may be that other factors contributed to the lack of success.

Those who reported on the experiments to the SPR noted that there were many successes that could not be attributed to hyper-acute hearing. Sometimes Murray would guess a scene from a book he had not read, and mention details about the scene or characters not spoken aloud when the subject was chosen. The only conceivable way he could have received this information was by telepathy with the agent, or with one of the other participants who knew the book.

A striking example of a miss that indicated a partial hit was an experiment in which a Mr. Mellor, acting as agent, said: "I'm thinking of the operating room in the nursing home in which I was operated [on]." Murray's response was: "I get an impression of a theater. No. I can't get it. I'm now guessing—Covent Garden and Oedipus." Although Mellor had used the phrase "operating *room*" rather than "operating theater," the concept of a theater

Telepathy Between Twins

of some kind had apparently been transmitted to Murray.

These experiments raise the possibility of telepathy being increased by the rapport existing between certain members of the same family—an aspect of parapsychology that is attracting some attention today. Murray seemed to be most successful when the agent was his daughter, Mrs. Toynbee. Whether this was due partly to a sympathetic relationship between them, or whether it was due to some exceptional ability of hers to concentrate on the subject remains an open question.

In evaluating the results of the experiments, the participants judged slightly over 33 percent to be complete successes; about 40 per cent to be failures; and the remainder, partial successes. Of course, given the nature of the material used, judgments of success or failure were to some extent subjective. More accurate means of measuring telepathy were to be developed in the years that followed, as psychical research adopted more of the methods of the laboratory.

Below: an early experiment by Dr. J. B. Rhine at his Duke University laboratory tested the telepathic abilities of twins. While one concentrated on a picture in a separate room (right), the other tried to reproduce it (left). It was found that twins do better in transmitting telepathic messages to each other than unrelated persons. This goes a step further than the Murray experiments, which seemed to show that family rapport could heighten telepathic powers. Rhine assumed that the extremely close rapport between twins would make them the most sensitive to telepathic communications.

Chapter 10 Harry Price and His Contemporaries

Is it possible for a medium to lower the temperature of an entire room during the course of a seance? Is this how she obtains the energy for her eerie manifestations? This was one of the questions tackled by the psychical researcher Harry Price, who spent years in his investigations of the foremost psychics of his day, inventing some fiendishly complicated equipment designed to detect any possible fraud on the part of the medium. Although he unmasked many cheats and charlatans, he undoubtedly had a taste for personal publicity. But some of the enigmas he uncovered remain unexplained to this day.

One winter evening in 1937 a group of six people were gathered together in a large house in a smart London suburb to witness an event which one of them later described as "the most remarkable case of materialization I have ever witnessed."

It took a lot to astonish Harry Price, who wrote these words, for he had been in psychical research for many years. He had sat with all the great mediums of Europe and America, and knew all the tricks of their trade. He had publicly denounced several of them when he had caught them cheating. But this "most remarkable" materialization was not produced by a professional medium. The group consisted of some women friends who gathered every Wednesday evening in this suburban house for a seance. Seances were, of course, being held all over London. What made this one remarkable, and of interest to Harry Price, was that the group claimed that one of their members' daughter, who had died 16 years before at the age of six, appeared physically in the room.

Price was skeptical but fascinated. He could see no reason why a private circle of respectable people should wish to perpetrate a fraud that would hold them up to ridicule if it were exposed. Nevertheless, he took all the precautions against fraud that he would have taken to an experimental sitting with a professional medium. Before the seance began he examined the room and its contents thoroughly, had all unnecessary furniture, ornaments, and pictures removed to another room,

Opposite: a so-called spirit photograph of Harry Price in which a woman's figure showed up only on the developed picture. It was taken by William Hope, whom Price exposed as a fraud in 1922. Price stated flatly that not one of the many spirit photographs produced for him during his tests had ever been genuine.

sprinkled starch powder on the floor on both sides of the door, and further insured that no one could enter the room by sealing the door and all the windows with masking tape. He initialled the tape so that if someone broke the seal and then reapplied other tape, he would be able to detect the substitution.

When the seance began the group sat in darkness for some 20 minutes and the bereaved mother, who was sitting next to Price, repeatedly whispered "Rosalie!" She sobbed quietly. Then she said, "My darling." Price became aware of a presence between them, and felt something soft and warm touch his hand, which was resting on his knee. Then he was given permission to touch the materialization. To his amazement he felt the nude figure of a little girl whose height he estimated at about three and a half feet. He felt her all over, put his ear to her chest and heard a heartbeat, and held her wrist in which he detected a fast-beating pulse. He was next allowed to examine the child by the light emitted from a luminous plaque which had been lying face down on the floor. His eyes confirmed what his hands had felt. Here was a pretty child, aged about six, with long hair falling over her shoulders. He asked her several questions, but the only one that got a reply was, "Rosalie, do you love your mummy?" Then the child lisped "Yes." The mother cried and clasped her to her breast, and all the women in the circle dissolved in tears. This highly charged emotional seance ended 15 minutes later, and when the lights were put on there was no sign of Rosalie. A thorough examination of the room, the seals, and the starch powder, showed that no one could have entered or left it during the seance.

Below: Price with Frank Decker, an American medium who agreed to undergo a series of tests in Price's laboratory in London. Under the stringent controls that Price contrived, Decker failed to produce any phenomena at all.

This is a fairly extreme example of a type of story that continually turns up in the literature of psychical research, and that leaves the reader only with a choice of improbabilities. In this case the improbabilities are: a) that Price was lying and made the whole thing up; b) that he was successfully duped; c) that Rosalie was actually a genuine spirit materialization. That he was lying is improbable because he included the story in his book *Fifty Years of Psychical Research* only reluctantly, at his publisher's request; it is not a story that would help his reputation as a serious psychical researcher. A friend who saw Price on the day after the Rosalie seance described him as "visibly shaken" by the experience—an unlikely state of mind if he were lying. That Price was duped is improbable because he took elaborate precautions, knew all the methods employed by fraudulent materializing mediums, and was convinced that the mother's emotions were genuine. If the materialization was a hoax she too was a victim of it. The third supposition, that Rosalie was a materialization, is improbable because there is no precedent for such a phenomenon outside legend and folklore. It violates all known laws of nature.

The Rosalie case exemplifies the problem that scientists have when confronted with the evidence of psychical research. To be stuck with a choice between improbabilities is not a situation that holds out much hope for the advancement of knowledge. It is an understandable reaction to shrug off the problem and get on with other work.

But let us stay with the problem for a while. An odd thing

The Skeptical Investigator

Left: one of Harry Price's precautions against fraud during a seance was to sprinkle starch powder to detect foot movements. He also marked chalk circles around such movable objects as the flower vase at top left.

about psychical research is that certain types of phenomena and certain avenues of research seem to prevail at particular times. Levitations and materializations are not much heard of nowadays, but both were frequently observed by the researchers of the period between the two World Wars. The founding members of the SPR, and its sister organization the American SPR, preferred to investigate mental phenomena—telepathy and clairvoyance—partly because experiments were easier to control and their results easier to assess, and partly no doubt because they were loath to demean themselves in the rough-and-tumble of the seance room. Their colleagues in continental Europe were less cautious, however, and apparently more

Fact or Fraud?

Fraud and physical mediumship often seemed to be inseparable.
Right: Eusapia Palladino at one of her seances. Even those who supported her mediumship admitted she would cheat on occasion.

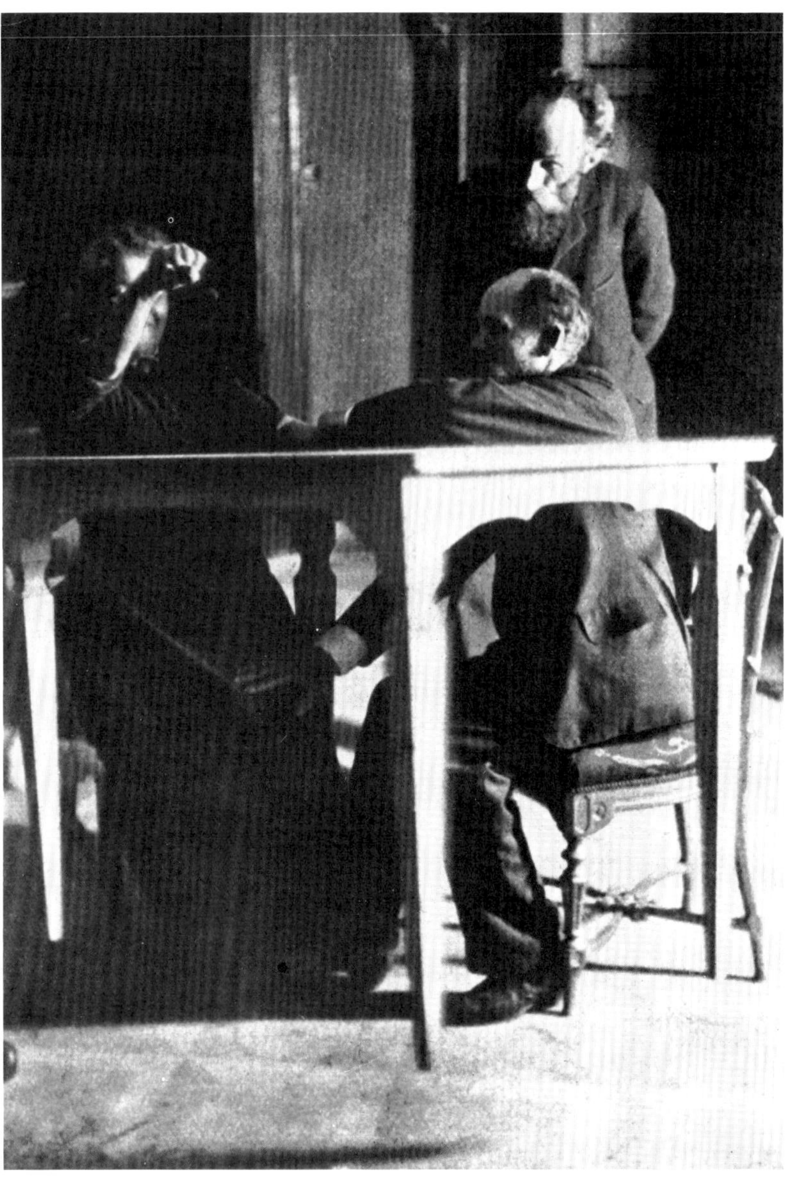

Above: a medium's accomplice of the 1890s, caught in the act with his ectoplasm trousers down.

ready to put their professional reputations in jeopardy by giving credence to the physical manifestations of mediumship.

On the subject of materializations, consider the words of Professor Charles Richet, a distinguished French researcher and winner of the Nobel Prize for his contribution to physiology: "I shall not waste time in stating the absurdities, almost the impossibilities, from a psycho-physiological point of view, of this phenomenon. A living being, or living matter, formed under our eyes, which has its proper warmth, apparently a circulation of blood, and a physiological respiration, which has also a kind of psychic personality having a will distinct from the will of the medium, in a word, a new human being! This is surely the climax of marvels! Nevertheless, it is a fact."[1]

No doubt Professor Richet was willing to commit himself so unequivocally because he was supported by distinguished contemporaries. His compatriots Dr. Gustave Geley and Dr. Eugene Osty, the German physician Baron von Schrenck-

Notzing, the great English physicists Sir William Crookes and Sir Oliver Lodge, were all convinced that they had witnessed genuine materializations under strictly controlled conditions. They could have been wrong. Nobel Prize winners and eminent physicists are no better qualified than anyone else to see through the wiles and sleight of hand of a clever conjuror. But that they were wrong *all* the time, and that *all* the phenomena they saw produced by mediums were fraudulent, is difficult to believe

Below: spirit phenomena were similar no matter where they occurred. Shown is a Danish seance during which a levitating chair sailed past the heads of sitters.

Mediums and Materialization

when one reads some of the accounts of their experiences and of the precautions they took against fraud. It is also difficult to imagine how some of the mediums, particularly the young women, could possibly have gotten access to the jealously guarded secrets of professional conjurors.

One of the most controversial physical mediums of the early 20th century was Eva Carriere (known in psychical research as Eva C.). Her real name was Marthe Beraud. The daughter of a high-ranking French army officer, she was brought up in Algiers. Her psychic powers were discovered by a general, who invited Professor Richet to investigate. Richet was impressed by what he saw—the full-form materialization of an individual who called himself Bien Boa. Although Richet noted a certain artificial quality about Bien Boa's beard, he remained convinced that the figure was produced paranormally by the medium. Subsequently, an Arab servant confessed that he was the spirit Bien Boa, and this confession was corroborated by Mlle. Beraud. However, her confession described a kind of trickery seemingly impossible to achieve under the conditions imposed by Richet, and Richet claimed that her statement simply indicated the mental instability typical of mediums.

A few years later Marthe Beraud appeared in Paris, where she produced impressive psychic phenomena. They were studied by a number of eminent researchers including Schrenck-Notzing—who gave her the pseudonym Eva C.—and Gustave Geley. She was also studied by the British SPR with less remarkable results. The most positive results were obtained by the French investigators, and in his book *Clairvoyance and Materialization* Geley published a series of photographs of materializations allegedly produced by Eva while in a trance. Some of the pictures show amorphous doughy masses, and others are of fully formed human heads. In a solemn and level-headed accompanying text Geley relates how on many occasions he saw a material substance (which Richet called "ectoplasm") emanate from various parts of Eva's body and form itself into organic shapes which were solid to the touch. Again we are faced with the problem of choosing to believe whether the distinguished professors were liars or the victims of a hoax, or whether, as they claimed, an actual materialization took place. Of course, no scientist is going to accept as evidence a man's sworn testimony on a phenomenon that violates the known laws of nature, even if that man is a Nobel Prize winner. He wants to see a repeatable experiment before he will acknowledge a fact proved, and one trouble with materialization is that the evidence for it cannot be produced on demand. Those who believe in it claim that it is a spontaneous phenomenon, and that one reason why physical mediums have sometimes cheated is that pressure has been put on them to produce the phenomena to order. Only when the effects do not come spontaneously, they say, does the medium resort to trickery.

Eva C.'s effects were almost commonplace compared to those produced by Franek Klusky. According to Geley, who devoted a large section of his book to him, Klusky was the supreme physical medium of the age. He was a Polish poet and banker who only discovered his strange gifts at the age of 46, and was

Above: a 1908 cartoon caricaturing Dr. Charles Richet, a famous French physiologist, for his interest in psychical phenomena. Richet went to Algiers to investigate Eva C. and her materialization of Bien Boa.

at first reluctant to exploit them. Finally, he was persuaded to participate in serious research. He certainly produced some bizarre effects. During a seance a bowl of paraffin wax, kept at melting point by being floated on warm water, was put near him. When a human form materialized it was asked to plunge a hand, a foot, or part of a face into the wax several times, then to plunge again in a bowl of cold water to set the wax. When the form dematerialized a wax molding of it would remain. This could be filled with plaster, and in this way several casts of spirit hands and feet were obtained, photographs of which are in Geley's book. In his accounts of the seances, Geley says there was no possibility that Klusky could have produced these effects fraudulently, for he was closely observed, and both his hands were held all the time. Moreover, the wrist openings of the wax "gloves" were too narrow for a living hand to have slipped through without breaking the mold. When the "spirit" hands were examined by experts they were found to be smaller than the hands of anyone who had been present at the seance.

Klusky also produced materializations of animals. It was not uncommon for cats, dogs, squirrels, and birds to appear in the room. Geley's book contains a picture of Klusky with an immense materialized buzzard on his shoulders. But the most

Below: Eva C. producing the materialization of an ectoplasmic face. The course of Eva C.'s mediumship was spectacular and highly controversial. By the time of her seances—from the 1900s to the 1920s—test controls had become so rigid that she was often made to sit in the nude. She even had emetics administered to check that she had not swallowed any material for faking her effects.

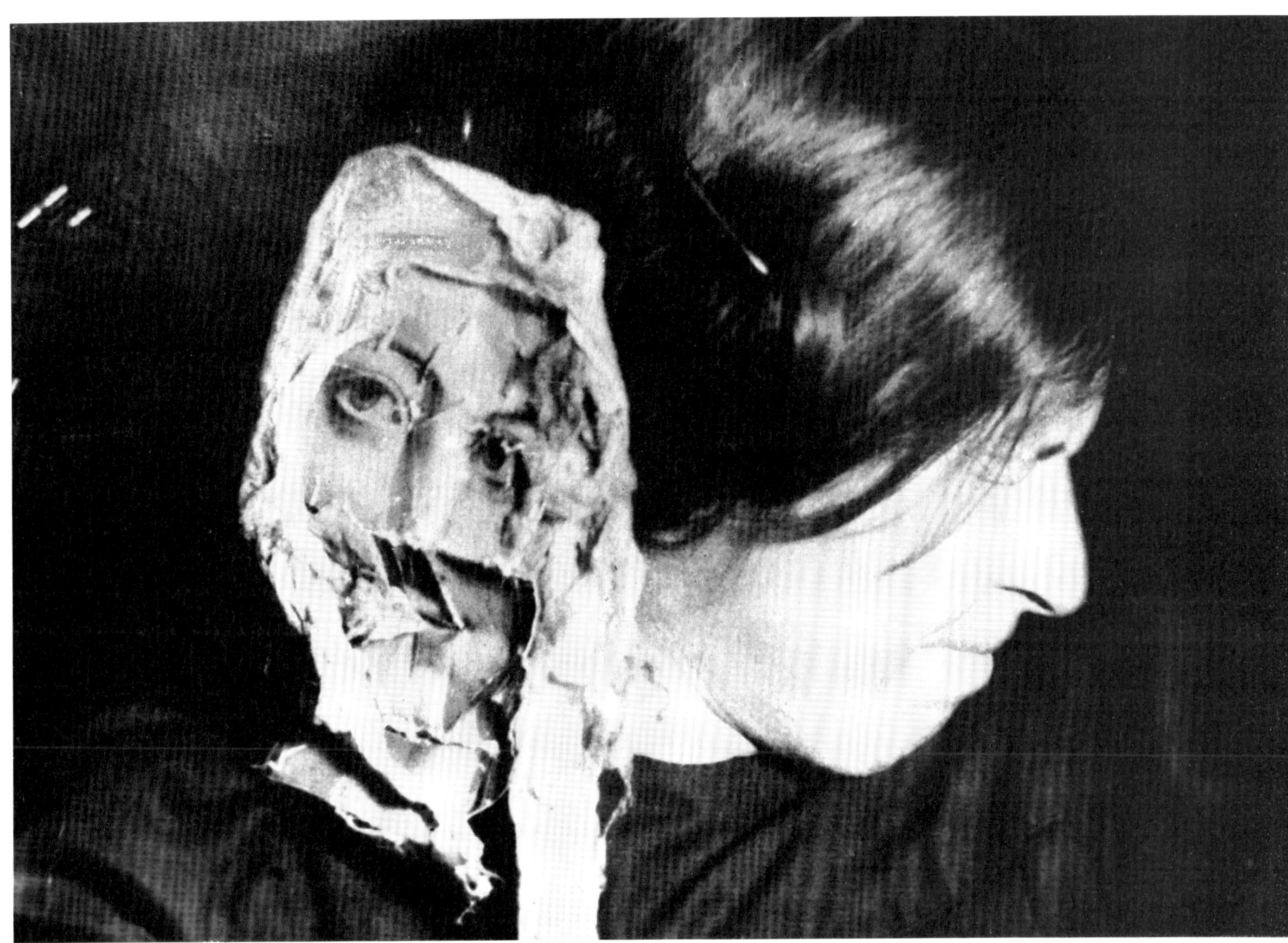

Klusky the Polish Medium

Below: Gustave Geley, who obtained the famous plaster casts of the hands said to be materialized by Polish medium Franek Klusky.

alarming experience for the sitters must have been the appearance of a creature they called *Pithecanthropus*, a large hairy ape man who grunted, ground his teeth, lurched around the room, and tried to lick the hands and faces of everybody present.

Klusky produced similar effects independently both for the French investigators and for the Polish SPR, but he would not sit with Harry Price. Price declared that Klusky's mediumship "is unsatisfactory from the point of view that no scientific body has investigated the alleged miracles." This must have annoyed Geley and Richet, who considered that their investigations were scientifically unimpeachable. For example, in order to insure that the "spirit gloves" obtained at Klusky's seances were actually made during the experiment and with their wax, the researchers mixed a small amount of a certain chemical with the wax. This chemical—undetectable at the time of the experiment—would later produce a discoloration in the wax when it was treated in a certain way. Richet was convinced that this and all the other evidence for the reality of materialization added up to a scientifically proved case. He wrote: "The fact that intelligent forces are projected from an organism that can act mechanically, can move objects and make sounds, is a phenomenon as certainly established as any fact in physics." He did not consider that this constituted a proof of survival of the spirit after death, however. He inclined rather to the view that materializations were thought-forms projected by the medium or in some cases, perhaps unconsciously, by one of the sitters participating in the seance.

That some kind of energy discharge takes place, both from the medium and from the sitters, during a physical seance was a hypothesis widely discussed during this period. In some sittings he conducted with a young London nurse named Stella Cranshaw, Price obtained objective evidence indicating that energy was absorbed from the environment during a seance. Self-recording thermometers showed a considerable drop in temperature—on one occasion as much as 11°F—and this drop coincided with the occurrence of the more vigorous physical manifestations, such as levitations. At the end of the seance the room temperature was always marginally higher than at the start, which was to be expected on account of the presence of the sitters. But the dramatic drop coinciding with the climax of the seance would seem to suggest that energy was somehow borrowed from the environment to produce the effects and then paid back at the end. Here, it seemed, was a genuine hard paranormal fact, a phenomenon objectively recorded, impossible to fake, showing the operation of a physical law quite unknown to contemporary science. It has not been satisfactorily explained to this day.

Harry price was a prolific inventor of ingenious devices for making his research methods foolproof and scientifically acceptable. To test Stella's powers to move objects by psychic force he constructed his "telekinetoscope." This elaborate invention contained two electrical contacts that normally required a two-ounce pressure to bring them together. They were protected from physical interference by a soap bubble, a glass shade, and

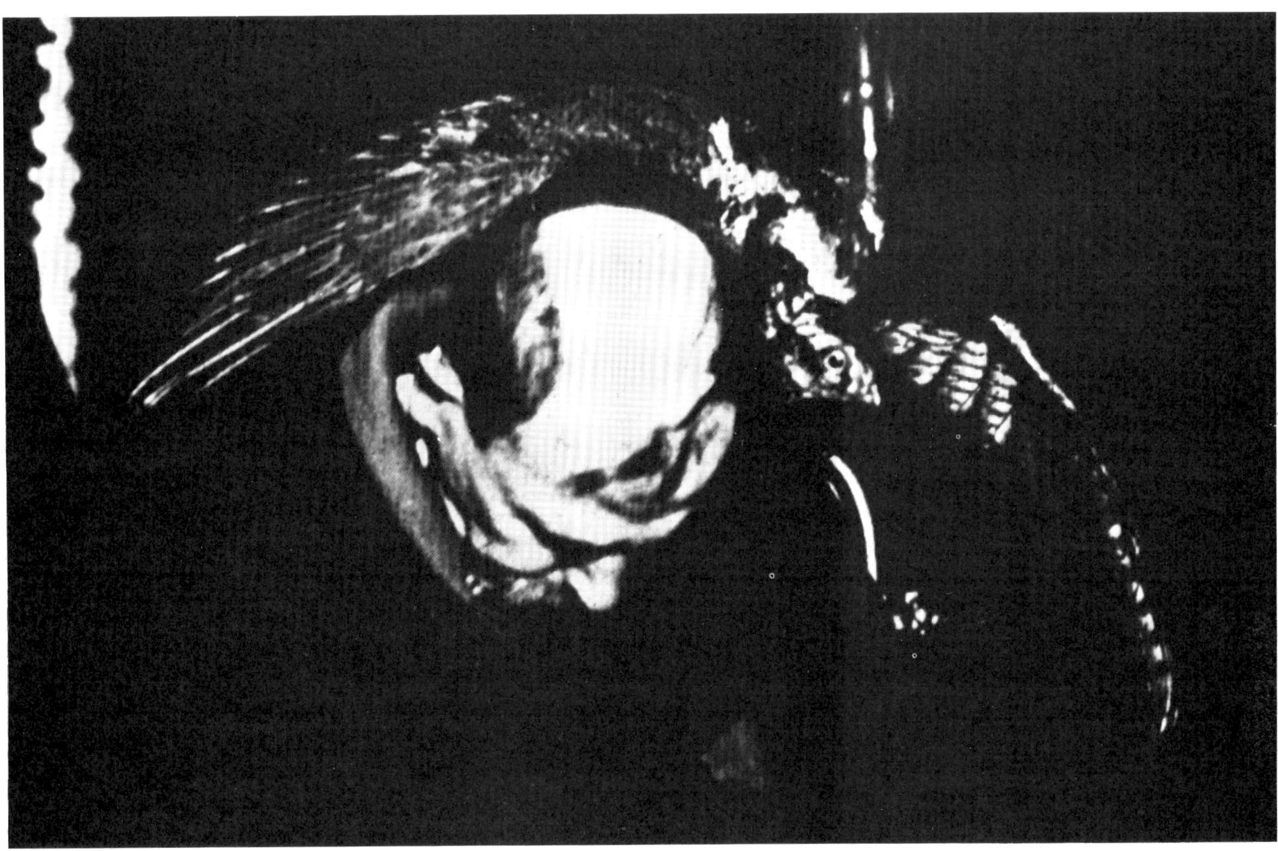

Above: Klusky during a seance with a buzzard he materialized perched calmly on his shoulders.

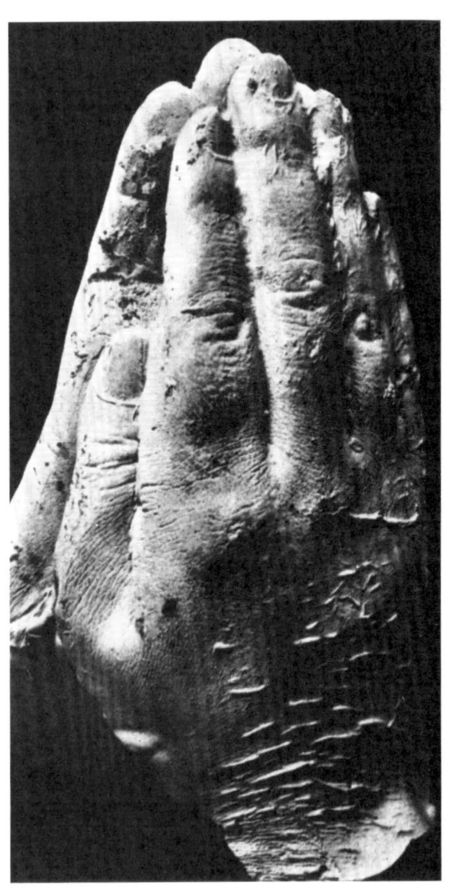

Right: one of several wax molds of materialized hands produced by Klusky. Spirits around the seance table were challenged to plunge their hands into a bowl of wax kept at melting point on the seance table. Plaster would then be poured into the mold.

a cage. When the electrical contact was made a red bulb would light up. At her first attempt Stella succeeded in completing the circuit and lighting the bulb, and when the telekinetoscope was examined, both the glass shade and the soap bubble were found intact. She had apparently brought the two electrical contacts together by the exertion of psychic force.

Most of Price's complicated inventions were designed to control the medium and prevent fraud. He had an "electric chair" in which the medium sat with head, arms, feet, hands, and seat all in contact with electric light circuits. At any movement a red signal light was automatically switched off. To insure further that psychokinetic effects were genuinely produced by psychic forces he developed his "counterpoise table." The object to be moved psychokinetically, which could be as light as a handkerchief, was placed on one side of the table. When the object was lifted, the other side of the table would fall, closing an electrical circuit that immediately activated a battery of cameras. Whatever moved the object would, if it were visible, be automatically photographed. Later Price devised a system of infrared ray projectors in the ceiling and walls of the seance room, which provided a more sophisticated

Above: Stella C., the medium discovered on a train by Harry Price. She was apparently not greatly interested in her psychic powers, and only reluctanctly took part in Price's various experiments. In spite of rigorous controls she produced electrifying effects.

and satisfactory method of control than the inhibiting electric chair. Each projector was aligned with a photoelectric cell. When mediums took position in a chair, certain rays were obscured by their body, and the resulting pattern was recorded in a nearby control room. Even if a medium were left entirely alone in the seance room, every movement could be observed on the control panel, which would also register the movement of any object in the room. In this way, not only was the medium controlled, but also any physical phenomena produced were automatically visible to the observer.

Obviously, such sophisticated apparatus required some form of permanent housing, and in 1926 Price opened his National Laboratory of Psychical Research in Kensington. One of the first subjects to be studied there was the Rumanian peasant girl Eleonore Zügun.

Eleonore was 12 years old when the weird effects that made her famous started to happen. In her presence, objects would fly about with no visible agent having thrown them. In other words, she was the focus of poltergeist activity. It seems unlikely that she would have tried to create the phenomena fraudulently, for because of them she was at first persecuted by the superstitious villagers who thought they were the work of the Devil. Eleonore was put in an asylum, where she might have remained had she not come to the attention of an Austrian Countess who was interested in psychic matters. The Countess secured her release, took her to Vienna, and wrote an article about her that was published in the Journal of the American Society for Psychical Research. When Harry Price read the article he decided to go to Vienna to investigate the phenomena for himself.

His investigation started with a rather alarming incident. He,

TABLE OF TEMPERATURES

No.	Date of Sitting	Time of Start	Temp. at Start	Time of Finish	Temp. at Finish	Min. (inter mediate)	Fall	Rise
1	Mar. 22	11.32 a.m.	60°	12.35 p.m.	62°	49°	11°	13°
2	Mar. 29	11.38 a.m.	61°	12.47 p.m.	65°	49.5°	11.5°	15.5°
3	April 5	11.20 a.m.	64.5°	12.43 p.m.	65°	57°	7.5°	8°
4	April 12	11.20 a.m.	62°	1.3 p.m.	66°	58°	4°	8°
5	April 19	11.18 a.m.	63.5°	1.15 p.m.	64.5°	43°	20.5°	21.5°
6	May 3	11.40 a.m.	67°	1.45 p.m.	74°	no fall		7°
7	May 10	11.5 a.m.	58.5°	12.25 p.m.	64°	57°	1.5°	7°
8	May 17	11.0 a.m.	57.5°	12.55 p.m.	64°	57°	0.5°	7°
9	May 24	11.15 a.m.	59°	12.55 p.m.	65°	58°	1°	7°
10	June 7	11.6 a.m.	62.5°	12.55 p.m.	68.5°	61.75°	0.75°	6.75°
11	June 21	11.15 a.m.	63.5°	12.45 p.m.	68.5°	62.5°	1°	6°
12	Sept. 27	10.45 a.m.	61°	12.35 p.m.	64°	no fall		3°
13	Oct. 4	10.40 a.m.	56°	12.35 p.m.	59°	55.5°	.5°	3.5°

Right: a chart of temperatures showing Stella C.'s remarkable quality of causing the room temperature to fall during a seance—apparently by absorbing the energy to produce the effects.

Eleonore, and the Countess were in the latter's study-bedroom in her apartment. He had brought the child a toy which came apart while she was playing with it. She ran over to where he and the Countess were sitting and asked them to fix the toy. They rose to attend to it, and while they were doing so a long steel paper knife shot across the room from behind them, just missing Price's head, and hit the door opposite. It clearly couldn't have been thrown by anyone, for there was no one else in the room, and the writing desk where it had lain was across the room in front of a window that was securely fastened.

Several other movements of objects in the room occurred during Price's brief visit, and he was so impressed that he persuaded the Countess to bring Eleonore to London. There, in the National Laboratory, under carefully controlled conditions and in front of some distinguished witnesses, numerous PK effects were recorded. One odd feature of these events was that they were accompanied by stigmata on the child's body. Red weals and what looked like teeth marks would appear. Her pulse rate rose in proportion to the violence of the phenomena. Eleonore must have been greatly relieved when, at the onset of puberty, the phenomena abruptly stopped.

Eleonore's case is a classic example of poltergeist activity, in that the events were spontaneous, uncontrolled, and unpredictable. A girl who suffered similarly when she was 12 but who retained her psychic powers in adult life was the Danish medium Anna Rasmussen. She was studied intensively between 1922 and 1928 by Professor Winther of Copenhagen, who in 1927 invited Price to witness a demonstration at his laboratory.

Anna had a "trance personality" (or "spirit guide" as Spiritualists would say) named "Dr. Lasaruz," who supposedly brought about the movement of objects. In order to study these

Tests in the Laboratory

Below: for its time, the Price laboratory in South Kensington, London, possessed remarkably sophisticated equipment designed to monitor seances and to detect any fraud. This photograph was taken in 1926, showing Price at work on one of his investigations.

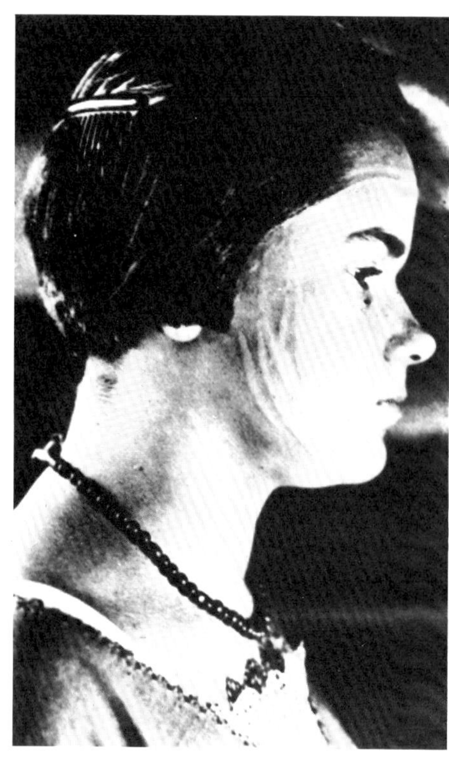

Above: Eleonore Zügun, the Rumanian child medium of 13, often had mysterious marks appear on her face—which she explained as the work of the Devil. She was one of Harry Price's first subjects for psychical research.

psychic powers, Professor Winther used a special device of a sealed glass case in which a number of pendulums of different weights were suspended by silk threads. In a sunlit room, under strict controls and before witnesses, Anna could make any one of the pendulums move in any direction as requested. All the experimenter had to do was ask Dr. Lasaruz to move a specific pendulum in a particular direction, and it would move accordingly. In his autobiography, Price wrote that he had never seen a more convincing example of psychokinesis than this.

The most famous psychics of the 1920s and 1930s were the Schneider brothers, Willi and Rudi. Like Hitler, they were born in the Austrian village of Braunau. From an early age the brothers showed remarkable psychic powers, and news of the so-called miracles taking place in Braunau reached Baron von Schrenck-Notzing. One of these miracles, witnessed and reported by retired warship commander Fritz Kogelnik, was the full materialization of Willi's spirit control "Olga," who "danced the tango very correctly and gracefully." Willi was the elder brother and the first to show psychic powers. In order to study Willi's powers thoroughly, Schrenck-Notzing arranged

Right: Eleonore with the Countess Zoe Wassilko-Serecki, who adopted her when she was being persecuted by her native villagers for her strange gifts.

for the boy to go to Munich, train for the dental profession at his own expense, and be available for psychical research experiments. He invited colleagues and scientists from all over Europe to attend the experiments, and in 1922 Harry Price did so.

The control conditions imposed in Schrenck-Notzing's seance room involved the use of a large wooden cage with gauze panels. A heavy table, a hand bell, and a heavy music box—all marked with luminous paint so that their movements could be seen in the semidarkness—were placed inside the cage, which was then locked. Willi was controlled by being dressed in one-piece black tights outlined with luminous bands and buttons. Luminous bracelets were put on his wrists, and he was held firmly by two men.

Soon after Willi had gone into trance the table inside the locked cage gave a resounding bump on the floor, and was seen to rise. Then the music box began to play and bump up and down. The music would stop and resume at the command of any of the sitters, and when the music box had run down it was rewound by some unseen agency—an operation that normally required two hands, one to hold the box and the other to work the lever. Then the luminous hand bell rang and jumped about inside the cage. Other phenomena occurred outside the cage. Price dropped a handkerchief on the floor, and it rose in the air. A hand-like form appeared, waved to the sitters, then slowly dematerialized.

Later Schrenck-Notzing discovered that Rudi Schneider's powers were even greater than Willi's, and he arranged similar tests of the younger boy. Price went to Munich again to see Rudi, and eventually brought the boy to London to be investigated in Price's own Laboratory.

That the Schneider brothers' effects were genuine was formally attested by more than 100 distinguished scientists and other scholars who attended Schrenck-Notzing's demonstrations. Nevertheless, they were not above cheating. On one occasion the cameras linked to Price's counterpoise table caught Rudi in the act of manually removing a handkerchief which, without the resulting photograph, would have been thought to have moved by paranormal means. (There is, however, some doubt about the authenticity of this photo.) In spite of this apparent evidence of cheating, Price was convinced that in most of his seances with Rudi—particularly those at which the electrical-contact method of control was used, as it always was after this incident—the PK affects were genuine. During many of Rudi's seances the automatic thermograph recorded a significant fall in temperature in the room, as it did at the Stella Cranshaw sittings.

In his autobiography Harry Price stated several times that he "would go a long way to see a miracle." Some of his critics have said that he sometimes went too far, pursuing his investigations in areas that only brought psychical research into disrepute. Any estimate of his contribution to knowledge of the paranormal must allow for the fact that there was a streak of the publicity seeker in him. He loved to be in the limelight, and he had a nose for a good story that would appeal to the press.

Children with Psychic Powers

Below: teethmarks such as these on Eleonore's hand were also said to be the work of the Devil.

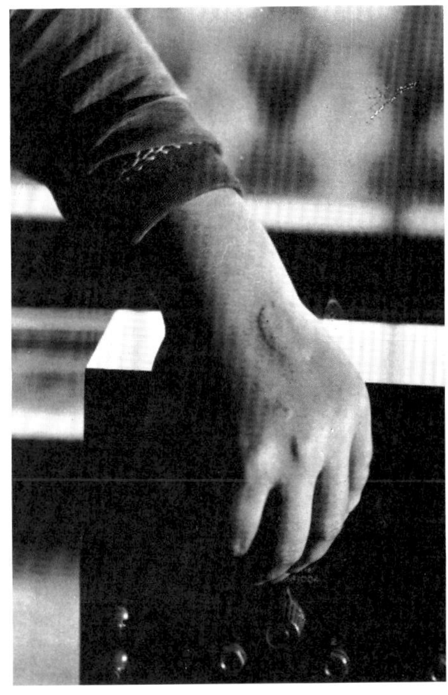

The Amazing Schneiders

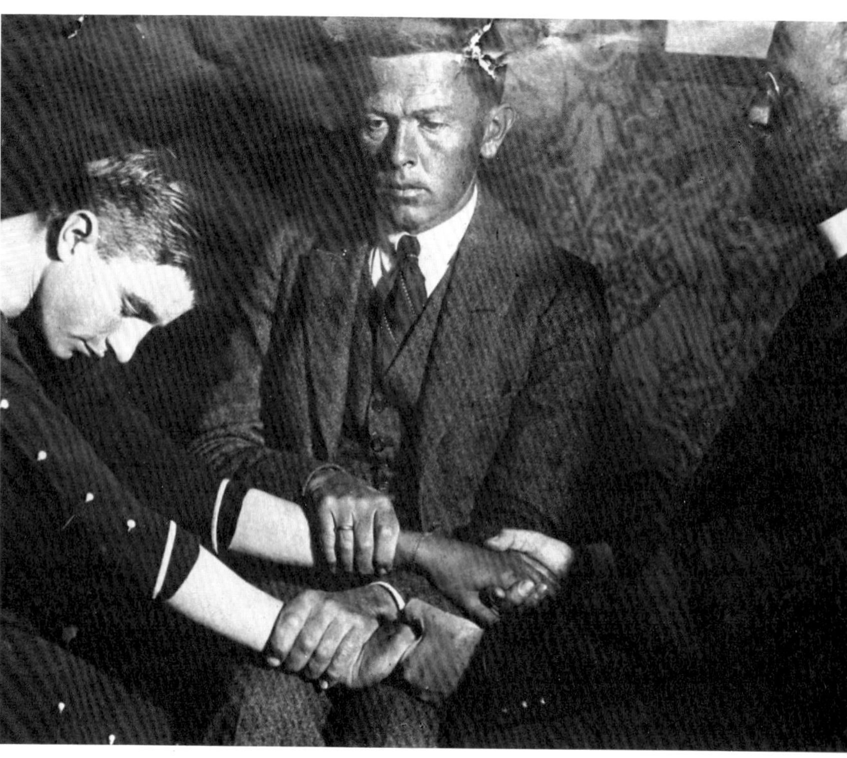

Right: Schrenck-Notzing tried to assure easy detection of fraud by dressing medium Willi Schneider in a tight one-piece costume and adorning him with luminous pins and bracelets. Two researchers also held Willi's hands firmly.

But personal profit was not among his motives, for he funded most of his research work himself and he donated the National Laboratory, which cost him a substantial sum to set up, along with his personal library of 17,000 volumes, to the University of London. He had the courage not to mind making a fool of himself, and he justified his more outlandish investigations with the argument that any alleged miracle was worth looking into if only to prove there was nothing in it. In this way, one could separate the hard core of the genuinely paranormal from the mass of superstition, fraud, and delusion that surrounded and obscured it.

In 1931 an old German magical manuscript entitled *The Blocksberg Tryst* fell into Price's hands. He was immediately interested, and, to the dismay of his scientific friends, he announced his intention of going to the Brocken, the highest peak in the Harz Mountains in central Germany, to carry out an experiment in ritual magic. One friend who was not dismayed and fell in with the plan with enthusiasm was the philosopher Dr. C. E. M. Joad, and in January 1932 the two improbable "magicians" set off for Germany. The ritual required the participation of a "maiden pure in heart" and a white goat, and it involved various incantations, magic formulae, and the preparation of a magic circle and a special ointment composed of bats' blood, scrapings of church bells, soot, and honey. Catching bats proved a hazardous and difficult exercise, but finally all the preparations were completed, and they had only to wait for a night when there was a full moon visible from the top of the Brocken. But month after month the moon was obscured by mist at the crucial time, and it was only after several postponements that the ritual was finally staged. If it worked, the

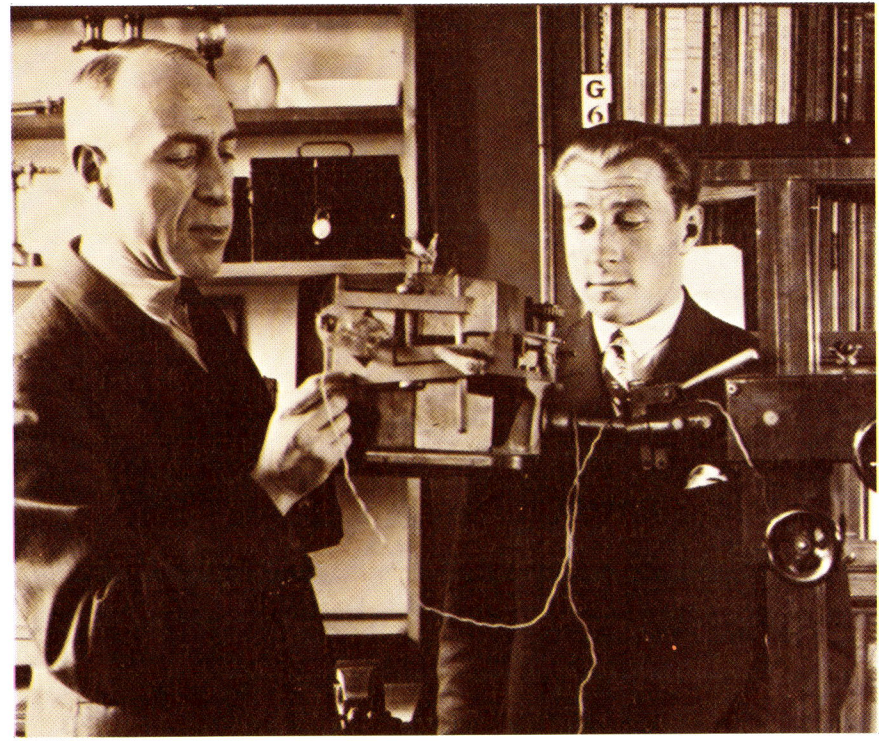

Left: Willi Schneider's brother Rudi, being tested by Harry Price. According to Price, Rudi became "the most convincing physical medium of whom we have any record." After about 1932, his powers also seemed to fade.

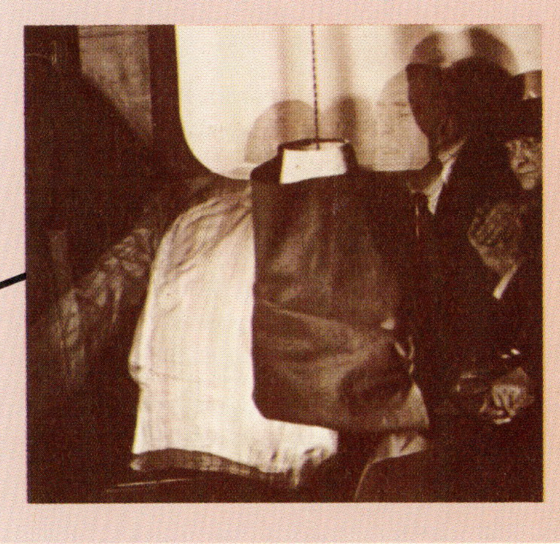

Above and left: the famous Price double-exposure showing Rudi in an act of fraud. His arm in the pajama jacket he wore at seances is apparently reaching out to take a handkerchief from the table and drop it on the floor—which would have been assumed to be the result of paranormal forces without the photograph.
A detail of Rudi is above. There was considerable controversy about this picture. It was said that Price had faked it out of jealousy because his protege was working with other investigators.

The Case of the Blocksberg Tryst

The Blocksberg Tryst

Right: this magical manuscript entitled *The Blocksberg Tryst* inspired Harry Price and Dr. C. E. M. Joad to set off for an adventure on the Brocken, highest peak of Germany's Harz Mountains. The ritual described in this excerpt from an old German book of black magic called for a goat and a maiden pure in heart. Price explained that the experiment had been carried out "in connection with the Goethe Centenary celebrations" of 1932.

Below: Price in close study of *The Blocksberg Tryst* manuscript.

"maiden pure in heart" would be rewarded by having the white goat transformed into a "youth of surpassing beauty." Needless to say, the goat remained a goat, and the newspapers had a field day. Price and Joad, however, returned to England satisfied that they had struck a blow for sanity and science by discrediting ritual magic and its devotees. The playwright Bernard Shaw expressed a general opinion of the experiment when he said that he might have been amused to be there but he "would not dream of making a special journey to see anything so silly!"

That Price was unashamed and unrepentant was proved by the fact that he undertook another and perhaps even sillier journey a short time after the Brocken adventure. A corres-

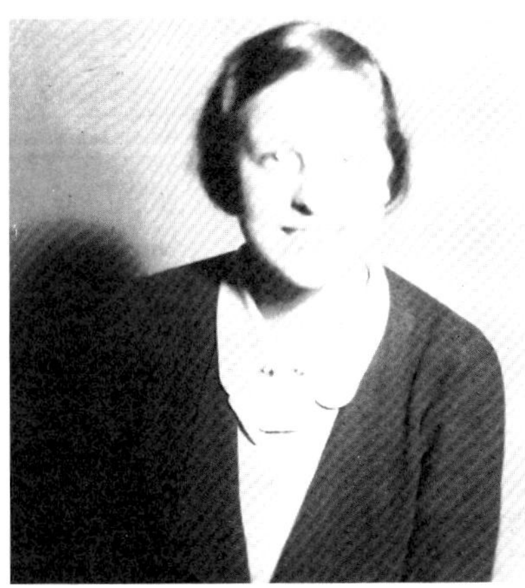

Left: Fraulein Urta Bohn, the "maiden pure in heart" found by Price and Dr. Joad for the magic rite on the Brocken.

Right: preliminary experiments with Urta Bohn, Price, Joad, and the goat while waiting for the appropriate night to come.

Below: the participants and their audience during the ritual. In spite of the best efforts of the two self-styled magicians, the goat didn't turn into a handsome young man as it was supposed to.

The Mongoose that Talked?

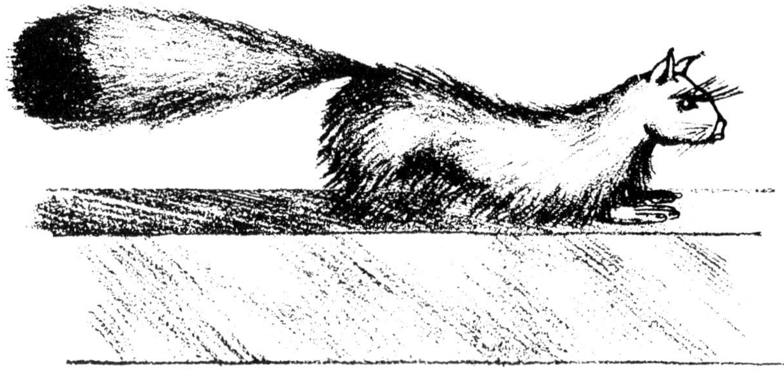

Right: Gef the talking mongoose, drawn from a description given by the farmer who discovered it. The animal kept entirely out of sight during Price's investigatory visit.

Right: the hole said to be used by Gef the talking mongoose—which could recite and sing—to enter the Irving home on the Isle of Man.

pondent in the Isle of Man informed him that a strange talking animal had attached itself to a family living in a farmhouse on the top of a mountain in the center of the island. Price wrote to the farmer, who confirmed that the animal was an Indian mongoose, and that it could not only talk but also converse intelligently, recite nursery rhymes and sing hymns. A friend of Price's, a Captain Macdonald, offered to investigate. When he returned from the island he reported that he had heard the "talking mongoose"—indeed had been verbally insulted by it—but had been unable even to catch a glimpse of it, and was unimpressed by the "phenomena." Reports of the mongoose's marvelous doings continued to reach Price, however, and some time later he investigated the matter for himself. He was hospitably received by the farmer and regaled with tales of "Gef's" marvels and mischief, but the "talking mongoose of Manx" remained as elusive as ever, and Price returned to London without any evidence of its existence. Nevertheless, he managed to write a book, *The Haunting of Cashen's Gap*, about his investigations into the strange case.

When Price died in 1948, an era in psychical research came to an end. His flamboyance and his flair for publicity had embarrassed some of his colleagues, but he had been a key figure in the field for a quarter of a century. His energy, enthusiasm, curiosity, and independence were qualities that enabled him to function as a link-man between American, British, and European researchers. And in the course of his own investigations he had turned up enough well-attested inexplicable phenomena to give the most thoroughgoing skeptic food for thought.

Below: Mr. Irving and his daughter on the doorstep of their farmhouse. The Gef affair was one of the most bizarre of Price's investigations.

Chapter 11
ESP in the Laboratory

Can a scientist get ESP to work under laboratory conditions? Research in the universities began in the 1930s and continues, each scientist attempting to produce an experiment that will isolate just one aspect of psi phenomena. Instead of the spectacular manifestations of the seance room, modern psychics concentrate on cards, attempting to transmit information about abstract symbols when all normal sensory contact has been rigorously excluded. What do these tests teach us about the possibilities of telepathic or clairvoyant contact? Have the scientists discovered powers we cannot explain? Some of their experiments have produced results which challenge the traditional concept of a logical world.

The scene is a room in the University of London. The year is 1937. A few people are about to engage in an elaborate guessing game, directed by the distinguished mathematician Dr. S. G. Soal. The person who is to do the guessing is Frederick Marion, a well-known stage telepathist.

Dr. Soal begins the game by handing Marion a small white handkerchief. Marion holds the handkerchief for a few seconds, hands it to one of the experimenters, and leaves the room accompanied by Soal and one of the other participants. The door, which has no keyhole, is closed behind them. The next stage of the game is to hide the handkerchief in one of six tin boxes which are located in various places in the room and numbered one through six. One of the group rolls a die in a box, silently showing the upturned face of the die to the recorder, who makes a note of its number. The handkerchief is then placed in the box whose number corresponds to the number on the die.

One of the participants now pulls over his head a stockinette hood that covers his features, and steps into a curious contraption—a kind of sentry box on wheels, open at the front. Another person slots into the front of the box several pieces of plywood, until the only visible part of the man in the box is his covered head. All of the participants except the man in the sentry box now step behind a curtain. The curtain contains eye-holes, which enable them to see what follows.

Dr. Soal, Marion, and the other experimenter reenter the

Opposite: an experiment by the American Society for Psychical Research. The person behind the curtain is trying to guess one chosen square out of 25 squares. The experimenter, in another room, watches him on closed-circuit TV and tries to influence the choice by her concentration.

Above: Frederick Marion, the gifted stage telepathist, taking part in a series of tests with Dr. S. G. Soal at the Harry Price Laboratory. He is trying to guess which is the preselected playing card. Soal is seated next to Marion in the center of the experimental group.

room. While Soal observes the proceedings carefully, Marion begins to walk around the room, trying to guess which of the boxes contains the handkerchief. He is followed by the man in the sentry box, who is wheeled by the other participant. Of the three people Marion can see, the only one who knows where the handkerchief is hidden is the man in the sentry box. As Marion walks around the room he frequently glances at the hooded head of this man. Eventually he goes to the correct box, lifts its lid, and removes the handkerchief.

This bizarre looking procedure was the final variation in a series of experimental games devised by Soal to determine whether Marion's ability to find hidden objects was in fact due to telepathy. The experiments had started out rather simply, with the half dozen or so participants remaining in the room seated around a table and watching Marion as he walked around the room trying to guess the correct box. Under these conditions he had guessed right 38 times out of 91 trials. The odds against scoring this high by chance are nearly 71 million to one.

It seemed probable, however, that Marion's success might be due not to telepathy but to physical cues from the sitters—cues they gave him unconsciously. In an effort to determine if this was the case and to what extent Marion depended upon such cues, Soal introduced various controls to obstruct cues from being given in the game: a curtain to hide all but one of the sitters; various kinds of hoods to cover the face of the person following Marion; cardboard boxes to cover his body down to his ankles. Even under these conditions, Marion continued to score high. It seemed possible that he was getting clues from another person's footsteps—the hesitations, accelerations, starts, stops. Hence the sentry box on wheels, eliminating telltale footsteps. Using the wooden panels, Soal varied the amount of coverage of the man's body. In the next-to-last series of experi-

Below: Marion during one of his night club performances, drawn by the artist Feliks Topolski in early 1940.

ments the front of the box was completely covered except for a tiny chink between the panels, through which the man could watch Marion and presumably will him to select the right tin box. Under these conditions, Marion's score dropped to chance level. With no cues, his apparent telepathic powers disappeared. In the final series, in which the man's hooded head was visible, they returned.

Dr. Soal's experiments with Marion clearly demonstrated that the man's extraordinary ability was not telepathy but an acute sensitivity to involuntary cues given by his audience—in this case by the hooded man in the sentry box.

"Let's not talk about extrasensory perception," say the critics of the ESP hypothesis, "until we know all that there is to know about sensory perception." Perhaps we will find that all the so-called paranormal powers of the human mind are just normal powers heightened to an extreme degree. Because telepathy, clairvoyance, and precognition appear to contradict our basic ideas of physics, time, and space, we certainly ought not to jump to the conclusion that they occur until we have exhausted every other possible explanation of the phenomena, goes the argument.

Laboratory research into ESP in the universities began in the 1930s, and it took full account of the skeptics' arguments. It was conducted by men trained in scientific method, and they understood clearly that no amount of spontaneous evidence would convince science of the reality of phenomena that conflicted with its basic assumptions. A telepathic apparition of one's cousin at the exact moment his plane is shot down, or a precognitive dream of the San Francisco earthquake, might be dramatic evidence of psi at work, but it is not the kind of evidence needed to convince a scientist. What was needed was to bring ESP into the laboratory where it could be observed and measured, and where experiments could be designed, as in the physical sciences, to test hypotheses about it.

The pioneer in this work was Dr. J. B. Rhine. In 1927 he and his wife Louisa, who had both taken Ph.D. degrees in botany, went to Duke University in North Carolina to pursue post-doctoral study in psychical research, They chose Duke because its Professor of Psychology, William McDougall—formerly President of both the British and the American SPR—had publicly campaigned for psychical research to become a university study, and was able to offer them his personal advice and the facilities of his department.

Six years later Rhine published his book *Extra-Sensory Perception*, which gave an account of the first years of parapsychological research at Duke. In scientific circles it was almost as great a bombshell of a book as Darwin's *Origin of Species* had been, and it stirred up a scientific controversy that is still raging.

The anecdotal evidence for ESP, such as that published in Gurney's *Phantasms of the Living*, suggests that it is a spontaneous faculty, often connected with crisis situations such as disasters and deaths. If this were true, then getting ESP to work under laboratory conditions would be virtually impossible. However, it is a basic principle of scientific research that small events produced in the laboratory can establish theoretical principles

The Marion Experiments

Below: Soal's sentry box. In it stood the one man in the room who knew where some given item was hidden. By removing or replacing the wooden panels, Soal could control how much of the man could be seen—and so determine to what extent he was giving Marion unconscious signals.

Right: the Amazing Randi, an American showman, with a pack of ESP cards. He claims to be able to duplicate psychic feats with a combination of sleight-of-hand, psychology, and theatrical gimmicks. Randi says matter-of-factly that he can do everything that Uri Geller has been seen to do, and also claims that there is nothing paranormal about any of it.

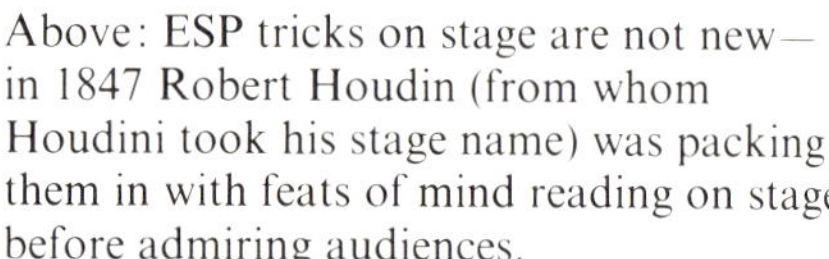

Above: ESP tricks on stage are not new—in 1847 Robert Houdin (from whom Houdini took his stage name) was packing them in with feats of mind reading on stage before admiring audiences.

relevant to much larger events. Men never understood thunderstorms until they discovered in the laboratory that sparks are produced between electrically charged objects. Similarly, an apparently trivial example of ESP, such as guessing what is on a card more often than chance would account for, might lead us to the principle underlying more dramatic spontaneous cases of ESP. It was in the hope of finding such a principle that Rhine began his research program at Duke University. It did not matter if the ESP effects produced in the laboratory were small and relatively undramatic. What did matter was that they should be measurable and repeatable, and that no other hypothesis except the operation of ESP could explain the phenomena.

Previous studies of ESP had used playing cards, numbers, or hidden objects as target material. Rhine and his colleagues realized that this was unsatisfactory, for people have favorite cards and numbers, and objects are loaded with associations for them. So new target material was developed using five relatively neutral symbols: a circle, a cross, three wavy lines, a square, and a star. A deck of ESP cards (sometimes called Zener cards because Dr. Zener suggested the symbols) consists of 25 cards, five of each symbol. In making a "run" through a pack, trying to guess each card or to identify it by extrasensory perception as it is separated from the rest, a subject might be expected to score five hits purely by chance. That is, over a series of runs through the deck, his average score would, according to the laws of chance, be five. If he consistently scores more than five hits through a long series of runs it is scientifically valid to assume that some factor other than chance is at work. Of course, the extra-chance factor may be some form of cheating, or collusion with the experimenter, or it may be due to some fault in the design of the experiment or to the subject's receiving and interpreting cues in a manner that neither he nor the experimenter is consciously aware of. But if these possibilities are adequately guarded against, and the subject continues to score significantly above chance expectation, it is scientifically legitimate to claim that ESP has been demonstrated to work.

In his controversial book *Extra-Sensory Perception* Rhine reported on the work done at Duke with eight subjects who consistently scored significantly above chance in card guessing trials. Of these the star performer was Hubert Pearce, a young student in the School of Religion at Duke.

Rhine's way of conducting his experiments—for which he was later severely criticized—was to start off informally with the subject, sometimes over a cup of coffee, and gradually to increase the controls. In his work with Pearce, Rhine found that the student usually took a while to adjust to the stricter conditions, but after a brief period of low scoring he would do as well, and sometimes even better, than before. His average score in 600 runs through the 25-card pack was slightly over nine hits per run. These results, said Rhine, "are positively breath-taking when one calculates their mathematical significance." The odds against chance accounting for such results, he added are "enormous beyond our capacity to appreciate."

Most of the work with Pearce tested clairvoyance. The experimenter did not look at the cards, so if Pearce was getting the information by extrasensory means, he was getting it from the

Genuine ESP or Stage Trickery?

Left: the calling card of Lady the talking horse. She picked successes in races, presidential campaigns, and on the stock market. She also located missing persons, spelling out the name of the place where they would be found. Dr. J. B. Rhine camped in a field to study her, and declared she had psychic abilities. But other investigators suggested it was all a case of the horse following almost imperceptible commands of her owner, Mrs. Fonda. Whether Mrs. Fonda was psychic or not was never tested.

Rhine and the Zener Cards

Below: Dr. J. B. Rhine, the American parapsychologist who set himself the job of creating repeatable and statistically measurable experiments on ESP.

cards themselves, and not telepathically from the mind of the experimenter. There is, however, another interpretation: that Pearce's high scores were due to precognition—that he was foreseeing the correct answers that would be revealed when the experimenter checked the cards.

In some of the early trials, Pearce and the experimenter—usually Rhine or his main assistant Dr. Pratt—would sit facing each other at a table. Pearce would shuffle the pack of cards, and the experimenter would cut the pack and place it between them. Pearce would call the top card and remove it from the pack still face down. The experimenter would record the calls and then check them against the pack.

Rhine soon discovered that Pearce could not only deliberately hit the target on an average of nearly 10 tries out of 25, but he could also deliberately miss it. In a series of 225 runs Pearce averaged less than two hits per run when he was instructed to make wrong calls. He could alternate high-scoring and low-scoring runs apparently by choice. But the most amazing discovery of these early trials with Pearce was that he could guess down through the pack without a single card being moved. Rhine would place a freshly opened and thoroughly shuffled pack of cards on the table. Pearce would concentrate and write down the order in which he thought the cards were arranged down through the pack. When the results of 65 such runs through the pack were tabulated, Pearce's score was an average of 7.4 hits—significantly above chance level. In one run, urged on by Rhine's offering him $100 for each hit he got in sequence, Pearce got all 25 cards right. He didn't get the $2500, though, for Rhine said the offer was understood to be "only a figurative one."

To test Pearce's powers of clairvoyance under stricter conditions, Rhine arranged a series of experiments at long distance. After synchronizing their watches, Pearce and the experimenter, Dr. Pratt, went into separate buildings on the Duke University campus. (At first they used buildings that were 100 yards apart; later the distance was increased to 250 yards). At a prearranged time, Pratt shuffled and cut a pack of cards, placed them face down on the table in front of him, then removed the top card and put it aside without looking at it. Pearce, in the other building, had a minute in which to write down his guess for that card. Then a second card was removed, and so on through the pack. At the end of the run Pratt made a record of the sequence, then shuffled the pack and ran through the procedure again. When two runs had been completed, Pearce and Pratt sealed up their record sheets and delivered them independently to Dr. Rhine. The results of these experiments were even more impressive than many of Pearce's trials at close range. After excluding the first three runs as an "adjustment phase," Rhine found that over nearly 300 runs at 100 yards Pearce was averaging 11.4 hits per run.

Pearce was just one of the eight people Rhine discovered among the faculty and students of Duke University who possessed extraordinary ESP ability. When he published *Extra-Sensory Perception* in 1934 he was convinced that he had demonstrated by unimpeachable scientific method that ESP occurs, and had presented a case that the scientific community as a whole must pay attention to. However, the scientific community remained skeptical for the most part, and in the ensuing controversy both Rhine's experimental methods and his statistical analysis of the results were criticized. Some of his critics even questioned his integrity.

One of the skeptics was Professor Bernard Riess of Hunter College in New York City. But unlike most other critics Professor Riess decided to test the ESP hypothesis by carrying out some experiments of his own. He discovered a promising subject, a young woman who lived near him in White Plains. Following the procedure used in the Pratt-Pearce experiments at Duke, he completed a series of 74 runs over a period of several months. At a prearranged time on certain evenings Professor Riess, sitting in his study, would go through a pack of cards while the girl, a quarter of a mile away, would write down the order of the cards. At the conclusion of the series she was discovered to have averaged the astonishing score of 18 hits per run. "Heaven knows there is no room for such results in my scientific philosophy!" Riess told a colleague. But with admirable scientific objectivity he accepted an invitation to publish a report on his experiments in the *Journal of Parapsychology*.

This is the best-ever record of success in ESP trials, but as it was not obtained under laboratory conditions and with qualified witnesses it remains on the level of anecdotal evidence. Like all other spectacularly high scorers in card guessing tests, the subject suddenly lost her powers. She underwent an illness, and when she recovered and was tested again her scores were not significantly above chance expectation. The same had happened to Hubert Pearce, who had suddenly lost his ability apparently as a consequence of receiving bad news from home. Parapsychologists are to this day puzzled by this tendency for ESP to manifest itself spectacularly but briefly in some people. However, the very fact that once-successful subjects eventually begin to fail is one indication that the original positive results were genuine.

One researcher who was highly skeptical when he read Rhine's report of the early work at Duke was the same Dr. Soal who later established—ingeniously if eccentrically—that the stage telepathist Frederick Marion possessed no paranormal powers. Soal's skepticism was not that of the hard-line materialist. Back in the 1920s he had already shown an interest in psychical phenomena. Soal was skeptical about Rhine's work because he found it difficult to believe that over a short period of time and in one place Rhine had discovered as many as eight high-scoring subjects. He had conducted similar experiments himself and had failed to discover even one gifted subject. For several years after Rhine's book was published he worked diligently with numerous subjects but still failed to get any results significantly above chance expectation. When the well-known photographer

Right: the five Zener cards developed by Rhine's associate Dr. K. E. Zener during the 1930s. They are still used as a reliable, standard testing unit around the world. Five correct guesses out of 25 cards can be expected to be made by chance alone; more than that may be significant of possible psychic powers.

Long-range ESP

Right: Hubert Pearce in a test with Dr. Rhine. He names cards before turning them over as Rhine records his calls. Pearce regularly scored well above chance, but suddenly lost his power at a time of great emotional stress.

Right: Duke University buildings used for "distance tests" of ESP. One series of tests was made with the subject and the experimenter in separate buildings B and C, 100 yards apart; a later series used buildings A and C, which were separated by 250 yards.

Basil Shackleton walked into his office one gloomy February afternoon in 1936 and volunteered as a subject, Soal had no reason to suspect that these experiments would yield one of the strangest discoveries of ESP research.

He still had no reason to suspect it after his first experimental session with Shackleton. The photographer had shown remarkable confidence when he volunteered. "I have come," he had declared, "not to be tested, but to demonstrate telepathy," and he claimed that with friends at home he could guess through a pack of playing cards from top to bottom and get most of them right. But he was disappointed in the results he produced under Soal's experimental conditions. His scores in six successive runs with the 25-card pack were 10, 7, 7, 6, 6, and 3 hits. He went away somewhat chastened, saying that he needed to have a drink or two before he could get his ESP functioning. But later, when Soal provided the "drink or two" and conditions in which Shackleton thought he could function effectively, the subject only averaged 4.1 hits per 25—well below chance expectation. A series of trials was completed, and at the end of it Soal filed away the unremarkable record of 165 hits out of 800 attempts. He forgot about Shackleton.

Three years later, Soal was persuaded to take another look at his records of the Shackleton experiments. The Cambridge psychical researcher Whately Carington had conducted some telepathy experiments himself, using pictures. On ten successive evenings he would draw a picture and hang it in a locked room in his house. His subjects, some of whom were on the other side of the Atlantic, would attempt to identify the picture by ESP and mail in their own drawings. Quite a number of these drawings, Carington noticed, matched well with a picture in his target

Above: the Duke distant ESP tests were generally conducted by having the sender in a room in one building concentrate on the card to be identified by the subject in another building.

ESP RECORD SHEET

No. ______

Subject H. Pearce Experiment Subseries D (copy)

Observer J.G.P. & J.B.R. Date Mar. 12-13, '34

Type of Test Clairvoyance BT Time ______

General conditions Distance test — 100 yards

Use other side for remarks. Total score ______ Avge. score ______

With ESP cards use ∧ for star, o for circle, L for square, + for cross. = for waves.

1		2		3		4		5		6		7		8		9		10	
Call	Card	Call	Card	Call	Card	Call	Card	Call	Card	Call	Card	Call	Card	Call	Card	Call	Card	Call	Card
∧	∧	o	L	o	=	+	+	o	=	L	L								
o	L	L	∧	=	o	∧	L	∧	∧	∧	+								
o	L	∧	L	∧	∧	o	o	L	=	L	o								
=	=	L	o	+	o	L	o	∧	∧	∧	∧								
+	∧	+	∧	=	+	+	+	+	=	+	L								
=	L	∧	=	o	=	L	+	=	∧	o	o								
L	L	=	=	L	L	o	o	+	+	+	L								
L	o	=	+	∧	o	+	∧	+	+	∧	=								
∧	o	o	=	L	L	o	=	o	o	+	+								
o	o	∧	+	L	∧	∧	L	+	L	+	o								
+	+	L	+	o	o	=	∧	o	=	=	∧								
+	=	o	+	+	+	+	+	+	+	o	o								
L	L	+	=	L	L	o	L	L	+	=	=								
o	∧	L	o	+	=	=	=	o	o	o	+								
∧	∧	=	L	=	+	o	∧	∧	o	∧	∧								
L	o	o	∧	L	=	∧	o	o	o	L	+								
o	=	=	o	∧	L	∧	∧	∧	=	o	L								
=	=	∧	o	+	=	=	=	=	L	+	∧								
o	+	∧	∧	L	o	o	L	=	+	=	∧								
+	+	+	o	∧	∧	+	+	L	L	o	o								
∧	∧	L	=	=	∧	o	L	=	∧	∧	=								
+	+	+	+	L	L	+	o	∧	L	+	L								
=	=	=	∧	∧	+	∧	∧	L	L	=	=								
L	o	+	L	∧	∧	=	=	+	o	+	+								
=	+	o	L	+	+	+	=	+	∧	o	=								
12		3		10		11		10		10									

Left: the scorecard from the first distant test with Pearce. The correct calls are circled. Five correct calls are predictable by chance. Pearce's results in six series of calls are, with one exception, at least twice that.

Below: the subject who is being tested records her impression of the card the sender is holding. The stopwatches are used to synchronize action between the two.

The Curious Displacement Effect

series, but not the one which was the target for the particular evening on which they were drawn. Many of them were uncannily accurate matches with the *next* picture in the series, or with one used as the target drawing on the previous night. The delayed hits were odd enough, but the advance hits indicated that precognition might be at work. At the time the subjects made these drawings the target drawing had not even been made. In some cases, Carington had not even thought of what he would draw.

Carington termed these advanced and delayed hits a "displacement effect," and he drew Soal's attention to it. He urged Soal to look through some of the records of his old experiments to see if further evidence of this displacement effect might be found. Soal followed his suggestion—though not very optimistically or enthusiastically, for it involved a considerable amount of work. But when he checked Shackleton's scores his perseverance was at last rewarded. He discovered that this subject, whose attempts at identifying the target card had barely come up to chance expectation, had called either the one before or the one after it in the series with remarkable frequency. When Soal mathematically analyzed the results he found that the odds against their being obtained by chance were more than 2500 to one. Shackleton's confidence in his powers of ESP had not been mistaken. He was like a marksman with a quirky bias to hit persistently just to the left or to the right of the bullseye.

Soal got in touch with Shackleton and in 1940 began a new series of experiments with him, using several different agents. He consistently scored one ahead of the target when his guesses were spaced at intervals of about 2.8 seconds, but when Soal speeded up the rate to approximately half the interval, he scored with equal consistency *two* ahead. Shackleton's ability to guess in advance in this way suggested precognition—the ability to foresee the future. Soal noted, however, that the results might also be explained by clairvoyance. Perhaps the subject was not foreseeing what would be in the agent's mind a few moments later, but psychically looking into the unturned cards as they lay on the table at that moment. As in Pearce's case, Shackleton's high scores might be attributed either to clairvoyance or to precognition.

Shackleton also improved his ability to identify the immediate target card. Once soal asked him to prepare himself for a session the following week when he would be scored only on the target card. Shackleton gave 76 correct calls in 200 trials, a score with odds against chance of more than 10 million to one. He also responded impressively when Soal secretly introduced another variation. Instead of a random arrangement of the five symbols, Soal used a pack consisting of only two symbols—12 of one symbol followed by 13 of the other. Shackleton's ESP was not thrown by this innovation. In three such nonrandom sequences introduced without warning in a series of normal random sequences, he scored 7, 12, and 13 direct hits.

When the distinguished Cambridge philosopher C. D. Broad studied the Soal-Shackleton experiments, he declared: "There can be no doubt that the events described happened and were correctly reported; that the odds against chance coincidence

Opposite: in this German ESP experiment, target symbols are produced by a random chance generator. The sender, on the right, then tries to transmit the images telepathically to the receiver at the left. Both the target symbols and the choices made by the receiver are automatically recorded, and then evaluated by a computer.

1 2 3 4 5
Start

Above: Soal's animal cards. He said he devised these because, after five years of using the Zener cards in his research, he had become tired of looking at the dull diagrams on them.

piled up to billions to one; and that the nature of the events which involved both telepathy and precognition, conflicts with one or more of the basic limiting principles [of science and common sense]."

Another Cambridge philosopher, Professor R. H. Thouless (who coined the umbrella-term psi) wrote in 1942: "The reality of the phenomena [of ESP] must be regarded as proved as certainly as anything in scientific research can be proved . . . Let us now give up the task of trying to prove again to the satisfaction of the skeptical that the psi effect really exists, and try instead to devote ourselves to the task of finding out all we can about it."

A great deal had in fact already been found out about ESP in the 12 years between the beginning of Rhine's work at Duke University and the time Professor Thouless wrote these words. But it was a puzzling body of knowledge, little more than a series of glimpses of a still mysterious paranormal faculty. This faculty could be demonstrated to work, and in some cases to work in obedience to certain laws, but it showed no overall pattern or lawfulness in its occurrence. Professor Thouless was right to emphasize that much remained to be discovered about the nature of ESP, and that it was a waste of time to persist with research designed to prove its already proven existence.

What precisely had been found out about psi up to this time? First, it had been demonstrated independently by researchers in different countries that in card guessing tests some people can show a consistent record of success that rules out chance as an explanation, and that can only be explained as the operation of ESP.

This ability seemed to be rare and short-lived. Consistently high scorers were difficult to find, and even they often lost their ability suddenly.

ESP, however, was not entirely an involuntary process. Gifted guessers like Pearce or Shackleton seemed able to score high or low, directly on the target card or on one of its neighbors, at will.

ESP was seen to operate most effectively when the subject was relaxed, and free from distractions. It could be temporarily destroyed by a depressant drug, such as sodium amytal, and restored (but not improved) by a stimulant, such as caffeine. In tests for telepathy, it tended to vary according to the relationship between the subject and the agent.

In the early days of research it had been assumed that telepathy was the most plausible form of ESP because it was easier to conceive of mind reacting with mind than of mind reacting with matter or transcending the limitations of time. But the discovery of Pearce's ability to guess down through the pack, and of the displacement effect in Carington's and Soal's researches, cast some doubt on this assumption. Some parapsychologists began to wonder if clairvoyance and precognition were perhaps more common than telepathy.

Such ambiguities in experimental results induced researchers to design some very careful and ingenious experiments, in which only one kind of ESP—telepathy, clairvoyance, or precognition—was tested and the others excluded.

ESP appeared to work equally effectively at any distance. This ruled out the possibility of its being explained in terms of any known physical law, for at that time all physical forces were believed to decline, however slightly, with the distance traveled. Although recently some exceptions to that rule have been discovered, we still don't know how ESP functions. We see only the results of its functioning.

The results themselves are fairly exciting even today—decades after Rhine reported his first experiments with Pearce. And although star subjects like Pearce are rare, some researchers now believe that everyone may possess ESP to some degree. Readers who would like to explore the possibility of ESP in themselves or their friends can easily set up their own simple experiments. This can be undertaken in the spirit of a game, but if it is properly conducted it could produce a valid contribution to current ESP research. The characteristics of the ESP faculty are by no means fully understood today, and any parapsychologist would be delighted to hear of the discovery of another consistently high-scoring subject like Hubert Pearce or Basil Shackleton.

Because the ESP faculty functions best when the subject is relaxed and uninhibited, it is a good idea to follow Rhine's approach of starting off informally and not making too much fuss

Carington and Soal

Far left: Dr. S. G. Soal, mathematician and psychical researcher. Before he began his statistical work on psychic phenomena he spent some time investigating mediums, among them Mrs. Blanche Cooper. During seances with her, Soal received long and detailed messages from his friend Gordon Davis—only to learn later that Davis was still very much alive. However, Blanche Cooper had been able to foresee where Davis would be living nearly a year before he had moved there.

Left: Basil Shackleton, the photographer whose great psychic gifts apparently included what was called Forward Displacement—consistently guessing the card ahead of the one he was to call.

over techniques and precautions. If a subject shows high-scoring ability the controls and conditions can be tightened up as the experimental series progresses. Initially, it is essential only to insure that the subject cannot obtain normal sensory information about the target cards. If he can see the backs of the cards, make sure there are no distinguishing marks on them. Also make sure there are no reflecting surfaces in the room that might enable him to glimpse the faces of the cards.

Preliminary experiments might be conducted with the subject and agent sitting at opposite ends of a five- or six-foot long table which was fitted with an improvised screen in the middle.

Zener cards are manufactured and sold commercially. The authorized distributor is Haines House of Cards, Norwalk, Ohio. Detailed instructions accompanying the pack explain how to test for clairvoyance and telepathy in several different ways.

Another kind of test can be constructed following a method adapted from one devised by S. G. Soal. Materials needed include five ordinary playing cards—the ace through the five—and five picture cards. Soal used cards with colored pictures of five animals: an elephant, a giraffe, a lion, a penguin, and a zebra. The idea was that animals were more easily visualized than the

Below: a distant ESP test at the Freiburg Institut in Germany conducted by Dr. Hans Bender. The receiver (at left) is two rooms away from the sender (at right). The sender tries to transmit his choice to the receiver, first letting the control room (center) know what it is, and then signaling the receiver to make her choice. The sender's choices are tape recorded, and the controller keeps a record of the calls from the receiver. This particular experiment had a high success rate—681 hits out of 2770 calls. The expected rate of success by chance would be 554 hits.

Telepathic Testing with Cards

abstract Zener symbols, and so might be more effective in pure telepathy tests. Cards bearing these symbols can easily be improvised or, alternatively, other picture cards may be used. Ideally, the names of the symbols should begin with different letters so that the subject need write only one letter for each trial.

Three people are required for this telepathy test: the subject, the agent, and the experimenter. The subject and the agent sit at opposite ends of the table with the screen between them, and the experimenter sits at the side of the table at the agent's end. The experimenter holds the five playing cards. The agent has the five picture cards, which he shuffles and lays face down in a row on the table in front of him. As an extra precaution they may be laid out in a cardboard box turned on its side, thus screening them from both the subject and the experimenter.

Both the experimenter and the subject have scoring sheets in front of them with lines numbered 1 to 25. To begin, the experimenter shuffles his five playing cards and shows one selected at random to the agent, saying as he does so, "one." This signals the subject to be ready to make his first guess. The experimenter then writes the number of the playing card on his scoring sheet and reshuffles the five cards. Meanwhile, the agent notes the

Modern Methods

number of the playing card shown to him, and looks at the face of the appropriate picture card in front of him. If it was a 3, for example, he will look at the third card from the left. The subject writes against the number 1 on his scoring sheet the initial letter (E, G, L, P, or Z if the animals pictures are used) of his guess at the target picture.

When a run of 25 guesses has been completed, the agent shows the experimenter the order of the target pictures. The experimenter can then assign the letters E, G, L, P, or Z to the corresponding numbers of the playing cards on his scoring sheet. The target cards are then reshuffled and laid out in a different order in preparation for another run. When the desired number of runs have been completed, the letters on the subject's scoring sheet are compared with the actual sequences on the experimenter's sheet.

The experiment can be converted into one testing clairvoyance if the agent does *not* look at the face of each picture card as its number is shown.

If private ESP experimentation is entered into seriously, it must be continued over several sessions and several hundred

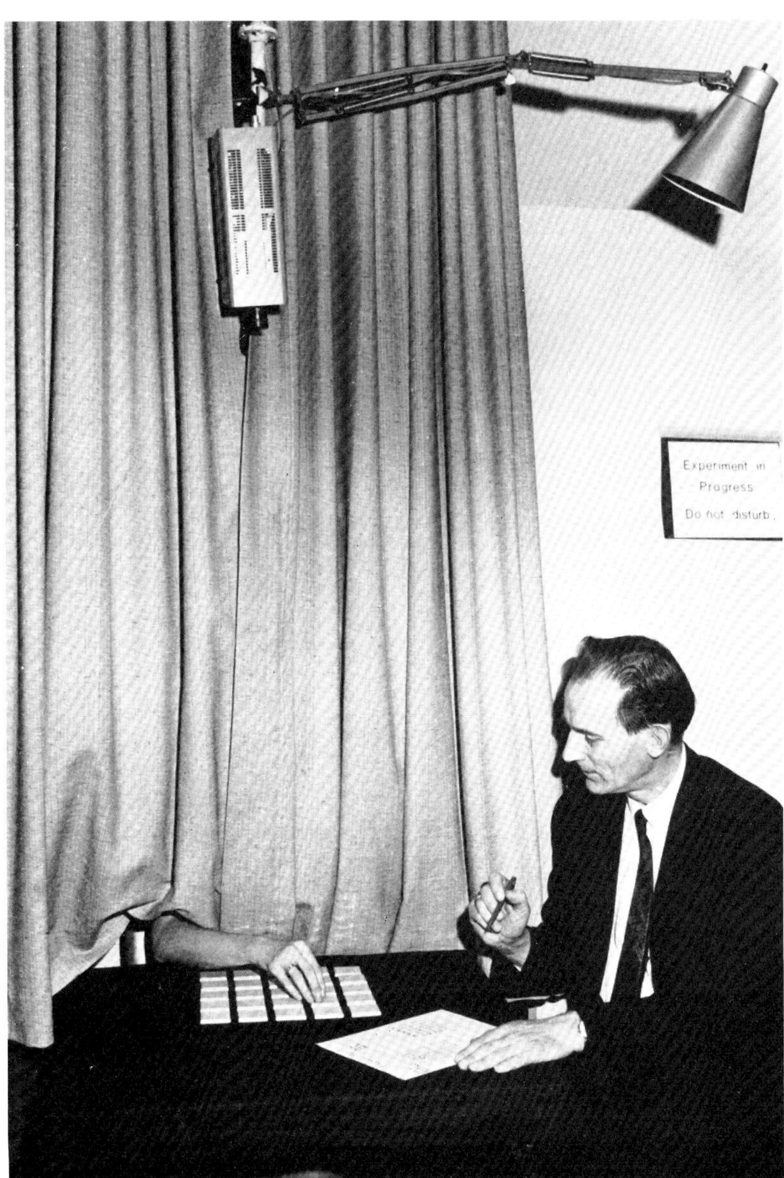

Right: another method of testing ESP. At a signal a person behind a curtain tries to guess the one of 25 squares chosen. His choices are recorded by the experimenter sitting on the right.

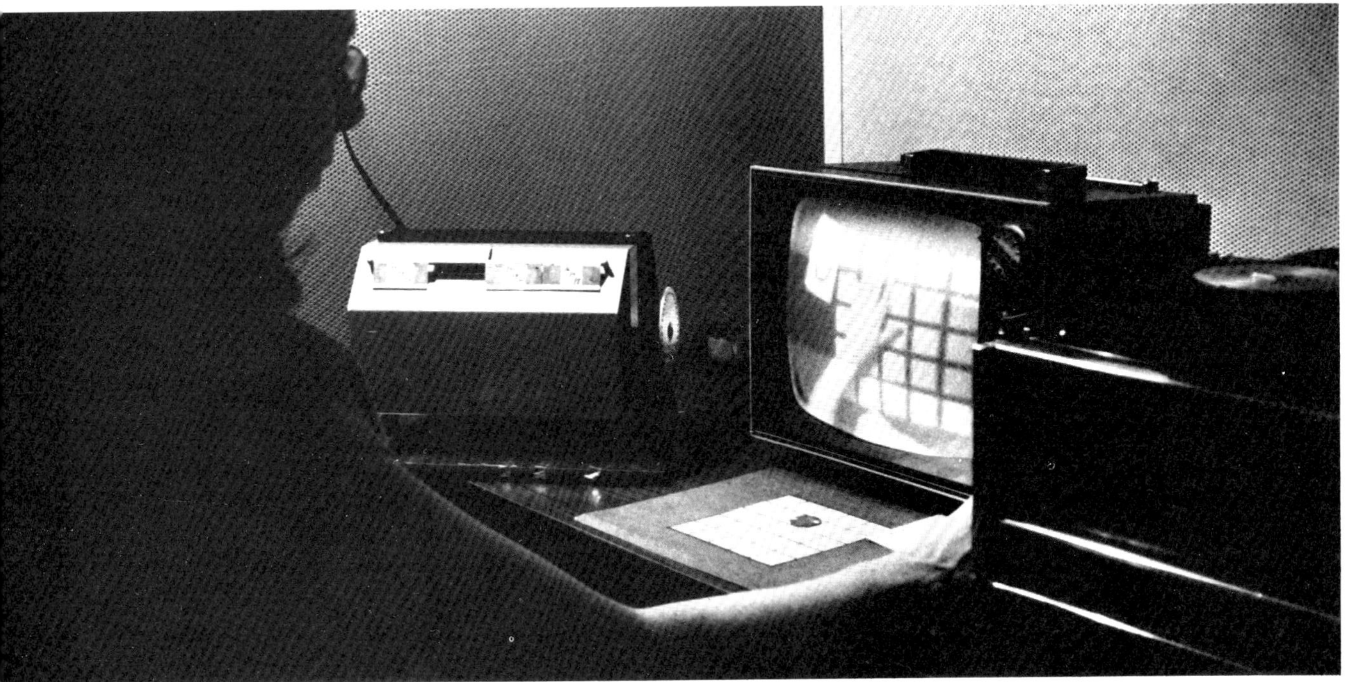

Above: in another room the sender concentrates on a TV picture of the receiver's hand moving over the squares, and tries to influence the choice by telepathy. The sender in this experiment was Janet Mitchell, a well-known American psychical researcher.

individual trials, or guesses. Rhine has said that most of his good subjects did not do particularly well in their first hundred trials.

To do well means to score consistently and significantly above the chance expectation of five hits per run of 25 guesses. On a series of 100 or more runs an average of even six or seven is significant. It would be premature to take it as signifying the operation of ESP, however. The high score might indicate a fault in the procedure. This would be the stage to introduce stricter controls and conditions.

The Soal-Shackleton experiments were conducted with the subject and agent in separate rooms with the door open so that the subject could hear the experimenter's cue-calls for the synchronization of his guesses. This is one improvement that could be introduced with a successful scorer after the preliminary trials. Another is to insure randomness in the numbers turned up by the experimenter. It is possible that in shufflling his five cards and picking one out for each guess he might, consciously or unconsciously, choose them in a certain order. This order might be picked up by the subject or it might correspond to an order that he favors. To eliminate this possibility the experimenter can prepare in advance lists of 25 random numbers, which he then communicates in sequence to the agent by holding up the corresponding playing cards. Such lists can be compiled from tables of logarithms or from a telephone directory, using the last digits of numbers down a column in the sequence in which they occur, and of course ignoring all digits except those falling into the range 1 to 5.

If, when these extra precautions have been taken, your subject continues to average seven or more hits per run over a long series of trials, you may have reason to suspect a serious case of supernormality—and should lose no time in calling in your nearest parapsychologist.

Chapter 12 Mind Over Matter

Can objects fly through the air, propelled by the power of thought alone? Unlikely as it may sound, well-documented evidence indicates that intelligent, reliable observers, time and time again, have been presented with situations that appear to offer no other possible explanation. While some scientists investigate poltergeist activity which occurs spontaneously, others attempt to pin down psychokinesis—PK—in the laboratory with long series of tests with dice or blank cubes. The results dictated by chance alone are easy to predict, but what does it mean when the results show that the rolling dice have apparently been influenced by a person thinking about them?

On January 14, 1966, the Miami police were asked to investigate some strange occurrences at a warehouse owned by Tropication Arts, Inc., a company that dealt in novelty items and souvenirs for the tourist trade. The complaint clerk at the station told Patrolman William Killam: "This person who called said he had a ghost in his place of business . . . going around breaking ash-trays, and he said they were just coming up off the floor and breaking." Patrolman Killam went off on his assignment muttering something about being sent to deal with "a lot of nuts."

When he arrived at the warehouse the owner told him that the breakages had started about a month earlier. At first he had put it down to carelessness on the part of the staff, but as weeks went by and the rate of breakage increased he realized that something very peculiar and unnatural was going on. Patrolman Killam listened skeptically, then said he'd better take a look around the warehouse. He walked along the aisles, sometimes stopping to stamp on the floor or shake one of the shelves in order to see if this would dislodge anything. Everything seemed normal and secure. Killam had walked the length of three aisles and was beginning to walk down a fourth when he saw something that stopped him in his tracks. A highball glass that was standing among others on a shelf suddenly rose into the air, traveled a few feet, and smashed onto the floor. Nobody else was near the spot, and when Killam shook the shelf roughly none of the other glasses moved.

Opposite: Polish medium Stanislawa Tomczyt during a psychokinesis experiment with Schrenck-Notzing. She seems to have succeeded in suspending a pair of scissors in the air.

Poltergeist Phenomena

Clearly this problem was beyond the capacity of the police. Psychical investigators were called in. They were Dr. J. G. Pratt of the Parapsychology Laboratory at Duke University, and Dr. W. G. Roll of the Psychical Research Foundation. Since their investigation of the "Seaford Poltergeist" that had tormented a Long Island family in 1958, they had become a kind of flying squad for the investigation of reported poltergeist phenomena. With a team of helpers they spent some weeks at the Tropication Arts warehouse, recording every incident in great detail, analyzing them, and looking for a common factor that would explain them. In all they recorded 224 incidents, 78 of which they themselves witnessed. The common factor turned out to be a 19-year-old employee, Cuban refugee Julio Vasquez. In most of the records of poltergeist happenings collected over

Photographic reconstructions of poltergeist activities that afflicted the Plach family of Vachendorf. Their teenage daughter may have caused them. Objects disappeared and reappeared, stones and coals flew through the air, and tools somehow escaped from a trunk on which Mrs. Plach was sitting. Right: Mr. Plach watches things flying around through the air.
Below: Professor Hans Bender, who investigated the case in 1948, with Mrs. Plach. She kept a careful diary recording all the peculiar manifestations.

the years there commonly is a mention of the presence of a young person, usually one who is going through some kind of emotional crisis. So the investigators had known what to look for. But their detailed recording of the incidents in this case yielded some interesting new discoveries.

The breakages had all occurred when Julio was in the warehouse, but not always when he was near the objects. Moreover, they nearly all occurred when he had his back toward the object that was moved, and the movements took place on his left side, never on his right. When the movements of the objects were plotted and the distances they traveled were measured, it was found that, as they had moved away from Julio, they had not traveled in a straight line but in a curve. Analysis of the distances the objects traveled in relation to their distance from Julio at the time of the incident revealed a precise mathematical ratio. This was found to agree with what is known in physics as the "law of exponential decay." This is the law that describes the weakening effect in many natural processes—for example, bacterial and radioactive decay, and the conversion of light to heat energy as it penetrates water. After studying and interpreting all the data, the investigators reached a conclusion: contrary to the warehouse owners' suspicions, no ghosts were involved. Julio was the poltergeist. The energy that caused the smashing of objects came from him.

The German word *poltergeist* translates as "boisterous or noisy spirit." But modern psychical researchers have come to the conclusion that poltergeist phenomena have nothing to do with spirits. Instead they are believed to be involuntary PK effects. They are caused by the release of pent-up psychic energy.

Below left: plates of food spilled.
Below: Mrs. Plach working on her diary as something flies past.

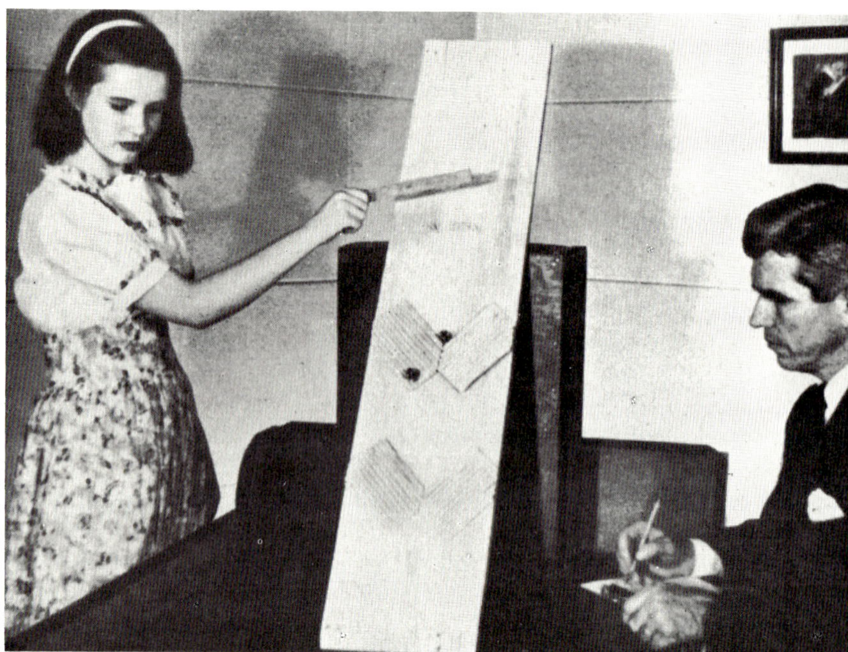

Right: one of the earliest PK tests at Duke University. Dice are mechanically released while the subject tries to influence the way they will fall. The experimenter who is keeping score is Dr. J. B. Rhine.

Right: in this variation of the Duke PK dice experiments, two dice have been specified as a target for the subject. An electrically rotated cage releases several dice, and the subject attempts to make the two target dice fall face uppermost.

The Pioneer of Parapsychology

J. B. Rhine pioneered scientific research into parapsychology in the United States. Rhine, who began his work in 1927, used the term "parapsychology" rather than "psychic research" because he thought it would make the subject more acceptable to scientists throughout the world. He tested telepathy, clairvoyance, precognition, and psychokinesis in strictly controlled laboratory conditions, but was also concerned with psychic phenomena in everyday life and with religious matters. He strongly believed that the question of survival after death should be investigated by scientific methods. In testing telepathy, Rhine found that certain people nearly always got a higher percentage of right guesses than the statistical possibility of one in five. In a series of tests over eight years, Rhine also showed that the mind can influence the fall of the dice, and that a person's psychic powers are greatest when he or she is alert and enthusiastic, but decline when tired or bored.

The mystery remaining is how this psychic energy gets converted to kinetic energy, capable of moving matter.

For most people, PK is a more difficult concept to come to terms with than ESP. It is difficult enough to accept that mind can interact with mind without any apparent channel of communication, but to propose that mind can interact with matter is even more implausible. Yet today the idea of psychosomatic illnesses and psychic healing, which most of the medical profession would have scoffed at not so long ago, is widely accepted. It is not so generally realized that these medical phenomena involve a mind-matter interaction that no known laws can explain. Still, the skeptic could point out that psychosomatic

The PK Effect

illness and psychic healing involve interaction between mind and matter in the same body. What is implausible is that mind can act upon matter outside the body, that a person can influence events in the external material world by pure will.

One day early in 1934 a young man walked into Dr. J. B. Rhine's office at Duke University and announced, "Hey, doc, I've got something to tell you I think you ought to know." He was, he explained, a professional gambler, and it was his experience that when he was in a certain state of mind, which he described as "hot," he could influence the dice to come up as he wanted them to by exercising his will. He had heard about Dr. Rhine's ESP research and thought that Rhine would be the man to take his discovery seriously and investigate it scientifically. He was right. Within minutes Dr. Rhine and the gambler were crouched on the floor in a corner of the office rolling dice.

Thus begun a long experimental program of PK research at Duke, the results of which were not published until 10 years later. Rhine and his colleagues had had enough trouble getting the scientific community to accept their evidence for ESP, and they didn't want to complicate the controversy prematurely by claiming to be able to demonstrate PK in the laboratory as well. So for nine years, the dice-rolling experiments continued quietly at Duke, and the results were carefully recorded and analyzed but not published.

The advantage of using dice in PK experiments is the same as the advantage of using cards to test ESP—the results can be statistically analyzed and an odds-against-chance calculation can be made. When two dice ("die" in the singular) are thrown together the sum of the faces can range from 2 to 12. There are 36 combinations of the two dice, 15 of which add up to values of 8 or more and 15 others to values of 6 or less, while 6 combinations produce the sum of 7. The two dice must be distinguishable from each other to produce this variety of results. For example, a three on die "a" and a four on die "b" can thus count as a separate score to a four on "a" and a three on "b", even though the numbers are the same in both cases.

The target in a PK test can be high scores, low scores, or sevens. Alternatively, a particular number can be made the target. At the end of a run, which at Duke was arbitrarily set as either 24 throws of separate dice, or 12 throws of pairs, or 8 throws of three dice, the deviation from chance expectation can be precisely calculated. The experimenter found that the most convenient procedure was to throw a pair of dice 12 times, and to will either high or low combinations to come up. The chance expectation for either result is five hits per run. This figure is arrived at by dividing the number of low or high combinations—which is 15 each—by 3, which is the number of times that 12, the number of throws, goes into 36, the number of possible combinations. In other words, the chances of a hit are reduced *in proportion* to the number of attempts. If there were 36 throws in a run, the chance of a hit would rise proportionately to 15. Of course, all such calculations of chance are based on a large number of runs. In the short term, results might deviate sharply from chance expectation without implying that factors other than chance are at work.

Below: a mechanical dice tumbler devised by the Duke Parapsychology Laboratory and still in use today. The dice are at the bottom of the set-up, on the right side.

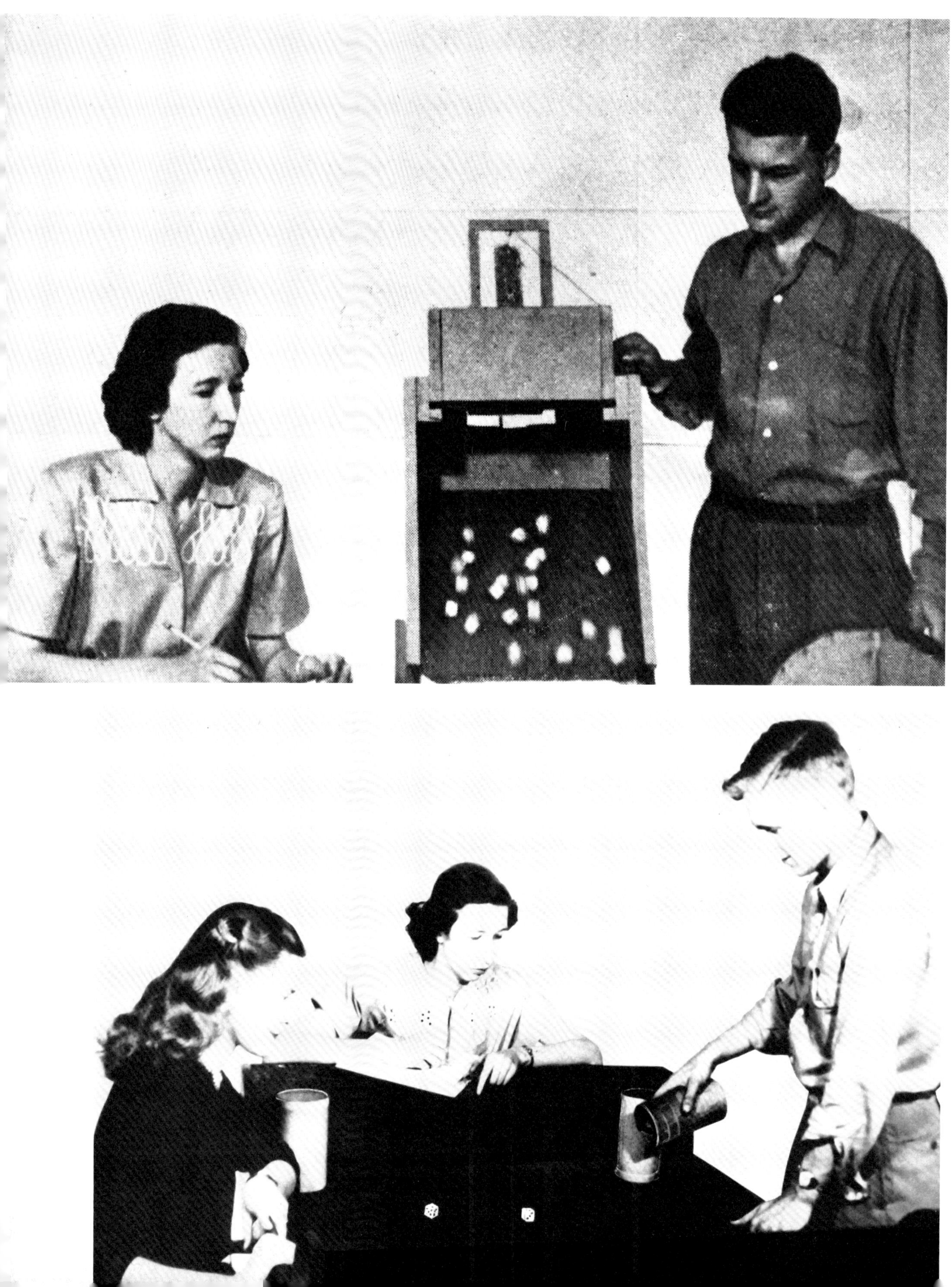

Psychokinesis Under Test

The first series of recorded experiments conducted at Duke consisted of 562 runs. There were 3110 hits, whereas the chance expectation was 2810 hits (5 times 562). So there were 300 more hits than pure chance would have produced. Calculations based upon probability theory showed that this result would not come up more than once in a billion times by chance alone.

After this encouraging exploratory stage the researchers at Duke felt it was time to vary and tighten up the conditions of the experiments in order to see if the results could be attributed to any cause other than PK. Two possible other causes were the employment of skill by the thrower of the dice, and the existence of a physical bias in the dice themselves. Dice on which the marker spots are hollowed out may slightly favor the higher numbers because their faces have had more material removed and are therefore fractionally lighter than the faces of the lower numbers. To rule out skill as a factor in throwing, the experimenters used various throwing devices, such as a chute with a corrugated surface and an electrically operated release mechanism. To prevent bias in the dice influencing the results, they used special precision-made dice. Also the targets within series of runs were systematically alternated so that the effect of any bias would be canceled out. Many more experiments were conducted under such improved conditions at Duke and elsewhere, and results significantly above chance were continually obtained. Unlike the ESP experiments, however, this research revealed no spectacularly high-scoring subjects. The work suggested that PK was a latent faculty that many, if not most people possessed, but that it rarely manifested itself as more highly developed in one subject than in another.

One of the most positive results in these trials was obtained in an amusing experiment that took the form of a contest between divinity students and gamblers. A student at the Duke Divinity School conceived the idea that PK might be an operating factor in cases of prayer apparently influencing events in the physical world. He put his idea to Rhine, who suggested that, because the divinity students would be highly motivated to succeed in order to demonstrate the efficacy of prayer, it might be interesting to compare their results with those of another group of strongly motivated individuals. So four young men noted for their success in crap shooting were found and matched against four prospective ministers. After a total of 1242 runs of a type in which the chance expectancy average was 4.00 hits per run, the gamblers had obtained an average run score of 4.52 and the divinity students an average of 4.51. This was virtually a tie. The interesting result of the experiment, though, was that when the results of both groups were combined and statistically analyzed, they were found to be likely to occur by chance only once in billions of tests. It was clear that motivation was a potent influence in PK trials, whether that motivation was religious or otherwise.

The most conclusive evidence for the operation of PK in the Duke experiments did not emerge in the course of the experiments themselves but later, when the results were analyzed. In 1943 active research at Duke was at a standstill because of the war, so Rhine and his only remaining research assistant dug out

Opposite top: in one of the PK tests devised by Dr. Betty M. Humphrey at Duke, 24 dice are used at once.

Opposite below: in another Humphrey test, the two subjects engage in a "tug of wills" experiment. Each of them wills a different side of the dice to appear uppermost.

Below: one of the Duke subjects trying PK tests after having been given a narcotic, sodium amytal, which made her very drowsy but didn't put her to sleep. The investigators found that large doses lowered the scoring rate. In contrast, small doses seemed to be followed by a rise in the subject's scoring.

the results of all the dice-rolling experiments of the previous nine years and had another look at them. They found a sharp drop in the above-chance scores from the first run in a test to the later runs. The experimenters had noted such declines at the time of making the tests, but had paid little attention to them. Now, when the separate tests were taken together and the overall pattern discovered to be one of a sharp drop in above-chance scoring, the scores acquired new significance. The same drop occurred in tests using mechanical dice-throwing machines, which, unlike humans, would not suffer the fatigue that often accounts for a scoring decline in many kinds of psychological tests. Reporting on the discovery of these "position effects" in the book *Mind Over Matter*, Dr. Louisa Rhine observed that they showed that PK was not just an ability sometimes to hit a target, "but a process connected with and expressed according to deep unconscious motivating factors, just as ESP had been found to be."

This delayed discovery armed the parapsychologists with a strong argument against the charge of fraud, for the evidence of the position effects had lain in the records for years without anyone suspecting it, and the patterns could not conceivably have been fraudulently introduced by the original experimenters, for no one had known at the time that such patterns would ever be significant.

When the accounts of the Duke experiments were published, more researchers became interested in PK. W. E. Cox, an amateur, became closely associated with Duke. He was a

Above: an example of a "placement PK" experiment, so called because the object is to influence something to fall in a certain place. W. E. Cox, a businessman who became an amateur researcher at Duke University, devised several placement experiments—and built a variety of original mechanisms and structures to use with them.

Right: Haakon Forwald, a Swedish scientist especially interested in placement PK. In this photograph taken about 1960, he is loading his special device for electrically releasing six cubes, which tumble down an incline and come to rest on a graded plane.

businessman with a talent for gadgetry. He devised several dice-throwing experiments using a variety of clock mechanisms, mercury switches, electrical relays, and complicated structures built in three and five tiers with different target areas for the dice to be directed to by PK. These experiments introduced a new skill that became known as "placement PK." In this case the object was not to influence a particular face of a die to come up but to influence freely rolling dice to come to rest in a particular place.

Placement PK

The outstanding contribution to research in placement PK was made by Haakon Forwald, a Swedish engineer-physicist. During the early 1950s he conducted independent experiments, rolling dice down an inclined plane and trying to will them to fall either on the left or the right side of a table. In 1957 he paid a visit to Duke and joined forces with Dr. Pratt. The Pratt-Forwald experiment subsequently became widely regarded as the most successful demonstration of PK.

In this experiment six wooden cubes were released mechanically and rolled down a chute onto a horizontal surface with a dividing line down the middle. The PK task was not to direct the cubes into one of the target areas but to influence those that fell in one area to roll farther than those that fell in the other. Lines drawn on the table parallel to the center line, at intervals of one centimeter, enabled the experimenter to measure the degree of displacement of the cubes from the center. A long series of trials produced a highly significant positive result with odds against chance of 5000 to one.

Left: after the cubes have all come to rest, they are measured on the horizontal and their positions are recorded.

The Healing Faculty

By the end of the 1950s the reality of PK was as firmly established by experimental method and statistical analysis as was that of ESP. But both ESP and PK as studied in the laboratory seemed to be relatively weak forces. PK research had only established the possibility of mental influence on small objects already in motion. Nobody had managed under laboratory conditions to make a stationary object move. Yet this is what happens in poltergeist phenomena and in some of the alleged physical effects produced by mediums in the seance room. All researchers in the field knew Professor Winther's report on the PK feats of the Danish medium Anna Rasmussen back in the 1920s, but no such talented subject had appeared on the scene since really scientific methods of control and analysis had been developed. There were, however, other areas of apparent PK activity that might repay scientific study. These included the phenomena of thought-photography, or "thoughtography," and psychic healing.

In 1910 the professor of psychology at Tokyo University, Tomokichi Fukurai, tested a woman of reported psychic ability for clairvoyance. He conceived the idea of having her identify clairvoyantly an image imprinted on a film plate which had not been developed. After the test he discovered that another plate had apparently been affected by the clairvoyant's effort at concentration. In later experiments he asked her to try to transfer specific images—usually geometrical figures or Japanese characters—onto unexposed film plates. No camera was used, and the target plate was sandwiched between the others. The woman consistently succeeded in imprinting the middle plate with the designated image, leaving the two outer plates entirely clear. Fukurai published a book on his strange discovery, and the ensuing controversy over his work on psychic phenomena forced him to resign his university position.

Below: Dr. Justa Smith, scientist and Franciscan nun who worked with the Canadian healer Oscar Estebany to investigate whether psi powers can affect enzymes.

Another important investigation—this time into psychic healing powers—was carried out in the 1960s. In this case a psychic healer, Oscar Estebany of Montreal, a former Hungarian army colonel, discovered his healing abilities in the 1930s in the course of massaging cavalry horses. He gained a reputation as a healer in Budapest in the 1940s, and continued to practice when he moved to Canada in the mid-1950s. Hundreds of cures, mostly of disorders that have defied the efforts of conventional medical practitioners, are attributed to him. In 1961 Estebany agreed to let Dr. Bernard Grad of McGill University test his healing power scientifically.

The obvious rational explanation of psychic healing is that it is effected by suggestion. In other words, the patient's faith in the healer effects the cure. Therefore Dr. Grad started his experiments with 300 patients that had no faith in, or knowledge of, Estebany's alleged powers. The patients were mice. Dr. Grad inflicted a small identical wound on all 300 mice, and divided them into three equal groups. The first group was treated by Estebany, the second by people who claimed no psychic healing powers, and the third was left untreated as a control group. The treatment consisted simply of the healer holding each cage of mice for 15 minutes twice a day. After 16 days the wounds were measured. It was found that those on the mice that Estebany had treated were only half the size of those on the other two groups of mice.

In another experiment Dr. Grad compared the growth of two

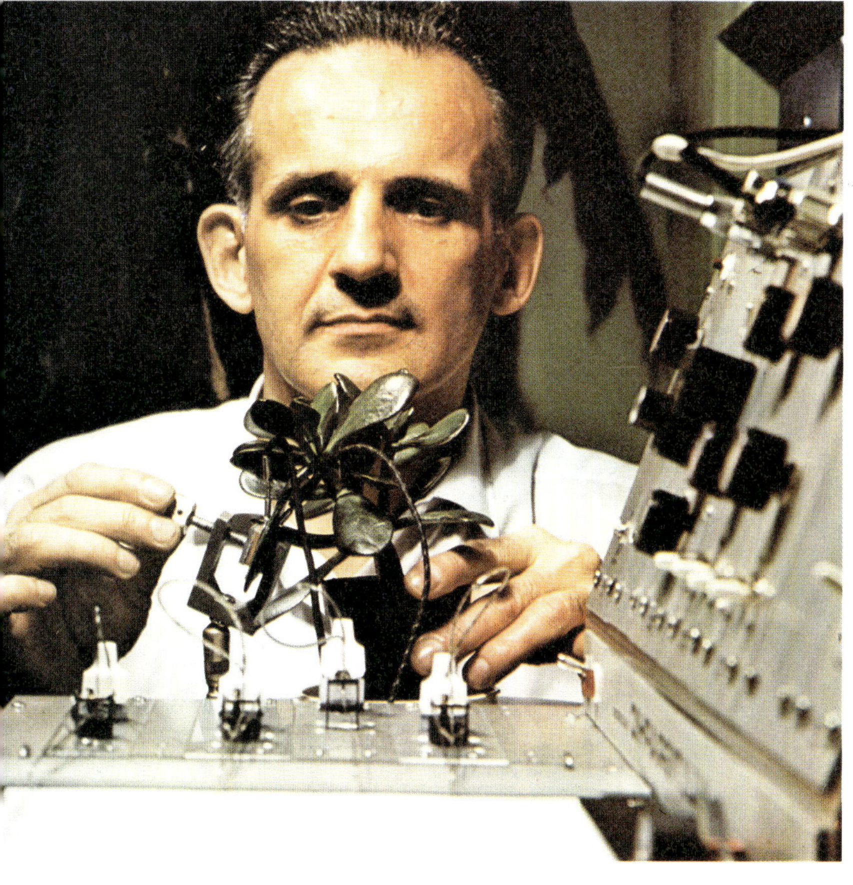

Left: animals and even microorganisms have been used in psi research, but Cleve Backster caused a stir when he claimed that plants react to stress caused by unkind thoughts and acts of humans. Backster, a lie-detector expert, calls this phenomenon "primary perception." So far he has not been able to successfully repeat his experiments—which he has carried out since 1966—under controlled conditions.

groups of potted barley plants. One group was watered with a solution that Estebany had held for 30 minutes, and the other was watered with some of the same solution that Estebany had not tried to influence. The psychically treated water consistently promoted stronger and healthier growth in the plants than the untreated water. Dr. Grad reported his experiments in the *International Journal of Parapsychology* but he was unable to offer an explanation of the results.

More searching investigations of Estebany's powers were conducted by Dr. M. Justa Smith, research director of the Human Dimensions Institute at Rosary Hill College in Buffalo, New York. Dr. Smith, a biochemist who is also a Franciscan nun, reasoned that if psychic healing works, it must work at the enzyme level in the body's cells. Enzymes are the substances that promote chemical changes in the cells, and enzyme failure is the root physical cause of disease. In order to promote health, the chemical reactions of certain enzymes within the body need to be accelerated and others to be slowed down.

Dr. Smith had done a great deal of research with the enzyme *trypsin*, which she knew can be severely damaged by exposure to ultraviolet light. She prepared a flask of trypsin in solution, damaged its molecular structure with ultraviolet light, and had Estebany hold his hands over the sides of the flask. Every 15 minutes she removed a small quantity of the solution and analyzed it in a highly sensitive machine called a *spectrophotometer*. In earlier experiments with Estebany, Dr. Smith

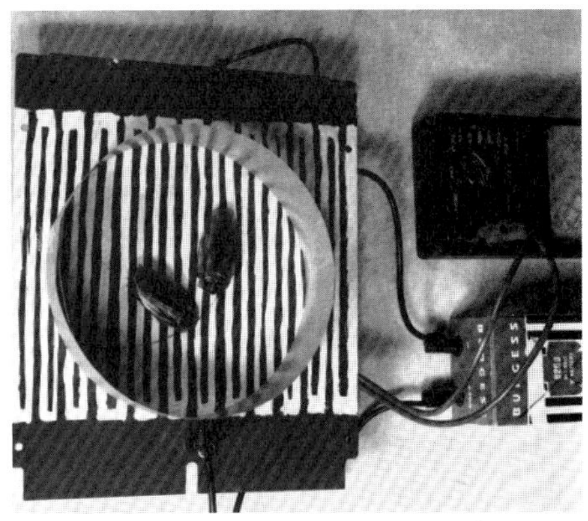

Above: cockroaches being tested for possible PK abilities in an experiment conducted by Dr. Helmut Schmidt. The insects were put on a wire grid fitted with a random number generator, and given intermittent shocks. The aim was to see if they could reduce the number of shocks by means of PK on the generator. Instead, their wild behavior produced 300 more shocks than chance would have.

Below: using equipment designed by Dr. Schmidt, a subject presses a button to indicate which light she thinks will flash next.

had discovered that he could accelerate reactions in healthy enzyme chains, but now she found that he could actually repair damaged molecules. Follow-up experiments with other healers and other enzymes confirmed the discovery. The psychic healers in Dr. Smith's experiments had no way of knowing which enzymes were in solution in the flasks they held, or whether an acceleration or deceleration of activity in a particular flask would have a potentially positive effect on the body. Yet invariably the healers caused chemical reactions of the kind appropriate in each case. When Dr. Smith presented the results of her research to the scientific world she appropriately titled her paper *Psychic Healing: Myth into Science.*

Whether psychic healing is brought about by energies emanating from the mind of the healer or from his body is still an open question. Only if it comes from his mind could we accurately term this healing a psychokinetic function. But this is a question of terminology that need not worry us at this point. What such research as Dr. Smith's has established is that some people possess powers that are outside the ken of modern physical science, and until these powers are more fully understood, it is convenient to group them under the general idea of PK.

An experiment that demonstrated PK influence at the cellular level, without involving the complicating factors in cases of psychic healing, was made by the English researcher Nigel Richmond. Richmond tried to influence by PK the movement of *paramecia*, which are single-celled organisms about .01 inch long, found in pond water. His method was to place a drop of pond water on a microscope slide, put a paramecium in the center of the microscopic field, and try to will the organism to swim where he wanted it to. For this purpose he divided the microscopic field into four quarters using two crossed hairs, and assigned each quarter to one of the four suits of playing cards. He determined the target area each time by turning up a card from the top of a shuffled deck.

Each attempt to influence the paramecium's direction of exit lasted 15 seconds. If a paramecium swam out of the field of view before the time had elapsed, it was still counted in the scoring by being assigned to the quarter through which it had passed. In all he made 1495 attempts. Chance expectation for a paramecium hitting the garget area was one-fourth of this number, or 373.75. Richmond found that the paramecia hit the target 483 times, a deviation of 109.25 over chance expectation. He also found that the creatures often went into the quarter diagonally opposite the target area. Out of the 1495 attempts, this area was hit 444 times—70.25 above chance. Richmond counted these diagonal scores as hits and grouped them with the target-hitting scores because, he wrote: "I suspect that influence applied in one direction would sometimes have its effects in the diametrically opposed direction. . . ." Whether or not he was justified in giving equal value to these opposite scores, the fact remains that he got considerably above-chance results for his target quarters. His experiment seemed to indicate that his mind influenced the movements of other living organisms by the power of PK.

Animal PK

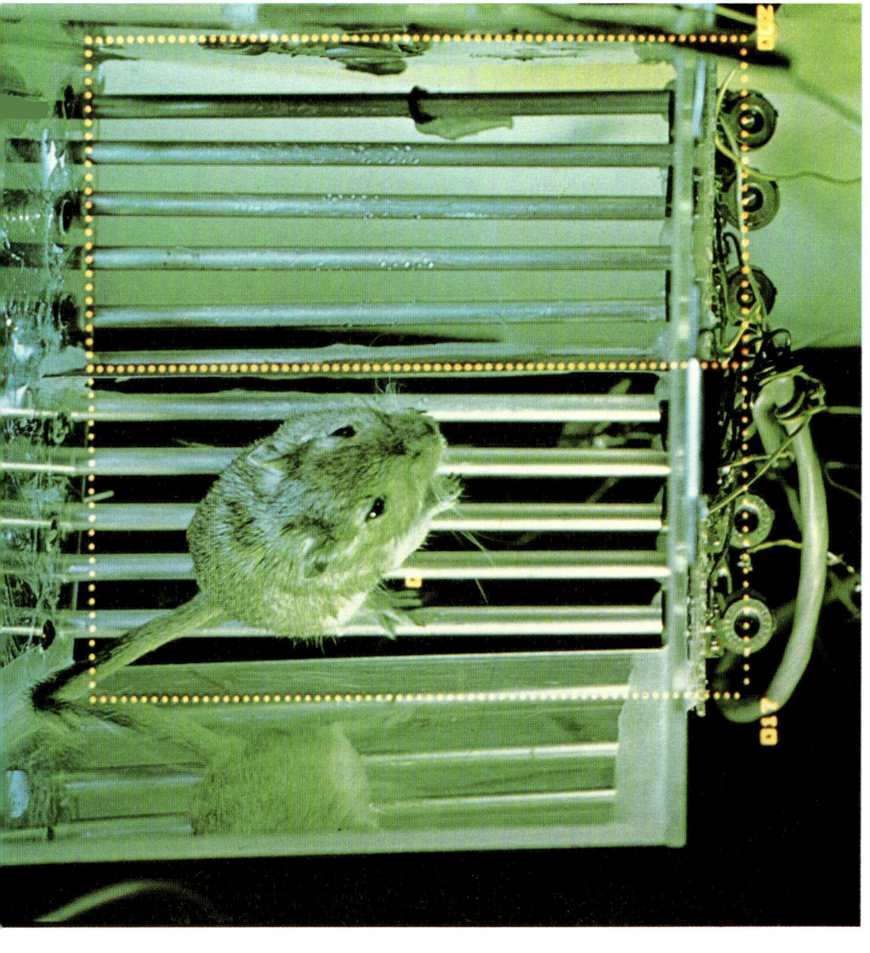

Left: a gerbil during tests for precognitive ability. Mild shocks are administered about once a minute to one half of the box, selected by a random number generator. The animal presumably guesses which side is about to be shocked and jumps to the other. In a fairly long series of tests, the results have been above those predicted by chance—indicating that even gerbils might possess some higher psi faculties.

Some parapsychologists, however, have raised the question whether the results might not show telepathy at work between the experimenter and the paramecia. This suggestion sounds preposterous, for telepathy is such an astonishing power that we tend to think of it as restricted to human beings, if we believe in it at all. But many experiments, particularly with dogs, cats, and horses, have indicated that the psi faculty—including telepathy and even PK—may not be confined to humans.

In 1970 Dr. Helmut Schmidt, now Research Director of the Mind Science Foundation, San Antonio, Texas, reported some experiments testing the PK ability of a cat. The point of the experiment was to see if the cat could manage to exert PK to turn on a lamp, by which it could warm itself, more often than the lamp would turn on by chance.

The governing mechanism for the lamp was a device called a random number generator. One of the chief problems in psi research is insuring randomness in the target materials. If one is testing for clairvoyance or for PK, it is important to eliminate the possibility of the experimenter knowing—even unconsciously—which card will turn up, for example, or which times the light will go on. If the experimenter or anyone else knows the answer, one would have to include the possibility of telepathy in any positive results. The most random known process in nature is the rate of decay of radioactive particles. In a pile

Above: Professor John Taylor of London University tests a child with psychokinetic ability to find a scientific explanation for such phenomenon. After appearing on a television show with Uri Geller in 1973, Taylor was convinced of the genuineness of PK powers.

of strontium atoms, for instance, half of the atoms will disintegrate over a period of 20 years. There is no way, however, of knowing which ones will disintegrate during this period, or at what time they will do so. When the disintegration takes place energy is emitted, and the random number generator uses this energy to turn on nine lights arranged in a circle, one at a time. The lights go on in a clockwise or counterclockwise direction depending on the decay rate of the strontium nuclei. The experimental subject's task is to make the lights go on in a given direction. This in turn governs the turning on and off of the generator. Success means that the subject has influenced, presumably by PK, the behavior of subatomic particles.

The cat used in Schmidt's experiments obviously couldn't know about the subatomic particles, but it clearly had an interest in turning on the lamp that was attached to the generator. For half an hour every afternoon, the cat was put into a shack inside which the temperature was 0°C—not cold enough to cause the cat serious discomfort, but not the kind of temperature a cat likes. In one part of the shack was the 200-Watt lamp, going on and off at intervals of a few seconds or less. Every second a number was being generated that would determine whether the lamp was on or off.

For the first five experiments in the series, the cat went straight to the lamp on entering the shack, and at the end of the 30 minutes was found curled up next to it. The experimenters found that the light had been on slightly more than 50 percent of the time. More specifically, out of the 9000 numbers generated one per second during the five sessions, 4615 had turned on the lamp—115 more than the 4500 expected according to chance. These results were interesting, but not startling.

Schmidt continued the experiment for another five afternoons. It was found that the cat's behavior changed. When the door was opened at the end of the sixth session, it dashed out of the shack. In none of the remaining sessions was it found sitting by the lamp as it had at first. "It seemed to have developed a dislike for the flashing lamp," reported Schmidt. Moreover, the generator turned on by chance fewer times than expected during the second series of five sessions. Was the animal capable of exerting PK but resentful at being bullied into performing? This is a tempting conclusion for anyone who knows cats. Unfortunately, the experiment was too short to prove anything. The onset of warm weather, affecting the temperature inside the shack, forced Schmidt to discontinue the tests. Over a period of 10 days, the variation from chance in both directions was too slight to indicate with any certainty the existence of feline PK.

A significant discovery about PK that has emerged from research done so far is that it is goal-oriented. That is, when it functions, it seems to accomplish an aimed-for result directly, without the person, animal, or lower organism that exercises it having any conscious conception, so far as we can tell, of the processes that lead to this result. This is the stumbling block for the rational mind. We can possibly conceive of will as a consciously controlled operative force influencing events in the material world. But the idea of will divorced from consciousness, working on the world without any guiding idea of *how* it works, without any program, is hard to swallow. It conflicts with our understanding of natural processes as being governed by laws of cause and effect. Yet there seems no way out of this puzzle. We just have to admit that Nature is under no obligation to conform to the laws that we have evolved to further our understanding of how it functions.

The most gifted psychics who produce PK effects never have any idea how they do it. Anna Rasmussen believed that her spirit guide, Dr. Lasaruz, was responsible for hers. In more recent years Uri Geller has attributed his powers to extraterrestrial beings. But such hypotheses are at present unprovable.

Psychics in the Laboratory

In the 1970s research into PK has entered a new phase with the discovery of extraordinarily gifted subjects comparable to Anna Rasmussen and the Schneider brothers. Early research at Duke University and elsewhere suggested that PK is a faculty that many people possess in a weak form, but that cannot be developed to a spectacular degree. The comparatively recent appearances of Uri Geller and Ingo Swann have challenged this idea.

The investigations of Geller and the resulting controversies have been widely reported, but the New York artist Ingo Swann is less well known. Like Geller, he has been studied by scientists at the Stanford Research Institute in Menlo Park, California.

Below: Taylor tests the level of radioactivity of the child's hands—which he thinks might explain her ability to bend metal.

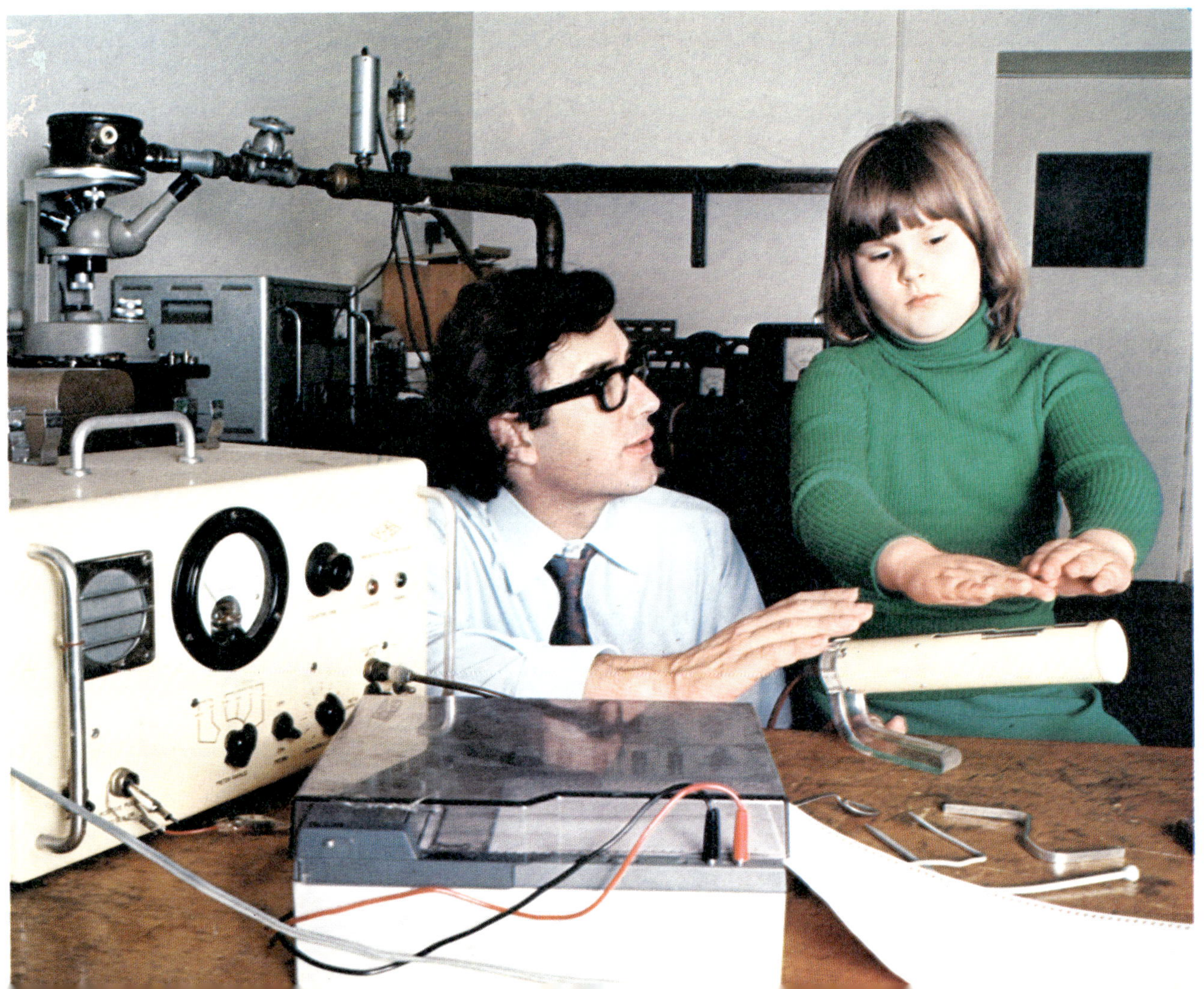

Above: an experiment designed by Dr. Gertrude Schmeidler of City College to discover whether PK energy generates heat. For it she used *thermistors*—temperature detectors—seen in the thermos bottles. The subject, artist Ingo Swann, was supposed to heat or cool the thermistors by PK power as directed by the experimenter.

At the Stanford Institute, physicists Harold Puthoff and Russell Targ supervised an experiment in which Swann was required to psychokinetically disturb the inner workings of a *magnetometer*. This is a device that produces electric current from a radioactive core sunk deep in a well. The current decreases at a uniform rate in relation to the decay rate of the magnetic field within the instrument. The output of current is recorded in the form of a continuous wave on a moving chart. The magnetometer is shielded by special metals so that no other magnetic influences can reach it. The physicists described to Swann how the magnetometer functioned, and told him that if he could affect the magnetic field within it the change would show on the output recording. Swann then focused his attention on the interior of the magnetometer, whereupon the frequency of the output immediately doubled. In the course of the experiment he was able to cause other changes, which show up clearly on the chart. Puthoff and Targ emphasize in their report that this was not a fully controlled scientific experiment, for it left open the question whether Swann had in fact disturbed the

The PK Energies of Ingo Swann

process of subatomic emission in the radioactive core, or whether he had affected the recording device. Either way, of course, the effect he produced in the laboratory equipment could only have been produced by the operation of PK.

Dr. Gertrude Schmeidler, a professor of psychology at the City University, New York, had also conducted experiments with Swann. Starting from the question of whether PK energy generates heat, as all other forms of energy do, she designed an experiment using *thermistors*—extremely sensitive temperature detectors—connected to the palms of Swann's hands and also lodged in thermos bottles on the other side of a large room. The thermistors in the bottles were the targets, and Swann was instructed to employ his PK faculty to heat or cool them as directed by the experimenter. He succeeded in doing this with an effort of concentration, and Dr. Schmeidler noted that his skin temperature correspondingly decreased and increased. She also noted that a thermistor in a bottle several feet from the target cooled down when the target bottle heated up. This fact raises an interesting speculation about psychic energy. As Dr. Schmeidler put it: "Rather than Ingo transferring all of his energy to the thermistor target, it appears that he drew on energy from the environment, and when he cooled the target he transferred the energy back."

This is exactly what the earlier researcher Harry Price inferred from the thermograph records obtained during sittings with the mediums Stella Cranshaw and Rudi Schneider. Such startling physical phenomena have only rarely occurred in the parapsychological laboratory, but the combination of sophisticated modern research methods and the appearance of gifted psychics like Geller, Swann, and a few others, has enabled contemporary parapsychologists to make rapid progress toward solving the puzzle of PK.

Left: Ingo Swann, artist and psychic, cooperates in many tests like this one on out-of-body experiences. He is able consciously to control his psychic powers. Here Swann is conducting an out-of-body experiment with researcher Janet Mitchell. Swann, seated in the room at the far right, is attempting to leave his body in order to identify colored images, preselected by the researcher and shown on the apparatus seen in the foreground.

Chapter 13 Parapsychology in Eastern Europe

Is there sophisticated psychical research being carried on behind the Iron Curtain? What are the amazing results of experiments into supernormal abilities, conducted by a society dedicated to an entirely rational and rigidly logical philosophy? Only isolated results and reports are available in the West, but they indicate an extraordinary interest in the functioning of psi abilities, and the discovery of several extremely gifted individuals. Is it possible to "see" with your fingertips? Is the color yellow slippery, as one psychic has reported? In one spectacular aspect of Soviet research, the "aura" around living organisms is actually photographed, using the Kirlian method.

Josefka had been trained to exercise her psychic faculty under hypnosis. On this particular evening she was going to try an experiment in precognitive clairvoyance. Her instructions were to think of a friend and try to foresee some unpleasant event that that friend might be able to avoid if warned about it in time.

Soon after Josefka was put into trance she started to show signs of agitation. She vividly began to describe a scene involving a girl friend who lived 50 miles away. The girl was in a restaurant. A stranger approached her and they talked for a while before leaving together. "She shouldn't go," Josefka kept saying. But in her vision her friend got on a motorcycle with the stranger and they sped away into the country. Then they stopped. "Oh my God!" Josefka cried in anguish, "He's torn her skirt." She went on to describe with mounting horror a scene of savage rape. The next day Josefka phoned her friend to tell her about the possibly precognitive nightmare she had had about her. But before she had said very much her friend interrupted. "You're too late," she said. "It's already happened—last night." Her description of what had happened to her matched Josefka's trance vision in every detail.

Josefka was one of several people who developed their psi faculty under the tutelege of Dr. Milan Ryzl, formerly of Prague, Czechoslovakia, and now resident in California. Dr. Ryzl, a biochemist turned parapsychologist, evolved a method of training people to be psychic which Dr. Leonid Vasiliev, the

Opposite: possibly the most important Soviet psychic research has been Kirlian photography, which shows the aura around living organisms. Western scientists are also investigating the phenomena, among them Dr. Thelma Moss. She is shown through a Kirlian photo.

The Strange Story of Josefka

pioneer Russian psychical researcher, called one of the most promising developments in parapsychology. During the last few years before he left his country in 1967 Dr. Ryzl trained more than 50 volunteers to become psychic in some way. He would put a subject into an hypnotic trance and ask him, or her, to visualize certain scenes or images that he would suggest. When the subject's visualizing faculty was sufficiently evolved, Ryzl would suggest that he or she try to visualize what was happening at a particular time to a friend or relative. Some of his subjects, like Josefka, developed their capacity for clairvoyance to the point that while in trance they could psychically "drop in" on friends and see what they were doing.

It was not necessary for the trance state to be deep. Ryzl reports that Josefka once went through a whole day in a light trance and pursued her normal family and working life without anyone noticing her state of mind. She was one of the students in Ryzl's group who eventually learned to induce the trance state in themselves without the help of the hypnotist. She sometimes found it amusing, and at other times perhaps embarrassing, to pick up people's thoughts telepathically. On several occasions she found her clairvoyance useful in locating missing objects such as keys and office documents.

While he was still in Prague, Ryzl became a research associate of the Duke Parapsychology Laboratory, and in some of his work he used the ESP card-guessing tests devised by Rhine and his colleagues. In one clairvoyance experiment, for which the Zener cards were individually enclosed in thick opaque wrappings, Josefka scored 121 hits out of 250 guesses. Chance expectancy would have been 50 hits, and Josefka's performance

Right: Josefka, the girl who became remarkably clairvoyant under the tutelage of Dr. Ryzl.

Left: Ryzl with Pavel Stepanek, his most brilliant ESP subject. He exhibited the extraordinary "focusing effect" in which he would always make the same guess for the same card, even though the guess might be wrong.

represented odds against chance of a trillion to one. This result was obtained when she was in an hypnotic trance. In a control experiment when she was in a normal state of consciousness she scored exactly at chance level.

Ryzl's star ESP subject, a quiet-spoken man named Pavel Stepanek, quickly learned to control his psi faculty without undergoing hypnosis. Throughout the early 1960s parapsychologists from America, Britain, and The Netherlands flew to Prague to test for themselves this reputed card-guessing prodigy. The busy Dr. J. G. Pratt of Duke was among them, and after his observations he declared that "Pavel Stepanek's achievement is one that has rarely, if ever, been equaled in the history of parapsychology." The remarkable aspect of Stepanek's ESP laboratory work was that he could achieve significantly above-chance results consistently, reliably, and with any experimenter testing him. Nor did he suddenly go into decline, as all other high-scoring subjects had done. He had a short off-period in the mid-60s when for a time his scores declined to chance level and below. But when he was invited to the United States in 1967 for tests in American parapsychology laboratories, he rewarded his sponsors by achieving spectacular scores under the strictest conditions of control. He also produced a new phenomenon, which researchers called the "focusing effect." For a given card he would make the same guess repeatedly, trial after trial. The guess might be a wrong one, but it was always the same guess for such favored cards, no matter how well they were concealed in wrappings and behind screens. Apparently he was recognizing the cards but, in some cases, consistently distorting the message he received from them. Parapsychologists are still perplexed by this focusing effect. Some think that it may be a key to a breakthrough in understanding of the psi faculty, while others think it is a freak effect and a red herring.

As a research technique, hypnotism has been used much more by Eastern European and Russian researchers than by Americans and Western Europeans. It is only in recent years that systematic research into the effects of altered states of consciousness (or ASCs) on psi has been pursued in the West. This delay might be attributed to our traditional reluctance to infringe the principle of individual liberty. Relatively few

Vasiliev, the Soviet Pioneer of ESP Testing

The late Dr. Leonid Vasiliev told a meeting of top Soviet scientists in 1960 that it was essential to research ESP because the American navy was testing whether telepathy could be used on atomic submarines. He said: "The discovery of the energy underlying ESP will be equivalent to the discovery of atomic energy." A year later Vasiliev became head of a special Parapsychology Laboratory at Leningrad University. During his work he ran hundreds of tests trying to think people into actions. For example, he tried to make people cross their legs or raise their hands by his thought power. They responded to these mental suggestions too frequently for mere coincidence to explain. Many of these Soviet experiments were in telepathic hypnosis with subjects hundreds of miles away. One of Vasiliev's most spectacular tests was with a subject in a room that excluded electromagnetic radiation, thus eliminating any possible physical communication as a medium of exchange in telepathy.

Western physicians, for example, will use hypnosis in treating illness. The Russians have had a different viewpoint. In the 1920s two psychologists, Professor Dzelichovski and Dr. Kotkov, ran some experiments in telepathic hypnosis with an unwitting girl student as subject. The girl had been asked to participate in some experiments with Professor Dzelichovski, but whenever she went to his laboratory for this purpose, he told her he was still waiting for some equipment to be delivered before they could begin. The girl began dropping in on the Professor on an impulse, and while she was with him chatting casually she sometimes fell asleep on her feet for a short time. She couldn't explain her behavior, but the delighted experimenters could, for both her impulsive visits and her sudden blackouts were telepathically willed on her by Dr. Kotkov. He was sitting in another room in the building, beaming his influence at her.

This story is reminiscent of the diabolical mad professor stereotype of the horror films, but we have it on no less an authority than Dr. Leonid Vasiliev, the most distinguished Russian parapsychologist and the only one whose books have been published in English translation. In his *Experiment in Mental Suggestion*, which appeared in 1962 several years before his death, Vasiliev revealed that Russian scientists had been doing research into telepathy since the 1930s. They had received orders to do so from a high authority—which suggests that Stalin may have thought that ESP would have some strategic value.

Most of these early Russian experiments were in telepathic hypnotism, and Vasiliev's accounts of them are at once fascinating and sinister. For a hypnotist to be able to knock a person out telepathically when that person is a thousand miles away, unsuspectingly conversing with someone else, is an alarming power for one human being to have over another. Yet this is what one of Vasiliev's colleagues did. He was in Sevastopol in the Crimea, and the subject, a girl, was in Leningrad. The knockout was timed to happen while the girl was with her psychiatrist, who was a party to the experiment. The Russian scientists estimate that four people in a hundred can be telepathically hypnotized at a distance, but no Western researcher has attempted to substantiate the claim.

One of Vasiliev's subjects was a woman who had been hospitalized for years suffering from psychosomatic paralysis of the entire left side of her body. Vasiliev, assisted by hypnotist Dr. Finne, made the woman move her paralyzed arm and leg by suggestion conveyed telepathically. They were so successful that a number of distinguished doctors went to the hospital to observe the phenomenon. First, the woman was put into trance. Then a piece of paper on which the command to be conveyed was written was passed around the group of observers. Vasiliev or Finne then concentrated mentally on the command until the woman complied with it. To rule out the possibility of her obtaining sensory cues from those present, her eyes were tightly bandaged and not a word was spoken. The degree of success was extraordinary. Finne was even able to focus on particular nerves in the paralyzed arm, and make the woman

Early Research in Russia

Left: Dr. L. L. Vasiliev, who was the father of Soviet parapsychology. Vasiliev's theoretical explanation for psi faculties was founded on a strictly physical basis: he said it was a remainder from earlier forms of evolutien, probably operating through some kind of energy in the brain so far undiscovered.

Below: Vasiliev (second from left) with his successor Dr. Paul Gulyaiev (third from left) in the Leningrad parapsychology laboratory with other scientists.

move it in the way she would if the particular nerve that he visualized had been mechanically stimulated. The woman always knew whether it was Finne or Vasiliev who had beamed the telepathic command.

A rumor that the United States Navy was experimenting with telepathy as a means of communication with submarines led to the publication of Vasiliev's books in the Soviet Union in the early 1960s. Until then his 30 years of research work had been

Above, the biophysicist Yuri Kamensky. He took part with Karl Nikolaiev in the long-distance telepathy tests in 1966 between Moscow and Novosibirsk, nearly 2000 miles away in Siberia.

top secret, for telepathy posed an ideological problem for the Russians. Unless it could be shown to have a physical basis which could be explained by some kind of wave theory, it would seem to subvert the official materialist philosophy. Much of Vasiliev's early work was designed to discover the energy underlying ESP. He went to great lengths to demonstrate that it involved waves.

He put his subject inside a Faraday cage, an immense and heavy metal box which resists penetration by radio and electromagnetic waves. Still she fell asleep when the telepathic sender, or agent, outside the cage willed her to do so. He then put the agent in a lead capsule which was sunk into a gully filled with mercury, but the girl in the Faraday cage nonetheless dropped off to order. The wave theory seemed insupportable and was quietly shelved, but the research program went on.

In 1966 a widely publicized telepathy experiment took place. The agents were in Moscow and the subject nearly 2000 miles away in Siberia. The subject was Moscow actor and journalist Karl Nikolaiev, and the agent was the biophysicist Yuri Kamensky. Supervised by a committee of scientists, Kamensky successfully transmitted to Nikolaiev mental images of six objects which were given to him in separate packages at the start of the experiment. In another test with a different agent Nikolaiev identified 12 out of 20 ESP cards as they were turned over in Moscow.

Clairvoyance is never mentioned in accounts of Soviet ESP research, in contrast to much American work suggesting that clairvoyance may be the primary mode of ESP. Nikolaiev's feat could be attributed to clairvoyance as well as to telepathy, but the Russians are sticking to the hypothesis of a type of "mental radio" to explain such phenomena, even though they have not been able to discover the elusive radio waves. Their research has brought to light some interesting facts about brain waves, however. In a distance experiment between Moscow and Leningrad, Nikolaiev was wired up to a battery of machines that monitored his physiological changes and brain wave patterns. He put himself into a receptive frame of mind and waited. He didn't know when Kamensky, 400 miles away, was going to begin his attempt at telepathic transmission, and he had no idea what kind of message to expect. The *electroencephalograph* (brain wave recorder) registered increased activity in Nikolaiev's brain at the exact moment when Kamensky began concentrating. It also indicated that the activity took place in the part of the brain appropriate to the type of message being sent. If Kamensky sent a visual image Nikolaiev's brain was activated in the area that controls sight, and if he sent an auditory signal like a whistle the receiver's brain registered a stimulus in the area involved with sound. Referring to this research in an article in the *International Journal of Parapsychology* in 1968, Dr. Milan Ryzl said, "These Soviet findings could bring us a long way forward in the control of ESP."

Since his defection to the United States in 1967, Ryzl has served as the main source of information about psi research in the Soviet Union and Eastern Europe for Western parapsychologists and students. But his writings on the subject

ESP Across 2000 Miles

Left: Nikolaiev (right) received the Kamensky messages. He is pictured with researcher Edward Naumov in front of a graph showing the high percentage of increase in the Soviet's popular publications on parapsychology in recent years. In the Moscow-Novosibirsk tests, Nikolaiev was able to receive messages better from Kamensky than from A. G. Arlashin, another sender in the experiment.

have all appeared in academic journals. The general public's knowledge of Eastern European parapsychology has come largely from a book entitled *Psychic Discoveries Behind the Iron Curtain* by the two young writers Sheila Ostrander and Lynn Schroeder. The authors gathered material for their book during a study-trip through the Communist countries in 1968, and published the book two years later. It was offered as a work of reportage, with the introductory caution that "Whether Communist observations and theories about psychic happenings are right or not, can only be determined by further investigations."

Despite this cautionary remark, the book gave rise to a myth that the United States and the Soviet Union are engaged in a psi-research race and that the Communists, with official backing, are forging ahead. Milan Ryzl, addressing an annual conference of the Parapsychology Foundation of New York, took a less dramatic view. He spoke of Soviet parapsychology as "cautious renaissance," and warned that, "The more spectacular ventures, which are most publicized, are more science fiction than solid pieces of scholarly study." However, he did cite a number of individual researchers and areas of investigation that he believes are contributing significantly to international progress in parapsychology. Among these important projects are Gulyaiev's research on the "electrical aura" of living bodies, Professor A. Novomeysky's investigations of "finger reading," and various studies of the PK effects

Right: Nelya Mikhailova with Dr. Zdenek Rejdak, one of the researchers who has worked on tests of her powers. On the table are some of the objects she had moved by PK. Dr. Rejdak strongly defended her powers as genuine.

produced by Mrs. Nelya Mikhailova.

Professor Ippolit Kogan designed and carried out the experiments with Nikolaiev and Kamensky. As head of the Bioinformation Unit of the A.S. Popov Society for Radiotechnics in Moscow, Kogan has completed many series of experiments in telepathy, and has also contributed to the theoretical study of the subject. He has continued Vasiliev's work on the telepathic control of consciousness using hypnotized subjects. In repeated trials, sleeping subjects have been made to wake up telepathically by an agent situated in another room. In another series of experiments with the gifted Karl Nikolaiev, Kogan's colleague Edward Naumov succeeded 13 times in 26 attempts in guiding Nikolaiev telepathically to find objects hidden in a room.

The Soviet term for telepathy, "bioinformation," indicates a bias toward finding a physical basis for the phenomenon. At one point Kogan demonstrated mathematically that if the existence of electromagnetic waves over a mile long could be assumed, telepathy might be explained in terms of this kind of radiation. Even so, the theory would not account for long-distance telepathy; and in his later theoretical work Kogan has tended toward the conclusion that telepathy can never be understood in terms of energy. Telepathy is transfer of information, and information must not be confused with energy, he maintains. Kogan illustrates his point with the example of light. To take a photograph in a dark room you need the concentrated light *energy* provided by a flashbulb. But when light conveys *information*, for instance in a warning buoy at sea, the faintest distant glimmer, requiring only minimal energy, can convey all necessary information. Bioinformation, or telepathy, Kogan suggests, may be analogous. The electromagnetic radiation of the brain is not powerful enough in terms of energy to push a message through space, but it can create a weak but detectable field of force around the body. In theory, it is possible that this

The Mysterious Mrs. Mikhailova

This extraordinary Soviet psychic apparently "sees" with her fingers and can move small objects by the power of her mind. A plump, attractive woman with dark expressive eyes, Mrs. Mikhailova discovered her powers when recovering from injuries in the hospital at the end of World War II. She recalls: "I was very angry one day and I was walking toward a cupboard when suddenly a pitcher moved to the edge of the shelf, fell, and smashed to bits." Gradually, Nelya Mikhailova found she could control her mental energy. Dr. Gerady Sergeyev, a neurologist at the Utomski Institute in Leningrad, set up numerous tests which found that Mrs. Mikhailova has a magnetic field surrounding her body only 10 times less than that of the earth itself. She also has an unusual brain wave pattern which generates 50 times more energy from the back of her head than from the front. Most people generate only three to four times more. After psychokinetic experiments, such as one in which she separated the yolk from the white of an egg by will power, she loses several pounds in weight and is physically and emotionally exhausted. When convalescing in the hospital in the 1960s she also found she could "see" the colors of her embroidery threads with her fingertips—powers that were later tested by Soviet researcher Dr. Leonid Vasiliev.

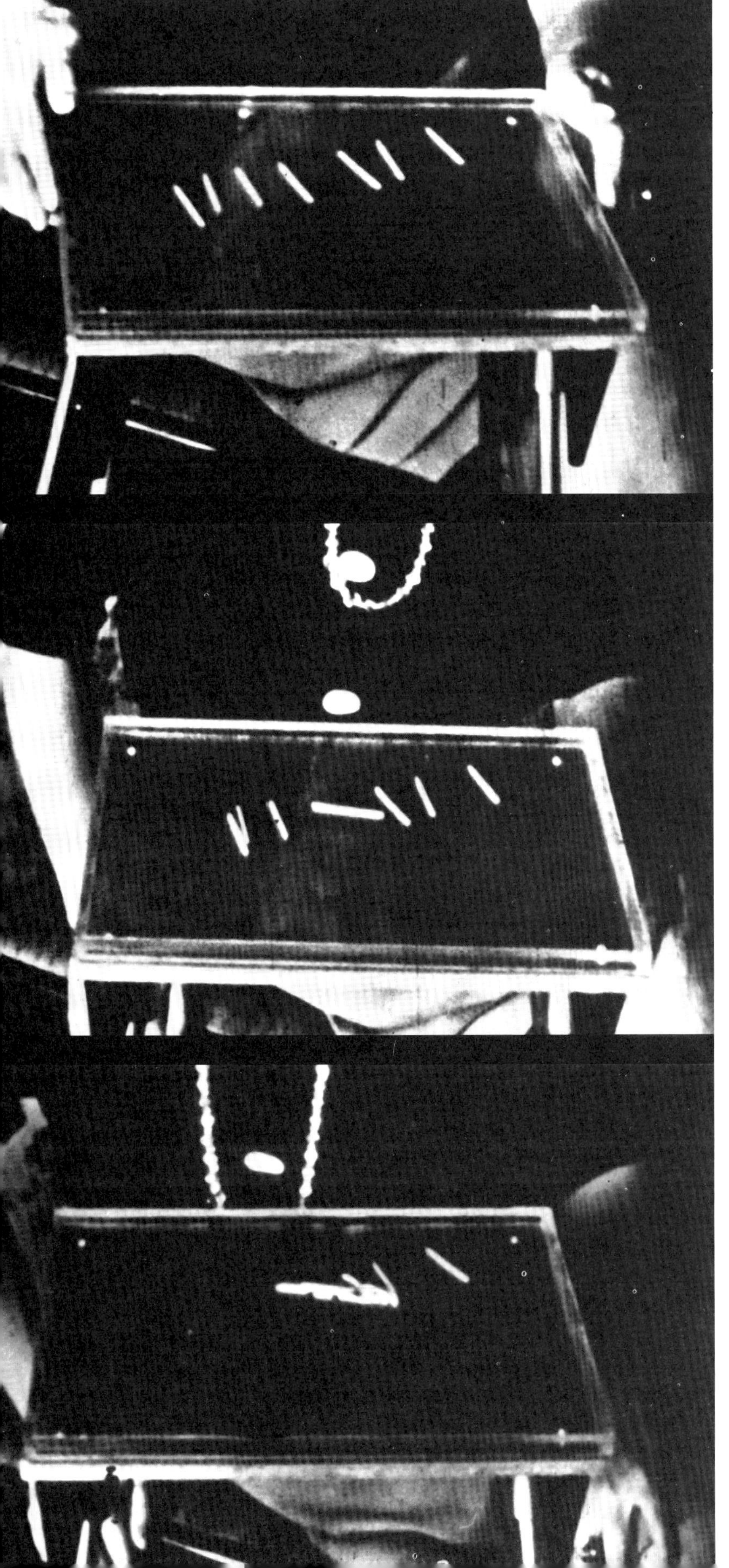

"Bioinformation," Soviet Telepathy

Left: stills from a movie of Mrs. Mikhailova, who is also known as Madame Kulagina, moving matches on a table by PK. The observers present said that at no time did her hands come into contact with the table itself.

Above: Nelya Mikhailova trying to exert her PK powers. The odd headgear is a device to monitor her brain waves during the test.

field of force—or psi field—can convey information to a person who knows how to interpret the faint signal.

This theoretical model for telepathic communication relies partly on the findings of Professor Pavel Gulyaiev, Vasiliev's successor as head of the Laboratory of Physiological Cybernetics at the University of Leningrad. Using extremely sensitive apparatus specifically designed for the purpose, Gulyaiev and his colleagues have discovered that all living bodies are surrounded by a faint electrostatic field, which they call the "electrical aura." This field undergoes constant changes, and even thoughts can cause changes in it which can be detected and measured. Gulyaiev has suggested that changes in the electrical aura may represent signals which carry information, and that this may be the means by which some fish, insects, and other animals communicate. It is also theoretically possible that changes in the aura, caused by mental activity, could be amplified to produce sufficient energy to move objects.

Moving With the Mind

The possible connection between PK and this electrostatic field has been investigated with the cooperation of a remarkable woman, Mrs. Nelya Mikhailova. This Leningrad housewife has dazzled Soviet parapsychologists for several years with her psychokinetic powers. Among those who have tested her is Dr. Gerady Sergeyev, who designed an instrument that picks up at a distance of up to four yards the electrostatic and magnetic fields of the human body. Sergeyev's detectors showed that Nelya Mikhailova generated 50 times more voltage from the back of her head than from the front, whereas most people generate only three or four times more. This was in a normal condition of rest. When Mrs. Mikhailova was actually exercising her PK, causing small objects on a table in front of her to move, the instruments showed that the magnetic fields around her body began to pulsate, and these pulsations kept in rhythm with pulsations of her heart and brain. Moreover, she appeared to be able to focus the force-field emanating from her in the direction of the object she was looking at.

Nelya Mikhailova has been observed and reported on by a number of Western parapsychologists and writers, who all vouch for the genuineness of her effects. She can make matches, cigarettes, pens, and other light objects move on a table by moving her hands over them or just looking at them. She can tilt a pair of scales which are equally balanced with weights of 30 grams, and continue to hold one side of the scale down when 10 extra grams are added to the other side. When she stops concentrating and moves her eyes the heavier scale sinks. To accomplish these feats she often has to spend considerable time revving up her powers. When she has finished she is fatigued, and she has sometimes been found to have lost weight.

The PK talent of Nelya Mikhailova was discovered by Vasiliev in the course of investigating a different paranormal faculty she possesses: the ability to "see" with her hands. Finger-reading or eyeless sight is a predominantly Soviet area of parapsychological research. Mrs. Mikhailova is reported to have discovered her ability one day in the early 1960s when,

Below: Mrs. Mikhailova is far from being the only Soviet psychic who has demonstrated PK powers in the laboratory. In these stills from a film, Alla Vinogradova is shown moving matches through PK.

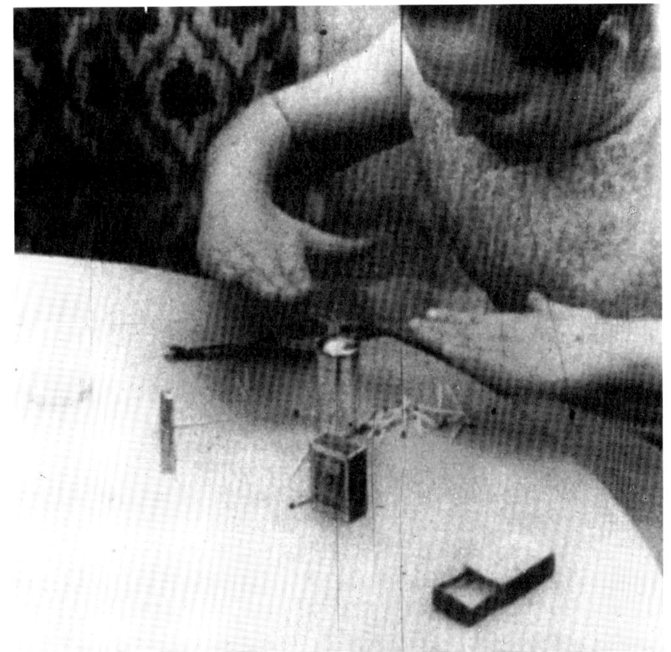

The Soviet Seeing Hands

convalescing from an illness in a Leningrad hospital, she was passing the time doing embroidery. She found that without looking she was able to pick out of the bag of thread any color that she wanted from among the many it contained. Some time later she happened to read an article about a young woman who lived in the Ural mountain city of Tagil, and who was said to be able to "see" with her fingers. Mikhailova reported her own experience to her doctor, who brought it to the attention of Vasiliev.

Rosa Kuleshova, the young woman in Tagil, really started something when she went to her doctor in 1962 and told him she had discovered that she could distinguish colors and read print with her fingers. Of course, the doctor was incredulous,

Right: Rosa Kuleshova reading a newspaper with her fingers rather than with her eyes. She caused a sensation in the Soviet Union with her psi power of seeing through the skin. The ability also extended to telling colors.

but Rosa demonstrated her ability to his satisfaction, and he informed professional colleagues of the discovery. Among these was Professor Abram Novomeysky, who tested her claims himself and was also satisfied that they were genuine. The provincial prodigy was then invited to demonstrate before top scientists in Moscow at the Biophysics Institute of the Soviet Academy of Sciences. After conducting their own experiments, which were carefully constructed to rule out alternative explanations such as telepathy and clairvoyance, the scientists confirmed that Rosa possessed skin sensitivity so acute that she really could "see" with her fingers.

If this were a freak phenomenon it would not be so important. But subsequent work by Professor Novomeysky and his col-

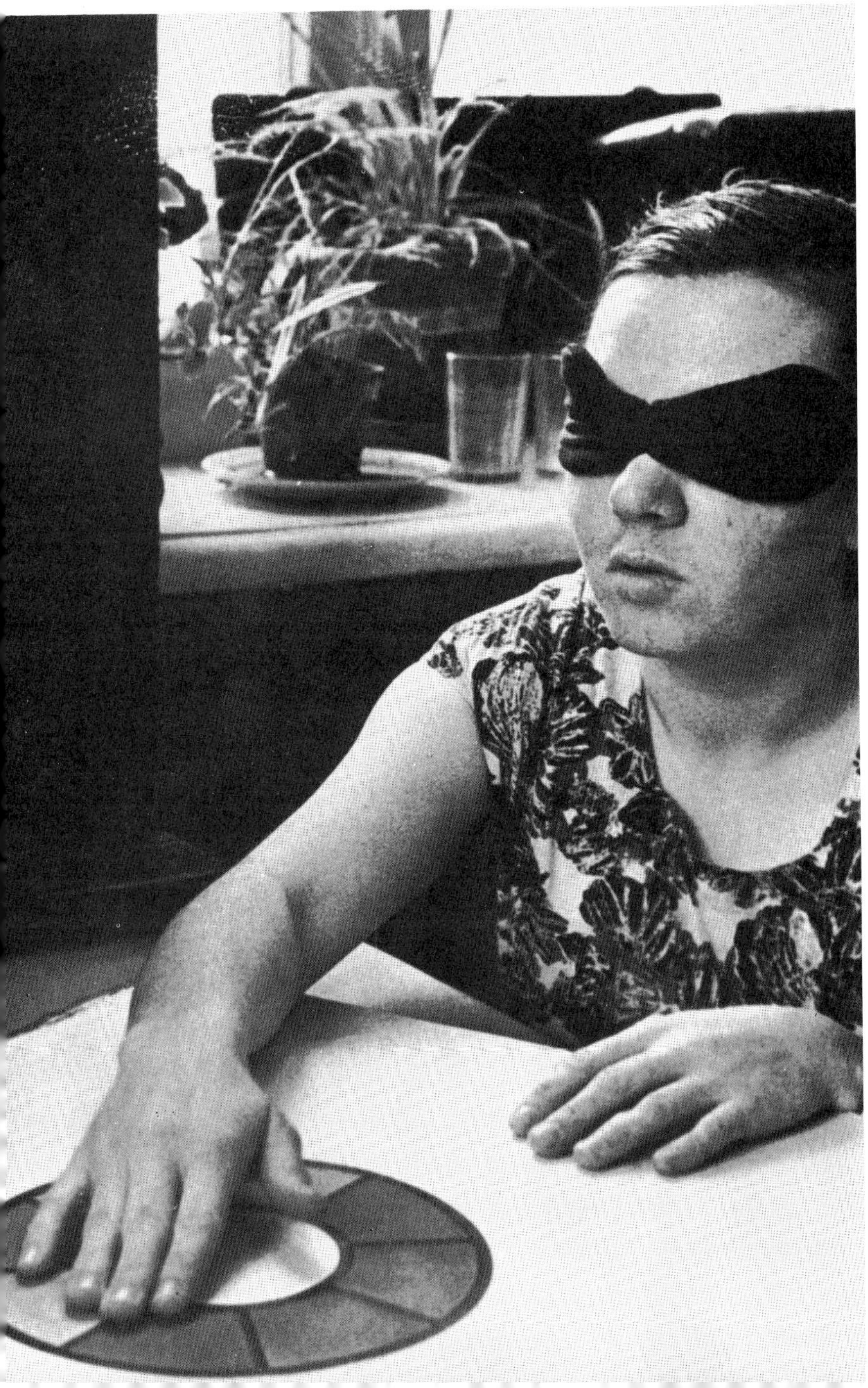

Above: even the placement of a piece of glass over the printed matter did not prevent Rosa Kuleshova from being able to read the numbers with her fingertips.

Left: Rosa Kuleshova seeing colors through her fingertips. At the beginning she could read only with the tips of the third and fourth fingers of her right hand, but as she developed her skill more, she could use all her fingers on both hands. After becoming famous, the young psychic went on the stage. Carried away by all the furor over her, she sometimes resorted to cheating to live up to her reputation.

Kirlian Photography

Opposite: a Kirlian photograph of the apparent interaction between a human finger and a magnet.

Below: Semyon and Valentina Kirlian, developers of Kirlian photography. They designed the apparatus that uses high frequency electrical currents to make visible the spectacular colored auras around all living things.

leagues showed that skin vision is a faculty that many people can develop. Rosa developed her ability gradually. At first she could only "see" with the fingers of her right hand, then she learned to do so with both hands and with other parts of her body, such as her elbow. Novomeysky found that one person in six of those he tested could learn within half an hour to tell the difference between two colors by touch. Some subjects eventually were able to distinguish all the colors, and they generally agreed on the distinctive feel of individual colors. Light blue is smooth, for example; yellow is slippery; orange is hard and rough. Subjects who actually developed the ability to distinguish colors merely by passing their hands over them found that different colors radiated their influence to different heights, as if they had a range of degrees of energy. Red appeared to extend highest and light blue the least. On the basis of this evidence Novomeysky conjectured that skin sight might be explained as an interaction between electromagnetic fields emanating both from the color and from the subject's body.

When the news of the discovery of Rosa Kuleshova and the phenomenon of eyeless sight reached the Soviet public, it caused a sensation. Many people found they possessed the faculty; others found they could simulate it; and Rosa herself, carried away by her fame, made extravagant claims that she

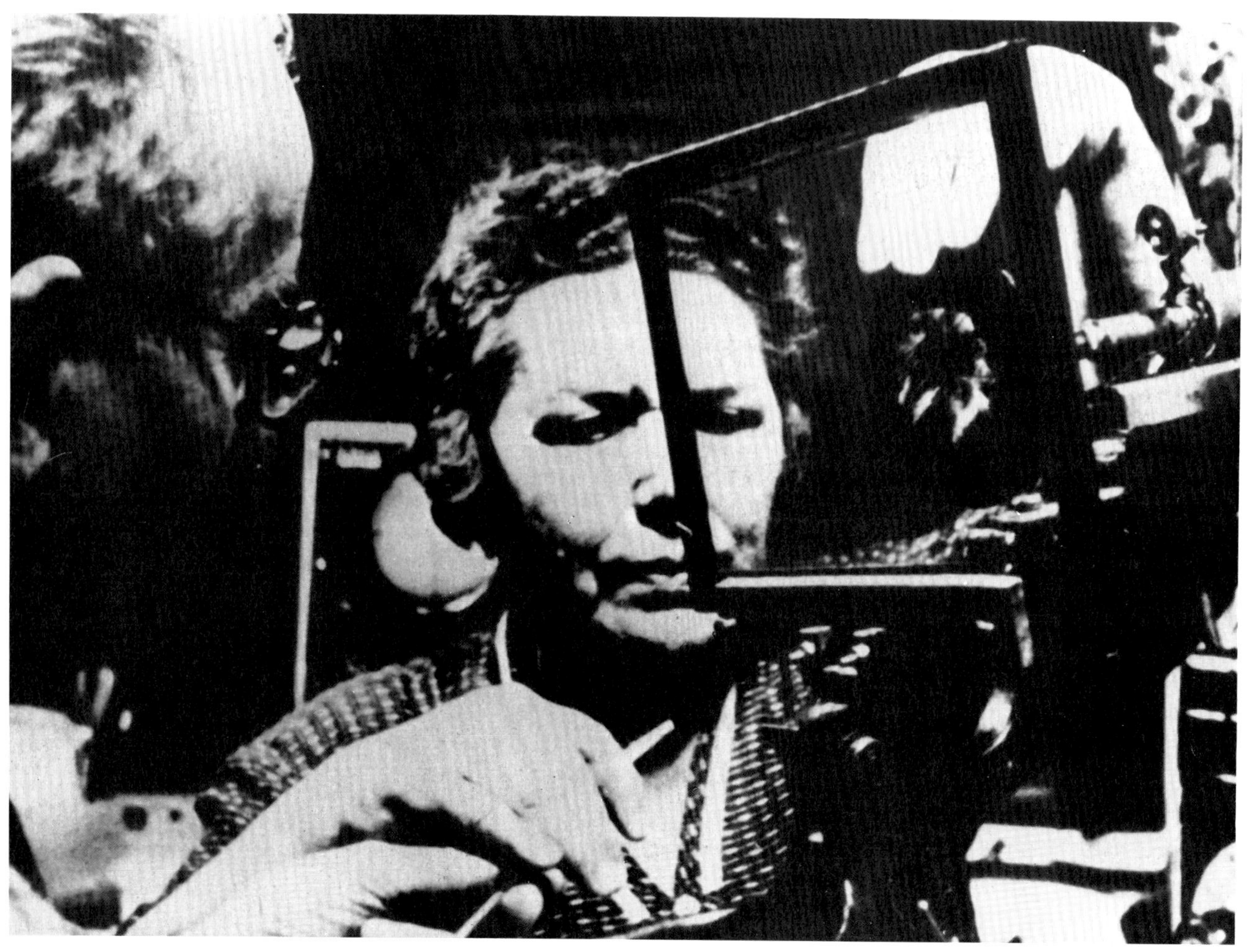

Photography of the Astral Body

Above: Dr. Thelma Moss, who has taken more Kirlian photographs and done more experimental work with them than anyone outside Russia.

Opposite: a Kirlian photo taken by Dr. Moss of Uri Geller's finger sending a burst of energy during one of his demonstrations. Uri Geller offers scientists the hope of a repeatable psychic experiment, and as a result he has spent days in laboratories with scientists all over the world.
Below: Geller's finger at rest.

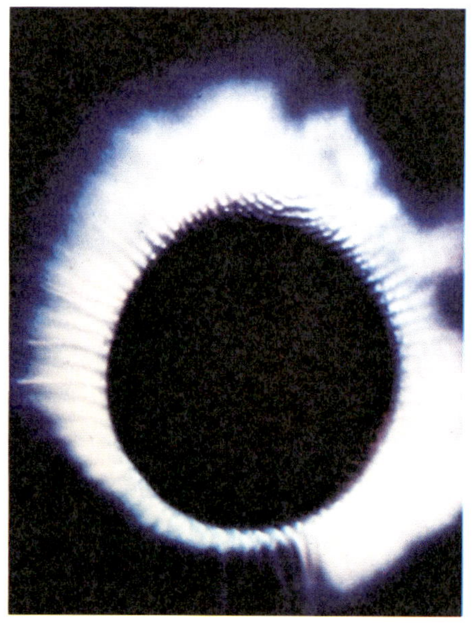

couldn't fulfill without cheating. But in Tagil and nearby Sverdlovsk, Novomeysky and his colleagues continued studying the phenomenon using blind subjects, most of them children who had been blind from birth. By playing colored beams on the palms of the children's hands and telling them, "this is red" or "this is blue," they trained them to distinguish colors, and later to "read" print. Research work in the field was pursued in other laboratories. In Odessa Dr. Andrei Shevalev taught a blind child to "see" with the aid of a lens attached to his forehead. In Sophia, Bulgaria, Dr. Georgi Lozanov trained 60 blind children to different degrees of competence in skin vision, and demonstrated their abilities at a meeting of distinguished physicians, psychiatrists, and psychotherapists. The evidence for the reality of this paranormal faculty, or sixth sense, accumulated until it was indisputable. To cap it all, the octogenarian French novelist and physician Jules Romains pointed out in an article in the *International Journal of Parapsychology* in 1965 that he had published a study of what he called "para-optic ability" as long ago as 1920.

Of all Soviet research relating to parapsychology, however indirectly, the most publicized is the process known as Kirlian photography. Using high-frequency electrical currents, Semyon and Valentina Kirlian discovered some 30 years ago that they could obtain pictures of living organisms that showed a surrounding aura of luminescence. This aura, which is called a "bioplasmic body," may be the same force field recently detected and measured by such scientists as Gulyaiev and Sergeyev. Theorists have conjectured that all living things possess a bioplasmic body. Kirlian photographs of leaves have clearly shown visible energy radiating from them, and variations in the aura of leaves of the same species have been proved to signal the onset of disease in a plant before the disease became visible by normal means. Similarly, changes in the aura of a human being may indicate changes in his mental and physical state.

Western parapsychologists have on the whole been slow to follow up the theory of a bioplasmic body, and have pointed out possible alternative explanations of the Kirlian effect. For example, Dr. Montague Ullman pointed out in an interview in *Psychic* magazine that some physicists believe the luminescence may be produced by ionization of the atmosphere. This caution on the part of Western investigators toward the bioplasma theory is understandable when one considers its resemblance to the ancient belief in an astral body coexisting with the physical body. The Kirlians' discoveries, and those of some other researchers in the Communist world, appear to support a belief generally regarded as a superstition by scientists in both the West and the East.

Nevertheless, the photographing and measuring of this force field, whatever its fundamental nature, may turn out to have important implications for parapsychology. It seems likely that this energy lies behind PK effects, and it may also play a part in psychic healing and even ESP. In the years ahead, even more exciting developments in parapsychology may emerge from laboratories in the Communist countries.

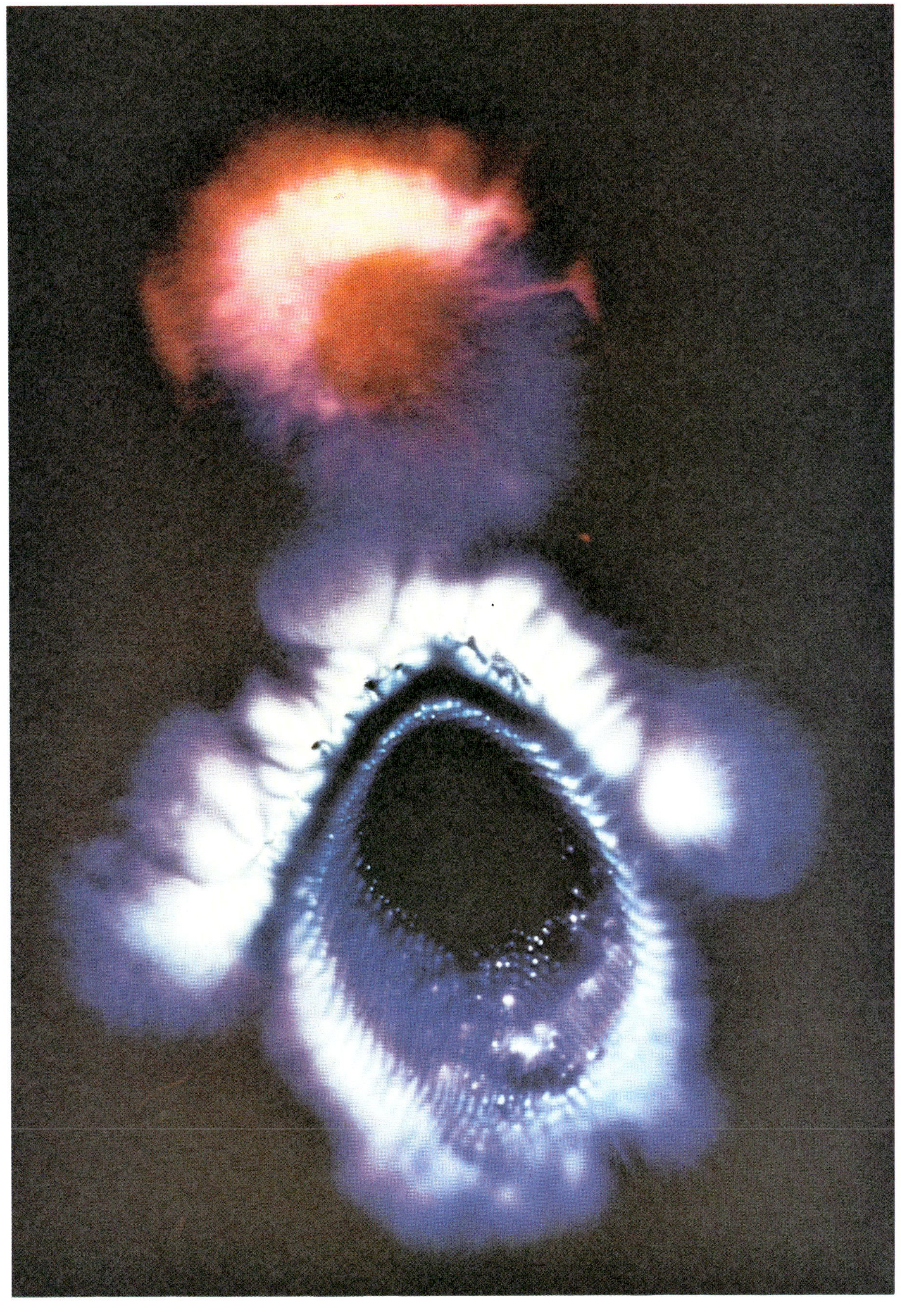

Chapter 14
Parapsychology Today

What is the future for parapsychology? Will it be possible for scientists to study psi phenomena more as they naturally occur, rather than in artificial situations using test card and dice? The trend now appears to be a concern with discovering under what conditions psi abilities function, and what they may indicate about the potential of the human mind. Is everybody capable of some degree of ESP? To what extent does personality influence the workings of psi? Parapsychologists today do not seem to need to prove that psi faculties exist—rather they seek to explore and develop them.

A young woman reclines at ease in a chair in a soundproof room. She can see nothing, because her eyes are covered by what looks like colored ping-pong balls cut in half. She can hear nothing, for she has on a headset through which comes only the uniform low hiss of "white noise." She is in a state of "sensory deprivation." She will remain in this state for a period of 30 minutes, and at some point during this time a friend in another room will view a series of stereoscopic slides, concentrate hard on the pictures, and try to communicate them telepathically to the young woman, who has no idea when during the 30 minutes the attempt will take place. Throughout the entire period she gives a running commentary on what she thinks and visualizes, which is tape recorded.

This experiment was designed by Charles Honorton, director of research in the Division of Parapsychology and Psychophysics at the Maimonides Medical Center, Brooklyn, New York. It tests his theory that "conscious sensory isolation increases access to internal mentation processes." In other words, when nothing is coming in from outside by way of the senses, a person will be more aware of what is going on inside on a purely mental level. The theory also proposed that in a state of sensory deprivation a person will be more susceptible than he normally is to nonsensory influences from outside, such as telepathic communication.

In this particular experiment the theme of the target series of

Some of the most interesting research in current parapsychology is in the area of sensory deprivation—isolation of the mind from stimuli. One of the goals is to see how the mind might then be influenced by ESP forces.

Opposite: this subject is undergoing a sensory deprivation test at New York's Maimonides Hospital.

Sensory Deprivation

slides is Las Vegas. The agent views the slides, concentrating on each picture in turn, and gradually the subject's commentary begins to home in on the target. She reports that she sees bright neon lights, street scenes with a lot of activity, theater marquees. . . . The brightly illuminated buildings could be nightclubs. . . . It could be some place such as Las Vegas. The sending period comes to an end, but the subject's continuous report on her thoughts and mental imagery continues until the prescribed time has elapsed. She is then shown four different sets of slides and asked to select one which has some correspondences with her recent stream of thought. She has no hesitation in selecting the target set, the scenes of Las Vegas. This experiment will be recorded as an unqualified hit.

Out of 27 series of such experiments, each series including 50 sessions with different subjects, Honorton reports that 20 produced a statistically significant proportion of hits. In one successful experiment the target theme of the slides viewed by the agent was "rare coins." Part of the subject's commentary during the sending period ran:" . . . now I see circles, an enormous amount of them. Their sizes are not the same . . . some are really large, and others are very tiny—no larger than a penny. They just keep flashing in front of me, all these different size circles . . . Now I see colors . . . two in particular, gold and silver, seem to stand out more than all the others. I sense something important. I can't tell what but but I get a feeling of importance, respect, value." On another occasion the target theme was "U.S. Air Force Academy," and part of the subject's commentary went: "An airplane floating over the clouds . . . planes passing overhead . . . thunder and angry clouds . . . airplanes . . . ultrasound . . . a blaze of fire, red flames . . . a giant bird flying . . . six stripes on an army uniform, V-shaped . . . the sensation of going forward very fast . . . ."

Not all the recorded hits are as unambiguous and direct as these. In assessing results, experimenters have to take into account the fact that there is not always a direct and literal correspondence between an external event and our mental reconstruction of it. For instance, on one occasion when the target pictures were taken from a news magazine story about the secret bombing of Cambodia, the subject reported images of former President Nixon cleaning his nose! Honorton doesn't say whether he counted that a hit.

This type of experiment exemplifies several characteristics of most of the current work in parapsychology. First, it is less concerned with proving that psi phenomena occur than with discovering under what conditions they occur and what they tell us about the properties and potentials of the human mind. Second, it doesn't necessarily revolve around work with exceptionally gifted individuals. There is a growing belief that most, if not all, people possess psi to some degree. Third, it depends less on the closed-option type of test, such as card-guessing, and gives the subject's mind freer range and more interesting challenges. Fourth, it seeks to create conditions favorable to the functioning of the psi faculty by putting the subject into an altered state of consciousness. Finally, it employs electronic and other technological aids to induce, observe, and measure psi

Left: Charles Honorton and Dr. Stanley Krippner flank Dr. Harry Hermon who is fastened into the witches' cradle, a device that disorients a subject spatially. Nicknamed after a trance-inducing device allegedly used by witches, it is used at Maimonides Hospital in sensory deprivation tests.

functions.

These characteristics, taken together, constitute a revolution in parapsychology. The subject has broadened out and converged with other areas of scientific investigation and with aspects of modern social and cultural life. Perhaps, in fact, this trend in parapsychology is less a revolution than a return to origins. One of the older generation of British psychical researchers, G. N. M. Tyrrell, said in his Presidential Address to the SPR in 1945: "Let us now, before the restricted view of the laboratory worker gains too firm a hold, try to realize how wide our subject is. We should try once more to see it through the eyes of Frederic Myers as a subject which lies at the meeting place of religion, philosophy and science, whose business is to grasp all that can be grasped of the nature of human personality."

Parapsychologists today are tending to return to this broader view of their subject, and to transcend "the restricted view of the laboratory worker." Many of them believe that the tradi-

"Telepathic Interaction"

tional methods of science as adapted to parapsychological research by Rhine and his colleagues in the 1930s are self-defeating in the study of psi functions, for they inhibit their operation. They believe that the little that can be learned about psi from card guessing, dice throwing and odds-against-chance computations has already been learned, and it is time for new and more imaginative approaches. Especially talented subjects are always interesting to parapsychologists, but the best and most interesting research being done today does not involve a quest for freak superminds. It combines the broadly humanistic outlook of the founders of psychical research with the technological sophistication of the modern physicist.

Modern studies in telepathy illustrate this. The eminent Cambridge philosopher C. D. Broad pointed out that to think of telepathy as transfer of information or imagery from one mind to another is too restrictive. He preferred to speak of "telepathic interaction." This phrase suggests the idea that one mind might act upon another without their thoughts or experiences necessarily corresponding, and he suggested that tele-

Below: Douglas Dean, shown using a *plethysmograph*, which monitors subtle variations in blood volume in any part of the body. It is used to measure a physiological reaction in a person of which he or she might be completely unaware consciously.

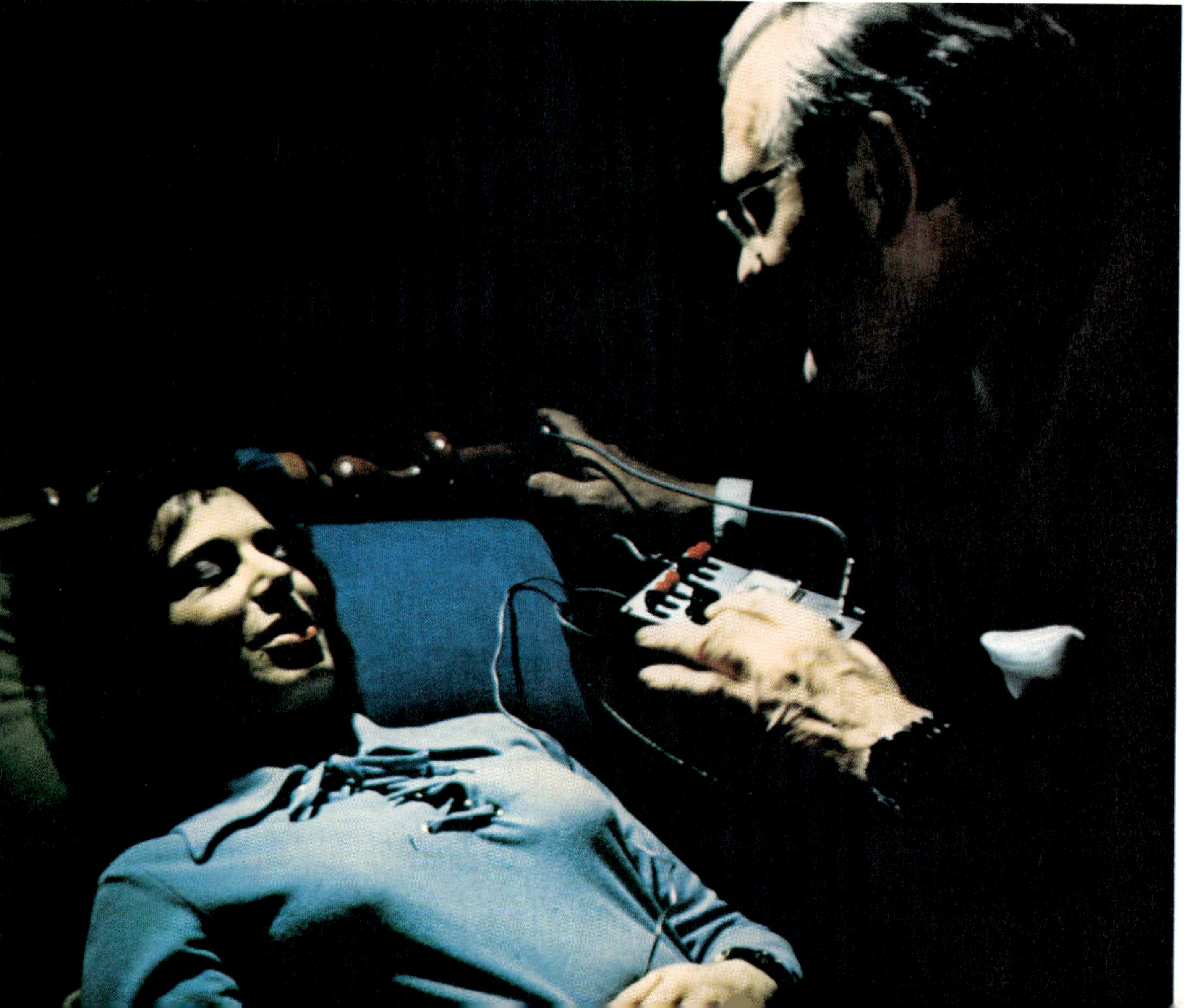

pathic interaction takes place in life more commonly than we might suppose and quite often without our noticing it. An experiment conducted by Douglas Dean of the Newark College of Engineering demonstrated Broad's concept.

Dean used a device called a *plethysmograph*, which measures fluctuations in blood volume in any part of the body. The index finger of the subject was connected to this device. In another room the agent was given a list of names and instructed to concentrate on the names one at a time in random order, making a note of the time at which he concentrated on each name. At the same time he was to visualize the subject and his location. Some of the names were of people listed in a telephone directory, but others were of people emotionally connected to the subject, such as his wife, his mother, or his child. Now when a person receives information that has emotional significance for him, his body may react in certain ways including change in blood pressure. In this experiment the plethysmograph frequently registered significant changes in the subject's blood volume when the agent concentrated on names of people the

Below: Research in 1971 at the Maimonides Hospital centered on the "alpha state," an extremely calm state in which psi seems to be able to function best. Honorton (right) and Dr. Krippner (left) observe a sleeping subject.

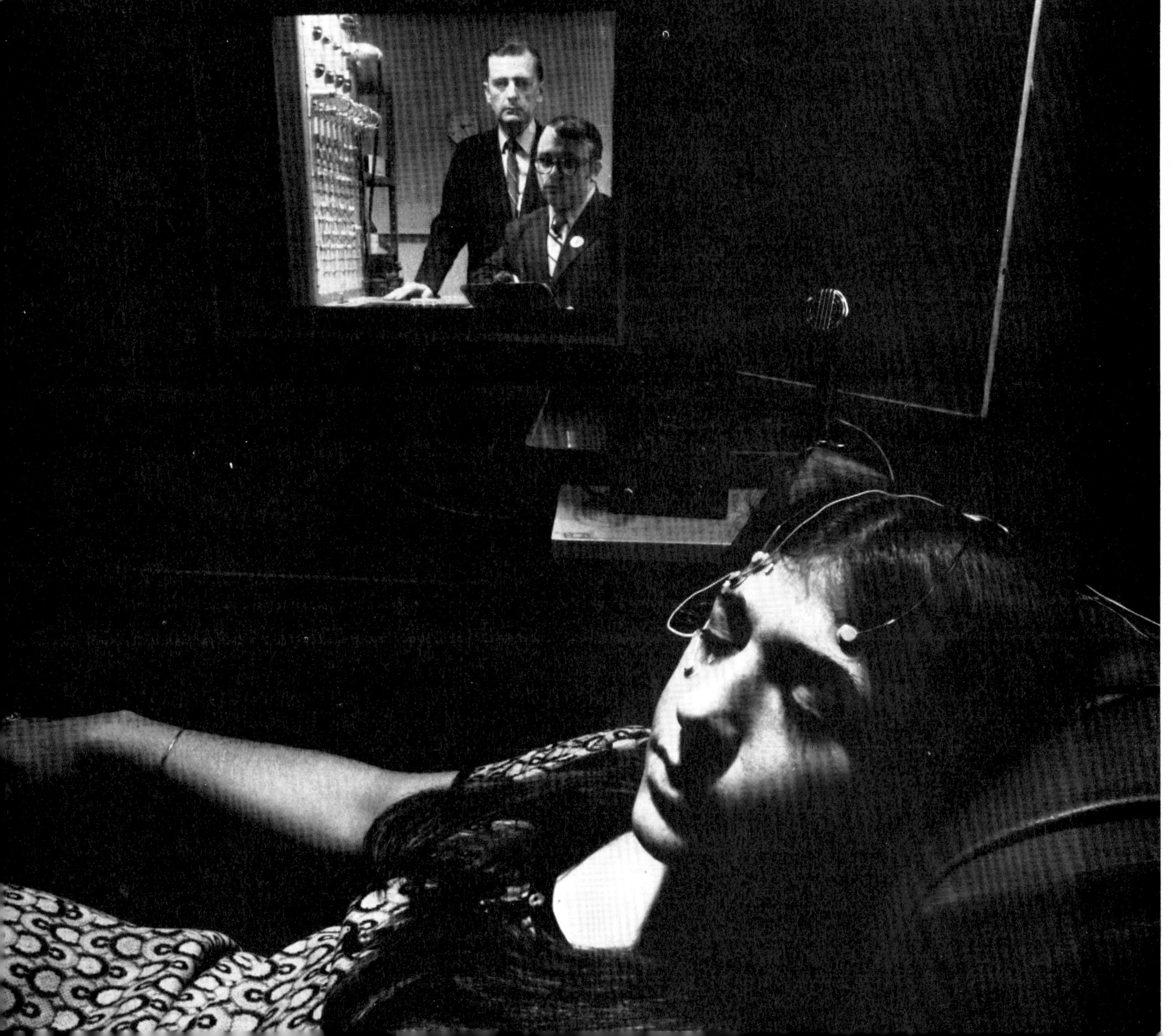

Dreams in the Laboratory

subject was close to. But when the agent was thinking about an unfamiliar name there were no such changes. The significant point of this experiment is that the subject was never *consciously* aware of what the agent was thinking. He never said, for instance, "Now he's thinking of Mary, my wife." Without the plethysmograph, nobody would have known that a telepathic interaction was taking place. In Dean's experiments about one person out of four showed a measurable response to telepathic messages of emotional content. The implication would seem to be that many of us may be physiologically reacting to other people's thoughts, even though we may not be able consciously to formulate the impressions they are making on us.

The dream telepathy experiments of Dr. Montague Ullman and Dr. Stanley Krippner at the Maimonides Hospital are perhaps the best-known modern investigations of telepathy. They have established clearly that telepathic communication is neither a rare occurrence confined mainly to times of crisis nor a special aptitude possessed by a few rare individuals.

The subject of Ullman and Krippner's experiments were ordinary people who volunteered to spend a night at the dream laboratory wired to an EEG (electroencephalograph) and to report on their dreams when they were awakened. It had been found that when a person is dreaming his eyes make rapid movements beneath the closed lids. The EEG monitored these movements and enabled the experimenter, in another room, to see when the subject was dreaming, and to awaken him to obtain a report on his dream while it was still vivid to him. In yet another room in the laboratory sat the agent. At the beginning of the session he selected an envelope from a group of 12, using a special method to insure a random choice. Each of the envelopes contained a postcard reproduction of a painting. The agent had to concentrate on this picture throughout the night and attempt to transmit his impressions of it to the sleeping subject. In the morning the tapes of the subject's dream reports and the target picture were given to independent judges who assessed the dreams for their correspondence, if any, to the target picture.

Above: during an experiment in dream telepathy at Maimonides, the sender sketches the picture she is trying to transmit to a sleeping subject. This is done to intensify the telepathic image.

What emerged strongly from hundreds of such experiments—and from the many spontaneous cases of dream telepathy collected by Ullman and Krippner—is that telepathic communication to a sleeping subject is a fairly frequent occurrence. However, the process is more of an infiltration of the dreamer's consciousness than a complete invasion of it. The target picture was never transmitted whole, as an image, but was broken up, and elements from it were interwoven with the sleeper's ongoing dream. Sometimes these elements were translated by the dreamer into an analogous form, just as in dreams we normally express material from real life in symbolic forms. For instance, one target picture was of two dogs standing with bared teeth over a piece of meat. The subject dreamed that she was at a dinner party with several other people, among them two friends who were noted for their greed and concern that others shouldn't get more than they did, especially of meat—"because in Israel," she explained, "they don't have so much meat." She was eating "something like rib steak" and was very aware of her friends eyeing her plate. There were no dogs in her dream, but it clearly incorporated the themes of greed and the eating of meat that were in the target picture.

A more literal correspondence was obtained with a picture showing a group of Mexican revolutionaries riding against a background of mountains and dark clouds. Part of the sleeper's account of his first dream of the night went: "A storm. Rainstorm. It reminds me of traveling . . . approaching a rainstorm, thunder cloud, rainy . . . a very distant scene . . . For some reason, I got a feeling, now, of New Mexico when I lived there. There are a lot of mountains around New Mexico. Indians, Pueblos. Now my thoughts go to almost as though I were thinking of another civilization."

This is pretty well a direct hit, and there are many others given in Ullman, Krippner, and Vaughan's book *Dream Telepathy*, which gives a detailed account of the work of the Maimonides Dream Laboratory team. Research such as this, along with Dean's work with the plethysmograph, has corroborated Professor Broad's idea that telepathy may not be a

Right: in the same experiment the person sending the telepathic message also held this boxing glove to reinforce the image. Although the subject did not dream about boxing at all, his dreams that night showed strong feelings of aggression and violence, and the experiment was evaluated as a hit by researchers.

Below: this painting of a boxing scene by George Bellows was used in a dream telepathy experiment.

"Sheep and Goats"

Below: Dr. Gertrude Schmeidler. In the field of psychical research, she is best known for her "sheep and goats" experiments in which she demonstrated that believers do better in psi tests than do determined disbelievers.

paranormal phenomenen at all but rather a feature of everyday life which generally goes unrecognized.

So perhaps all of us are psychic. This is one of the conclusions that contemporary parapsychologists are reaching. Clearly, however, some are more psychic than others, and another major area of present day research is into the conditions and personality factors that favor psi functions.

The pioneer of this type of research is Dr. Gertrude Schmeidler of the City University of New York. In the late 1940s and early 1950s Dr. Schmeidler conducted thousands of clairvoyance experiments with standard Zener cards, asking each subject before the test began whether he or she believed that ESP was possible under the conditions of the experiment. The purpose of the question was to "separate the sheep from the goats." Believers in the possibility of ESP were called sheep and disbelievers goats. Analysis of thousands of runs showed that

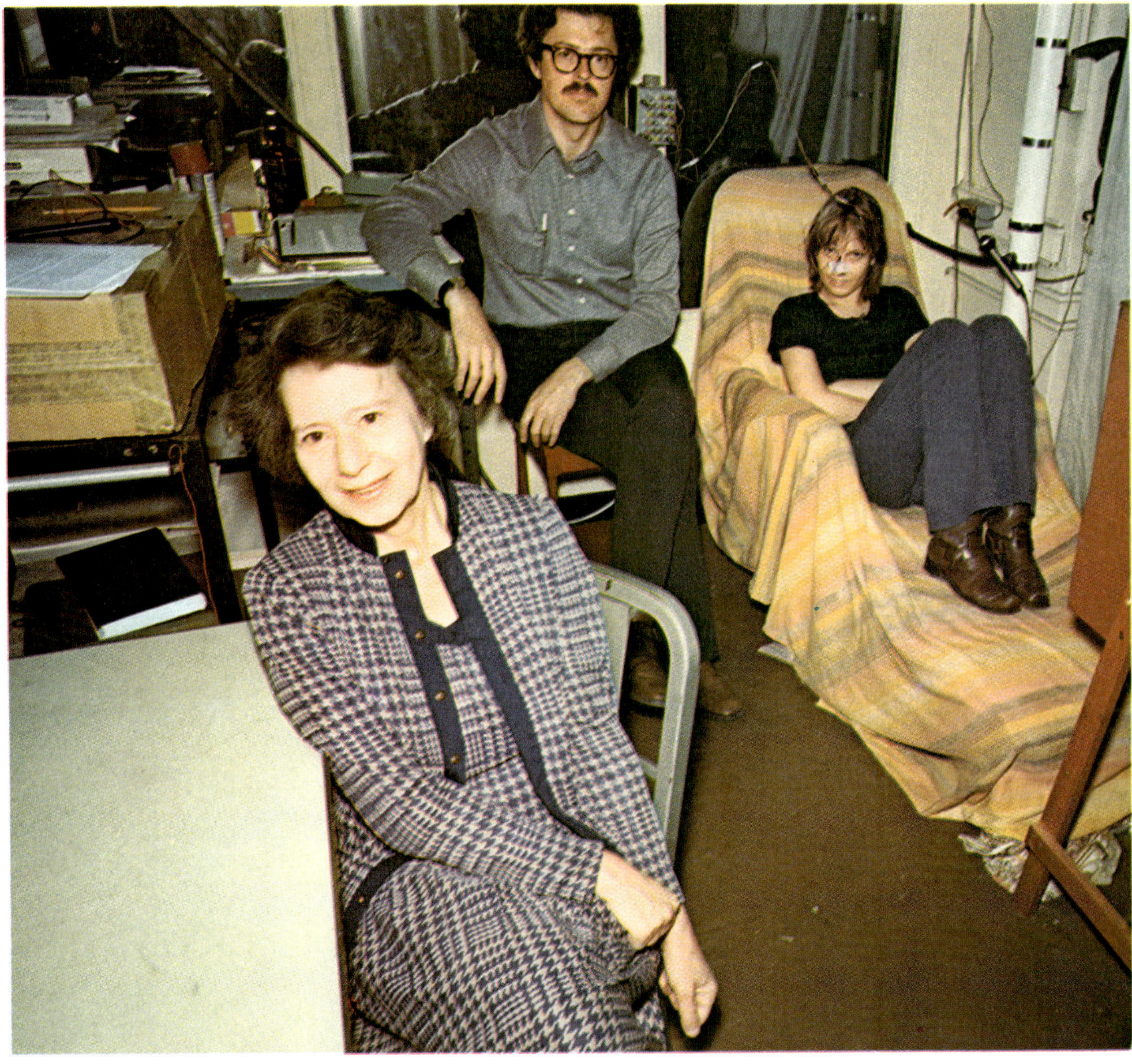

Far left: target picture used by Dr. Betty Humphrey in a test relating ESP and personality factors.

Left: a clairvoyant reproduction as drawn by an "expansive" person—the type that has been shown to score better in most ESP tests.

Below: the same target picture drawn clairvoyantly by a "compressive" person. Such people are less likely to have psi ability.

sheep consistently scored slightly above chance, while goats scored slightly below it. Belief in success appeared to have a positive influence on scoring, and disbelief a negative influence. Dr. Schmeidler also discovered that the difference between the two groups was sharpened by making the experimental conditions pleasanter for the sheep than for the goats.

Another early researcher into the effect of personality factors was Dr. Betty Humphrey of the Duke Parapsychology Laboratory. Before administering an ESP test she asked the subject to draw anything he wished on a blank sheet of paper. This is a standard psychological test. People who produce bold, uninhibited drawings using all available space are categorized as "expansive" types, and those who produce drawings that are small, timid, or conventional are categorized as "compressive." The terms correspond more or less to the more common ones of "extravert" and "introvert." Dr. Humphrey found that her expansive subjects consistently scored positively in standard ESP tests, whereas the compressives tended to score below chance.

Dr. Margaret Anderson and Rhea White carried research into the classroom in order to study the effect of interpersonal relations on psi functioning. They found that the highest scores were turned in by pupils who liked and were liked by the teacher who administered the test. Approximately chance results were obtained when the teacher-pupil relationship involved no particular feeling on either side, and significantly below chance results were obtained when the pupil and teacher positively disliked each other.

These relatively simple pioneer experiments of the 1940s and 1950s established that personality factors and interpersonal relationships affect psi functioning. A great deal more research has been and is still being done in this area, and it has become increasingly sophisticated.

All the experiments described so far were with subjects in normal states of consciousness. The next logical step after examining the factors that encourage psi in normal states was to find out whether deliberately induced alterations in states of

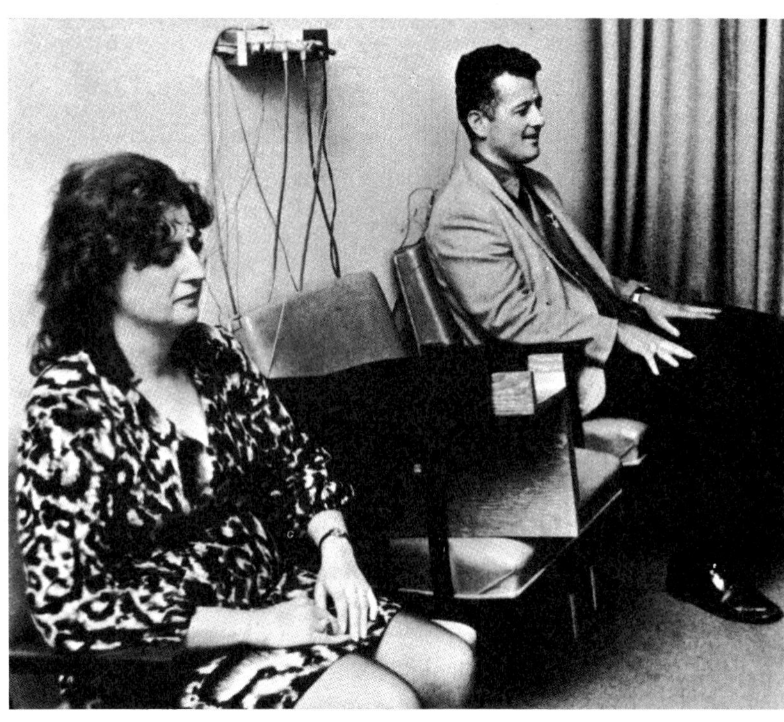

Above: two researchers connected with the American Society for Psychical Research watch the read-out on a polygraph machine during an experiment. The subjects, in another room, are trying to achieve an alpha state.

Above right: the subjects in the experiment. Their aim is to reach a state in which their brain transmits alpha waves. The electrodes fixed to their heads send their brain waves to the control room's polygraph machine.

consciousness would amplify the psi faculty. Rhine, in his early work at Duke, had discovered that the depressant drug sodium amytal adversely affects the psi faculty, and that the stimulant caffeine restores it to a normal level. Dr. Schmeidler went into hospitals and discovered that in the passive states of mind following concussion or childbirth psi functioning was significantly enhanced. Evidence from the fields of religion and anthropology, as well as early psychical research with mediums, testified to the fact that the trance state is conducive to psi. Now, with the development of the EEG and other electronic aids, it has become possible for a person after a little training to induce, at will, a state of mind favorable to psi.

The psi faculty has always been thought to be elusive and uncontrollable, but a new medical technique called "biofeedback" may succeed in bringing it under control. The principle of biofeedback is that a person who is provided with immediate knowledge of his internal body processes can learn to control some that normally operate involuntarily. In a typical biofeedback session a subject sits comfortably in a chair with electrodes attached to the back of the head, right forearm, and two fingers of the right hand. He wears a special jacket equipped with a respiration gauge. He aims to self-regulate muscle tension, body temperature, and brain wave rhythm. The electrodes detect changes in these internal states and relay the information back to the subject by means of three bars of light on a screen in front of him. The bars, like that of a mercury thermometer, become taller or shorter in response to changes in the physiological state that each is monitoring.

The subject first aims to achieve complete relaxation, and can watch the progress of this effort on the feedback meter wired to the muscle in his forearm. Having achieved this, he concentrates

Studying the Alpha State

Left: biofeedback moves into the commercial field through a group called Silva Mind Control, an American organization which conducts sessions leading to "functioning in the alpha." This is a group of Silva graduates.

on raising temperature, while the electrodes attached to his fingers measure his success and relay the information to the second bar on the screen. He then tries to induce an extremely calm yet alert state of consciousness that is characterized by distinctive patterns of brain activity called alpha rhythms. When the subject manages to produce alpha rhythms for a period of 10 seconds the third bar on the screen rises to its maximum height.

An alpha state has been found to be the state of consciousness most favorable to psi functioning. In 1971 Charles Honorton ran a significant experiment with subjects who had been trained to put themselves into an alpha state. It was a straightforward clairvoyance card test, but each subject was required to go through two series of guesses. For the first series, the subject lay in a semidark room with his eyes closed, and made his guesses when the EEG indicated that he was in an alpha state. For the second series he sat with open eyes under bright light—conditions which inhibit the production of alpha rhythms. The results showed a consistent and highly significant difference between the scores attained under the different conditions, and demonstrated that the alpha state of profound calm combined with alertness is especially favorable for the occurrence of psi.

Dr. Elmer Green of the Menninger Foundation in Topeka, Kansas, is an expert on biofeedback and voluntary control of internal states. He has conducted experiments with two masters of mind-body control, the Indian yogi Swami Rama, and the American mystic Jack Schwarz. Swami Rama demonstrated control of the arteries in his wrist by simultaneously warming up one spot on the palm of his hand and cooling another spot only two inches away until there was a difference of 9°F between them. He slowed down his heartbeats from 70 a minute to 52,

Above: as part of biofeedback tests, Dr. Elmer Green of the Menninger Foundation prepares the well-known Indian yogi Swami Rama for a test in which he will record his brain waves. He hopes to determine how the Swami exerts control over his normal physical reactions.

taking less than a minute to effect the change. Then, for the sake of the experiment and to demonstrate what yogic training could achieve, he offered to stop his heartbeat completely for three or four minutes. Dr. Green said that an arrest of 10 seconds would be enough to prove his point, and the Swami promptly obliged, but extended the period to 17 seconds. This made some of the observers start to panic. He also demonstrated what he called "yogic sleep." He went into a deep sleep, snoring gently, and the EEG showed heavy delta waves that are characteristic of a mental state of total oblivion to the world. Every five minutes a laboratory assistant made a statement in a very low voice. When the prearranged period of 25 minutes had elapsed, Swami Rama promptly sat up and repeated word for word every statement that the assistant had made. It was as if he had been deeply asleep and wide awake at the same time.

Jack Schwarz, says Green, is "one of the greatest talents in the country and probably the world in the realm of voluntary bodily controls." In his early teens he was drawn to Eastern philosophy and began to practice meditation regularly. He taught himself to perform many of the feats attributed to Hindu and Muslim fakirs. At the age of 16 he was able to lie on

Biofeedback and Yogic Sleep

Left: yoga has traditionally been a method by which students gain conscious control of their involuntary actions. The techniques of Eastern meditation are now being scientifically measured and investigated in many prominent Western laboratories.

a bed of sharp nails and to allow a man to stand on his stomach while he was doing so. At Green's laboratory he demonstrated his powers of pain control by allowing burning cigarettes to be held against his forearm, and by driving a knitting needle through his biceps. When the needle was removed a little blood appeared, but Schwarz said, "Now it stops," and the bleeding immediately stopped. While he was performing these and similar feats, the EEG recorded a steady production of alpha rhythms.

According to Green, both Swami Rama and Jack Schwarz are able to report correctly on the past, present, and future conditions, both physical and mental, of people they do not know and have never seen. Schwarz claims also to be able to read people's auras. He amazed a visiting psychiatrist at the Menninger Foundation by giving a detailed account of the doctor's own medical history and condition.

Anyone, says Schwarz, can do what he does. It is a matter of training and practice. Today, with the EEG and biofeedback techniques, the training can be greatly speeded up. Some years ago the so-called autonomic physiological systems, which include blood flow, temperature, and brain waves, were thought to be inaccessible to control by the will, but today students can

Above: Lawrence LeShan, who set up the experiments with medium Eileen Garrett in an independent investigation into the powers of sensitives. He also taught himself to be a psychic healer, mainly by using techniques of meditation.

learn to regulate them after just a few training sessions. There are indications that psi faculties may also be brought under control by similar methods.

A man who has developed psychic faculties in himself and others without using the biofeedback method is the New York psychologist Lawrence LeShan. In an important recent book *The Medium, the Mystic and the Physicist*, LeShan describes how he made himself a psychic healer. His training as an experimental psychologist predisposed him to believe that the alleged evidence for the paranormal "must be due to bad experimental design, false memories, hysteria, and chicanery." On the other hand, he thought that if the evidence were valid it could be of tremendous importance for science and life, and he decided to try to discover the truth for himself. He remembered that the great French chemist Lavoisier had stated authoritatively that meteorites were an impossible fable because it was obvious that there were no stones in the sky, and LeShan didn't want to risk committing a similar error by dismissing psi as impossible just because it didn't fit in with prevailing scientific ideas of reality.

LeShan started his independent inquiry by investigating the evidence provided by sensitives. (The term "sensitive" is generally used instead of "medium" today because it doesn't suggest an intermediary between the world of the living and the spirits of the dead.) He was fortunate in that one of the most gifted, serious, and respected sensitives of modern times, the late Eileen Garrett, was then living in New York and willing to cooperate with him. He spent more than 500 hours questioning Eileen Garrett and designed several experiments in which she willingly participated. On one occasion when Mrs. Garrett was in Florida and LeShan was going to join her the following day, he prepared an experiment in psychometry in advance. While in his office in New York, he collected several different objects including an old Greek coin, a woman's comb, a fossil fish, a bit of stone from Mt. Vesuvius, a scrap of bandage, and an ancient Babylonian clay tablet. He wrapped each object in tissue, sealed it in a small box, and put the box into a manila envelope. Another person put the envelopes, which were numbered, into larger envelopes marked with different numbers. This person had the list of both code numbers but did not know which objects were in which envelopes. Thus, no one, including LeShan, could convey any information about the content of any envelope to Eileen Garrett. Mrs. Garrett was to be given the envelopes in turn and would attempt to describe details of the history of the object it contained.

While assembling the materials LeShan found that he needed another box, so he went to a neighboring office and asked a secretary, whom he only knew by sight, if she could provide one. The secretary went into his office to find out what size of box would be needed, and in the course of their conversation she picked up and examined the clay tablet. A suitable box was found in LeShan's own office, and he forgot the whole small incident. Two weeks later and 1500 miles away, LeShan and Eileen Garrett tried the psychometry experiment. She picked up an envelope—later found to contain the clay tablet—and immediately said there was "a woman associated with this." She described the secretary in such detail, LeShan says, that it would have been possible to pick her out of a line-up of 10,000 women. She even mentioned two scars that proved to be there.

Such evidence as this convinced LeShan of the reality of paranormal faculties. After examining the testimony of Eileen Garrett and other sensitives, as well as the writings of the great mystics and some modern physicists, he formulated a theory that two distinct orders of reality exist. One he called "Sensory Reality" and the other "Clairvoyant Reality." Paranormal faculties develop, he says, when a person moves out of the Sensory and into the Clairvoyant Reality. The difference between the two is largely a difference of thought and attitude, of ways of looking at the world. Most of us live most of the time on the level of Sensory Reality, basing our thoughts on the information conveyed through our senses. We see people and things as separate entities, and we consider the most important things about them to be the properties that make them individual. From the other point of view, that of Clairvoyant Reality, the important thing about an individual is her relationship to the rest of the universe. All beings—and even inanimate substances like rock, water, and earth—are seen as parts of a whole. Time, also, is perceived differently; it does not necessarily flow in one direction at an even pace. Our everyday concepts of past, present and future are seen as illusions.

Two Distinct Orders of Reality

In distinguishing and describing these two kinds of reality, LeShan quotes several modern physicists. The atomic physicist J. Robert Oppenheimer, for example, acknowledged the existence of two realities in these words: "These two ways of thinking, the way of time and history and the way of eternity and timelessness, are both parts of man's efforts to comprehend the world in which he lives. Neither is comprehended in the other nor

Left: Mrs. Eileen J. Garrett, one of the most famous mediums of the 20th century. Interested in trying to understand her own psychic gifts, she cooperated fully with LeShan and other psychical researchers who tested her.

Parapsychology - a Science of Today

reducible to it. They are, as we have learned to say in physics, complementary views, each supplementing the other, neither telling the whole story."

Having provisionally accepted the existence of a separate plane of reality in which psi is possible, LeShan wanted to test this theory with reference to a particular aspect of psi. He chose psychic healing as his area of study. After reading the available literature on the subject and observing and talking with a number of healers, he came to the conclusion that there are two basic types of psychic healing. In Type 1 the healer goes into an altered state of consciousness in which he views himself and the patient as one. He doesn't touch the patient, or attempt to do anything; he just concentrates on a sense of being at one with the patient and with the universe, and on deep intense caring. In Type 2 the healer tries to heal, to turn on a flow of energy. He lays his hands on the patient's body on either side of the affected area, and often the patient remarks that he feels heat in that part of his body.

LeShan then began to train himself to achieve the state of consciousness required for Type 1 healing. His goal was to attain awareness of Clairvoyant Reality and in that state to become one with the patient for a few moments. His training consisted of learning to meditate. After a period of a year and a half, he learned to achieve a state of mind in which he could heal.

His attempts were not always successful. He also points out that when healing did take place, it might in some cases be due to other causes. Yet in many cases the positive biological changes that occurred seemed almost certainly due to the healing encounter. Sometimes he supplemented the Type 1 approach with a Type 2 laying on of hands, frequently with successful results.

As a scientist LeShan couldn't accept a successful experiment as valid unless it was repeatable. It was possible, he suggested, that he had been a natural psychic healer all along without realizing it. If the technique he had developed was the cause of his success, then it should work for others, he reasoned.

It does. Since 1970 LeShan has been holding training seminars for groups of psychologists and students, and many acts of healing have been carried out by these people in the course of the work. Various side-effects have been noticed, particularly intense telepathic communication between members of the groups and between healer and patient.

Le Shan's work is characteristic of some of the best being done in the area of parapsychology today, for it does not aim primarily to prove the existence of the psi faculties but rather to explore and develop them and to bring them into operation in daily life. It demands a degree of personal commitment and a shift of theoretical viewpoint that perhaps few orthodox scientists would be capable of. In the last analysis, however, such work is a genuine contribution to science, for it is bringing what was thought to be unknowable and unpredictable into the realm of the known and the controllable. It suggests that what today we call paranormal we may in the not too distant future regard as entirely normal.

The early psychical researchers asked, "Is there life after death?" Today's parapsychologists are asking, "Are there latent faculties in man that can be developed to enhance life *before* death?" And that is a revolution.

Opposite: trustees of the American Society for Psychical Research. Parapsychology has moved into a respectable middle age, recognized by scientists of all kinds as a challenging field for investigation.

Index

References to illustrations are shown by italics.

Picture Credits

Fievet/AAA 131; R. Magritte, *La Reconnaissance Infinie*, 1933 © by A.D.A.G.P., Paris, 1974 123; Aldus Archives 49, 59, 62, 64(L), 65, 70(R), 71, 76, 84, 87(L), 88; © Aldus Books 155, 187, 192, 193(R), (Mike Busselle) 135(B), (Gianetto Coppola) 60–61, 96–97, (Ann Dunn) 57, (Bruno Elettori) 140–141, (Dmitri Kasterine) 22, 112–115, 136(L), (Eileen Tweedy) 63, (John Webb) 146(T), (Bibliothèque de Troyes) 69(L), (Musée de Versailles) 70(L); Jean Overton Fuller, *The Magical Dilemma of Victor Neuburg*, W. H. Allen & Co., Ltd., London, 1965 78; Archiv Gerstenberg, Frankfurt 149; Milan Ryzl, *Hellsehen in Hypnose*, published by Ariston Verlag, Geneva, formerly Ramòn F. Keller 218–219; Ashmolean Museum, Oxford 85; Associated Press 110(L); Estate of J. G. Bennett 16(T); The Bettmann Archive, Inc. 184(L); Bibliothèque Nationale, Paris 54, 66–67; Reproduced by permission of the British Library Board 29, 32, 34(T), 36–38, 48; British Library (Photo R. B. Fleming © Aldus Books) 33; Reproduced by permission of the Trustees of the British Museum 82; Camera Press Ltd. 134(R), (E. J. Dingwall) 164(L); ed. John Symonds and Kenneth Grant, *The Confessions of Aleister Crowley*, Jonathan Cape Ltd., London, and Farrar, Straus & Giroux, Inc., New York 79, 92, 93(BR), 98–102, 104–105; Photos J.-L. Charmet 58, 137, 147, 166; Elda Hartley/ Colorific! 238, 246; Photo Dr. Lewis Creed 15; Milbourne Christopher, *Seers, Physics and ESP* with permission of Thomas Y. Crowell Co., Inc., 1970 185; John Cutten 134(L), 151, 193(L); John Cutten and Dr. Helmut Schmidt 206(T); *Daily Telegraph* Colour Library 139, 153; Photo John Freeman © Aldus Books, By courtesy of the Trustees of the Dickens House Museum 142; Trevor H. Hall, *The Strange Case of Edmund Gurney*, Gerald Duckworth & Co. Ltd., London 154(L); Jule Eisenbud, *The World of Ted Serios* 118–119; Dr. Christopher Evans 232(T); Mary Evans Picture Library 52, 124, 146(B), 148(T), 152; Field Museum of Natural History, Chicago 121(R); Haakon Forwald 206(B), 207; Frater Volo Intellegere 90; Leif Geiges, Staufen, Germany 108–109, 164(R), 186, 189(L), 191, 194–195, 200–201, 221(L), 226, 249; Musée du Louvre, Paris/Photo Giraudon 64(R); Reproduced by Gracious Permission of Her Majesty The Queen 28; Raghubir Singh/ The John Hillelson Agency 41; From J. G. Bennett, *Witness: The Story of a Search*, Hodder and Stoughton Limited, London, 1962 14; Michael Holford Library Photo 50, 81; Institut für Grenzgebiete der Psychologie und Psychohygiene, Freiburg 135(T); The Institute of Parapsychology, Durham, North Carolina 158–159, 188, 189(R), 202–205, 210, 243; Alix Jeffry 196–197, 244, 248; © Yale Joel 1974 8–11(C), 12–13, 116; Photo by Ann Johnson. Taken at the American Society for Psychical Research 132; From Rolf Alexander, M.D. *The Power of the Mind*, T. Werner Laurie, Ltd., London, 1956 23; Gunther Leeb 230; Montague Ullman, Stanley Krippner, and Alan Vaughan, *Dream Telepathy*. Reprinted with permission of Macmillan Publishing Co., Inc., New York, © 1973 240, 241(T); MacQuitty International Collection 68; The Mansell Collection, London 30(L), 35, 73, 75, 89, 95, 144–145; The Metropolitan Museum of Art. Catherine D. Wentworth Fund, 1950 27; Bretos Y Miro 20–21; Janet Mitchell 133; Courtesy Thelma Moss, Neuro-psychiatric Institute, University of California 231, 232(B), 233; Vincent van Gogh: *The Starry Night* (1889). Oil on canvas 29 × 36¼ inches. Collection, The Museum of Modern Art, New York. Acquired through the Lillie P. Bliss Bequest 51; National Gallery of Art, Washington, Gift of Chester Dale 241(B); National Gallery of Ireland 94; National Portrait Gallery, London 156; Nordisk Pressefoto, Copenhagen 165; Photos courtesy of S. Ostrander and L. Schroeder 221(R)–224; © Paraphysical Laboratory, Downton, Wiltshire 225, 227; Reproduced with permission of *Parapsychology Review* © by Parapsychology Foundation, New York 130; Harry Price Library, University of London 46–47, 160–163, 170–174, 175(B)–179, 182(T), 183; *Psychic News* 136(R); Psycho-Physical Research Foundation 120, 121(L); René Fulop-Muller, *Rasputin, the Holy Devil*, G. P. Putnam's Sons, 1928 74; *Radio Times* Hulton Picture Library 69(R), 103, 148(B), 150, 154(R), 168; Rex Features Ltd. 110(R), 247; Christopher McIntosh, *Eliphas Lévi and the French Occult Revival*, Rider & Co., London, 1972 86; Roger-Viollet 87(R), 167, 175(R), 198; Photo Donald Cooper for the Royal Shakespeare Company 34(B); Siena Cathedral/Scala 80; Upton Sinclair, *Mental Radio, Does It Work, and How*, 1930 127–129; Francis King, *Ritual Magic in England*, Neville Spearman Ltd., London, 1970 93(T); *The Gospel of Sri Ramakrishna*, translated by Swami Nikhilananda, Sri Ramakrishna Math, Mylapore, Madras, 1957 44; Süddeutscher Verlag-Bilderdienst, München 31; © Time Inc. 1975, Henry Groskinsky 106, *Life*, (A. Eisenstaëdt) 16(B), 17, (Don Snyder) 19, (Julien Wasser) 111, *Time Magazine* (Bill Eppridge) 216, (Henry Groskinsky) 2, 138, 180, 184(R), 209, 211, 234, (Valerie Shustov) 228, (Don Snyder) 208, 237, 242, 245, 251, (John Zimmerman) 239; © Time Inc. 1976 (Henry Groskinsky) 215; Courtesy Feliks Topolski 182(B); Transworld 212–213; UPI Photos, New York 229; Gustav Geley, *Clairvoyance and Materialisation*, T. Fischer Unwin Limited, London, 1927 169; Victoria & Albert Museum, London (British Crown Copyright) 45, (Photos Eileen Tweedy © Aldus Books) 18, 24, 30(R), 56; From André Sollier and Zsolt Györbiró, *Japanese Archery: Zen in Action*, John Weatherhill, Inc., Tokyo 42–43; Colin Wilson 11(B)

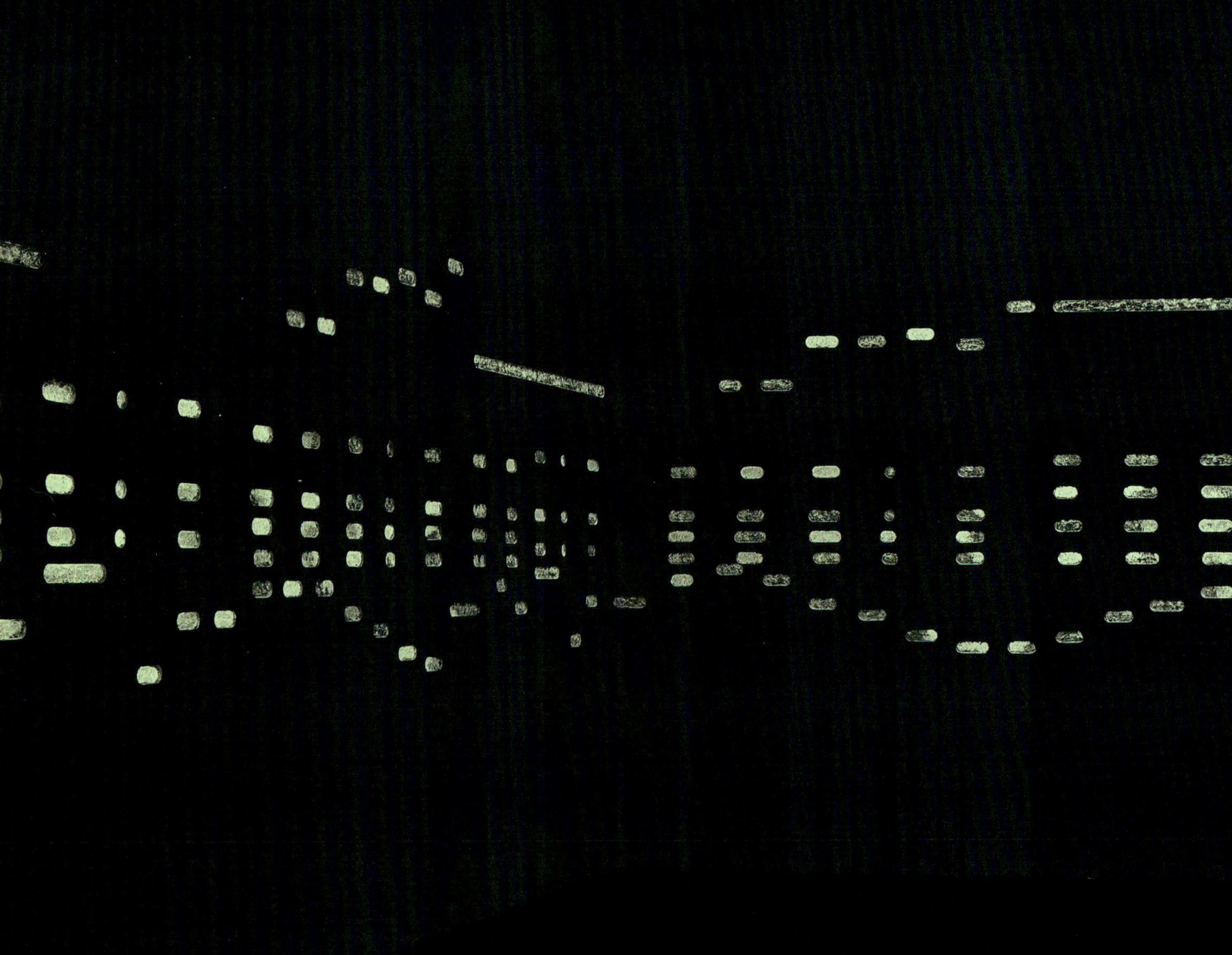

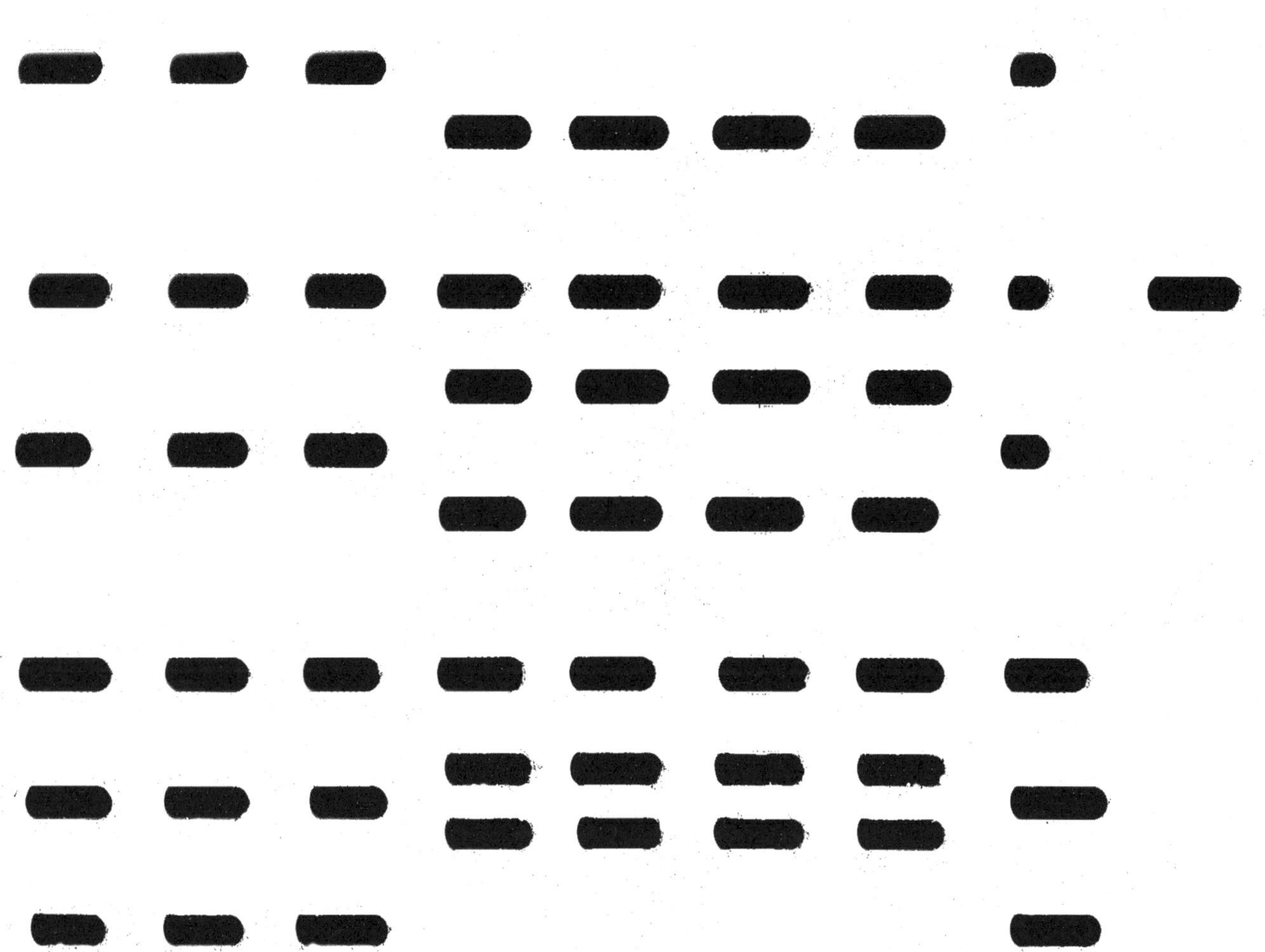

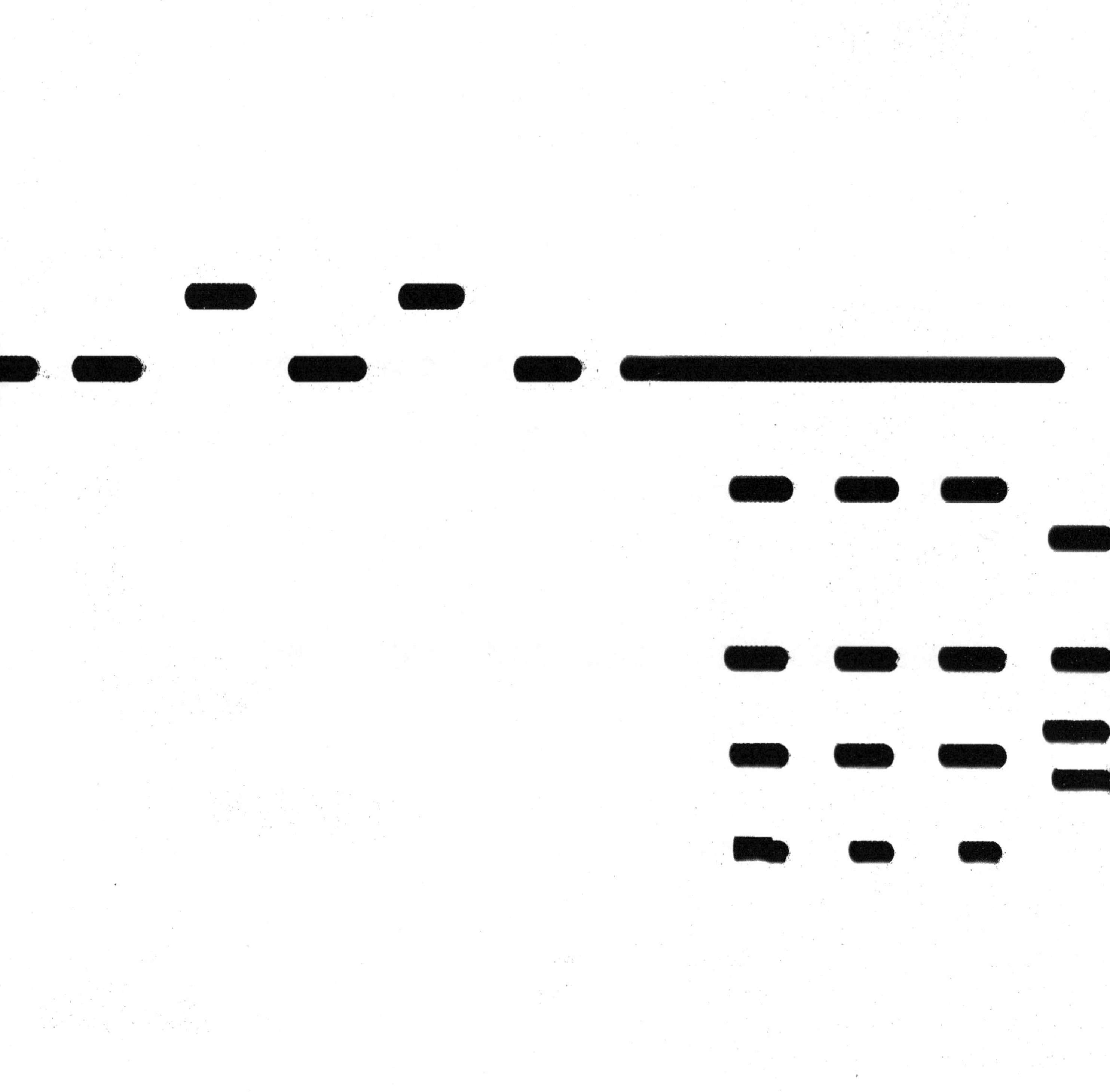

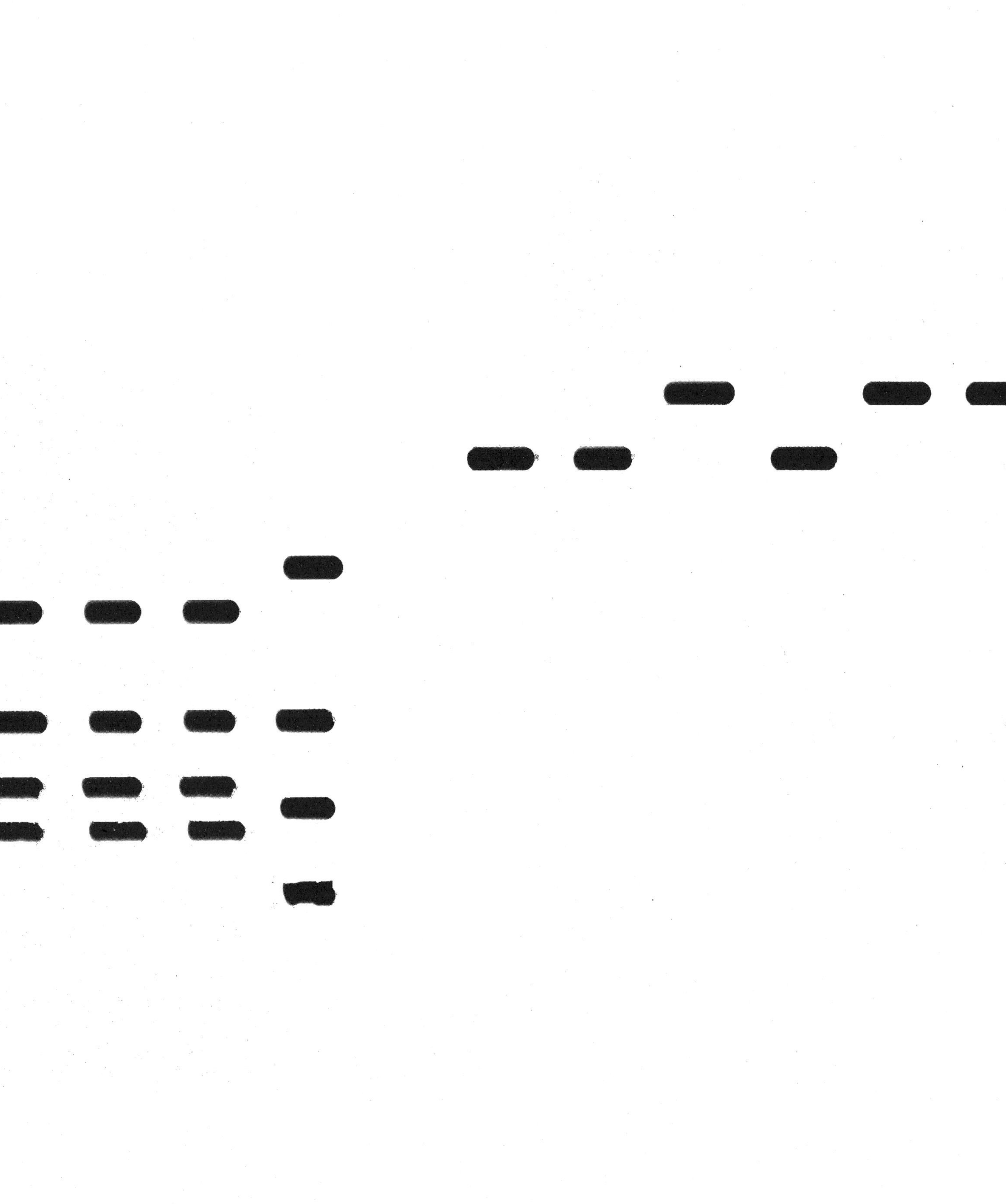

CONTENTS

DIRECTORS' FOREWORD

The Serpentine Gallery is delighted to present this exhibition dedicated to the work of leading artist Anri Sala (born 1974, Tirana). Since the late 1990s, Sala has worked predominantly with the moving image; his early videos and films mined his personal experience to reflect on the social and political change taking place in his native Albania. More recently, Sala has attached a growing importance to sound, creating remarkable works in which he recasts its relationship with the image. Linked to this development is Sala's long-standing interest in performance, and particularly musical performance, which is keenly felt through this exhibition as well as in earlier works such as *Mixed Behaviour*, 2003, and *Now I See*, 2004. A central premise of this exhibition is that most of the works presented at the Serpentine either use a live performance as their starting point or could lead to a performance in the future. This thread is developed further in this publication, which features a selection of Sala's earlier 'scores' including *A Spurious Emission*, 2007, *Ulysses*, 2007, and *5 Flutterbyes*, 2007/2010.

The exhibition is conceived as a cycle, or loop, structured around pairs of works that echo each other. *Answer Me*, 2008, was filmed in the abandoned dome of a Buckminster Fuller-designed surveillance station and uses the structure's unique architecture to investigate the effect of space on the production of sound. The dome's distinctive echo, triggered in the film by a man playing the drums in the large, empty space, drowns out all of the dialogue spoken by the female character, with the exception of the words that give the film its title. The siting of this work in the Serpentine's central gallery, itself with a domed ceiling, draws a parallel between the space of the film and the space of the exhibition. Similarly, the drum that is 'played' by the dome's echo in *Answer Me* appears in the first room of the exhibition as *Doldrum*, a snare drum activated by the inaudible low frequencies of the film's soundtrack.

Two of Sala's most recent films deconstruct and reconfigure a well-known punk song. In *Le Clash*, 2010, performers outside a derelict concert hall in Bordeaux play renditions of the song *Should I Stay or Should I Go* through a barrel organ and a music box. While in *Tlatelolco Clash*, 2011, shown for the first time at the Serpentine, figures among the ruins of the Tlatelolco area of Mexico City randomly insert fragments of a musical score into a barrel organ, creating a disjointed version of the same song. Both films play at the same time in the exhibition, the continuous and disjointed renditions of the song echoing each other across the space. Accompanying *Le Clash* is *No Window No Cry*, 2010, a music box fitted in a window, which allows visitors to add a further layer to the film's soundtrack. For *Score*, the barrel organ's score is given a different form. The perforated pattern is carved through walls covering the windows, translating sound into a different materiality and creating openings to the outside that allow the sounds of the park and the gallery to intertwine.

Long Sorrow, 2005, filmed on the eponymous public housing estate in Berlin, is an enigmatic record of a performance orchestrated by the artist. Sala invited noted free jazz musician Jemeel Moondoc to perform while suspended on a platform located outside the window of an apartment on the eighteenth floor of the building. The film was the starting point for a series of live performances that culminated recently in the project *3-2-1*, 2011, in which Sala invited saxophonist Andre Vida to respond live to an audio recording of Moondoc improvising along with his own earlier performance in *Long Sorrow* (resulting in a 'trio'). Vida then played live with the film (a 'duet') and finally performed a solo. *3-2-1* is restaged at the Serpentine, punctuating the fixed cycle of the show with an unpredictable and improvised element and integrating the strands of film and performance that run through Sala's recent work.

We are thrilled that Anri Sala accepted our invitation to show his work at the Serpentine. It has been a great pleasure and a privilege to work with him to realise his vision for this exhibition and we cannot thank him enough for his thoughtful engagement throughout every stage of the project. We are also grateful to Sala for very generously producing a beautiful Limited Edition to accompany the exhibition and for allowing the Gallery to benefit from its sale. Sound echoes and relocates throughout the Serpentine's spaces charting a path through this exhibition. Sala worked closely with Olivier Goinard to mix the soundtracks of each film for the Serpentine and we are indebted to them both for realising this remarkable element of the show. We have benefitted greatly from the involvement of Lewin Quehl from Anri Sala's studio, whose skill and experience was invaluable in the planning and installation of the exhibition. We would also like to thank Frank Bode for lending his considerable technical expertise.

The LUMA Foundation has generously supported *Anri Sala* and we extend our heartfelt thanks to the Foundation, and to Maja Hoffmann in particular, for playing such a vital role in making it possible for the Serpentine to deliver this ambitious exhibition and for their continued support of all of the Gallery's programmes.

The Council of the Serpentine Gallery is an extraordinary group of individuals whose involvement is critical to the success of the Gallery. We are enormously grateful to the members of the Council for their sustained commitment.

We are very fortunate to have been able to rely on the support and advice of Hauser & Wirth throughout the development of this project. We extend our warm thanks to Iwan and Manuela Wirth and to their team at the Gallery.

We are indebted to the group of exhibition patrons who share a passion for Sala's work and have come together in support of this exhibition, including Ramdane Touhami and Zumtobel Group. We would also like to thank Agnès Troublé and the agnès b. London, Endowment Fund for their important contribution toward the realisation of this project. *The Independent* is the Gallery's media partner and we are grateful to the paper for helping to bring the Serpentine's programme to a larger audience. We would also like to gratefully acknowledge Galerie Chantal Crousel, Paris; Marian Goodman Gallery, New York; and kurimanzutto, Mexico City, who have provided important assistance in producing the exhibition.

Sala's frequent collaborator Quentin Walesch has conceived and designed this catalogue with the artist and our heartfelt thanks go to him for overseeing every aspect of this handsome publication. We remain grateful to Michael Fried for his insightful study of Sala's work *Mixed Behaviour* and to Joshua Simon whose essay provides a fascinating introduction to recent developments in the artist's work. We would also like to thank Andre Vida for his assistance in realising *3-2-1* and for his commitment to this part of the exhibition from an early stage. We are also delighted that Vida participated in an interview with the artist for this catalogue. Finally, we would like to acknowledge the team at the Serpentine who produced this exhibition. Kathryn Rattee, Exhibition Curator, Mike Gaughan, Gallery Manager, Sally Tallant, Head of Programmes, and Claire Feeley, Assistant Curator, have worked closely alongside all members of the wider team to realise this project and we thank them for their enthusiasm and commitment.

Julia Peyton-Jones
Director, Serpentine Gallery
and Co-Director, Exhibitions & Programmes

Hans Ulrich Obrist
Co-Director, Exhibitions & Programmes
and Director, International Projects

Inversion – Creating Space Where There Appears To Be None (Anri Sala), 2010

Tirana Rally Speech.doc Page 2 of 2

citizen seriously and vote on June 28th. Vote for change. Vote for the new politics. Vote for the new spirit of Albania. Vote for your children and grandchildren. Vote your h[illegible] and dreams. Vote. Thank you.

Students

Vote stealing

Emigrants

Paving roads

http://mail.google.com/mail/?ui=1&[illegible]w=att&th=1221191d2a4c63df&attid=0.2&disp=va[illegible] 6/26/2009

Inversion – Creating Space Where There Appears To Be None (Edi Rama), 2010

Intervista (Finding the Words), 1998
(Transcript)

Tirana, 1998

Anri Sala: Mum, I have a surprise for you.
Valdet Sala: I'm wary of your surprises. Come sit down!
Anri Sala: I was unpacking my things from the moving cartons, and I found a reel of film.
Valdet Sala: What a surprise! I didn't know we had this film. It's from the time I was a militant.
Enver Hoxha, regime boss
Valdet Sala: So that's your surprise...
Anri Sala: Are you moved?
Valdet Sala: I don't think so.
Anri Sala: Do you remember? What year was it?
Valdet Sala: In '77, I think. 20 years ago
Anri Sala: What was it?
Valdet Sala: The Albanian Youth Congress.
Anri Sala: How old were you?
Valdet Sala: I'm 52 now... minus 20... I was 32.
Anri Sala: You remember what you were saying in the interview?
Valdet Sala: No. I'd be curious to know.
Anri Sala: There is no soundtrack.
Valdet Sala: Too bad the sound's lost. I don't remember, but – Oh, Pushkin. It's Pushkin Lubonia.
Anri Sala: Is he still in Albania?
Valdet Sala: I think so. Funny, I don't remember him interviewing me.
\- - -
Anri Sala: Hello, is this Mr. Lubonia's residence? May I speak to Pushkin? – This is Anri Sala, Valdet's son. I think you know her. – I'm a film student in Paris. – I found an interview with my mother from the late '70's, in which you figure. I would like to meet you, and film you, if possible. – Because you're a witness and you can help me find the text. – No, it's not for television! It's a personal project. It's for a film school.
Pushkin Lubonja: I did over 2000 interviews. What could I tell you! In all my interviews, even the one with your mother, my questions were foreseeable, just like all the answers. Even the TV audiences could predict the contents of the interview. The questions were set in advance. You could only give positive answers.
\- - -
Todi Lubonja: What happened to the sound?
Anri Sala: I only found the picture.
Todi Lubonja: And why isn't there any colour?
Anri Sala: The film's in black and white.
Todi Lubonja: Let me have a look. I will tell you which congress it is.
Liri Lubonja: You can tell from the First Secretary.
Todi Lubonja: It might be '78. We were gone by then.

Liri Lubonja: Just as I said, we have to see who the Secretary was. If it was Mero or Monari or Bardhi.
Todi Lubonja: Pirro, you old devil!
Liri Lubonja: God rest your soul. – And that's Leka! – That looks like Pipi.
Todi Lubonja: Where?
Liri Lubonja: Behind Fiqirete.
Todi Lubonja: I don't think so.
Anri Sala: Then you weren't at this congress.
Liri Lubonja: No, it was held after our expulsion. We didn't even know it was taking place. Liri and Todi Lubonja were sentenced to 16 years in prison, after having been members of the Party's Central Committee at the head of the Albanian Youth Union.
- - -
Anri Sala: You were the soundman for the interview. And now you're a taxi driver.
Taxi driver: I'm one of the pioneers of the Kinostudio. I worked there for more than 30 years. I wasn't fired. I left for financial reasons. My pay was ridiculously low, prices were rising, so I bought this car and became a cabbie.
Anri Sala: Why is there no sound in the interview?
Taxi driver: We didn't film then as you film now. We didn't have a synch sound here.
Picture and soundtrack were separate. The camera on the one side, the tape recorder on the other. That's why the sound is missing. It was probably lost. At the time I was terrified of there being a technical hitch during interviews with the bosses of the nomenclatura. – Nowadays, there's the fear of the street, robberies, muggings, it's another kind of fear. I prefer this new fear, because it has an end. The other was endless, it only stopped with death.
- - -
'This meeting was held to clearly express the polticial situation of the country, in terms of the struggle against imperialism, revisionism and the two superpowers, which is only possible with the Marxist-Leninist Party. And only if youth unites its efforts under the guardianship of the Marxist-Leninist Party….'
- - -
'…examining the current political situation, not only in certain countries, but around the world as well, and by discussing problems, we can appreciate the importance of a people's revolutionary movement.'
Valdet Sala: I don't believe this! It's absurd! I just can't believe it! It's just spouting words. There's no sense to it.
I know how to express myself!
Anri Sala: Look, Mom. I had deaf-mutes decipher it. They are the only ones who can.
I'll read the subtitles, while you read your lips.
Valdet Sala: It's not the political view, but it makes no sense.
Anri Sala: Read your lips, Mom! …'was very clear… in terms of the struggle… against imperialism and the two superpowers…'
Valdet Sala: But it's gibberish!
Anri Sala: '…with the backing of the Marxist-Leninist Party… if the youth pools its efforts…'
Valdet Sala: Do I talk that way?
Anri Sala: '…the guardianship of the Marxist-Leninist Party…it will achieve victory…'
Valdet Sala: 'In this struggle.'
Anri Sala: '…in this struggle. Even if we follow the current political situation…'
Valdet Sala: Where?
Anri Sala: '…in certain countries…'

Valdet Sala: Not at all!
Anri Sala: There aren't any cuts in the film!
Valdet Sala: Those aren't my words.
Anri Sala: Sure, they are! Read your lips! I'll read the text.
- - -
Anri Sala: When did you do this interview?
Valdet Sala: It was after a Communist Youth Meeting.
Anri Sala: What about?
Valdet Sala: About the world revolution, so that all men would be equal, without oppression or exploitation. It still has a nice ring to it!
Anri Sala: Did you believe in that ideal?
Valdet Sala: I often asked myself those questions, where does compromise with power and one's self begin, and rebellion end?
Anri Sala: How do you feel about only deaf-mutes reading into your past?
Valdet Sala: It's an irony of fate!
Anri Sala: Do you see anything in common?
Valdet Sala: Yes, we were living in a deaf and dumb system, where we only spoke with one mouth and one voice. It's symbolic, because, in certain milieux, things were less strict. Among us, things were more open. You wrote a poem at 9 about your fear of politics. How could you have written it, if it had been against our family's beliefs? Things weren't all black and white. We could live, fall in love, have children. We thought, we'd change the world, and little by little, we lost everything. Our generation was the victim of past errors, whereas our parents were luckier. They'd just won the war, and everything was possible. Long live the revolutionary spirit! Vote for the Party on 20 September!
Valdet Sala: The positive side is you can learn from our experience in order to do things differently. If I could go back, I wouldn't act differently. I believed in what I was doing, that much I can say. I really believed.

For you, my motherland,
the loveliest song
I sing for you from the bottom of my heart.
For your mountains and wild valleys,
for you this motherland,
where I live happily today.
You are so beautiful
and full of greatness
of an impregnable fortress…
- - -
Liri Lubonja: I think there were several kinds of people. Those who knew what was going on, and those who continued to cling to their ideals. Your mother was a young militant, honest, sincere. I don't think she acted out of hypocrisy. She believed in those ideals, she really did. Then came the great disenchantment. We touched bottom in a system meant to create the ideal society.
Todi Lubonja: When someone couldn't find fish at the market, and he'd complain, he'd be tried for challenging authority and sentenced for threatening the State. So they'd throw him in prison. Had I asked him: 'Why are you here?' – 'I complained about the lack of fish.' That's how they legalized injustice, oppression and violence. We lived under 50

years of dictatorship. Dictatorships don't expose evil, they hide it. They hide crime. Dictatorships don't provide security, they impose a false sense of security.

- - -

Valdet Sala: The commandments of communism were to be honest, social-minded, idealistic, energetic, optimistic, etc. I was all of those things. I am still that way. And I still work for that today. So that society can be more social-minded, more attentive to the individual, more humane.

Anri Sala: And the enthusiasm in the archive footage was real?

Valdet Sala: I can talk to you about concrete experience, about the efforts of young people. We built all the orchard terraces, we built the northern roads, we built the railroads. It was real, Anri, because we were building. Then there was the phoney enthusiasm, the hysteria! The delirious enthusiasm of congresses and ceremonies. It was a forced enthusiasm, which had lost all its significance. It was a crowd's hysteria for its Leader, who was like an icon. The farther away the Leader was, the more mythic he seemed. The closer you got, the more banal he became, until he lost all significance.

Anri Sala: Mom, does my filming this bother you?

Valdet Sala: I don't know. If you weren't my son, I don't know if I'd have agreed. I have mixed feelings. I can't give you a simple answer. Personally it doesn't bother me, since I'm talking about a reality and my rapport with that reality which belongs to the past, and concerns the present as well.

- - -

'Albania is on the brink of civil war. Tanks are moving towards the southern cities held by armed rebel forces. The city of Vlora is torn by violent clashes, which claimed two more lives in the last few hours. The rebels demand the resignation of President Berisha just re-elected by the parliament. Albanians are preparing for their first cease-fire since the last world war.' 'Their money vanished in the local pyramid company bankruptcies. They led the revolt of the small investors. Hospital staff didn't know which way to turn nor how to treat victims of beatings or stray bullets.'

- - -

Valdet Sala: I'm frightened because I don't see a way out. I don't understand what's happening anymore. I'm frightened. I'm very confused! When I talk about the future, I'm thinking about those close to me, but also the country's future. The recent events have crushed lots of hopes. It's as if a destructive force had swept away all constructive energy. I'm frightened. I'm frightenend for you and me. For me what matters most is that you and your sister have a future. That's my greatest desire. My desire for a future for Albania is just as great. That's logical, since I can't see you apart from this country. If this country has a future, you'll have one too. But if it doesn't, neither will you. As they say in Albania: 'Ask for one thing, and you'll get two.' I think we've passed on to you the ability to doubt. Because you must always question the truth.

Intervista (Finding the Words), 1998

5 *Flutterbyes*, 2007/2010

5 Flutterbyes, 2007/2010
(Score assignment for five Butterflies and two Pinkertons)

B1: Vogliatemi bene, un bene piccolino, un bene da bambino quale a me si conviene.
B2: Vogliatemi bene, un bene piccolino, un bene da bambino quale a me si conviene.
B3: Vogliatemi bene, un bene piccolino, un bene da bambino quale a me si conviene.
B4: Vogliatemi bene, un bene piccolino, un bene da bambino quale a me si conviene.
B5: Vogliatemi bene, un bene piccolino, un bene da bambino quale a me si conviene.
P1:
P2:

B1: Vogliatemi bene, noi siamo gente avezza alle piccole cose umili e silenziose
B2: Vogliatemi bene, noi siamo gente avezza alle piccole cose umili e silenziose
B3: Vogliatemi bene, noi siamo gente avezza alle piccole cose umili e silenziose
B4: Vogliatemi bene, noi siamo gente avezza alle piccole cose umili e silenziose
B5: Vogliatemi bene, noi siamo gente avezza alle piccole cose umili e silenziose
P1:
P2:

B1: ad una tenerezza sfiorante e pur profonda come il ciel, come l'onda del mare.
B2: ad una tenerezza sfiorante e pur profonda come il ciel, come l'onda del mare.
B3: ad una tenerezza sfiorante e pur profonda come il ciel, come l'onda del mare.
B4: ad una tenerezza sfiorante e pur profonda come il ciel, come l'onda del mare.
B5: ad una tenerezza sfiorante e pur profonda come il ciel, come l'onda del mare.
B6: ad una tenerezza sfiorante e pur profonda come il ciel, come l'onda del mare.
P1:
P2:

B1:
B2:
B3:
B4:
B5:
P1: **Dammi ch'io baci le tue mani care. Mia But**terfly! Come t'han ben nomata
P2: Dammi ch'io baci le tue mani care. Mia **Butterfly! Come t'han ben nomata**

B1:
B2:
B3:
B4:
B5:
P1: **tenue** farfalla.
P2: tenue **farfalla.**

B1: **Dicon ch'oltre mare** se cade in man dell'uom, ogni farfalla da uno spillo é trafitta
B2: Dicon ch'oltre mare **se cade in man dell'**uom, ogni farfalla da uno spillo é trafitta
B3: Dicon ch'oltre mare se cade in man **dell'uom**, ogni farfalla da uno spillo é trafitta
B4: Dicon ch'oltre mare se cade in man dell'uom, **ogni farfalla** da uno spillo é trafitta
B5: Dicon ch'oltre mare se cade in man dell'uom, ogni farfalla **da uno spillo é trafitta**
P1:
P2:

B1: **ed in ta**vola infitta!
B2: ed in tavola infitta!
B3: ed in tavola infitta!
B4: ed in tavola infitta!
B5: ed in ta**vola infitta**!
P1: **Un po' di vero c'è. E tu lo sai per**ché? Perché non fugga **più**.
P2: Un po' di vero c'è. E tu lo sai **perché**? **Perché non fugga** più.

B1: Sì, per la vita.
B2: **Sì, per la** vita.
B3: Sì, per la vita.
B4: Sì, per **la vita**.
B5: Sì, **per la** vita.
P1: **Io t'ho ghermitta**… **Ti serro palpi**tante. Sei mia. **Vieni**, **vieni**.
P2: Io t'ho ghermitta… Ti serro palpi**tante. Sei mia.** **Vieni**, **vieni**.

B1:
B2:
B3:
B4:
B5:
P1: Via dall'anima in pena l'angoscia paurosa. É notte serena! Guarda, dorme ogni cosa!
P2: Via dall'anima in pena l'angoscia paurosa. É notte serena! Guarda, dorme ogni cosa!

B1: Ah! Dolce notte! Quante stelle! Non le vidi mai si belle!
B2: Ah! Dolce notte! Quante stelle! Non le vidi mai si belle!
B3: Ah! Dolce notte! Quante stelle! Non le vidi mai si belle!
B4: Ah! Dolce notte! Quante stelle! Non le vidi mai si belle!
B5: Ah! Dolce notte! Quante stelle! Non le vidi mai si belle!
P1: Vieni, vieni! É notte serena!
P2: Vieni, vieni! É notte serena!

B1:
B2:
B3:
B4:
B5:
P1: Vieni, vieni! É notte serena! Guarda, dorme ogni cosa!
P2: Vieni, vieni! É notte serena! Guarda, dorme ogni cosa!

B1: Dolce notte! Quante stelle! Non le vidi mai si belle! Trema, brilla ogni favilla
B2: Dolce notte! Quante stelle! Non le vidi mai si belle! Trema, brilla ogni favilla
B3: Dolce notte! Quante stelle! Non le vidi mai si belle! Trema, brilla ogni favilla
B4: Dolce notte! Quante stelle! Non le vidi mai si belle! Trema, brilla ogni favilla
B5: Dolce notte! Quante stelle! Non le vidi mai si belle! Trema, brilla ogni favilla
P1: Vieni, vieni! Vieni, vieni! Vieni
P2: Vieni, vieni! Vieni, vieni! Vieni

B1: col baglior d'una pupilla. Oh! Oh! quanti occhi fissi attenti
B2: col baglior d'una pupilla. Oh! Oh! quanti occhi fissi attenti
B3: col baglior d'una pupilla. Oh! Oh! quanti occhi fissi attenti
B4: col baglior d'una pupilla. Oh! Oh! quanti occhi fissi attenti
B5: col baglior d'una pupilla. Oh! Oh! quanti occhi fissi attenti
P1: sei mia! Via l'angoscia dal tuo cuor! Ti sento palpitante.
P2: sei mia! Via l'angoscia dal tuo cuor! Ti sento palpitante.

B1: d'ogni parte a riguardar! pei firmamenti, via pei lidi, via pel mare.
B2: d'ogni parte a riguardar! pei firmamenti, via pei lidi, via pel mare.
B3: d'ogni parte a riguardar! pei firmamenti, via pei lidi, via pel mare.
B4: d'ogni parte a riguardar! pei firmamenti, via pei lidi, via pel mare.
B5: d'ogni parte a riguardar! pei firmamenti, via pei lidi, via pel mare.
P1: É mia. Ah! Vien, vien, sei mia. Ah! Vieni, guarda, dorme ogni cosa.
P2: É mia. Ah! Vien, vien, sei mia. Ah! Vieni, guarda, dorme ogni cosa.

B1: Ah! quanti occhi fissi attenti, quanti sguardi
B2: Ah! quanti occhi fissi attenti, quanti sguardi
B3: Ah! quanti occhi fissi attenti, quanti sguardi
B4: Ah! quanti occhi fissi attenti, quanti sguardi
B5: Ah! quanti occhi fissi attenti, quanti sguardi
P1: Ti serro palpitante. Ah, vien! Guarda dorme ogni cosa.
P2: Ti serro palpitante. Ah, vien! Guarda dorme ogni cosa.

B1: ride il ciel! Ah! Dolce notte! Tutto estatico d'amor ride il ciel.
B2: ride il ciel! Ah! Dolce notte! Tutto estatico d'amor ride il ciel.
B3: ride il ciel! Ah! Dolce notte! Tutto estatico d'amor ride il ciel.
B4: ride il ciel! Ah! Dolce notte! Tutto estatico d'amor ride il ciel.
B5: ride il ciel! Ah! Dolce notte! Tutto estatico d'amor ride il ciel.
P1: Ah, vien! Ah, vieni, vieni! Ah, vien, ah, vien!
P2: Ah, vien! Ah, vieni, vieni! Ah, vien, ah, vien!

ANRI SALA

Joshua Simon

Translation is the language of Anri Sala. As Boris Buden and Stefan Nowotny write in their essay 'Cultural Translation':

> Etymologically, translation evokes an act of moving or carrying across from one place or position to another, or of changing from one state of things to another. This does not apply only to the words of different languages, but also to human beings and their most important properties. They too can be moved across all sorts of differences and borders and so translated from one place to another, for instance from one cultural and political condition to another. Thus, one can culturally translate people – for a political purpose and with existential consequences.[1]

Communicating voice into speech, sound into image, space into time, feelings into temperatures, exhaustion into virtuosity, breath into music, Sala's work is preoccupied with translation as a language.

Translation

It is said that the opening theme of the third movement of Mozart's *Piano Concerto No. 17 in G Major* is a transcription of the song of his pet starling. This anecdote helps shed light on Sala's work: the reversed relationship between music and score, the balance between random occurrence and meticulous formation, improvisation and virtuosity, are key to the way in which Sala's works operate. At the Serpentine Gallery, he plays with these relationships both between the works themselves and in relation to the exhibition space, its environment and visitors.

From *Intervista*, 1998, to *Tlatelolco Clash*, 2011, Sala proposes a reversal of transcription and performance through translation. In his video *Intervista*, he attempts to reconstruct the lost soundtrack of a film shot at the Albanian Youth Conference of 1977, in which his mother gave an interview as a young woman. Since she can no longer recall her statements, Sala embarks on an investigation that leads him to seek the help of lip-reading deaf-mutes. In this way, he is not only able to decipher his mother's words, but also to bring back a language that no longer exists – that of Albania's Communist past – to the degree-zero of pronunciation: the actual physical movement of the mouth. Yet this is not a mere restoration of sound back to image; it is also a reevaluation of the soundtrack through translation. Rephrasing, rewording, reapplying – these techniques are of key importance to Sala's work, since meaning,

1 Boris Buden and Stefan Nowotny, 'Cultural translation: An introduction to the problem, and Responses', in *Translation Studies*, Volume 2, Issue 2, 2009, p. 196. Since translation as a linguistic concept has come to dominate our concept of cultural exchange, Buden and Nowotny respond to Naoki Sakai's question: 'What sort of social relation is translation?', a question with which Sala's work also seems to be occupied.

we learn, is actually enhanced by translation. For Sala, there is no language but translation.[2]

Ulysses, 2007, and *Why The Lion Roars*, 2008, are both elaborate translation mechanisms that are enacted either by visitors to the installation or through the environmental conditions outside. In *Ulysses*, the notation for the drum section of an unreleased Franz Ferdinand song, interpreted by Sala and Jeremy Millar, can be performed by visitors. Sheets of paper with the song's lyrics are attached to screens in front of a drum kit, along with the instructions taken from onomatopoeic indicators in James Joyce's *Ulysses,* for when and how the drums should be struck. Each visitor performs an improvisation of a song that he or she does not yet know. *Why The Lion Roars* is a thermo-activated database containing dozens of movies. More than fifty feature films are continually programmed in relation to the outdoor temperature. Each film represents a degree from minus 10°C to plus 40°C. Thus the temperature outside is translated into a film projected inside. This kind of 'weather programming', as Sala calls it, a not-so-random shuffle, brings together different genres, allowing for new phrasings that abruptly cut some films while playing others repeatedly. Sala's channel-flipping machine translates narrative into event, sensation into subjectivity. As he told curator Raphaela Platow, regarding *Why The Lion Roars*: 'We share subjectivity, something we're not supposed to.'[3]

Describing Sala's use of sound and the way it takes over spaces, curator Marie Fraser has stated: 'He doesn't use sound to create a particular effect, as in cinema, but attempts rather to film the effect of a sound produced by a particular situation.'[4] This is true of the pair of works *Air Cushioned Ride*, 2006, and *A Spurious Emission*, 2007, where Sala followed the Mozartian logic of composing as mimicry. Based on Arizona radio transmissions, these two works share the same soundtrack, performed differently. The film *Air Cushioned Ride* is a single shot of a highway rest area full of freight trucks. As Sala's car circles them, their interference causes the radio to flicker between a country music station and the baroque music he was listening to. The process of constantly being in motion sets up a relationship between location and sound – when Sala drives to the east of the trucks, we hear the baroque music, and when he drives to their west, we hear country music. This kind of radio interference is called 'spurious emission', the title chosen by Sala for the companion piece, where he commissioned a composer to transcribe the soundtrack of *Air Cushioned Ride* as a musical score and then had it performed by a baroque trio and a country band. The translation

2 Following Roman Jakobson's statement that 'the meaning of any linguistic sign is its translation into some further, alternative sign', Buden and Nowotny write: 'translation is crucial for the actual putting into practice of any presumably homogeneous "sign system", and this not only with respect to distinct linguistic unities in the sense of Saussurian languages, but already at an intralingual level as a capacity of "rewording".' Ibid, p. 202.
3 Anri Sala in conversation with Raphaela Platow, in *Anri Sala: Purchase Not by Moonlight* (Museum of Contemporary Art, North Miami/Cincinnati Contemporary Arts Center, 2008), p. 22.
4 Marie Fraser, 'Filming Sound', in *Anri Sala* (Musée d'art contemporain de Montréal, 2011), p. 54.

of coincidence into performed musical notation is also the translation of spaces connected by sounds into sounds connected by space. The music is now played in an acoustic environment and what was overlapping is now chronological – sharing a space, the trio and the band play one after the other.

Exhibition

With translation as language we are dealing with a collective project of idiosyncrasy. This is realised in Sala's exhibition at the Serpentine Gallery through a juxtaposition of asynchronicity and polysynchronicity.

Showing alternately in the Serpentine's North Gallery are two films defined by architecture. In *Answer Me*, 2008, Richard Buckminster Fuller's geodesic domes for the Teufelsberg Intelligence Station, a relic of the Cold War era in West Berlin, produce a wonderful echo as a setting for the film's drama of aggression and miscommunication. In *Long Sorrow*, 2005, we see the saxophonist Jemeel Moondoc performing a free jazz improvisation while hanging out of an upper floor window in the *Langer Jammer* (Long Sorrow) apartment building in Berlin. Both films were inspired by their locations. They were scripted based on the drama the locations suggest through their effect on sound. By this, Sala inverted the process of scouting for a specific location for a film, instead developing the film based on a specific location.

Le Clash, 2010, and *Tlatelolco Clash*, 2011, showing in the Serpentine's East and West Galleries, feature the same Clash song, *Should I Stay Or Should I Go*. Shot outside the dilapidated La Salle de Fêtes in Bordeaux's Grand Parc, *Le Clash* features a dreamy rendering of the song played by a man walking alone with a music box and a couple carrying a barrel organ on a cart while singing parts of the chorus. The music they make echoes around the buildings as the man follows the sound. Both the couple and the man seem to be devoted to playing the song. As the man holds his music box tightly, we see the mechanism rolling inside. At one point, we also see the organ's punch cards piling up against a modernist mosaic in the background, which echoes their perforations. Sound is being *produced*: the song is not a soundtrack, but diegetic sound that comes from the scene itself.[5] Reminiscent of the characters in François Truffaut's 1966 adaptation of Ray Bradbury's novel *Fahrenheit 451*, who memorise novels, becoming living books, Sala's protagonists seem to have become receptacles for the music.

Tlatelolco Clash is based on a performance that Sala made at the opening of an exhibition featuring *Le Clash* in Mexico City.[6] The punch cards for *Should I*

5 Both the music box and barrel organ were enhanced by wireless microphones that fed speakers in La Salle de Fêtes, making the song into a kind of a sound sculpture. The film is based on a performance by Sala from 2009, *Tease tease tease*, which took place in front of and around the mosaic facade of the building. In the performance and the film, the music from the music box and barrel organ, together with the echoing speakers from inside La Salle de Fêtes, creates an un-equilibrated stereo of asymmetrical synchronicity.

6 Sala named the performance *Invitations*. It took place at the opening of his solo show at kurimanzutto, Mexico City, 19 February, 2011.

Stay Or Should I Go were chopped up into thirty-four segments with a duration of four seconds each, and sent to guests as their invitation to the opening, making them objects that held not only part of the score, but also time itself. The guests handed their cards to a musician who fed them into the organ, varying tempo, pitch and volume. When these were inserted in the random order of the visitors arriving, the song played like a broken record, jumping back and forth between some parts and repeating others. Sala restaged this collective performance over the course of a day at Tlatelolco square, a highly charged site in the heart of Mexico City, where a massacre of some 300 people took place during the 1968 student demonstration. The site is home to an Aztec temple, a Catholic Church, and the Square of the Three Cultures, designed by Mario Pani in his signature modernist style. The earthquake that hit Mexico City in 1985 left large parts of the area vacant, where no new buildings have been erected. The film records the gradual change of light as night falls and we see the shadow of one Aztec pyramid climbing up the stairs of another as the punch cards are randomly inserted into the barrel organ. Yet, at a certain moment, the film moves from its image-based chronological structure to a music-based edit where the song plays coherently from beginning to end. Now it is the images that are ruptured and disturbed, going back and forth between night and day.

Recalling the regime of the assembly line, the collective performance echoes the industrial age, with its notions of standardised factory labour and collective synchronicity. In this sense it contrasts with *Le Clash*, where the man produces the music alone. Here it is useful to think of Paolo Virno's notions on the general intellect. For Virno, we perform collective improvisations of synchronised virtuosity, creating a score together by 'acting-in-concert' with other virtuosos.[7] Like the man in *Le Clash*, we carry the assembly lines with us wherever we go. Participation is seen as a process which generates different forms of collectivity. This polysynchronisation of labour that Virno describes is performed by Sala's Mexico City guests, feeding the barrel organ with their invitations.

Exhaustion

In an essay of 1995, Gilles Deleuze discussed the works of Samuel Beckett in terms of 'the exhausted' a mode that goes beyond being tired and that 'exhausts the possible' through what he calls 'inclusive disjunction', in which 'everything divides, but into itself'.[8] He then sets out four ways in which Beckett 'exhausts the possible' in his works:

7 Paolo Virno, 'Virtuosity and Revolution: The Political Theory of Exodus', in *Theory Out Of Bounds: Radical Thought in Italy*, Paolo Virno and Michael Hardt (eds.), (Minneapolis: University of Minnesota Press, 1996), pp. 189–210. Here I draw on Kai Van Eikels' reading of Virno, as presented at a Curatorial/Knowledge seminar in Berlin, January 2011.

8 Gilles Deleuze, 'The Exhausted', in *Essays Critical and Clinical*, trans. Daniel W. Smith and Michael A. Greco (London: Verso, 1998), pp. 153–154.

9 Ibid, p. 161.

Forming exhaustive series of things
Drying up the flow of voices
Extenuating the potentialities of space
Dissipating the power of the image[9]

These also seem appropriate when thinking about the combinatory aspects of Sala's work. As the works unfold in space, we find ourselves in need of a vocabulary to name the new potentials that they bring. Deleuze speaks of a metalanguage in which 'words no longer give a realisation to the possible, but must themselves give the possible a reality that is proper to it, a reality that is precisely, exhaustible.'[10]

In an interview with Sala, Hans Ulrich Obrist observed: 'There is a point where you do not use the space just to show your work, but you use your work to release the space.'[11] At the Serpentine, the space is both opened and blocked at the same time. The barrel organ's perforated score is carved into the walls, which allows the music from the works to leak out of the gallery into the park, and the park's noises to penetrate inside the exhibition. The movement here is thus not only inside-out but also outside-in. The exhibition, as a community of works about and involving translation, allows for both sound and light to enter and participate in its syntax. Sala defines the opening of the space as 'improvising rules yet not letting them become a contract. An occurrence of de-railing without having rails'.[12]

In the hallway leading from the East Lobby to the East Gallery is *No Window No Cry (Le Corbusier, Maison-atelier Lipschitz, Boulogne)*, 2011, a window containing a music-box comb mechanism on which the visitor can play *Should I Stay Or Should I Go*. In the South Gallery *Doldrum*, 2008, a snare drum with drumsticks is installed. The drumsticks are caused to beat on the skin of the drum by low frequency vibrations emanating from *Answer Me* and *Le Clash*. The projections operate according to a program with two cycles. One cycle revolves around a pairing of *Le Clash* and *Tlatelolco Clash*, running in parallel in the East and West Galleries, followed by *Answer Me* playing alternately in the North Gallery. *Tlatelolco Clash* is 3 minutes, 30 seconds longer than *Le Clash*, so that the correctly reconstructed version of *Should I Stay Or Should I Go* plays on its own, after *Le Clash* has ended.

The second cycle is a live performance entitled *3-2-1*, 2011. In dialogue with *Long Sorrow,* Sala has conceived this performance that is based on improvisation and can also be seen as a walking piece.[13] In 2006 Moondoc was recorded responding to his original solo improvisation in *Long Sorrow,*[14]

10 Ibid, p. 156
11 'Hans Ulrich Obrist in conversation with Anri Sala', in *Anri Sala*, Mark Godfrey, Hans Ulrich Obrist and Liam Gillick (London: Phaidon, 2006), p. 27.
12 Conversation with the artist, 20 August, 2011.
13 First performed at VeneKlasen/Werner, *Symphony Movement VI,* curated by Clara Meister and Soundfair, Berlin, 24 June, 2011.
14 The recording took place at Galerie Chantal Crousel, Paris, 22 April, 2006.

thereby creating a duet. Now, saxophonist Andre Vida is invited to answer and echo this duet, live in the gallery, expanding the soundscape from solo, to duet, to trio. The improvisation takes place in the space nine times a day, seven days a week over seven weeks. In this way, the spontaneous virtuosity of the performer is met with the mundane organisation of time and of waged labour. The weekly work, day in and day out, of a series of virtuoso performances, brings together Deleuze's idea of 'inclusive disjunction' with that of collective synchronisation. The event of the possible, that no longer needs to be realised in body or object, is performed through the exhibition. Simultaneous and spontaneous, this performance offers itself as a one-time repeating score based on an exhaustive series that dissipates the power of the image and extenuates the potentialities of the space.

In a conversation with Raphaela Platow, Sala states that he tries in his exhibitions 'to compose interrelationships that link works and anticipate their togetherness in the space.'[15] Marie Fraser has defined this attempt at synchronicity in terms of music versus space:

> the idea is not to impose a direction or suggest a possible scenario, but to synchronise the works as in a musical score … [I]t seems clear that the idea of a musical score introduces both an abstract dimension and a more powerful, extreme experience of space and time … [The works] tend to synchronise with one another and to produce a space that interacts with the visitor's experience. As with a musical composition, it is essentially a matter of *relationship, combination, harmony.*[16]

The works in Sala's exhibition at the Serpentine operate through disjunctions, additions, reversals and repetitions. These works operate in concert, exhausting the possible and translating it into a language that does not yet exist.

15 Anri Sala in conversation with Raphaela Platow, in *Anri Sala: Purchase Not by Moonlight*, p. 27.
16 Marie Fraser, 'Filming Sound', p. 53.

Tlatelolco Clash, 2011

Tlatelolco Clash, 2011

Le Clash, 2010

Le Clash, 2010

Tlatelolco Clash, 2011

Tlatelolco Clash, 2011

Le Clash, 2010

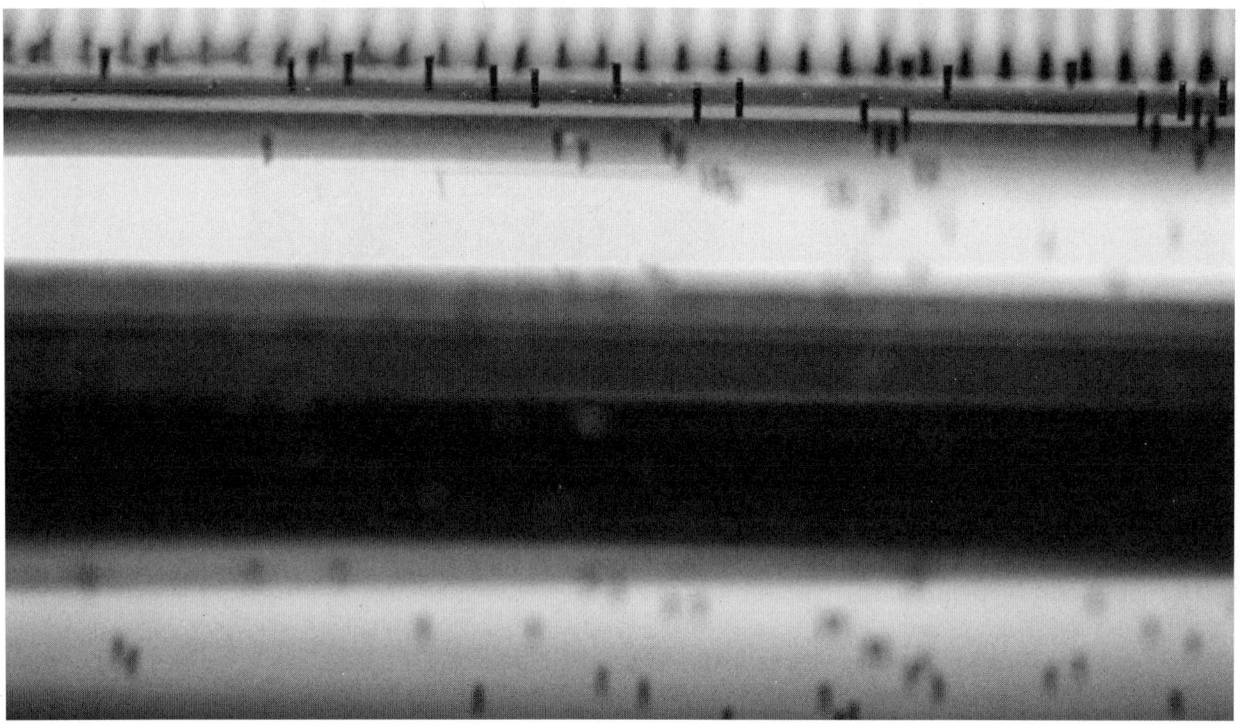

Le Clash, 2010

ANRI SALA INTERVIEWED BY JULIA PEYTON-JONES AND HANS ULRICH OBRIST

Julia Peyton-Jones
What was the first work you ever made?

Anri Sala
That's a difficult thing to say because it depends which one we'd consider to be a work.

Peyton-Jones
Which one do you consider to be a work?

Sala
I think the first were these drawings of eggs that I did every day. I started painting when I was ten, so I could go back to the first oil painting I did, for example. But there was a moment when I was preparing for the exam to enter the High School for Art in Tirana, and there was very tough competition. Everybody was preparing by doing these drawings, very Soviet-like, of flowers. For the exam everyone had to make a drawing of the same bas-relief flower and they would all prepare by practicing with the flowers from previous years. And Edi Rama said to me, 'Forget about it! This is exactly how one can destroy one's own sensibility of drawing. What you should do, which is the most difficult thing to do, is to draw eggs.'

Hans Ulrich Obrist
Edi Rama is now the opposition leader in Albania, but at that time he was an artist who taught you. He was your mentor.

Sala
Yes. He started in politics as Minister of Culture when he was thirty-three, and then became Mayor for nine years.

Obrist
And Edi's advice to you as a young artist was to draw eggs?

Sala
Yes. So I did more than 1,000 eggs – it was a daily activity. When, much later in 2010, I did an exhibition of Edi's daily drawings called *Inversion, Creating Space Where There Appears To Be None* at About Change

Studio in Berlin, I remember this conversation between Philippe Parreno and Edi where Philippe said, 'Drawings could be seen as scores, like musical scores ... But if you take them as scores you could imagine being able to restage the event that produced them, like following a map.' He wondered if one could look at the drawings and be able to replay the Mayor's day. In a way, the eggs had this kind of diary or score aspect too. The most difficult part was the tone. There are white eggs and there are brown eggs, and I had to draw the brown ones, and, because I was using a pencil, I had to filter out the colour, which is a very difficult thing to do. When you do a white one, it's easier because you know exactly the tonality of the shade. So, as a process of endurance and a kind of score, I think this was maybe my first work, conceptually: a notation of eggs.

Peyton-Jones
And was it a different egg every day or the same egg?

Sala
The eggs would change, because otherwise it would go bad, and you couldn't afford to let an egg go bad because they were rationed at that time. You were allowed a certain number of eggs a week as a family. I could only use it for as long as it could be still cooked.

Peyton-Jones
But this is a very sophisticated start: you were making conceptual artworks of 1,000 eggs.

Sala
Yes. But I must give credit to Edi, because it's not like I was aware that I was doing something conceptual. Now, when I look back on it, I see that it was almost a conceptual discipline.

Obrist
Your sister mentioned to me that when you were a child you did these television drawings. You'd sit in front of the television, and you'd 'score' what you saw on the screen. So it all started when you were five. Is that true?

Sala
Yes. It could be a film with war scenes, or with archers, or it could be a football match. I'd draw it in such a way that at the end, if you looked at the directions of the arrows I made, you could see who won: from the way the arrows were pointing at people, you'd see that only one was alive at the end of the battle. And the football was the same: you could see who'd scored from the drawings.

Obrist
I think it's interesting that connection between score and diary. Does Rama still do these daily doodles?

Sala
I'm sure he does.

Obrist
It would be interesting to hear a little bit more about Rama. How did you meet him? Do you remember the day you met him?

Sala
No. I only remember that it was when I was ten years old. Before that, I'd studied violin for almost seven years. But there was a moment when I suddenly got fed up. I just wanted to leave it behind. And that's when my interest in visual things grew. It became like a space of freedom in response to these violin studies, which at some point became like a suffocating experience. And when I stopped, I started painting more and more and that's how, through my parents, I met first Edi Hila, and then at the same time Edi Rama. Edi Hila is a very good artist in Albania who was also my Professor at the Academy of Fine Art. He has been recognised, but not as much as he deserves.

Peyton-Jones
Do you think it would be true to say that the seeds of your work were planted as early as your music lessons? The discipline of learning to play an instrument is similar to the kind of repetition and endurance and that went into the 1,000 eggs.

Sala
I would say that's at least partly right, in the sense that it created my awareness of tempo – whether it translates into music or whether it translates into daily variations of shadow and light. Either way, it's still a matter of a diary, a matter of tempo, a matter of music and rhythm – the tempo in the drawings of the eggs is how the shades changed every day. So maybe we can trace the beginning, which at that time was intuitive, to back then. It was only later that I realised how the qualities of one medium translate into another medium and become stronger. Tempo, for example, might be felt more strongly in a series of drawings than in a musical score. For me, it was always about realising that at the edge of one medium is the possibility for another.

Peyton-Jones
It's just a step from one to another?

Sala
Exactly, but not at all in the sense of an interdisciplinary approach. This is precisely what I'm not interested in. I'm not interested in one medium including the other, but in one medium taking on the qualities of another. There is something about tempo that can be visualised and it becomes about an image that you *hear* rather than see but that still remains with you as an image. And this quality also makes the image self-effacing. *Title Suspended*, 2008, for example, is a sculpture but it has a filmic nature in that it is a constantly changing form. Two gloves rotate very slowly and it is only for a few moments of every rotation that they assume the shape of a pair of complete hands.

Peyton-Jones
Your early works are often linked to scores, but they could also be considered as transcripts. Intervista, *1998, is a sort of transcript. Can we jump now to how you moved from painting to the moving image with films like* Intervista *that all somehow have to do with transcripts?*

Sala
I think before my work went from this static image into the moving image, before it went faster, first it went slower. There was this period where I got very interested in frescos and I studied how to make them. This again has something to do with endurance, and with the daily activity, because what you start in a day you have to finish. And if you can't finish in the day, then you have to start all over again. And you finish something anticipating what you'll be doing tomorrow, because you have to be able to make sure that the density of the layers in each individual daily section ends up at the same level. The divisions or 'seams' can't be visible because otherwise you would have a kind of patchwork effect. This idea of anticipating what comes next and of building continuity out of a series of breaks or ruptures connects to how I work when I make a film, and even to how I work when I do a show, in the sense that sometimes, when I think of an exhibition, this is what triggers me to think of making a film – not because I need to do another work for the show, but because there's something that may still be incomplete in the proposal. So I don't always go from the new work into a new show; sometimes it's the existence of the new show that makes me think of how to articulate what's missing.

Obrist
Where did you execute these frescos?

Sala
They were in the Academy of Fine Art, but over the years, they've repainted the walls. But also what's interesting is that this was a response, at least by intuition, to what was happening politically and socially: my interest in fresco took place exactly in those years after the regime fell. Suddenly, everything was possible: it was an acceleration of information, of desires not being forbidden anymore. But at the same time, this created a feeling of disorder in the sense that, before, we were all doing more or less the same thing – we were all different, yet our paintings couldn't be too different because they were all based on Socialist Realism. So there was a restrictive frame. And then, all of a sudden, everything that was forbidden

became possible. After the regime fell and we returned to classes, I discovered that one of my friends had become a surrealist and another had become an expressionist, which was great because it was a sign of all the possibilities, but at the same time I was terrified of this. I wasn't terrified of the fragmentation in itself, but of the fact that these new directions weren't based on an internal development – on emancipation in the practice of being an artist. They happened just because one could suddenly do anything. And it was at this point that I chose a kind of slowdown – a slowdown through the medium of fresco. So the fact that life changed, that the system or values changed, that the politics and the whole society changed, didn't make me go directly from painting to video, which, at first sight, might have been considered the most appropriate medium to record the changes. Instead I approached it with a twist.

Obrist
So you went from painting to fresco to moving image. If you do a catalogue raisonné of your works in the future, what would be number one?

Sala
I think it would be the one I realised as my final project for my Diploma at the Academy of Fine Art. Students had to present a final work, which was usually expected to be a painting or a sculpture, but I made a video. And it was the very first time that a video was presented there. Each student had to choose an advisor for their final project, and I chose another Edi: Edi Muka. So that was the very first video and I'm sure he must still have the text that he wrote for his speech to the jury. People were a bit shocked and now it seems like a deliberate provocation, but it wasn't like that at the time. And Edi Muka surprised them as much as my video did because he started talking about Walter Benjamin. I think it was the first time that this name had intruded on discussions about art in Albania.

Peyton-Jones
Did you feel it was your role or your desire to be different, to be in some way provocative or to take a stand? Or was it driven by your work?

Sala
I think when I look back from a distance it could be seen as provocative, in the sense that when everybody started to be different, I slowed down and did fresco, which was an anachronism in the context. Even during the Communist era, people didn't really study fresco, or, if they did, it was because it was part of the classes and they were obliged to. But I really chose it. And then still later on, I went into video. But, like I said, this moment of slowing down before running was because I needed to find my own tempo and to find a reason from within instead of simply doing it as a reaction or in order to shock. Maybe intuitively we all want to break the rules, or at least to question the rules, to arrive at unexpected questions and unexpected answers. So maybe that was part of it, but it wasn't my goal.

Peyton-Jones
And was sound part of that first work?

Sala
No. There was no sound at all because I wanted it to remain very abstract. I don't want to sound like I'm complaining about how few means we had, but just to give you the context, when I did this video, it took me a long time to find a camera. There was only one VHS camera accessible to students in the whole of Tirana and that was at the Open Society Foundation for Albania (Soros). I had the camera for only one day, and it could record sound, but I wanted the film to be silent since it enhanced the abstraction in this very concrete image. So sound became important by being absent, and it was a deliberate choice: I didn't include sound just because the camera came with sound.

Peyton-Jones
When did you make your first film with sound?

Sala
The first film where sound – and its absence – plays an active role was *Intervista*. The process of interviewing my mother was as important to me as the end result. Finding the film of her being interviewed by state television, investigating the lost soundtrack and eventually recovering my mother's words with the help of deaf-mutes who were able to read her lips and then insisting on having her see the film again with her words restored in order to shed light on the changes that had taken place over this period of thirty years were all part of an important process that occupied my mind as much as knowing in advance that it was going to become a film, or that I'd edit this together with that. So it was more like the editing was embedded in the process, it was like scratching a silent film until the words come out. I wasn't aware from the outset that it was going to become a film. The quality of the approach was as important as the quality of the framing, of the filmmaking, and this is not always the case. Sometimes the way you approach something, the way you film it, can be very uneven. But in this work, it had to be perfectly balanced, morally speaking. Luc Barnier and Liria Bégéja played an important role in the making of *Intervista* and in a broader sense in my initiation with moving images.

Obrist
One of the things that I'm interested in is the idea of space in relation to these film works. Very early on you said that you didn't just use the space to show your work, but that you used your work to release the space. And that's something that obviously became more important as your work has matured. Entre chien et loup/When the Night Calls it a Day *at the Convent de Cordeliers, ARC, Musée d'Art moderne de la Ville de Paris in 2004, was an extreme example, where you played with the light between dusk and dawn. Your show in Warsaw at the Centre for Contemporary Art in 2005 was another example, where your work actually released the space, and at Hauser & Wirth in London in 2007 you achieved this through a temporary ceiling that bisected the space horizontally. Could you talk a little about this?*

Sala
To answer, I'll just take a moment and go back to *Intervista* to say that while it would be easy to think that *Intervista* is about a woman dealing with her past, and who struggles to believe what she said in her youth, to me it was very clear, and it's also very clear in the film, that in this moment of puzzlement, my mother wasn't surprised by the political content of what she said, because everybody knew that at that time there was only one avenue of political talk; she was surprised by how inarticulate it sounded when she saw it again. And that's where, together, we became aware that the syntax of the language had changed, had broken, because it had become so calcified in order to serve a regime and a certain message – a kind of mono-message. So that's where I became very aware that in moments of extreme pressure, a language breaks. That's where it all starts for me: this becoming aware of things that are forgettable so long as they are transparent. When it comes to the shows, one thing that's always been very important for me is that when people see a film, I don't want them to feel projected into what they see, but to remain aware of where they're standing. And this awareness can be facilitated by the syntax of an exhibition. At ARC, for example, it was about creating this continuous twilight where one could see the videos and, at the same time, be aware of this space where you couldn't really see the corners. So it gave the impression of a kind of psychological space that wasn't real enough to have corners. Twilight lasted eight hours, which of course visitors knew was artificial because it usually lasts no more than 20 minutes. The films all together were much longer than the duration of natural twilight and the aim of this intervention was to set up a different relationship to duration.

And after ARC, another example is Warsaw, where, again, I didn't want to launch the viewer into the other realities contained in the films, like you would in a classic cinema setting where everything's done to make the space disappear. I don't want people to feel that they're in an anonymous space, because I want them to remain aware of the space where they are. In Warsaw I did this by constructing a series of slopes that would start and end, not at the doors in between the spaces, but more or less in the middle of the spaces, so that it became like a de-synchronisation between floors and walls. And because when you were watching certain films, you felt you were on an uphill slope, and these slopes triggered the feeling of gravity, the film would 'resist' you, or you would resist it.

Obrist
And were you aware at that time of the French architect Claude Parent and his work on the oblique?

Sala
No, not at all. It came out of this idea of how to trigger awareness of where you are. I'd tried it once with light, and then I wanted to try it with something that was not to do with the field of visibility. I wanted to articulate an awareness of the body using gravity. And later on, I used low-frequency sounds, which is again a form of articulating an awareness of things that are neither really audible nor visible.

Peyton-Jones
These are strategies that destabilise people and make them reconsider where they are. It makes them more conscious of their surroundings. It's a heightened level of consciousness. In your exhibition Purchase Not By Moonlight *at the Museum of Contemporary Art North Miami in 2008 you also reconfigured perception using these low frequencies.*

Obrist
And there, drums became a display feature.

Sala
Drums became a display feature, which rendered sound visible. And several films were simultaneously displayed. I pursued the idea of choreographing time in this show, of using the distribution of time and of sound to make a cartography, a map, of the exhibition. It creates a flow of movement in the space. And it has this unifying aspect, not at all in a metaphoric or symbolic sense, but in the sense of unifying how one experiences the exhibition. I was increasingly interested in how one can make an exhibition with the media that I use – which is mainly video, but also sound and light and sometimes photography and sculpture – in a way that's like a normal show, where you can see a sculpture and behind it is a drawing, and then a painting further on, etc. It's slightly frustrating this idea that because you work with film and video and sound you have to create these boxes that oblige you to forget the rest of the space. And like I said, I don't want people to forget the space. And I don't want them, because they're concentrating on something, to forget that there's a background to it – not only the context of the film, but the fact that in the background, elsewhere in the exhibition, there's yet another film. So this was my intention: to articulate all these elements in a space with open borders and no walls.

Peyton-Jones
This reconfiguring of perception is also what you were doing with your mother in Intervista: *you were reconfiguring her perception of that time in which she lived. It's both autobiography and biography. And then it goes into something entirely different, which is about history and politics. And there was the whole reversal of roles: you're showing her something, as her son, that happened in her youth, which echoes the way in which, as the child grows up, the parent goes through a process of looking at herself through the child's development. But you did it in a way that was very gentle and careful but also tough. It was an extraordinarily sophisticated film on the one hand but also a very tender biography on the other. And a number of things come up in relation to this work. Reconfiguring of perception is one thing, but also time. You marked time in a variety of different ways in this film, and of course it's very much present in the works about music, which is all about time. Could you say something about why time is important to you?*

Sala
We often say that time puts things in perspective, but what I'm more interested in is how time can put itself in perspective and how time can measure the perspective

Long Sorrow, 2005

Agassi, 2006

of itself. So the wider question is how to show time as something subjective and something objective, how to create these loose units of time that everyone experiences differently depending on their individual sensibilities.

My video with the horse called *Time after Time*, 2003, for example, is five and a half minutes long, but to some people it feels much longer. We all have different perceptions of the duration of things. There's this beautiful saying that three minutes of pain are much longer than three minutes of mathematics. This was exemplified by the experience of the musician Jemeel Moondoc in *Long Sorrow*, 2005, who was suspended, playing his saxophone, from the eighteenth floor of this building in Berlin. Just below him there was a bus station, and he knew more or less the time it takes for a bus to stop, to let people out, to let people in, to leave. He said he tried not to look at the bus because it would make time seem to go more slowly and would add to the psychological strain caused by his fear of the void and the drop. Here again we have this de-synchronisation of objective and subjective time. Jemeel and I had an agreement that whatever happened, I wouldn't leave him outside for more than ten minutes. And I fully respected that. It was one of the reasons why I wanted to shoot on 16 mm film rolls, which are ten minutes long. When the film reel stopped, we'd need to change it, so I knew that it was also time to bring Jemeel back into the apartment again. And there were moments of tension where he didn't believe that I was doing it, because it felt to him like it was thirty minutes between breaks. And I said 'It can't be thirty minutes because we're shooting on ten-minute reels.'

Obrist
I met a fascinating American neuroscientist, David Eagleman, at this year's SciFoo conference, who also writes novels. And he gave this speech where he said that he had a near-death experience as a child, when he fell from a roof. And he said the same thing that many people have said: that when you have this near-death experience, time becomes very drawn out. It only took him a few seconds to fall from the roof, but it felt like an eternity, and all these images came to him. As a neuroscientist he found out that it's to do what happens in the brain. Under such extreme stress with shock, all these substances are liberated that make you enter into a second or third tier of your memory, which would explain why people see their lives flashing before them before they die. And he also said that when we experience the present, we always experience it with a small delay, so what we think is now is actually a few seconds ago, because our perceptions have to get to the brain in order to be processed.

Sala
It's beautiful that we experience the present with a delay, because it means that time always includes its future. We always think that the present includes the past, but scientifically speaking, it includes the future because of the delay element. And this idea of delay was also explored in another of my films called *Agassi*, 2006.

Peyton-Jones
In what sense?

Sala
I saw this photograph of Andre Agassi, where the tennis ball is passing by him, and because it's going so fast, his eyes aren't looking at it – there's a delay. His eyes are looking to where the ball *was*, not to where it is in the photograph. And I thought that was very interesting. In a film projection, there's this round mark on the print that becomes white when it's time to change the reel. It's there to synchronise the different reels. And when I made this image of Agassi as a 16 mm film, I put a round mark like that exactly where the ball should be according to the position of his eyes, like another ball. So we see the ball twice – the real one and the abstract one. And the gap between the first time it comes and the second time it comes is not the usual gap that allows the projectionist to change the reel and preserve the continuity but is the time it takes the ball, after an Agassi serve, to travel over the net and hit the other player's side of the court, which is approximately 0.79 seconds or precisely 19 frames. When one sees the first hole, one 'sees' the noise of the

ball being hit by the racket and then, with the second hole, it hitting the ground.

Obrist
A score always hides another score. It's interesting that many of your scores come after the fact. It's not that you create a score that is a master plan for something; it's the other way around.

Sala
It's both, actually, because, as you say, the score comes after the event, but sometimes the score that comes after the event also becomes the precursor of a new event. So *Air Cushioned Ride*, 2006, for example, was a film I made when country music began to interfere with the baroque music playing on the radio in my car. Then I asked a musician to transcribe it. So the score came after the event. But then, based on this score, I did a performance called *A Spurious Emission*, 2007, with a country band and a baroque trio.
In *Why The Lion Roars*, 2008, on the other hand, there's this idea of a daily forecast controlling a composition of feature films. Each film represents a temperature in degrees, from minus 11°C to 45°C. A thermometer measures the temperature outside the projection space and simultaneously edits the film programme, which changes in correspondence with the actual outdoor temperature. At the exact moment of an increase or decrease in temperature, each film is interrupted and replaced by another. So the weather forecast becomes like a score, but it's a score that's not only dependent on time but also on place. With *Air Cushioned Ride* and *A Spurious Emission* the relationship between time and space really hangs in the balance. The film was very space-bound, because I had to circle the trucks continuously so that the radio channels would swap between each other: the moment I stopped, it was only one channel. It was the fact that I was going from one side of the group of trucks to the other that created the score. The moment that this was transcribed and translated into annotations like a score and played by a country band and a baroque trio for *A Spurious Emission*, then it becomes a score governed by time – because the North or the South or East and West of the trucks in the previous situation becomes before and after in the new score.

Obrist
It's a different kind of coding?

Sala
The syntax changes all the time. And then there is *Ulysses*, 2007, which includes a score that I did in collaboration with Jeremy Millar based on the song *Ulysses* by Franz Ferdinand, which had not yet been released. It was two years before the song came out. People were invited to 'perform' the song, guessing what it might sound like, based on this score. Rather than using traditional musical notation, the score represented the drum part through descriptions of the sounds to be produced and directions as to how these sounds might be made. Given the title of the song, it seemed only appropriate that all of the words used in the score were onomatopoeic descriptions of the suggested drumbeat and also that the phrases provided as instructions were taken from James Joyce's novel.

Peyton-Jones
A score is also a cut: if you score paper you mark it, you cut it. And it's interesting that the score for you is a notation, a record, but you move from that to making a cut: you actually incise material. In Tlatelolco Clash, *2011, for example, the profile of a girl has the barrel organ score, which takes the form of a perforated card, projected onto her, or reflected on her arm.*

Sala
Yes because she's using it as a sunshade.

Peyton-Jones
Yes. But it's also like a cut. It's a violent sort of …

Sala
Incision, like a marking. Instead of saying 'You scarred me for life', you could say 'You scored me for life.'

Obrist
We haven't spoken of the 5 Flutterbyes, *2007/2010, performance, which was first presented as part of* Il Tempo del Postino *at the Manchester International Festival in 2007. We are reproducing the score for the performance in this catalogue.*

Sala
5 Flutterbyes is based on the aria *Vogliatemi bene, un bene piccolino* from the first act of *Madama Butterfly* by Giacomo Puccini. Instead of only one Madama Butterfly, the performance features five sopranos. When one soprano sings, the other sopranos mime the libretto. The instant the singing soprano withholds her voice and continues only moving her lips, another soprano's voice takes over. Each soprano has a precise part in the score, which describes when she sings and when she silences her voice, so that it is only ever *one* Butterfly that is heard fluttering around in the space. The Butterfly's presence floats in the room from one body to another and is incarnated in the wandering voice.

Peyton-Jones
This discussion of performance brings us to something that's integral to the Serpentine show, which is the free jazz performance in 3-2-1, *2011. Free jazz, of course, has no notation. It has no score.*

Sala
Absolutely. But it's embedded in the score of the show, because the musician plays to and with *Long Sorrow*. So a free jazz sax player is improvising with the free jazz sax player in the film. And it's called *3-2-1* because it takes place through three spaces, first as a trio, then a duet and finally as a solo. It's a performance that I first did a couple of months ago in Berlin, which was part of a project curated by Clara Meister.[1] In the first room, the live saxophone player improvises with a recording of a performance at Galerie Chantal Crousel, in which Jemeel Moondoc improvises with his performance in *Long Sorrow*, so it is a duet, and when the musician in the live performance joins in, it becomes a trio. And then the musician goes into the second room and he plays to the film, so it becomes a duet between the musician in the exhibition and the musician in the film. And then he finishes the improvisation on his own in the third room. So it's *3-2-1*.

Peyton-Jones
Which is also like a conductor's countdown to get everybody together at the start of a piece. I'm wondering whether there's any way of capturing the improvisation? Because one of the things about a score is that it captures what's ephemeral, that which has gone. Unless you record it, it no longer exists apart from in the minds and the ears and the hearts of the people who were a part of that performance. And all that unforeseen notation is going to be circulating in the atmosphere of the Serpentine Gallery, and will be compounded layer upon layer over the duration of the exhibition. And I just wonder whether there's any value or interest in trying to synthesise it into some kind of concrete form, whatever that may be?

Sala
Yes I think it is interesting, because in the performance *3-2-1*, the musician will respond and improvise to an already recorded free jazz improvisation. But what the musician will be doing nine times a day over two months, will always be different. It is a way of constantly renewing something that is recorded or fixed. It's like a 'breeze' that will blow through the show, crossing from east to west and from one gallery to the next. This 'breeze' creates a dynamic between fixed and not fixed – the sequence of the show runs according to a time code but the performance sweeps through nine times a day and introduces something unpredictable, something whose nature is to be in flux. It's like a score where the time is notated but some of the notes are missing. It's like a breeze blowing through a tree, and each time the breeze blows through the tree it changes the pattern of light passing through the leaves. And this is connected to an idea that I mentioned before: that instead of being a performance that becomes a film, it goes further,

1 The project, entitled *Symphony*, was a collaboration between VeneKlasen/Werner and Soundfair and invited musicians, composers, and visual artists to make works expanding on the traditional concepts of concert and exhibition, and to present these works as unique events in the gallery.

because it becomes a film – *Long Sorrow* – that leads to a new performance.

Peyton-Jones
Is it like a diary?

Sala
Yes and one that's open towards the future. It's not about the found object, it's not about the found situation, but it's about the found future, in the sense that the future comes in and scores itself in the present. So how could this be put physically into a notation? I have no idea. I'm afraid with free jazz, it would be like a kind of blasphemy. But on the other hand it's interesting because it's a reaction to an already existing improvisation but which is no longer improvisation because it's time coded. And it will repeat itself again and again and again in the course of the show.

They say that the early musical scores were like a language that wasn't very precise. It was only later that the composers started to develop further symbols and instructions to make the 'sentence' as precise as possible. So it's a little bit like this idea of an early score in that it's so open to interpretation that you can make it different every time you play it. The free jazz in *Long Sorrow* isn't a score, but a recorded piece. But at the same time, because it's free jazz and because of the nature of my invitation to the musician, the performance is a very open one, because the musician will be able to change it and he will change it every time.

Obrist
The first thing people will see in the Serpentine exhibition will be Doldrum, *2008, a snare drum whose drumsticks appear to beat on their own. This isn't the first time this work has appeared. It's like a character in a movie who pops up every now and then. It was the central display feature in your shows in Miami, which we have already discussed, and at the Contemporary Arts Center in Cincinnati. In fact, the drumsticks are triggered by the soundtrack of* Answer Me, *the film projected in the North Gallery. In the film, the drums' echo is so loud that it makes the drumsticks vibrate. And this is the kind of overture to the show.*

Sala
It's the overture, and it's also like a visual speaker for the show. Because *Doldrum* responds only to the lower frequencies of the soundtrack of *Answer Me*, we don't actually hear the sound coming through the speaker inside *Doldrum*. But those low frequencies have animpact on the skin of the drum that makes the drumsticksbounce. It's a reversed situation, because normally when you play a drum it's the drumstick that makes the skin bounce and this creates the sound inside the drum. *Doldrum* will also react to the low frequency of *Le Clash*, 2010.

Now what I think is interesting is that in *Answer Me* there are a lot of low frequencies because the soundtrack of the film was recorded inside a Buckminster Fuller dome. That's where the idea of *Doldrum* originates: with the drum that's able to play on its own just because of the strength of the frequencies in the dome. In the case of *Should I Stay or Should I Go*, which in my film is played on a barrel organ and a music box, it doesn't have low frequencies. It's very melodic and stays in the mid-to-high tones. So what I want to do is to bring in the low frequencies of the original song. And what I like in this dynamic is that the low frequencies for *Le Clash* don't come from the film, but they do come from where the film came from. Very often the melody of a song finds itself in the high frequencies, and the experience is in the low frequencies. So the thing that's the least translatable afterwards is the low frequencies and the thing that you could always communicate to somebody else by whistling or by humming is the mid-high frequencies. A melody, like a story, travels better in time. But low frequencies travel better in space and then they die in space. So what I like about this connection with *Should I Stay or Should I Go* is that it's a punk song, and the moment it's translated in the present into a music box or barrel organ it loses its low frequencies. So the present has lost its present-ness, because, like I said, low frequencies are in the present, in space not time.

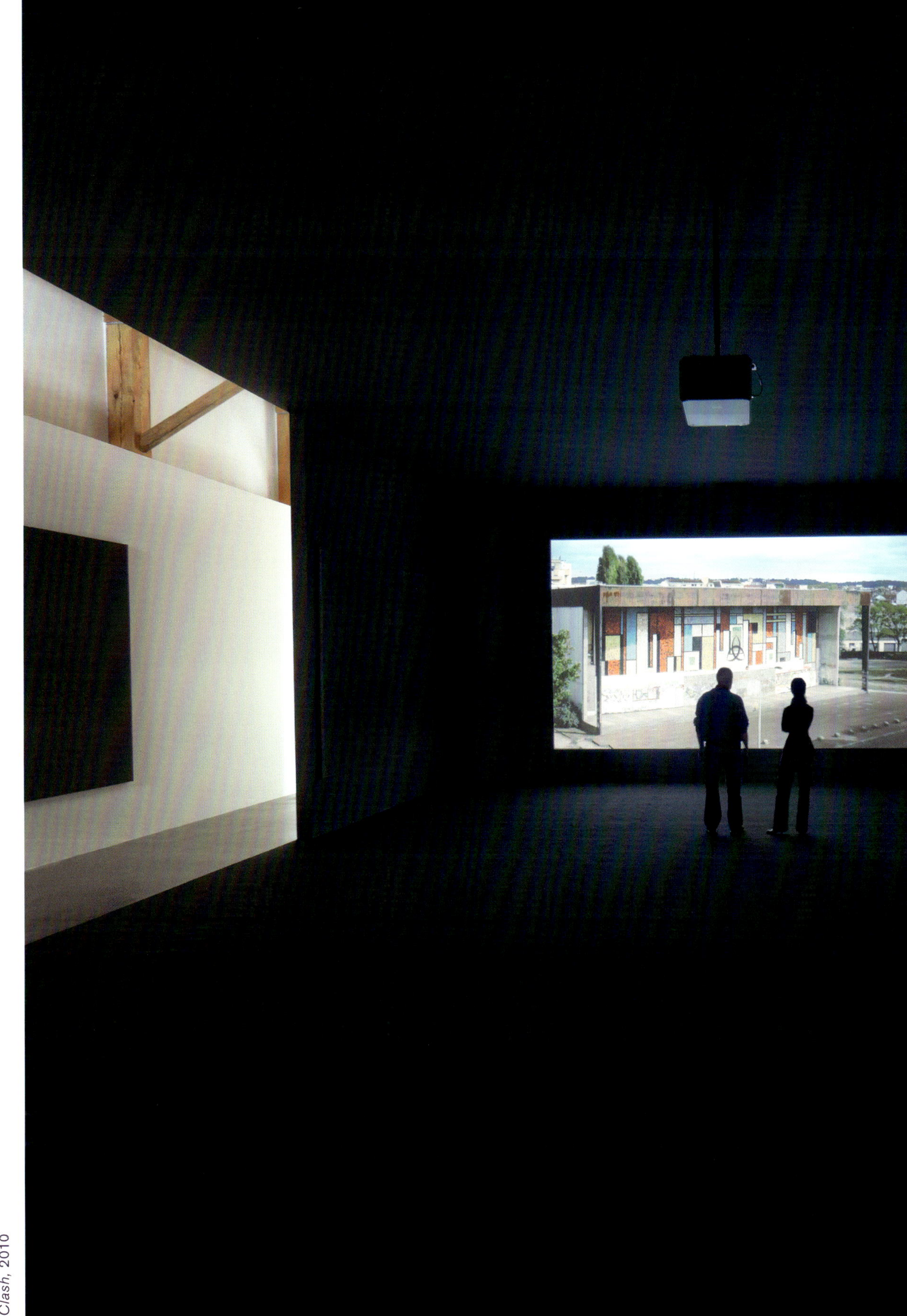

Le Clash, 2010

Doldrum, 2008 *Answer Me*, 2008

By losing its low frequencies, *Should I Stay or Should I Go* becomes like a melody from the past, which is interesting because the film is 2010 and the song was 1982. The song sounds more like the present and the present sounds more like the past because the sound of a music box or of a barrel organ remind us of the melodies of the past. So I like this past and present having swapped places. And in the exhibition I like this idea that the drum will feature the low frequencies not in the film, but in the past, when the song was in the present.

Obrist
Answer Me *is constructed around a conversation and you have also conceived your exhibition at the Serpentine as a series of conversations?*

Sala
This exhibition stages several conversations and pairings. There's a conversation between *Doldrum* and *Answer Me*. There's the conversation between *Le Clash* and *Tlatelolco Clash*, whose soundtracks share the same musical element. But this is a different kind of dialogue from the one between *Answer Me* and *Doldrum*. Where these two works are in sync, *Le Clash* and *Tlatelolco Clash* are technically in sync but sonically out of phase. *Le Clash* is based on the continuity of the song and *Tlatelolco Clash* is based on the deconstruction of the song. And I used this as an element to create a fiction that took place in the ruins of Tlatelolco, which is a very important place in Mexico City. It's where the Aztecs were decisively beaten by the Spanish. But it's also the place where the student massacre happened in 1968 – they were shot in those ruins from these remarkable modernist buildings that you see around them.

Obrist
It's an important area in the history of Mexico.

Sala
Yes, it's an area where the identity of the nation was questioned. It's a place of a very sad story where Cortes won against the Aztecs, but at the same time, if it hadn't been for that moment, the nation of Mexico wouldn't exist, which is a mix between the Aztecs and the Spanish. And it's an interesting place because it's a mix between three periods. It's the ruins of the pyramids, and next to it is a church, which was made by stealing stones from the pyramids, and all of it is surrounded by this modernist architecture, which was partially destroyed by an earthquake. So it's full of rupture, the architecture surrounding this place. And the barrel organ is in the ruins and the people come with their individual cards, which are punched with four seconds of the score for the barrel organ. And they come there and they play their section of the song themselves. It's a bit like going to vote. It becomes like the ballot box where your political thought becomes a vote or a voice. So your invitation becomes four seconds of the song. And in the film, as they arrive and put in their cards they deconstruct the song, because each person has a different section and they come out of order. It becomes like an offspring of the song, with lots of silences in between, as we see people come and leave. And this is filmed over the course of a day and a night. And then there's a moment where there's a U-turn in the film, where the song reconstructs itself. It totally deconstructs the timeline of day and night. And that's the moment when the film is reorganised in the editing so that the song is put into the right order but the reality of day and night is now in total disorder. So it plays with the idea of continuity. By following one continuity, you rupture another one, and by refining the continuity of another logic you rupture the previous one. And so this will be in a dynamic de-phasing with *Le Clash*, because as we enter the show, they'll both be playing together. The effect is like a strange echo, where continuity and rupture both play the same tune. On the one side we'll hear the continuity of the song and on the other side we'll hear the discontinuity of the song at the same time. But because the new film is a bit longer, it is only after *Le Clash* finishes that the discontinuity in *Tlatelolco Clash* stops and the song plays in the right order.

Obrist
You mention the editing of Le Clash *and we recently recorded a conversation with Liria Bégéja, with whom you*

have worked very closely for many years on the editing of your films.

Sala
Liria's contribution to my films is very important. She has a talent for composing different scenes and their succession in such a way that gives a feeling of tempo and time rather than a narrative that can be 'read'. This is crucial because I conceive the films as open structures that can sustain the feeling of a continuous present. They do not simply convey meaning but also let meaning in. The difficulty in filming open-ended narratives is that sometimes it can result in a labyrinth of possibilities at the stage of editing. Finding the path can be complex because the more doors you leave open when shooting the more doors need to be shut during editing. The challenge is how to create intent without creating definition, and Liria's input helps bring a further resolution and clarity.

Obrist
I want to ask you about how you have responded to the Serpentine space and return to Answer Me, *which obviously has to do with the architecture of the dome. Does this relate to the architecture of the Serpentine Gallery?*

Sala
There are two domes in the Gallery: there's the little one in the first room of the show and there's the bigger one in the North Gallery. Under the little dome will be *Doldrum*, and the film *Answer Me* is under the larger dome. There is a set of drums under each of the Serpentine's domes. And the principle of a snare drum is a dome, so there is also a dome under each of the Serpentine's domes. With both works, the architecture of the film – or of the sculpture – mirrors the actual architecture of the exhibition space.

Every enclosed space, especially those that are circular, like a dome or a snare drum, has its own specific frequency response to which it responds best. And there's a mathematical formula to find out the frequency: you measure the perimeter and you translate it into the frequency. This is how, when working on *Answer Me*, we composed the music with the drummer in the film. I asked him to compose music that included the dome's frequency as much as possible. This is what makes the other drum play by itself: the frequency response gives life to the other drum. And when it came to making *Doldrum* itself, the same principle was used. With Olivier Goinard, who has made the sound for almost all my films and will be mixing the sound in the show, we used the formula to find the frequency to which the snare drum responds best, and then all the low frequencies in *Answer Me* and *Le Clash* were pushed down to that level.

Peyton-Jones
And I'm fascinated by why you picked the title Doldrum *for this piece. It's a very poetic work, but it's a negative word. It's a word of sadness.*

Obrist
Or melancholy.

Peyton-Jones
Melancholy, yes. If you're in the doldrums, you're kind of stuck.

Sala
The word was originally a nautical term. In certain areas of water in the Caribbean, the Trade Winds can suddenly stop for months, and in the past, boats would be unable to sail. And because this wasn't allowed for in the rations of food and water, many people died or their ships disappeared. And so being in the doldrums means that you're stuck, and you never know for how long. So this is why I chose the title, because the drum responds only to the low frequencies, so you don't know when the drumsticks will start playing again. Will it be in the next two seconds? Will it be in the next five measures? And in the exhibition, *Doldrum* won't be playing during *3-2-1*, so that will be a very long doldrum.

Obrist
After having worked such a long time with the moving image in the 1990s and early 2000s, you've shown with your performances a desire for more direct experience: you made the performance 5 Flutterbyes, *and now at the Serpentine, this full durational performance, where again, it's a live experience. Can we talk a little bit about where this desire comes from?*

Sala
For me, it's this idea of the tension that comes with live experience, the fact that you don't have it on a tape, you don't have it in a box, it's not there forever. And it's continuously to be negotiated, it's continuously to be brought back. For me it's a little bit like an offspring, or a branch; something that goes out but at the same time it's within. It goes out *because* it is within. So the live performance is the offspring of the show. What I like about it is this continuous present: the next part is not here yet. And in many of my films there's this idea of the continuous presence but at the same time they include the past and the future because they are either based on a performance or could lead to a performance in the future. *Long Sorrow* is a very good example of filming something that's continually in the present: the next moment is always being negotiated. So the relation between performance and something that's recorded, or already mediated, is like the relationship between raw and cooked. I'm not interested in one without the other. I've said before about *Long Sorrow* that I wasn't interested only in the music, because if I had been, I'd have filmed the saxophone. And I never filmed the saxophone. I filmed the lips. It was almost as if I could film the air in the moment that it becomes music.

Peyton-Jones
How does No Window No Cry, *2010, relate to* Le Clash *and* Tlatelolco Clash?

Sala
No Window No Cry relates to *Le Clash* through the music box. First of all there's a relation between *Le Clash*, the music box and architecture because *Le Clash* was based on a performance that I did outside a derelict concert hall in Bordeaux, intertwining renditions of the song on a barrel organ and a music box.[2] In fact, in this exhibition all the works are either the result of a performance or they lead to a performance. So *Answer Me*, *Long Sorrow* and *Le Clash* are all the result of a performance, and *Long Sorrow* leads to another performance. *No Window No Cry* stems from the music box in *Le Clash*. It opens up the soundtrack of the film to its new surroudings and makes it possible to add another layer to it. It's something I did first in the Ciccillo Matarazzo Pavilion designed by Oscar Niemeyer for the São Paolo Biennale in 2010, where *Le Clash* was also shown. And then I did this piece again in Mexico City for my exhibition at kurimanzutto in 2011 and for this show I located the window in the Central Library of the Universidad Nacional Autónoma de México in Mexico City, which is a building that was designed by Juan O'Gorman. The window in this show is based on a window in the Maison-atelier Lipschitz which is a Le Corbusier-designed house where Philippe Piccoli lives. Philippe is someone with whom I have worked on a few projects and he is also the main character in *Le Clash*. The window creates the possibility of adding a new layer to *Le Clash*.

Obrist
This work makes another connection between architecture and sound. Many of your works, such as Answer Me, Long Sorrow, *or* Dammi i Colori, *2003, which shows Edi Rama's attempts to reinvigorate the city of Tirana, and your film* 1395 Days Without Red, *2011, relate to architecture or to the city. Can you talk about this aspect of your work?*

Sala
There's a kind of bond between architecture and sound. Architecture is like the frame of sound. So when we think of moving images or photography, we think of the frame and what's inside and what's outside. But sound has two frames: it's either the score or the architecture off which it bounces. In some cases it is the location that suggests the content. With *Answer Me* I saw the dome and thought, 'This place has such an amazing echo due to its architecture', and then I asked myself what story

2 The performance, *Tease tease tease*, took place at La Salle des Fêtes du Grand Parc in Bordeaux as part of *Evento* festival of the arts in 2009 curated by Didier Fiùza Faustino.

could take place there and be influenced by it. So the architecture adds its own layer of narrative, which, in this case, is not built around words but around frequencies. The story of *Answer Me* is based on a little script about the divorce of a couple, but because this conversation is taking place inside the dome, it's no longer a couple, because there's always the echo. So again, it becomes three. *Jamais deux sans trois*.

Peyton-Jones
And the barrel organ score is also carved into walls built to cover the windows on the east and west sides of the Serpentine. This work also makes a connection between architecture and sound.

Sala
Yes. To me it's very important how there's this relation, like a double helix, between structure and content. So this score, which is transposed onto the wall and is the transcription of the barrel organ music that we hear in the film, becomes a sort of sculpture in the space. These walls will cover the windows but the windows will nevertheless be open. So we will have an opening between the gallery and the surroundings and not only will it let the sound of the exhibition go outside, but it will also let the sounds from outside come in. So in a way, it's like a Trojan horse. Instead of letting the message out, it becomes a hole that lets the outside in. The aim is to juggle frequencies and narratives so that the syntaxes of both loosen, opening up a space for new perspectives of meaning to come in. And this is something that has always interested me – the idea that where sound and space meet they create resonance beyond reverberation.

Doldrums, 2008

Air Cushioned Ride, 2006 *A Spurious Emission*, 2007

Viol.
Gamba
Cemb.
Vocals
Guitar
P. Steel
Bass
Drums
mf
B
say let's try a gain beg ging me to let you back in___ ev' ry
A Maj7
B Maj7
E

(Hold Tempo)
59
Viol.
mf
tr
Gamba
mf
59
Cemb.
mf

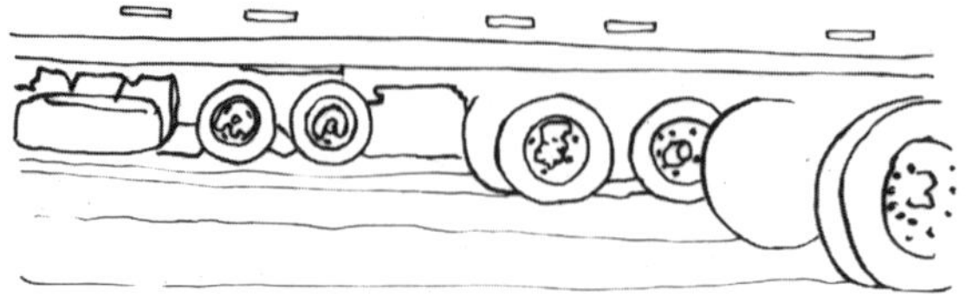

65
Viol.
Gamba
Cemb.
Guitar
P. Steel
Bass
Drums
A
f

71
Viol.
Gamba
Cemb.
Guitar
B
f
Bass
Drums

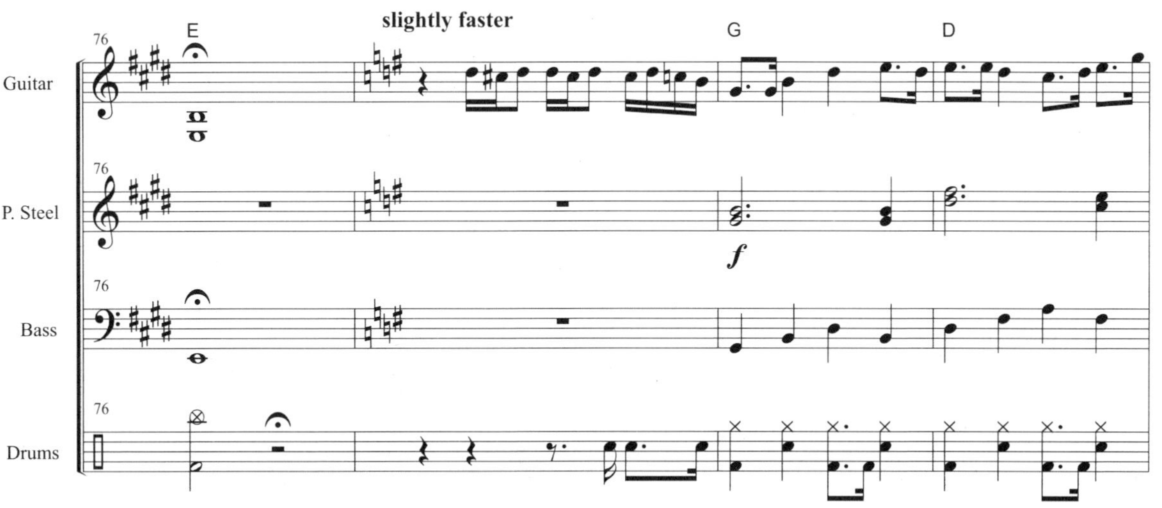
slightly faster
E
G
D
Guitar
P. Steel
Bass
Drums
76
f

G
C
G
D
Guitar
P. Steel
Bass
Drums
80

84
slightly slower
Viol.
mf
Gamba
mf
84
Cemb.
mf

slightly faster
89
Viol.
Gamba
Cemb.
Vocals
drink - ing in this bar
C
D
Guitar
G
D
P. Steel
Bass
Drums

slightly slower
94
Viol.
Gamba
Cemb.
Vocals
'ded
Guitar
G
P. Steel
Bass
Drums

Air Cushioned Ride, 2006 *A Spurious Emission*, 2007

No Window No Cry (Juan O'Gorman, Biblioteca Central de la UNAM, Mexico City), 2011

No Window No Cry (Oscar Niemeyer, Ciccillo Matarazzo Pavilion, São Paulo), 2010

No Window No Cry (Le Corbusier, Maison-atelier Lipschitz, Boulogne), 2011

3-2-1
ANRI SALA AND ANDRE VIDA IN CONVERSATION

Anri Sala
This performance, *3-2-1*, which features your improvisation, is like an offshoot that grows out of the body of the show and reinserts itself at precise and regular intervals.

I've been thinking about the idea that in the exhibition there are two kinds of openings. There are the holes in the walls covering the windows – these follow the pattern of the barrel organ score and create openings between the gallery and the park outside. They allow the exhibition to breathe in and out and let sound pass from inside to outside and vice versa. And at the beginning of your performance you'll place the bell of the saxophone into one of these holes, so that you'll be playing to the outside.

These are openings in space, which let the exhibition spread and unfold. But there are also what we could call holes in time and, in this exhibition, for me you are like an opening in time. In theory, your improvisations will be different every time. You will take the show in unpredictable directions each time you perform and, in a sense, this introduces a different kind of hole or break in the exhibition.

Andre Vida
When you're improvising you have to be as open as possible to the moment, to your responses to it, to what you can actually achieve on your instrument. But also to what you can't achieve, to what you don't know about yourself and what you don't know about your instrument. This idea of being like a hole immediately makes me think of this kind of openness and presence within the moment. But, of course, because of the repetition involved in this performance, I'm curious about how that's going to operate in 3-2-1. *During the 52 days of the exhibition, this performance is*

going to happen 468 times and I will participate in approximately 400 of these performances. I'm curious about how responses are going to start registering. After a week it could become mechanical and yet I will constantly be fighting against anything mechanical. I'll want to be continuously perceiving things, to be listening, to be focussing in on different aspects every time.

Sala
You'll be focussing on everything that can help you find new possibilities for your improvisation, that can help you to not get stuck by the repetition of the reference, which is *Long Sorrow*. And although *Long Sorrow* was originally an improvisation, the moment it was recorded it stopped being an open improvisation and became closed and fixed. I said before that *Long Sorrow* could be understood as a type of hole in the exhibition because it's a point of entry or exit from the exhibition for you. You will use it as a point of departure and go in and out in unexpected ways – musically but also psychologically, as you were just saying. The question is whether, at some point, *Long Sorrow*, which was originally an open improvisation performed outside an open window, stops being an inspiration and becomes a prison.

The performance has its own structure. You play with a recorded duet, then with the film and finally on your own, as a solo. And it's interesting to hear you say that after one week it could become mechanical. That's exactly what we both want to avoid because the whole idea is to keep it out of the known possibilities, to keep it open, unscripted and unscored. The aim is to exhaust all possibilities. How do you think *Long Sorrow* will operate within the daily practice of this performance? Where will the balance be between inspiration and impediment?

Vida
I was thinking about this and there are basically three choices: to accompany, to respond, or to ignore. You can play along with it. You can respond, which is a variation on that – playing against it or being antagonistic towards it. Taking in the images and sounds of Long Sorrow *and playing as a physical counterpoint. Or you can just totally ignore it. This is another option – to not look at it, to stand in a corner, to not play anything, to be silent. I mean that's also an option. That's something I was already thinking about – at what point is silence an acceptable response?*

Sala
It depends on whether silence comes as something active or as a form of failure. In *3-2-1* you first respond to a recording of Jemeel Moondoc responding to his own improvisation as captured in *Long Sorrow*. In a sense, there are two Jemeels playing. You encounter it as a duet and make it a trio. Then you improvise only with *Long Sorrow*, that is with Jemeel's improvisation in the film, making it a duet. And finally you play a solo, which is the end of the performance. Within each of Jemeel's improvisations there are silences – they are brief but well marked. And within each of your improvisations there might be moments when, if you fall silent, a trio becomes a duet and a duet becomes a solo. And this would be different from your solo at the end of the performance as it would be a moment when *Long Sorrow* has a recorded solo incorporating music and image. This will depend on how you use silence. How do you adjust the tempo and find a balance between when you fill in any space in the music and when you don't?

3-2-1, 2011

3-2-1, 2011

How do you play silence? Will silence become another musical element?

Vida
The quality of silence is so particular. It's difficult in the context of the trio, for instance, in the first room, when I'm playing with the recording of the two Jemeels, because it gets overwhelming at some points. You know there's so much saxophone and it just occupies so much space. Sometimes I feel like I'm obligated to take a moment of silence so that I can think. And when there are people in the room then it makes it even more important to tailor this experience for them. Having visitors in the galleries is going to have a huge effect on silence and also on sound. The silence in Long Sorrow, *for instance, is a great moment. I think it happens almost in the middle of the film. It's already marked in my mind where it happens so I have been playing with that particular silence. I also wondered, if I were to turn '3-2-1' into '3-1-1', that is, if I were silent in the second room, do you think it would be a transgression?*

Sala
If you are silent in the second room, the performance won't realise '3-2-1' as a concept. Rather than a deliberate attempt to change the concept of the piece, I think the decision about how much silence you need at a given moment in the day should be approached from a musical or organic perspective. '3-1-1' instead of '3-2-1' doesn't interest me as much because I want to keep the idea of a decreasing presence. Of course decreasing presence in number does not mean decreasing presence in intensity. When we did this performance in Berlin the intensity of your solo was totally overwhelming. The intensity doesn't have to do with the number of the saxophones in the space. I wouldn't agree that you should not play at all during *Long Sorrow*. But on a given day, do you play only a few notes in the very middle exactly in the moment where Jemeel stops playing? This is possible, and could be interesting. Anything is possible, it's not scored. You continue to have a critical musical approach and response to the thing and I want you to respond musically and organically to the concept of the invitation.

Vida
What is really interesting for me is to have an open and ongoing dialogue with you about the contours and limits of this performance. It allows me to think more specifically about my responses and to locate areas of tension.

Sala
For me you are not only playing notes you are also playing silence. And the moment you take a conceptual decision not to play at all during *Long Sorrow* then you're not playing silence you are playing a concept. Whereas if you only play one note then all the rest becomes played silence.

Vida
I think that behind every sound and every silence there's an intention, that both sound and silence carry intention. And that it would be possible to not play anything and still have presence. If the intention was right it would still be possible to properly enact the concept that you're describing.

Sala
This leads us to the question of how you are present during a long absence and how you are present during a short absence. I've seen you present during a short silence during the performance in Berlin. But what I don't yet know is at what point your presence during

a long silence becomes an absence. At what point do you become like anybody else in the space but just with the saxophone in your hand. And this is not the aim.

Vida
I like this idea of being between absence and presence. Going to the other extreme, if I were to play the exact same thing that Jemeel Moondoc plays in Long Sorrow, *is it possible you that would consider this a '1'?*

Sala
No because you would nevertheless be two presences in the space. There is a deliberate asymmetry between the majority of the music in the show, which is scored, and your performance, which is not. So if you were to play the same melody, the same notes as Jemeel does in *Long Sorrow* (while *Long Sorrow* is playing) you would be playing a 'score' even if it isn't written down as a succession of notes before you. It's something that might be interesting once but if it is repeated I think it upsets the balance between what is scored and what is improvised.

Vida
I think it's possible, after having completed so many of these daily performances, that one day I'm going to play it exactly as I've heard it all these times. It would simply be a musical response to having heard it so many times. And if something like that were to happen, it would be magic.

Sala
But this is very different and it would be magic because, as you say, it would be a musical response and not directed by a score. It follows the logic of improvisation but it comes to the same musical result.

Vida
Yes exactly. In my experience these moments, they just happen. You never know when they're coming.

Sala
Today, for the first time, you did a full rehearsal where you undertook the full daily set of nine performances. When we did this performance for the first time in Berlin at VeneKlasen/Werner it was a one-off. At the Serpentine it will, of course, be very different – because of the physical stamina required but also because psychologically you will enter into a different territory. I'm curious about how you think this will affect the music you will be playing.

Vida
When I consider the prospect of performing nine times a day over the 52 day period of the show, the most important question for me is how to maintain not only my focus and presence in the moment, but also the perspective and distance from my performance that allows me to make interesting decisions about the direction of the music. It's really hard to say once you get to day 35 what's going to happen. I know that psychologically, as a performer, when I see even one person in the room it totally alters the way that I play. I know already that I'm going to be addressing myself as much as I can to that person.

Sala
This leads to another idea I want to raise, which is about the exhaustion of improvisation. Do you think it is possible to reach a point where you exhaust all possibilities? That you could reach a point when all possible directions are exhausted?

Vida
I don't think it's possible although I think it's a good question and it's one that I'm curious about. It's part of the reason I'm interested in this project – I want to see where it pushes me. I haven't ever put myself in a position like this. This term 'improvisation' is maybe not the best term to use. Steve Lacy talked about 'spontaneous composition', which I always thought was a better way of describing it because it really is an act of composition. Improvisation gives this impression of freedom and in fact what I've learned is that freedom is sometimes not so useful. Having something to work off, a structure to fight against can be more productive.

A piece of mine that addresses this theme is called Tie me Up. *It's for two violins and a viola. The musicians wear these complicated straightjackets that are connected to each other at multiple points by ropes. They have to really fight against each other to be able to touch the bow to the string. This visceral struggle is closer to what interests me in improvisation or 'spontaneous composition'. It's similar to what we have been discussing – this very rigid time structure that you've come up with for this installation. You are, in a sense, putting me in a kind of straightjacket; I have to always play within the same framework and yet try to do something compelling each time. The challenge is to see it anew every time and to find something inspiring in it, in the music and in the actual rooms.*

Sala
The idea of movement is very important to this performance. I see this piece as a breeze that passes through the show. It cuts through it, like an incision, like the holes we spoke of earlier.

Vida
That's interesting – I have been thinking about the importance of movement in these performances. In the first room I play just with audio played back – it's as if there are ghosts in the room with me. And in the second room there is the actual image of Jemeel, which is moving and there is a play of movement and light and it opens up my ability to walk and move in the room, which is a whole other dimension that interests me.

Sala
We spoke earlier about 'dead' moments and the differences between active and passive silences – the idea that silence has to be 'played' and not be a result of not being able to do anything else. And we were discussing the possibility that you could scratch a score on the wall, which would be like help from a friend. And I have seen some of your scores and they look very dynamic. It's almost like they are scores that are there to give you ideas and not to tell you what to do.

Vida
That's exactly how I think of them. Sometimes, when I make a score, it's actually a way of remembering an improvisation, a spontaneous composition, the things you discover when you're playing that you can't verbalise. The physicality and tension of performance and the ways that notes get stretched and broken and collide. I learned a lot about notation from my teacher, Anthony Braxton, but for me notating is never really a tool for enacting something specific.

Sala
In a way your scores are like anti-scores because what they do is remind you that improvisation is possible in moments where you might fall back on repetition or on

something mechanical. As long as they inspire improvisation, they are about an opening up rather than a closing down.

Vida
Exactly. It makes me think of how every time I pick up my instrument, I'm always in this immediate battle to reinvent my relationship to it. So these scores are like snapshots from an ongoing long term relationship. They tell me where I've been and give me suggestions of things that I could discover.

In preparing for this project, I did an eight-hour solo improvisation. It was such an extreme experience that it made me realise that I needed to find an alternative to visualised notation, one that could be deployed and reinterpreted over a long duration. And one of the types of notation I thought of was using a poem. The first poetic logic that came to me after that eight-hour day was 'trust the silence'. Because one of the challenges in constantly creating sounds over a course of 30 minutes, nine times a day, is that it becomes difficult to forget about your task and just trust that the silence is going to lead you.

Sala
It's interesting that you speak of this. There is a moment in *Long Sorrow* where Jemeel improvises with church bells that play nearby and that's where I realised that he was so open but at the same time completely focused on his situation, which was that he was suspended outside the 18th floor of a building. In a sense he grasped at the bells as a way of making himself forget where he was. He attached himself to the details of his situation. You will be grasping for these details, outside of *Long Sorrow* and other than the exhibition, whether it is some form of notation or poem, as you describe, the features of the audience or the sound coming from outside through the holes in the walls, in order to deal with the repetition and this 'void' of time. Where Jemeel was suspended in the void of space, you will be suspended in the void of time.

3-2-1, 2011

Ulysses, 2007

[Intro]

Two bar entrance with faintly beating feelers.

Bootless Bootless Bootless Bootless

Bootless Bootless Bootless Boot Boot Bootless

And there was music.

Bootless Bootless Lickitup Bootless

Bootless Bootless Lickitup Bootless

Bootless Bootless Lickitup Bootless

[Riff 1]

To the refrain in a funk.

Boo Entity Boo Entity Boo Entity Boot ti boot ti

Boo Entity Boo Entity Boo Entity Boot ti boot ti

Boo Entity Boo Entity Boo Entity Boot ti boot ti

Boo Entity Boo Entity Boo Entity Boot ti boot ti

Clash Boo Entity Boo Entity Boot ti boot ti

Boo Entity Boo Entity Boo Entity Boot ti boot ti

Boo Entity Boo Entity Boo Entity Boot ti boot ti

Boo Entity Boo Entity Cacarracarracarraca

Ulysses, 2007 (Score)

[Verse 1]

Bootless Bootless Lickitup Bootless
I sit and hear sentimental footsteps,

Bootless Bootless Lickitup Boot Boot Bootless
then a voice say “hi so?

Bootless Bootless Lickitup Bootless
So what you got? What you got this time?

Bootless Bootless Lickitup Boot Boot Bootless
Come on let’s get high_______________

Bootless Bootless Lickitup Bootless
Come on Lexxo what you got next-o?

Bootless Bootless Lickitup Boot Boot Bootless
Walking twenty five miles__________-o?

[Chorus 1]

Part A

	And snares		And snares
Bootless	**Bootless**	**Bootless**	**Bootless**
I've	found a	new	way
	And snares		And snares
Bootless	**Bootless**	**Bootless**	**Bootless**
I've	found a	new	way
	And snares		And snares
Bootless	**Bootless**	**Bootless**	**Bootless**
So	don't	amuse	me
	And snares		And snares of the devil
Bootless	**Bootless**	**Bootless**	**Bootless**
I don't	need	your	sympathy

It repeats itself again.

Part B

	And snares		And snares
Bootless	**Bootless**	**Win - dow**	**sash**
	Oh	La La	La La
	And snares	And snares	
Bootless	**Bootless**	**Win - dow**	**sash**
		Ulysses______________	
	And snares	And snares	
Bootless	**Bootless**	**Bootless**	**Clash**
	I found a	new way	
	And snares	And drums rolling	
Bootless	**Bootless**	**Diddleiddle ooddleooddle**	
	I found a	new way	baby

Tara Tara. Great chorus that. Taree Tara.

[Riff 2]

After myriad metamorphoses of symbol, it blazes.
Booming over bombarding chords.

Boo Entity — And snares Ca Entity — Boo Entity — And snares Ca tea Ca

Boo Entity — And snares Ca Entity — Boo Entity — And snares Ca tea Ca

Boo Entity — And snares Ca Entity — Boo Entity — And snares Ca tea Ca

Boo Entity — And snares Ca Entity — Boo Entity — And snares Ca Teats

Boo Entity — And snares Ca Entity — Boo Entity — And snares Ca tea Ca

Boo Entity — And snares Ca Entity — Boo Entity — And snares Ca Teats

Boo Entity — And snares Ca Entity — Boo Entity — And snares Ca tea Ca

Boo Entity — And snares Ca Entity — Boo Entity — And snares Ca Entity

[Verse 2]

Bootless Am I	And snares enters softly **Bootless** Ulysses?	**Bootless** Am I	And snares **Bootless** Ulysses?
Bootless No, but	And snares **Bootless** you are	**Bootless** now,	**Boot Boot Bootless** boy______
Bootless You're a	And snares **Bootless** hedonist.	**Bootless** Dead	And snares **Bootless** hedonist,
Bootless well	And snares **Bootless** last night	**Bootless** was	And snares **Boot Boot Bootless** wild______
Clash What's	And snares struck boldly **Bootless** the matter there?	**Bootless** Feeling kind of	And snares **Bootless** anxious?
Bootless Felling that	And snares **Bootless** hot blood	**Bootless** grow	And snares **Boot Boot Bootless** cold?_____
Bootless Yeah	And snares **Bootless** everyone,	**Bootless** everybody	And snares of the devil **Taratarataratara** knows it,
Clash Yeah	**Bootless** everyone,	**Bootless** everybody	**Bootless** knows it,
Clash everybody	**Bootless** knows you're...	**Boot** **Boot**	**Boot** **Boot**

His hand moved faithfully the unsteady symbols.
Repeat capriciosly.

[Chorus 2]

Sings the chorus.

Part A

Bootless I've	And snares **Bootless** found a	**Bootless** new	And snares **Bootless** way
Bootless I've	And snares **Bootless** found a	**Bootless** new	And snares **Bootless** way
Bootless So	And snares **Bootless** don't	**Bootless** amuse	And snares of the devil **Bootless** me
Bootless I don't	And snares **Bootless** need	**Bootless** your	**Bootless** sympathy

It repeats itself again.

Part B

Bootless	And snares **Bootless** Oh	**Win - dow** La La	And snares **sash** La La
Bootless	And snares **Bootless**	**Win - dow** Ulysses___________	And snares **sash** ___________
Bootless	And snares **Bootless** I found a	**Bootless** new way	And snares **Bootless**
Clash	And snares **Bootless** I found a	And drums rolling **Diddleiddle** new way	 **ooddleooddle** baby

It repeats itself again.

With care repeated, with greater difficulty remembered,
forgot with ease, with misgiving remembered, repeated with error.

[Middle]

But wait. Chords dark. Lugugugubrious. Low. Lumpmusic.

<table>
<tr><td>Boom</td><td>Chi Ca Chi</td><td>Boom</td><td>Chi Ca Chi</td></tr>
<tr><td>Boom</td><td>Chi Ca Chi</td><td>Boom</td><td>Chi Ca Chi</td></tr>
<tr><td>Boom
Oh</td><td>Chi Ca Chi</td><td>Boom</td><td>Chi Ca Chi
Then</td></tr>
<tr><td>Boom
sud-</td><td>Chi Ca Chi
den-</td><td>Bom Bom
ly</td><td>Bladder Bom
you</td></tr>
<tr><td>Boom
know</td><td>Chi Ca Chi</td><td>Boom</td><td>Chi Ca Chi
You're</td></tr>
<tr><td>Clash
ne-</td><td>Chi Ca Chi
ver</td><td>Bom Bom
go-</td><td>Bladder Bom
ing</td></tr>
<tr><td>Clash Tschunk
home</td><td>Boot Tschunk</td><td>Boot Tschunk
You're never</td><td>Boot Tschunk
You're</td></tr>
<tr><td>Boot Tschunk
never</td><td>Boot Tschunk</td><td>Boot Tschunk
You're never</td><td>Boot Tschunk
You're</td></tr>
<tr><td>Boot Tschunk
never</td><td>Boot Tschunk</td><td>Boot Tschunk
You're never</td><td>Boot Tschunk
You're</td></tr>
<tr><td>Rolywholyover
Boot Tschunk
never</td><td>Boot Tschunk</td><td>Boot Tschunk
You're</td><td>Boot Tschunk
never</td></tr>
<tr><td>Bom
going</td><td>Bom
home________________</td><td>Bladder</td><td>Bom</td></tr>
</table>

[Coda]

Bootless No	And snares Bootless	Bootless Not going	And snares Clash
Bootless home	And snares Bootless	And snares Clash baby______________________	Carr Carr Carra
Bootless No	And snares Bootless no	Bootless not	And snares Clash Ulysses___
Bootless ________	And snares Bootless	And snares Clash baby______________________	Carr Carr Carra
Bootless No	And snares Bootless	Bootless not	And snares Clash Ulysses___
Bootless ________	And snares Bootless	And snares Clash oo-hoo-hoo______________	Carr Carr Carra
Bootless	And snares Bootless	Bootless Not	And snares Clash Ulysses___
Bootless ________	And snares of the devil Carracarracarracacarracarracarracacarracarraca		

The endlessnessnessness...
He hummed, prolonging in solemn echo the closes of the bars.
Low sank the music, air and words.

Answer Me, 2008

Answer Me, 2008

Answer Me, 2008

Answer Me, 2008

Answer Me, 2008

Answer Me, 2008

SALA WITH SCHILLER: WORLD, FORM, AND PLAY IN *MIXED BEHAVIOUR*

Michael Fried

In the twelfth of Friedrich Schiller's 'Letters on the Aesthetic Education of Man' (originally written in 1795), a foundational text on aesthetic thought for the modern period, the German poet, playwright, and thinker Friedrich Schiller posits two fundamentally opposed drives within the human psyche – first, a purely receptive drive to experience the sheer succession of sensations, which is also to say the sheer flow of time (or succession as such); and second, a drive to assert control over such material, to give it form, which is also to say (as Schiller does toward the end of the eleventh 'Letter') to annul time, to affirm persistence within change, and to subjugate the manifold variety of the world to the unity of the self.[1] As he also writes: 'In order … not to be mere world, [man] must impart form to matter; in order not to be mere form, he must give reality [to form]' (117). Schiller calls these drives the *sensuous drive* and the *formal drive*, and further imagines, first, that each naturally seeks to realise itself to the maximum, and second, that the essential task of culture (his ultimate concern) is precisely to do justice to both drives equally, to maintain each against the other: '*first*, to preserve the life of sense against the encroachments of freedom [the will, the drive to autonomy]; and *second*, to secure the personality against the forces of sensation. The former it achieves by developing our capacity for feeling, the latter by developing our capacity for reason (122). (Needless to say, Kant's philosophy, in particular the *Critique of Judgment*, hovers in the immediate background.) There follows a passage of particular interest in the present context. Schiller writes:

> Since the world is extension in time, i.e., change, the perfection of that faculty that connects man with the world will have to consist in *maximum changeability and maximum extensity* [my emphasis]. Since the person is persistence within change, the perfection of that faculty that is to oppose change will have to be *maximum autonomy and maximum intensity* [my emphasis]. The more facets his receptivity develops, the more labile it is, *and the more surface it presents to phenomena* [my emphasis], so much more world does man *apprehend*, and all the more potentialities does he develop in himself. The more power and depth the personality achieves, and the more freedom reason attains, so much more world does man *comprehend*, and all the more form does he create outside of himself. His education [the work of culture] will therefore consist, *firstly*, in procuring for the receptive faculty the most manifold contacts with the world, and, within the purview of feeling, *intensifying passivity to the utmost* [my emphasis]; *secondly*, in securing for the determining faculty the *highest degree of independence from the receptive* [my emphasis] and, within the purview of reason, *intensifying activity to the utmost* [my emphasis]. Where both these aptitudes are conjoined, man will combine the greatest fullness of existence with the highest autonomy and freedom, and instead of losing himself to the world, will rather *draw the latter into himself* [my emphasis again] in all its infinitude of phenomena, and subject it to the unity of his reason. (122–23)

1 Friedrich Schiller, 'Letters on the Aesthetic Education of Man', in *Essays*, trans Walter Hinderer and Daniel O Dahlstrom (New York: Continuum, 1993), pp. 118–21; the statement about annulling time and affirming persistence within change is p. 118. Further page references will be in parentheses in the text. See also the discussion of the 'Letters' in Frederick Beiser, *Schiller as Philosopher: A Re-Examination* (Oxford and New York: Oxford University Press, 2005).

In the next 'Letter,' indeed, Schiller suggests that were it possible for a human being actually to maximise both drives, to combine receptivity and autonomy at something like full strength, he (Schiller means he or she) 'would have a complete intuition of his human nature, and the object that afforded him this vision would become for him a symbol of his *accomplished destiny* and in consequence (since that is only to be attained in the totality of time), serve him as a manifestation of the infinite (126).

Assuming that such cases could actually occur, Schiller says, they would awaken in the subject a new drive, a third drive, which he calls the *play drive*, and which he claims 'would be directed toward annulling time *within time* [an extremely interesting claim in view of what will follow], reconciling becoming with absolute being and change with identity (126).' Or again: 'The sense drive wants to *be* determined, wants to receive its object; the form drive wants *itself* to determine, wants to bring forth its object. The play drive, therefore, will endeavor so to receive as if it had itself brought forth, and so to bring forth as the intuitive sense aspires to receive (126).' In other words, following some difficult sentences on contingency, the play drive will 'introduce form into matter and reality into form. To the extent that it deprives feelings and passions of their dynamic power, it will bring them into harmony with the ideas of reason; and to the extent that it deprives the laws of reason of their moral compulsion, it will reconcile them with the interests of the senses (127).'

In the following 'Letter,' the fifteenth, Schiller explains that 'the object of the sense drive, expressed in a general concept, we call *life*, in the widest sense of the term: a concept designating all material being and all that is immediately present to the senses. The object of the form drive, expressed in a general concept, we call *form*, both in the figurative and in the literal sense of this word: a concept that includes all the formal qualities of things and all the relations of these to our thinking faculties. The object of the play drive, represented in a general schema, may therefore be called *living form*: a concept serving to designate all the aesthetic qualities of phenomena and, in a word, what in the widest sense of the term we call *beauty* (128).' At this point, or rather just before it, I want to leave Schiller behind: the notion of beauty will be of no use whatsoever in what follows, and indeed strikes one almost as an atavism when it suddenly comes to the fore in the passage I have just cited. For we are on the threshold of the decisive turning in aesthetics that will be represented by Hegel, in whose *Lectures* on the topic the concept of beauty, as is well known, plays a structurally minor role.[2]

Nor do I wish to follow Schiller in maintaining that the opposition between the sense drive and the form drive is determining for the human psyche as such, or that ideally both drives are reconciled, brought into relation with each other, via a third or play drive also within the psyche, so to speak. Not that it is hard to imagine, not that one is not familiar with, less convincing claims than these about the nature and structure of the human psyche. But my aim in what immediately follows is more narrowly focused: I want to use the terms in which Schiller seeks to define the drives as a means of characterising, perhaps I should say of framing, an exemplary work of video art by Anri Sala.

2 See Ludwig Wittgenstein, *Culture and Value*, rev. ed., ed. Georg Henrik von Wright with Heikki Nyman, rev. ed. of text by Alois Pichler, trans. Peter Winch (Oxford: Basil Blackwell, 1998), p. 91: 'The way whole periods are incapable of freeing themselves from certain concepts – e.g. the concept "beautiful" & "beauty"'. Obviously Wittgenstein feels that it is imperative that we do so free ourselves, and I am with him on this.

The work is *Mixed Behaviour* and was made by Sala in 2003. Ideally it would now be possible for the reader to leave this essay and view the actual piece, which lasts exactly eight minutes and nineteen seconds, preferably more than once. Of course that isn't possible. Nevertheless I shall proceed by describing the video *as if* the reader had just watched it.[3] A few preliminaries:

First, *Mixed Behaviour* was filmed in Sala's native Tirana on New Year's Eve, 2003 (and then worked on extensively afterward). According to Sala, in the course of the 1990s and the first years of the new decade the New Year's Eve celebration in Tirana became more than a little dangerous, with individuals setting off their own fireworks and also firing guns the sound of which was masked by the fireworks, so that the next morning it would turn out that people had been killed and no one had realised it. In important respects, *Mixed Behaviour* represents an inspired response to this situation. Second, *Mixed Behaviour* brilliantly exemplifies one of Sala's chief concerns throughout his career to date: the relation of image to sound, or perhaps more accurately image track to sound track, which in many of his videos or short films are treated as essentially autonomous elements that nevertheless – or rather, precisely by virtue of that autonomy – are made to articulate each other in fascinating and productive ways. This is true of *Long Sorrow*, 2005, in which the noted free jazz saxophonist Jemeel Moondoc has been filmed at extremely close range improvising on his instrument – which we no more than glimpse – while suspended outside a window on the eighteenth floor of a large apartment complex in Berlin.[4] *Mixed Behaviour* takes a similarly inventive approach to the same basic issue. But its import goes beyond even that, as I shall try to show with the help of the preceding summary of Schiller. Finally, if the reader were about to watch (and hear) the actual video I would say at this point: above all keep your eyes open; don't let yourself be lulled by an expectation that the video will simply continue as it starts – in fact about two minutes and fifty seconds into the piece distinctly strange things begin to happen. As follows:

The video opens confusingly. It is dark, nighttime, and we hear the sound of raindrops striking some sort of surface (a plastic tarpaulin, it turns out). We then become aware of a light source – a flashlight of some sort? – the other side of a transparent plastic sheet that seems to be covering... what? Some sort of equipment: we first see a dark rectilinear form with wiring coming out of its top – probably a battery, a power source of some kind. We notice too that someone is moving just beyond the plastic sheet, we see the sheet being lifted, we glimpse an earphone gripped in a hand, we sense the person beyond the sheet ducking to get his head under its protection, then we are given a glimpse of his head and face and realise that he – a young man with short-cropped dark hair – has put on the earphones, and as all this is taking place we first become aware of a few crackling noises, like firecrackers or gunshots, and then, as the young man seems to do something with his hands to the equipment in front of him, we also hear music, a disco beat... All this takes less than a minute, in fact after fifty seconds our point of view shifts

3 I saw *Mixed Behaviour* under ideal conditions at Sala's 2009 exhibition at the Contemporary Art Center in Cincinnati. It was shown on a 4:3 format video monitor suspended in the middle of a dark (but not pitch black) room, with stereo speakers sitting behind the monitor more or less at the same (imagined) distance as that between the viewer and the DJ in the video. It was hard to break off watching and listening.

4 I discuss *Long Sorrow* at length in my recent book *Four Honest Outlaws: Sala, Ray, Gordon, Marioni*. (London and New Haven: Yale University Press, 2011). For the reading of *Long Sorrow*, see pp. 32–49.

decisively to a position directly behind the young man and the plastic sheeting-covered equipment and perhaps fifteen feet away, and when this happens we also become aware of the larger situation: the young man and the equipment (on a table), indeed we too, in a manner of speaking, are on the roof of a building from which we look past the young man and the equipment toward the dark city beyond. Most conspicuously there is a large building right of center which we feel must be several hundred feet away, part of which remains dark and part of which shows lighted windows (possibly, though, we are seeing two different buildings at somewhat different distances from us), plus there are various smaller buildings in the distance, but the upper half of the image is taken up by the night sky and the rocketing or exploding fireworks. And along with the sound of the fireworks, and the background sound of the rain, there is now equally prominently the sound of music with its Latin-sounding beat (actually the music started up around forty seconds into the piece, when we were still under the plastic sheeting), music we quickly gather is somehow being controlled – actually it is being 'remixed' – by the young man, who in effect is playing the role of a DJ on this curious occasion.[5]

And that is the basis of the entire work: the camera now stays fixed, we are shown the young man always from the rear, sometimes bent considerably over so as to get his entire upper body under the plastic sheeting, sometimes only partly bent over, but always his hands and the equipment are covered by the sheeting, and within a minute or two our attention shifts almost exclusively to the sky and the fireworks, or rather to the interplay between the remixed music and the fireworks – the latter as both visual and sonic phenomena – which are clearly meant to be experienced in some at least partly motivated relation to each other. In the upper left corner of the image we see the scalloped bottom of an awning that presumably has been lowered to help protect the camera (and in a sense us) from the rain.

As for the overall structure of *Mixed Behaviour*, two points should be stressed. First, I count four more or less distinct phases or 'movements' based on shifts in the music, which as I have said begins roughly forty seconds into the piece; a second phase begins around the four minute mark; then shortly after five minutes the music stops and for nearly forty seconds we hear only fireworks (and rain), until around 5:50 a new burst of music comes on, supplemented at around 6:28 by voices chanting something we cannot quite make out (there were voices earlier, too); finally a last phase begins around 6:55 with music of a different beat, though the voices return shortly before the 8-minute mark. Then there is silence except for a few fireworks until the piece ends at 8:19.

Second, an absolutely crucial point, about two minutes and forty seconds into the piece something altogether out of the ordinary happens: two fireworks *go into reverse*, by which I mean that instead of simply exploding into a large number of brilliant fragments that then (often) explode again and slowly fall, extinguishing themselves en route, the explosion and fanning out of fragments are followed by an exactly opposite movement as the fragments contract back to the originating explosion (and beyond). Following the first few reversals, however, the explosions return to normal for roughly 20 seconds, then another explosion goes into reverse, and starting just after three

5 The DJ is using two CD players and a mixer, not that there is any way of knowing that from the video itself. According to Sala, his choice of music was inspired by that of Kruder and Dorfmeister, an Austrian duo who came to the fore starting around 1993. My thanks to Sala for providing this and other information about his piece.

and a half minutes the reversals return in force to great effect – they cannot now be missed. And just over one minute later, around 4:37, we see a single explosion expand then contract and then expand and contract again twice more; this takes place in the sky right of center, where most of the more spectacular fireworks go off, and the effect of playfulness as well as of what can only be called authorial control – but this will call for qualification – is extremely strong. Something of the sort also happens just over one minute later, the fireworks this time being more than usually dramatic and the reversals much speedier, more palpably 'in one's face,' than any until now. In the last minute and a half we are made particularly aware of the awning at the upper left, as well as of rockets exploding overhead, beyond the limits of the 'frame,' drenching the DJ-figure and his protected equipment with bursts of red and green illumination. (Something similar happens toward the beginning of the piece.) Toward the end of the video there is music alone for maybe half a minute; then we see the DJ stand up as if to leave the scene though not quite in the flesh – rather he appears superimposed over a shot of the equipment as if he were a ghost rather than an actual person. We hear the voices again and a few last explosions, then the screen goes black and the video is over. Not that the foregoing amounts to a thorough inventory of what *Mixed Behaviour* offers to be seen and heard: for example, at various moments skyrockets or Roman candles whiz by at what seems dangerously close range, and in general more seems to happening than can be readily inventoried, even after repeated watchings. Plus there is the impression the piece conveys, both visually and sonically, of all this taking place not just some distance away but also overhead, in close proximity to where we seemingly are. (Of course, almost every time I have said 'we' I have meant the camera.)

The question that now arises is how exactly Sala's video relates to Schiller's account in the 'Letters on the Aesthetic Education of Man' of the interaction among the three drives – the sensuous drive, the formal drive, and the play drive – assuming that such a relation between the two exists. Let me say for a start that after I had watched *Mixed Behaviour* several times, Schiller's text irresistibly came to mind, and that when I sat down and reread the latter – it had been years since I had last done so – I was powerfully struck by the affinity between the two. Take for example Schiller's account of the sensuous drive, which you will remember he equates in the first place with the sheer succession of sensations as well as with the flow of time (or succession as such): what could better exemplify these than a display of fireworks exploding in a night sky, which is to say successively albeit unpredictably rising from the ground, bursting into brilliant, different coloured outward-expanding patterns, the individual fragments of which then fall back to earth, losing brightness as they do so, as other fireworks arise and explode, to be replaced in turn by still others (fireworks as an 'art' of pure sensation, visual and aural)? And then there is the rain, which, like the fireworks, we both see and hear, with the further implication that were we actually on the roof we might be feeling the impact of the rain as well. Indeed the sound of the rain on the plastic sheeting chimes with Schiller's claim that the 'perfection of that faculty that connects man with the world will have to consist in maximum changeability and maximum extensity... The more facets his receptivity develops, the more labile it is, and the more surface it presents to phenomena...' – the surface of the plastic sheeting serving in this context as a figure for the heightened or 'extended' receptivity of the self. (The presence of the sheeting both was and was not fortuitous. The original idea for *Mixed Behaviour* did not call for it; but as New Year's Eve approached Sala realised that rain was likely – it had been raining all week, apparently – and provided for that contingency. Brilliantly, as matters turned out.) As for the form drive, it is exemplified in the first instance by the DJ, whom we soon come to perceive as seeking to use the music he is remixing as a means of gaining control over the fireworks, or at least of 'including' the fireworks in the music; and up to a point the video may appear to suggest that he succeeds in this, at least some of the time, most notably at those moments when the fireworks go into reverse, or rather – to quote Sala from an unpublished discussion with Hans Ulrich Obrist – when their movements 'go forward and backward depending on the movements of the music.' In any case, we quickly sense that the DJ has no audience for his music beyond the immediate situation, however the latter is described.

Here it is crucial to get the sense of competition or struggle between the two drives both in Schiller's 'Letters' and, in my account, as figured in Sala's video exactly right. Most important, it would be faithful neither to Schiller's thought nor to the logic of the video if one came to see the DJ – avatar of the form drive in this reading – as simply or unequivocally mastering the flow of sensations as figured by the fireworks (and indeed the rain). I think of him rather as fictively absorbed in pursuit of that aim. That he is forced to do so under the plastic sheeting in order to keep the rain off his equipment – a state of affairs that in obvious respects would tend to separate him from the fireworks (as would, for that matter, his wearing of earphones) – reinforces one's sense of the difficulty of his project, hence of the magnitude of his absorption in it. Our somewhat distanced view of him from behind activates a familiar structure from absorptive painting of the 18th and 19th centuries – think of Chardin, Courbet, Caillebotte, Hammershøi and others – and from recent photography – Struth's first museum series and various works by Jeff Wall, in particular. The rain doubly matters, in other words, as a figure for the successiveness of sensations and because it requires that the DJ work under wraps, so to speak. Or rather triply, in that the sheeting comes to stand for the receptiveness of the self.[6] More broadly, in Schiller's text both the sensuous drive and the form drive are understood to strive for maximum expression. To the extent that in a particular instance this proves attainable – to the extent to which the two drives operating at full strength turn out to be harmonisable with one another – that will be the work of the play drive, which Schiller associates with the 'aesthetic qualities of phenomena and, in a word, what in the widest sense of the term we call beauty' or, let us simply say, with art. And *that*, I want to suggest, is figured or expressed in *Mixed Behaviour* by the work of the artist, Anri Sala, though of course it is also possible to see the DJ as a surrogate for the artist – but again only up to a point. Indeed the non-documentary or say fictional status of the DJ is insisted on at the end of the video when he is rendered ghostlike as he stands up to leave. And even before that moment, though it is difficult to make out, the DJ's actions themselves go into reverse whenever the fireworks do – Sala had no way of reversing the exploding fireworks other than by reversing the image track as such. (One can see this in the way roman candles and the like streak downward toward their points of origin at those moments.) Finally, the very theme of 'connection' between the fireworks and the music is consistent with Sala's larger concern throughout his career with the relation of image-track to sound-track; the special character of *Mixed Behaviour* in this regard is that it thematises that relation as one in which the sound of the remixing seeks to master the image, also in a sense the sound, of the fireworks. But as I have said, it is crucial to recognise that this is only a fiction, and that Sala's project, as distinct from the DJ's, is at once to create that

6 Was Sala lucky that it rained, then? No doubt. But he has repeatedly shown, as in the dazzlingly opportunistic *Air Cushioned Ride,* 2007, that he knows what do with his luck. A story for another occasion.

impression and to acknowledge, in the modernist sense of the term, that the truth of the piece is more complex – more playful, one might say. In this connection it is interesting to note that much of the post-filming work concerned the sound; for example, Sala went back to Albania with recording equipment and set off his own fireworks to make sure the sonic dimension of the piece would be exactly as he wanted it.

Something else one wouldn't know simply from experiencing the video is that Sala himself was crouching under the plastic sheeting covering the battery and mixers throughout the duration of the shoot; it was he who filmed the opening seconds of *Mixed Behaviour* from that cramped vantage point. During the rest of the filming there was no one behind the camera – but of course the directorial intelligence throughout is his.

It's in this light, too, that I understand one of the features of *Mixed Behaviour* that most surprised me when I first viewed it, and for some time afterward – I refer to the fact that the initial reversal of exploding fireworks occurs relatively early in the piece, after no more than two minutes and fifty seconds. One might have expected that Sala would have chosen to make the viewer wait longer before introducing that patently unnatural effect. But then (after repeated viewings) I realised that introducing it early on meant that the viewer had ample opportunity to become accustomed to the fact of reversal, with the result that by the time reversal comes back at just over three and a half minutes and again just after four and a half minutes and five and a half minutes, and not only comes back but is increasingly activated in syncopation with the music, the viewer – I'm taking my experience as typical – has begun at least somewhat to lose hold of the 'natural' tendency of the fireworks to explode outward and then fall to earth, and thus to accept reversal as something other than anomalous within the structural logic of *Mixed Behaviour* as it unfolds over time. In other words, the cumulative effect of temporal reversal in Sala's video is not so much that of contravening or dominating the natural order of events – in Schiller's terminology, the mastering of sensation and succession by a drive toward form – as it is something like what Schiller provocatively characterised in his fourteenth 'Letter' as the 'annulling of time *within time*,' which in this case I understand to mean preserving the effect of temporal succession while taking radical imaginative liberties with temporality as ordinarily experienced. (Transforming temporal succession from within, so to speak.) More broadly, Schiller says of the play drive that it 'will endeavor so to receive as if it had itself brought forth, and so to bring forth as the intuitive sense aspires to receive' – a rather prescient paraphrase of the overall import of *Mixed Behaviour* as I have described it. As is the notion that if the two drives could be conjoined, 'man … instead of losing himself to the world, will rather draw the latter into himself in all its infinitude of phenomena …'

Let me be clear about what I take all this to mean: I am not suggesting that Sala conceived of *Mixed Behaviour* in terms of the argument of Schiller's text – nothing could be less likely, or indeed more foreign to Sala's general approach to his art. In particular the fact that the video is set in Tirana has everything to do with Sala's personal history as well as with a certain 'ethical' or 'political' impulse – to neutralise or even to redeem artistically a situation, the firing of guns throughout New Year's Eve, of which he disapproved. And as I have already noted, Sala's work

7 (New Haven and London: Yale University Press, 2008).

from the start has been concerned with relating image track to sound track in original and compelling ways. I *am* suggesting, though, that the basic argument of the 'Letters' with respect to the three drives bears a surprisingly close relation to Sala's video, or to put this slightly differently, that the medium of video in Sala's hands turns out to have lent itself to an artistic project that can usefully be understood in terms of Schiller's exalted but also quite specific vision of the stakes of art and the mission of culture. This may appear to defy common sense of a contextual sort: between Schiller's 'Letters' and Sala's *Mixed Behaviour* there looms a chronological gulf of more than two centuries, not to mention the disparity in almost every cultural regard between the Weimar of Schiller and Goethe and the Tirana or Paris or Berlin (Sala's cities) of the early 2000s. But it may be that contextual considerations are an unreliable guide in situations such as this one. In my 2008 book *Why Photography Matters as Art as Never Before*[7] I tried to show that as regards the practice of a number of leading contemporary photographers, the antitheatrical artistic regime or episteme that first emerged in the course of the 1750s and 60s in France and of which Diderot in his writings on painting and drama was the most lucid advocate is still in force – dialectically transformed, that can't be stressed too strongly, but nevertheless in force. And in my book *Four Honest Outlaws* I extend that account to cover the diverse work of Sala, Charles Ray, Joseph Marioni, and Douglas Gordon. I would not want to launch a comparably sweeping claim about the contemporary relevance of Schiller's aesthetics, and yet there is an important sense in which it was precisely the technology of video that established the conditions for the belated realisation of his vision especially with regard to the issues of play and temporality as these are theorised in the 'Letters.'

Needless to say, this is to take Sala's achievement in *Mixed Behaviour* extremely seriously – much more seriously than is usual in commentaries on contemporary art. And it is to take Schiller's ideas extremely seriously as well – if not more seriously then in a different, less strictly historicist spirit than is usual in commentaries on German post-Kantian thought.[8] To which I will add that the treatment of temporality in *Mixed Behaviour* is consistent with what in *Four Honest Outlaws* I seek to show has been Sala's intense concern with one or another version, also dialectically transformed, of the high modernist ideal of 'presentness'.[9] Just as the conspicuous trumping of mechanical causality – the normal progress of exploding fireworks – by the artist's intentions is in line with the high modernist insistence on intentionality all the way down, or rather with the redoubling of that insistence in the work of contemporary artists such as Thomas Demand and Charles Ray.

A final pair of claims: the strongest art of today is far more philosophically interesting and at the same time more genuinely ambitious than standard accounts of the present situation often suggest; and Sala, not yet forty, is at the cutting edge of the developments that make it so.

8 A notable exception: the writings of the philosopher Robert Pippin. See for example Robert B. Pippin, 'What Was Abstract Art? (From the Point of View of Hegel)', *Critical Inquiry* 29 (Autumn 2002), pp. 1–24.
9 This is a major theme in my 1967 essay *Art and Objecthood.*

Mixed Behaviour, 2003

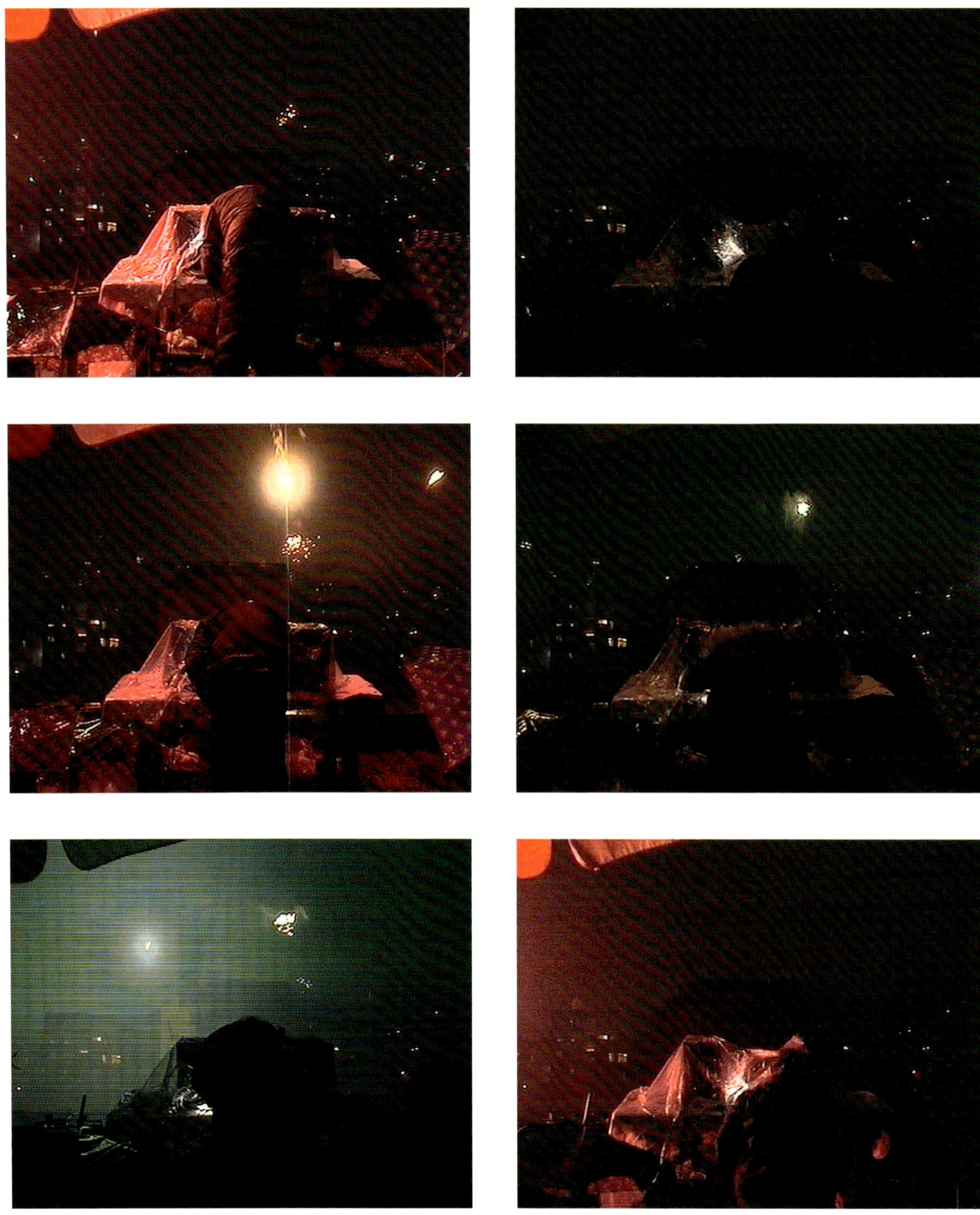

Mixed Behaviour, 2003

ALEKSANDR NEUSKIY

UZAK

YOL

UZAK

ALEKSANDR NEUSKIY

REVERSAL OF FORTUNE

ALEKSANDR NEUSKIY

Why The Lion Roars, 2008 (Forecast 01.01.2009)

NINOTCHKA

ALPHAVILLE
KÁRHOZAT

NAKED

sans toit ni loi

DER LETZTE MANN

sans toit ni loi
NAKED

KÁRHOZAT
ALPHAVILLE
NINOTCHKA
DUEL I HESHTUR

HAROLD AND MAUDE
ZIDANE, UN PORTRAIT DU 21E SIÈCLE
RASHOMON

After HOURS
THE TROUBLE WITH HARRY
MAT I SYN

THE TROUBLE WITH HARRY

After HOURS
RASHOMON

ZIDANE, UN PORTRAIT DU 21E SIÈCLE
HAROLD AND MAUDE

Why The Lion Roars, 2008 (Forecast 01.04.2009)

JALSAGHAR

Rosemary's Baby

Out of the Present

Play Time

L'AVVENTURA

MAT I SYN

L'AVVENTURA

Play Time

Out of the Present

Rosemary's Baby

JALSAGHAR

LE RAYON VERT

THE GREAT GATSBY

Sud sanaeha

THE SWIMMER

MORTE A VENEZIA

UNE PARTIE DE CAMPAGNE

12 angry men

Los Olvidados

DOG DAY AFTERNOON

ET LA LUMIERE FUT

LEPOTA POROKA

ET LA LUMIERE FUT

DOG DAY AFTERNOON

Los Olvidados

12 angry men

UNE PARTIE DE CAMPAGNE

MORTE A VENEZIA

THE SWIMMER

Sud sanaeha

Why The Lion Roars, 2008 (Forecast 01.07.2009)

ZIDANE, UN PORTRAIT DU 21E SIÈCLE

HAROLD AND MAUDE

DUEL I HESHTUR

NINOTCHKA

ALPHAVILLE

KÁRHOZAT

ALPHAVILLE

NINOTCHKA

DUEL I HESHTUR

HAROLD AND MAUDE

ZIDANE, UN PORTRAIT DU 21E SIÈCLE

RASHOMON

After HOURS

THE TROUBLE WITH HARRY

After HOURS

RASHOMON

ZIDANE, UN PORTRAIT DU 21E SIÈCLE

HAROLD AND MAUDE

Why The Lion Roars, 2008 (Forecast 01.10.2009)

Title Suspended (Sky Blue), 2008

Title Suspended (Sky Blue), 2008

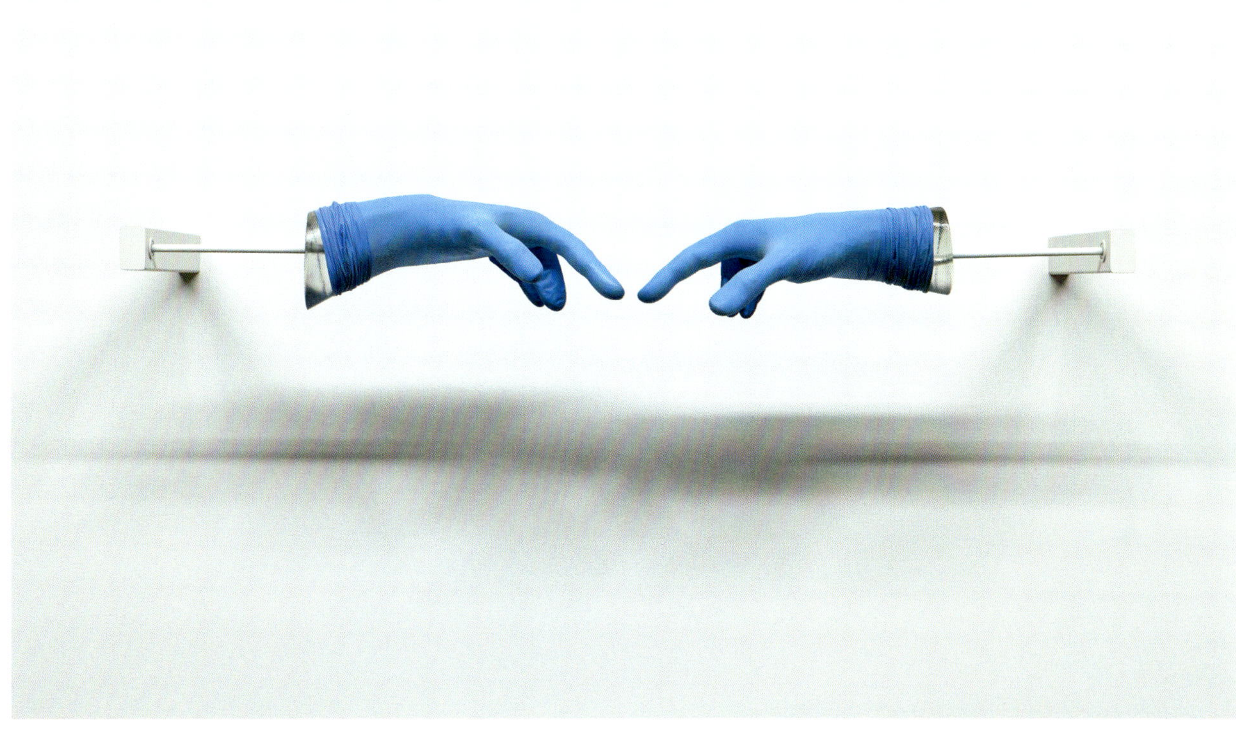

Title Suspended (Sky Blue), 2008

Untitled (Cactus 2), 2011

WORKS IN THE EXHIBTION

Tlatelolco Clash, 2011
HD video projection,
Dolby Digital 5.1
11 min, 49 sec
With Manuel Martínez, Alejandra Arroyo, Petra Salgado, Gerardo Muñoz, Leonor Madera, Manuel Jiménez, Rodolfo Navárez, Patricia Kurczyn, Regina Flores, Maricarmen Martínez, Isidro Vargas, Efraín Rosas, José Valdés, Toña Maldonado, Rodolfo Baltazar, Alejandra España, Mercedes Adalid, Manuel Rocha, Norma Flores
Patrick Ghiringhelli, Lazare Pedron, Olivier Goinard, Nicolas Cantin, Liria Bégéja, Nelly Ollivault, Manola Samaniego, Alejandra España, Cesar Covarrubias, Axel Muñoz
Special thanks to Monica Manzutto; Jose Kuri; Rosario Nadal; Luc Barnier; Manuel Rocha; Lic. Maria del Perpetuo Socorro Villareal, National Coordinator of the Instituto Nacional de Antropología e Historia; Lucia Sánchez Bustamante, Head of the Archeological Site of Tlatelolco; Sergio Raúl Arroyo, Director of the Centro Cultural Universitario Tlatelolco, UNAM; Julieta Giménez Cacho, Coordinación de Difusión Cultural UNAM; Cristina Faesler; Anapaula Zamacona; Philippe Picoli; Grazia Cattaneo; Anaïs de Balincourt; Agnès Fierobe
Courtesy of kurimanzutto, Mexico City; Marian Goodman Gallery, New York; Hauser & Wirth, Zurich, London; Galerie Chantal Crousel, Paris; Kaikai Kiki, Tokyo

3-2-1, 2011
Live performance featuring Andre Vida on saxophone responding to *Long Sorrow*
Duration variable
Special thanks to Clara Meister, Soundfair and VeneKlasen/Werner, Berlin

No Window No Cry (Le Corbusier, Maison-atelier Lipschitz, Boulogne), 2011
Music box, glass, wooden window-frame
135 × 108 × 10 cm
Built by Philippe Picoli, Paris
Special thanks to Grazia Cattaneo Picoli.
Courtesy of Galerie Chantal Crousel, Paris

Score, 2011
Score of *Le Clash* for barrel organ carved into wall
Dimensions variable
Courtesy of the artist

Le Clash, 2010
HD video projection,
Dolby Digital 5.1
8 min, 31 sec
With Philippe Picoli, Martin Denis (Paulo), Sonia Terhzaz
Patrick Ghiringhelli, Olivier Goinard, Liria Bégéja, Luc Barnier, Clara Meister, Lara Blanchy, Xavier Marchand, Augustin Barbaroux
Special thanks to Didier Faustino
Courtesy of Galerie Chantal Crousel, Paris; Marian Goodman Gallery, New York; Hauser & Wirth, Zurich, London; Johnen Galerie, Berlin; kurimanzutto, Mexico City

Doldrum, 2008
Altered Brady snare drum, loudspeaker parts, snare stand, drumsticks
75 × 56 × 41 cm (approx)
Built by Sehring Audio Systeme, Berlin
Sound design and mixing by Olivier Goinard
Special thanks to Stefan Sehring and Manuel Miseur
Courtesy of the artist and Marian Goodman Gallery, New York

Answer Me, 2008
HD video, stereo sound
4 min, 51 sec
Upon an invitation by Nico Dockx
With Ruth Rosenfeld and Krist Torfs
Nico Dockx, Krist Torfs, Kris Delacourt, Patrick Ghiringhelli, Liria Bégéja, Luc Barnier, Lazare Pedron, Stephan Blosche, Jean-Pascal Flavien, Manuel Miseur
Special thanks to Clara Meister, Jochem Vanden Ecker, Rik Desaver, Helena Sidiropoulos and Šejla Kamerić
Courtesy of Marian Goodman Gallery, New York; Hauser & Wirth, Zurich, London; Galerie Chantal Crousel, Paris; Johnen Galerie, Berlin

Title Suspended (Sky Blue), 2008
Resin hands, rubber gloves, motor
67 × 110 × 36 cm
Built by Philippe Picoli, Paris
Special thanks to Yasko Pinard, Laurent Legall, Olivier Favard, Grazia Cattaneo Picoli, Yves Noras, Bruno Coupchoux, Amanda Riffo
Courtesy of Hauser & Wirth, Zurich, London

Long Sorrow, 2005
HD video transferred from super 16 mm colour film, stereo sound
12 min, 57 sec
With Jemeel Moondoc
Produced by Fondazione Nicola Trussardi, Milan
Patrick Ghiringhelli, Lazare Pedron, Olivier Goinard, Julio Rodriguez, Trefor Proud, Kerstin Viot, Henryk Bhme, Jörn Lachmann, Nawrocki Alpin, Holger Nawrocki, Thilo Kosack, Matthias Kahle, M. Günther, Thomas Franke, Manuel Miseur, Jean-Pascal Flavien, Sebastian Schobbert, Matthias Rick, Holger Mischke, Angelo Strobel, Sven Geppert, Liria Bégéja, Luc Barnier, Marion Monnier, Eduardo Villanueva
Special thanks to Karin Dietz, Gesobau; Massimiliano Gioni; Friedrich Meschede; Eduardo Villanueva; Karina Daskalov; Klaus-Dieter Rath, Gesobau
With the support of D.A.A.D., Berlin
Courtesy of Marian Goodman Gallery, New York; Hauser & Wirth, Zurich, London; Galerie Chantal Crousel, Paris; Galerie Rüdiger Schöttle, Munich; Johnen Galerie, Berlin

BIOGRAPHY

1974
Born in Tirana, Albania

1998–2000
Postgraduate Studies,
Le Fresnoy, Studio National des Arts Contemporains, Tourcoing, France

1996–98
École Nationale Supérieure des Arts Décoratifs, Paris

1992–96
National Academy of Arts (BA Painting), Tirana

Lives and works in Berlin

SOLO EXHIBITIONS

2011
Anri Sala, Galerie Chantal Crousel, Paris
Anri Sala, kurimanzutto, Mexico City
Anri Sala, Musée d'art contemporain, Montreal

2010
Anri Sala: Creating Space Where There Appears To Be None, About Change Studio, Berlin

2009
Anri Sala: Purchase Not By Moonlight, Marian Goodman Gallery, New York
Answer Me, Johnen Galerie, Berlin

2008
Anri Sala: Purchase Not By Moonlight, Museum of Contemporary Art North Miami; Contemporary Arts Center, Cincinnati (2009)
Why The Lion Roars, CENTQUATRE, Paris (in collaboration with the Commande artistique de la Ville de Paris 2008)
Long Sorrow, De Pont museum voor hedendaagse kunst, Tilburg, Netherlands
La Mano di Dio, Alfonso Artiaco Gallery, Naples
Anri Sala, Galerie Chantal Crousel, Paris
Anri Sala: Overthinking, Galerie Rüdiger Schöttle, Munich
Anri Sala: Hand of God, Center for Contemporary Art, CCA Kitakyushu
Kabinett für aktuelle Kunst, Bremerhaven

2007
Anri Sala: Long Sorrow, Museu Nacional de Arte Contemporânea – Museu do Chiado, Lisbon
A Second Look, Hauser & Wirth, London
Anri Sala, Marian Goodman Gallery, New York
Thinking Architecture #1: Anri Sala, Extra City, Antwerp
Air Cushioned Ride, Johnen Galerie, Berlin

2006
Galerie Rüdiger Schöttle, Munich
Galerie Chantal Crousel, Paris

2005
History Started Playing With My Life, Kosovo Art Gallery, Prishtina
Long Sorrow, Fondazione Nicola Trussardi, Milan
Anri Sala, Centre for Contemporary Art Ujazdowski Castle, Warsaw
Anri Sala: Artist in Focus, Museum Boijmans van Beuningen, Rotterdam
Anri Sala: Artist in Focus, The 34th International Film Festival Rotterdam
Anri Sala: Time after Time, The Museum of Art, Rhode Island School of Design, Providence
Dammi i Colori, DAAD Galerie, Berlin
Anri Sala: Dammi i Colori, The Mildred S. Lee Gallery, Waltham, Massachusetts

2004
Anri Sala, Yeans Gallery, Gothenburg
Anri Sala, Gallery EXIT, Pejë, Kosova
Alfonso Artiaco Gallery, Naples
Hauser & Wirth, London
Entre chien et loup/When the Night Calls it a Day, Musée d'Art moderne de la Ville de Paris/ARC, Paris; *Wo sich Fuchs und Hase gute Nacht sagen,* Deichtorhallen, Hamburg
Now I See, The Art Institute of Chicago
Marian Goodman Gallery, New York

2003
Galerie Johnen & Schöttle, Cologne
Anri Sala, Kunsthalle Vienna
All Gone, Center for Contemporary Art, CCA Kitakyushu

2002
Oficina Para Proyectos de Arte, Guadalajara, Mexico
Anri Sala, Ikon Gallery, Birmingham
Amplified Absorbers, Hauser & Wirth, Zurich
Missing Landscape and Promises, TRANS>area, New York
Concentrations, Dallas Museum of Art
Naturalmystic (tomahawk #2), Galerie Rüdiger Schöttle, Munich
Programa Gallery, Mexico City

2001
It Has Been Raining Here, Galerie Chantal Crousel, Paris
Galerie Rüdiger Schöttle, Munich (with Martin Creed)
Nocturnes, Delfina Project Space, London

2000
De Appel Arts Centre, Amsterdam (with Christian Jankowski)
Galerie Rüdiger Schöttle, Munich (with Torsten Slama)
Galerie Johnen & Schöttle, Cologne (with Martin Boyce)
Nocturnes, Mamco/Le Musée d'art moderne et contemporain, Geneva

SELECTED GROUP EXHIBITIONS

2011
1395 Days Without Red: A film by Anri Sala in collaboration with Liria Bégéja from a project by Šejla Kamerić and Anri Sala with Ari Benjamin Meyers, The Whitworth Art Gallery, Manchester; Museu d'Art Contemporani de Barcelona/MACBA; Club Marbeuf, Paris
Animal Kingdom: There Was An Old Lady Who…, Schinkel Pavillon, Berlin
Les cadeaux du présent, Centre d'Art Neuchâtel, Switzerland
Chamber of Lights, Muzeum Sztuki w Łodzi, Poland
Electric Nights, LABoral Centro de Arte y Creación Industrial, Gijón, Spain
French Window: Looking at Contemporary Art through the Marcel Duchamp Prize, Mori Art Museum, Tokyo
8 1/2: A Selection of Works from the Exhibitions Organised by the Fondazione Nicola Trussardi from 2003 to the Present, Stazione Leopolda, Florence

2010
Faux Amis/An Ephemeral Video Library, Jeu de Paume, Paris
Haunted: Contemporary *Photography/Video/Performance,* Solomon R. Guggenheim Museum, New York
There is always a cup of sea to sail in, 29th São Paulo Biennial
Les Promesses du Passé. Une histoire discontinue de l'art dans l'ex-Europe de l'Est, Centre Pompidou, Paris
Catch Me! Grasping Speed, Kunsthaus Graz, Austria
Photo I, Photo You, Calvert 22, London
…on the Eastern Front. Video Art from Central and Eastern Europe 1989–2009, Ludwig Museum, Budapest

2009
Gender Check. Femininity and Masculinity in Eastern European Art, MUMOK, Vienna
The Spirit of the Haus – 20 Years, Haus der Kulturen der Welt, Berlin
Look Again. Five Visions in Contemporary Video, Tabakalera, Donostia-San Sebastian
Invasion of Sound. Music and the Visual, Zacheta National Gallery of Art, Warsaw
Vidéos Europa, Le Fresnoy, Studio national d'arts contemporains, Tourcoing, France
Closer, Beirut Art Center, Lebanon

2008
Medium Religion, ZKM Zentrum für Kunst und Medientechnologie, Karlsruhe, Germany
Ego-Documents, Kunstmuseum Bern, Switzerland
Thinking the World, Centrale électrique, Brussels
Modern Ruin, Queensland Art Gallery, Brisbane
Lost Paradise – The Angel's Gaze, Zentrum Paul Klee, Bern
Eclipse – Art in a Dark Age, Moderna Museet, Stockholm
Die Lucky Bush, Museum van Hedendaagse Kunst, Antwerp
God & Goods. Spirituality and Mass Confusion, Villa Manin, Passariano
Falling right into place – The Fold in Contemporary Art, Kaiser Wilhelm Museum Krefeld, Germany
Archive Fever: Uses of the Document in Contemporary Art, International Center of Photography, New York
Signals in the Dark: Art in the Shadow of War, Blackwood Gallery, University of Toronto Mississauga; Leonard & Bina Ellen Art Gallery, Concordia University, Montreal; Model Arts & Niland Gallery, Sligo (2009)

2007
Euro-Centric, Part 1: European Art from the Rubell Family Collection, Miami
Existencias, Museo de Arte Contemporáneo de Castilla y León/MUSAC, Spain
Rethinking Dissent, Gothenburg International Biennial for Contemporary Art, Sweden
Imágenes del otro lado, Centro Atlántico de Arte Moderno, Las Palmas de Gran Canaria
Il tempo del Postino, Opera House, Manchester (in collaboration with Manchester International Festival); Theater Basel, Basel (2009)
Her(his)tory, Museum of Cycladic Art, Athens
MARTa is silent, MARTa Herford, Germany
Silence. Listen to the Show, Fondazione Sandretto Re Rebaudengo, Turin
In the Eye of the Storm, Kunstmuseum St. Gallen, Switzerland
Airs de Paris, Centre Pompidou, Paris
The Morning After – Videoarbeiten der Sammlung Goetz, Weserburg Museum of Modern Art, Bremen
L'oeil – écran ou la nouvelle image, Casino Luxembourg – Forum d'art contemporain
2nd Moscow Biennale of Contemporary Art, Russia
Between Borders, Museo de Arte Contemporánea de Vigo/MARCO, Spain
Sensorium Part II – Embodied Experience, Technology and Contemporary Art, List Visual Arts Center, Cambridge, Massachusetts

STAFF OF THE SERPENTINE GALLERY

Director, Serpentine Gallery and Co-Director, Exhibitions and Programmes
Julia Peyton-Jones

Co-Director, Exhibitions and Programmes and Director of International Projects
Hans Ulrich Obrist

Deputy Director
Diane Lennan

Business Assistant
Poppy Parry

Executive Assistants to Julia Peyton-Jones
Katie Doubleday
Natasha Jenkins

Executive Assistant to Hans Ulrich Obrist
Lorraine Two

Junior PA to Hans Ulrich Obrist
Alicia Harrop

Head of Programmes
Sally Tallant

Assistant Curator
Claire Feeley

Gallery Manager
Mike Gaughan

Education Project Curator
Janna Graham

Education Curator
Joceline Howe

Education Project Assistant
Amal Khalaf

Public Programmes Curator
Nicola Lees

Exhibition Curators
Sophie O'Brien
Kathryn Rattee

Assistant Gallery Manager
Jen Wu

Head of Communications
Rose Dempsey

Head of Press
Tom Coupe

Web Editor
William Barret

Communications Co-ordinator
Varind Ramful

Communications Print Manager
Mary Lehner

Head of Development
Louise McKinney

Head of Events
Michelle Anselmo

Head of Grants, Trusts and Foundations
Lee Rodwell

Trusts and Foundations Co-ordinator
Olivia Brinson

Researcher
Victoria Foord

Corporate Development Co-ordinator
Charlie Hill

Editions and Information Manager
Tom Harrisson

Events Manager
Katie Hollingworth

Senior Corporate Development Manager
Katherine Holmgren

Prints Assistant
Matthew Johnstone

Individual Giving Manager
Arianne Lovelace

PA to Head of Development
Susie Murphy

Membership Manager, Individual Giving
Rachel Stephens

Head of Finance
Stephen Rider

Financial Accountant
Vanessa Teixeira

Finance Assistant
Annand Wiffen

HR Co-ordinator
Elizabeth Clayton

Head of Projects
Julie Burnell

Duty Managers
Josh Dowson
Katherine Kiorgaard

Senior Buildings Manager
Chris Gerlach

PA to Head of Projects
Nicola Mitchell

Senior Gallery Assistants
Anna Curtis
Alex Flowers
Amy Gee
Rene Songui
Mary Toal

Gallery Assistants
Bill Rousseau
Charrise Hoult
Claire Dorsett
Daisy Janes
Duncan Woolridge
Hannah Lees
Jeanne Mirodatos
Laura Martin
Laura Meade
Lavinia Singer
Mark Dillon
Nathan Williams
Phil Thompson
Rosalind Inett
Rosie Gibson
Sophie Boyd
Sophie Neilson
Steven Burridge

ACKNOWLEDGEMENTS

Trustees of the Serpentine Gallery
Lord Palumbo Chairman
Felicity Waley-Cohen and Barry Townsley Co-Vice Chairmen
Marcus Boyle Treasurer
Patricia Bickers
Mark Booth
Roger Bramble
Marco Compagnoni
David Fletcher
Bonnie Greer
Zaha Hadid
Rob Hersov
Colin Tweedy

40th Anniversary Founding Benefactors
Jeanne and William Callanan
The Highmont Foundation
The Luma Foundation

And Founding Benefactors who wish to remain anonymous

Council of the Serpentine Gallery
Rob Hersov Chairman
Marlon Abela
Mrs Basil Al-Rahim
Shaikha Paula Al-Sabah
Goga Ashkenazi
Mr and Mrs Harry Blain
Mr and Mrs F. Boglione
Mark and Lauren Booth
Sarah and Ivor Braka
Alessandro Cajrati Crivelli
Jeanne and William Callanan
Raye Cosbert
Aud and Paolo Cuniberti
Carolyn Dailey
Russ DeLeon and Serge Tiroche
Griet Dupont
Denise Esfandi
Jenifer Evans
Mark Evans
Lawton W. Fitt and James I. McLaren Foundation
Kathrine and Cecilie Fredriksen
Olivier de Givenchy
Jonathan Goodwin
Mr and Mrs Lorenzo Grabau
Richard and Odile Grogan
Jennifer and Matthew Harris
Susan and Richard Hayden
Michael Jacobson
Mr and Mrs Tim Jefferies
Mrs Kristi Jernigan
Ella Krasner
Mr and Mrs Jonathan Lourie
The Luma Foundation
Giles Mackay
Pia-Christina Miller
Catherine and Franck Petitgas
Eva Rausing
The Red Mansion Foundation
Yvonne Rieber
Thaddaeus Ropac
Spas and Diliana Roussev
Robin Saunders and Matthew Roeser
Anders and Yukiko Schroeder
David and Simone Sproul
Ahmed and Cherine Tayeb
Robert Tomei
Andrei Tretyakov
Andy Valmorbida
Robert and Felicity Waley-Cohen
Bruno Wang
Andrew and Victoria Watkins-Ball
Mr and Mrs Lars Windhorst
Manuela and Iwan Wirth
Anna and Michael Zaoui

And members of the Council who wish to remain anonymous

Council's Circle of the Serpentine Gallery
Eric and Sophie Archambeau
Len Blavatnik
Wayne and Helene Burt
Nicholas Candy
Edwin C. Cohen and The Blessing Way Foundation
Ricki Gail Conway
Guy and Andrea Dellal
Marie Douglas-David
Johan Eliasch
Joey Esfandi
Mala and Oliver Haarmann
The Hon Robert Hanson
Petra and Darko Horvat
Mr and Mrs Michael Hue-Williams
Dakis Joannou
Jolana Leinson and Petri Vainio
Elena Bowes Marano
Jimmy and Becky Mayer
Matthew Mellon, in memory of Isabella Blow
Tamara Mellon
Martin and Amanda Nowoon
J. Harald Orneberg
Stephen and Yana Peel
Silvio and Monica Scaglia
Olivia Schuler-Voith
Mrs Nadja Swarovski-Adams
Phoebe and Bobby Tudor
Hugh Warrender
Beatrice Warrender
Michael Watt
John and Amelia Winter

And members of the Council's Circle who wish to remain anonymous

Founding Corporate Benefactor
Bloomberg

Exclusive Professional Services Adviser
Deloitte LLP

Platinum Corporate Benefactors
Arup
Bloomberg
Burberry
Finch & Partners
Hiscox
The Independent
J.P. Morgan Private Bank
Mace Group
Maybach
Meyer Sound
Omni Colour Presentations
Stanhope Plc
Weil, Gotshal & Manges

Gold Corporate Benefactors
Elliott Thomas
The Kensington Hotel
Laurent-Perrier
Stage One
The Times
Viabizzuno
Wallpaper

Silver Corporate Benefactors
H. Stern
Knight Frank LLP
mlogic
The Portman Estate

Bronze Corporate Benefactors
Boujis
By Word of Mouth
The Coca-Cola Company
De Beers Diamond Jewellers Ltd
DLD Media GmbH
DP9
DPA Microphones
The Groucho Club
The Hub
The Landscape Group
Morgan Stanley
Samsung
SCA
Site Engineering Surveys Ltd (SES)
Smoke & Mirrors
T.Clarke Plc

Education Projects supported by
Bloomberg

Education Programme supported by
The Annenberg Foundation
Big Lottery Fund Awards for All
Camden Council
City Bridge Trust
Marie Donnelly
Eranda Foundation
Ernest Cook Trust
David Fawkes and family
The Haskel Family Foundation
Heritage Lottery Fund
J G Hogg Charitable Trust
Housing Corporation
ICE Futures Charitable Trust
The Kobler Trust
John Lyon's Charity
London Councils
The Mercers' Company
The National Lottery through Arts Council England
PRS Foundation
The Rayne Foundation
The Dr Mortimer and Theresa Sackler Foundation
The Scotshill Trust
Westminster City Council

And kind assistance from
The Lone Pine Foundation
The Nyda and Oliver Prenn Foundation
Old Broad Street Charity Trust

The Philip and Irene Gage Foundation
The Royal Borough of Kensington and Chelsea
The N. Smith Charitable Settlement
Westminster Arts

Exhibition Programme supported by

Marlon Abela, Morton's Club
Charles Asprey
Colección Helga de Alvear, Madrid-Cáceres, Spain
The Colwinston Charitable Trust
Culturesfrance
Galleria Continua
Galerie Daniel Buchholz, Berlin/Köln
Larry Gagosian/Gagosian Gallery
Gavin Brown's enterprise
Barbara Gladstone, New York
The Graham Foundation for Advanced Studies in the Fine Arts
Hauser & Wirth Zürich London
The Stanley Thomas Johnson Foundation
Mrs Katrin Henkel
The Henry Moore Foundation
The Luma Foundation
Catherine and Pierre Lagrange
Lia Rumma Gallery
Lisson Gallery
La Fondation Louis Vuitton pour la création
Luhring Augustine, New York
Matthew Marks, New York
The National Lottery through Arts Council England
Pro Helvetia
The Red Mansion Foundation
The Robert Mapplethorpe Foundation, Inc.
Ruth and Richard Rogers
Simon Lee Gallery
The Swiss Cultural Fund in Britain
The Embassy of Sweden
Thea Westreich/Ethan Wagner

Learning Council Committee

Jeanne and Willian Callanan
Gilberto Pozzi
Selina S. Sagayam
Hugh Warrender

Learning Council Members

Brian and Melinda Carroll
Andrew and Jane Partridge
Alta Thorne

Patrons

Marie-Claire, Baroness von Alvensleben
Sofia Barattieri di san Pietro
Humphrey and Ginny Battcock
Colleen de Bonis
Christina Boothe
Mr and Mrs Charles Bracken
Patrick Brennan
Mr & Mrs W. S. Broeksmit
Clarissa Alcock Bronfman
The Rory and Elizabeth Brooks Foundation
Mrs Susan Burns
Dr Martin A. Clarke
Sir Ronald and Lady Cohen
Terence and Niki Cole
Alastair Cookson
Davide Costa
Giulia Costantini
Christie's
Andrea Dibelius
Frank and Lorna Dunphy
Dr Paul Ettlinger
The Edwin Fox Foundation
Mrs Carmen Engelhorn
Fares and Tania Fares
David Fawkes
John Frieda and
Avery Agnelli Frieda
Francesca von Habsburg
The Harman Foundation
Ivana Hasecic and Laurent Cadji
Mrs Katrin Henkel
Ariadna Garcia-Ayats
Yassmin Ghandehari
Karine Giannamore
Francesca Guagnini
Sara Harrison
Jasmine Horowitz
Eva and Iraj Ispahani
Mr and Mrs Karim Juma
Mrs Ghislaine Kane
Tessa Keswick
Ms Audrey Lynn Klein
Martina and Yves Klemmer
Catherine Lagrange
Pierre Lagrange
Mr and Mrs Simon Lee
Natalie Livingstone
Andrew and Jacqueline Martin
Eileen and Liad Meidar
Jeff and Valerie Montgomery
Mr Donald Moore
Gregor Muir
Paul and Alison Myners
Joseph and Chloe O'Sullivan
Christina Pamberg
Andrew and Jane Partridge
Mr A.S. Rahman
Mr and Mrs Ivan Ritossa
Kim Samuel-Johnson
Rupert Sanderson
Mr and Mrs Mark Shanker
John Stefanidis
Siri Stolt-Nielsen
Ian and Mercedes Stoutzker
Simon and Fiona Thomas
Alta Hagan Thorne
Laura and Barry Townsley
Rebecca Wang
Helen and Peter Warwick
Peter Wheeler and Pascale Revert
Mrs Pauline Witzenfeld
Cynthia Wu
Poju and Anita Zabludowicz

Future Contemporaries Committee

Alia Al-Senussi
Flora Fairbairn
Tim Franks
Rebecca Guinness
Liz Kabler
Dan Macmillan
Bobby Molavi
Jake Parkinson-Smith
Cristina Revert
Andreas Siegfried
Stan Stalnaker
Christopher Taylor
F. Uribe
Marcus and Alexa Waley-Cohen
Jonathan Wood

Future Contemporaries Members

Sharifa Alsudairi
Abdullah Alturki
Kamel Alzarka
Mr and Mrs Ben Arbib
Marco Assetto
Flavie Audi
Anja and António Batista
Philip Beatty
Max Bergius
Margherita Berloni
Elena Bonanno di Linguaglossa
The Hon. Alexander Brennan
Ben Bridgewater
James and Felicia Brocklebank
Chris Byrne
William Burlington
Jessica Carlisle
C. Cartellieri
Antony Clavel and Maria Novella Vecere
Patrick C. Cunningham
Indi Davis
Roxanna Farboud
Mrs Selma Feriani
Mrs Deana Goldstein
Marie Guerlain
Michael Hadjedj
Mr S. Haq
Matt Hermer
Carolyn Hodler
Nicholas W. Hofgren
Julia Hofmann
Olivia Howell and Michael Patterson
Kamel Jaber
Karim Jallad
Marina Jovanovic
Zoe Karafylakis Sperling
Chloe Kinsman
John Krasner
Niels Kroner
Mans Larsson
Maged Latif
Arianne Levene
Kai Lew
James Lindon
Dan Lywood
Sonia Mak
Jean-David Malat
Marina Marini
Jose Mazoy
Anne Mellentin
John Paul Micalleff
Laura Modiano
Fernando J. Moncho Lobo
Sheryl Needham
Isabelle Nowak and Torsten Winkler
David Olsson
Sophie Orde
Samira Parkinson-Smith
Catherine Patha
Anja Pauls
Julia Pincus
Carlos and Francesca Pinto
Mike Radcliffe
Farah Rahim Ismail
Laurent Rappaport
Piotr Rejmer
Claudia Ruimy

Poppy Sebire
Xandi Schemann
Alyssa Sherman
Tammy Smulders
Christopher Thomsen
Jonathan Tyler
Andy Valmorbida
Mr and Mrs Vincent Van Heyste
Rachel Verghis
Sam Waley-Cohen
Trent Ward
Lucy Wood
Omar Giovanni Zaghis
Mr and Mrs Nabil Zaouk
Fabrizio D. Zappaterra

Benefactors

Mr and Mrs Allahyar Afshar
Shane Akeroyd
Mr Niklas Antman and Miss Lisa Almen
Paul and Kia Armstrong
Jane Attias
Anne Best and Roddy Kinkead-Weekes
Roger and Beverley Bevan
Anthony and Gisela Bloom
Mr and Mrs John Botts
Marcus Boyle
Mervyn and Helen Bradlow
Vanessa Branson
Benjamin Brown
Ed Burstell
Mrs Tita Granda Byrne
Lavinia Calza Beveridge
Azia Chatila
Paul Clifford
Sadie Coles
Carole and Neville Conrad
Matthew Conrad
Gul Coskun
Yasmine Datnow
Mr and Mrs Colin David
Mr and Mrs Christopher Didizian
Robin and Noelle Doumar
Mike Fairbrass
Mr and Mrs Mark Fenwick
John Ferreira
Hako and Dörte, Graf and Gräfin von Finckenstein
David and Jane Fletcher
Eric and Louise Franck
Alan and Joanna Gemes
Zak and Candida Gertler
Leonardo and Alessia Giangreco
Hugh Gibson
Peter Gidal
David Gill
Dimitri J. Goulandris
Richard and Judith Greer
Linda and Richard Grosse
Louise Hallett
Liz Hammond
Jeremy Hargreave
Susan Harris
Timothy and Daska Hatton
Maria and Stratis Hatzistefanis
Alison Henry-Davies
Mrs Christine Johnston
Marcelle Joseph and Paolo Cicchiné
Jennifer Kersis
James and Clare Kirkman
Mr and Mrs Lahoud
Geraldine Larkin
Anne and Sydney Levinson
George and Angie Loudon
Sotiris T.F. Lyritzis
Mr Otto Julius Maier and Mrs Michèle Claudel-Maier
Cary J. Martin
Mr and Mrs Stephen Mather
Ruth and Robert Maxted
Viviane and James Mayor
Warren and Victoria Miro
Gillian Mosely
Dr Maigaelle Moulene
Paul Munford
Georgia Oetker
Tamiko Onozawa
Teresa Oulton
Desmond Page and Asun Gelardin
Maureen Paley
Dominic Palfreyman
Midge and Simon Palley
Julia Peyton-Jones OBE
Sophie Price
Mathew Prichard
Mrs Janaki Prosdocimi
Ashraf Qizilbash
Bruce and Shadi Ritchie
Kasia Robinski
Kimberley Robson-Ortiz
Jacqueline and Nicholas Roe
Fabio Rossi
Victoria, Lady de Rothschild
James Roundell and Bona Montagu
Michael and Julia Samuel
Ronnie and Vidal Sassoon
Joana and Henrik Schliemann
Nick Simou and Julie Gatland
Bina and Philippe von Stauffenberg
Tanya and David Steyn
Simone and Robert Suss
The Thames Wharf Charity
Britt Tidelius
Gretchen and Jus Trusted
Audrey Wallrock
Lady Corinne Wellesley
Alannah Weston
Helen Ytuarte White
Dr Yvonne Winkler
Mr Ulf Wissen
Henry and Rachel Wyndham
Mr and Mrs Nabil Zaouk

And Learning Council, Patrons, Future Contemporaries and Benefactors who wish to remain anonymous

Supported by

Arts Council England
The Royal Parks
Westminster City Council

This catalogue is published on the occasion of the exhibition *Anri Sala* at the Serpentine Gallery, London, 1 October – 20 November 2011.

Exhibition curated by

Julia Peyton-Jones
Director, Serpentine Gallery and Co-Director, Exhibition and Programmes

Hans Ulrich Obrist
Co-Director, Exhibition and Programmes and Director, International Projects

Kathryn Rattee
Exhibition Curator

Supported by

LUMA
FOUNDATION
Council of the Serpentine Gallery and
Hauser & Wirth

Exhibition Patrons
Ramdane Touhami
Zumtobel Group
and those who wish to remain anonymous

With additonal support from

agnès b. london endowment fund !!

Media Partner

THE INDEPENDENT

The Serpentine Gallery is supported by

Edited by
Kathryn Rattee and Melissa Larner

Designed by
Studio Quentin Walesch
(Quentin Walesch, Julian von Klier)

Printed at
Pöge Druck, Leipzig (DE)
Bound at
Buchbinderei Mönch OHG, Leipzig (DE)

ISBN 978-3-86335-098-7
(Koenig Books, London)

ISBN 978-1-908617-00-2
(Serpentine Gallery, London)

Opening Pages:
pp. 1 + 128: *Score,* 2011
pp. 2 + 127: *Score,* 2011
pp. 3 + 126: *Tlatelolco Clash,* 2011
pp. 4 + 125: *Tlatelolco Clash,* 2011
pp. 5 + 124: *Le Clash,* 2010
pp. 6 + 123: *Le Clash,* 2010
pp. 7–10: *Score,* 2011

Cover Image:
Tlatelolco Clash, 2011

Dust Jacket:
Tlatelolco Clash, 2011
Long Sorrow, 2005

Credits:
pp. 1, 22, 128: Installation view, Galerie Chantal Crousel, Paris, 2011, photograph by Florian Kleinefenn
pp. 2, 54, 59, 111–113, 127: Installation view, Musée d'art contemporain de Montréal, 2011, photograph by Guy L'Heureux and Richard-Max Tremblay
p. 47: Installation view, Fondazione Nicola Trussardi, Milan, 2005, photograph by Marco De Scalzi
p. 53: Installation view, kurimanzutto, Mexico City, 2011, photograph by Estudio Michel Zabé
p. 72: Photograph by Juliana Santacruz
pp. 75–76, 81: Performance at VeneKlasen/Werner, Berlin, in collaboration with Soundfair, 2011, photograph by Friederike Seifert
p. 82: Installation view, Museion – Museo d'arte moderna e contemporanea, Bolzano, 2008

All photographs by the artist unless otherwise stated.

The artist would like to thank:
My deepest appreciation to Julia Peyton-Jones, Hans Ulrich Obrist and Kathryn Rattee for their approach, commitment and synergy; Andre Vida for his unique input; Michael Fried and Joshua Simon for their insightful thoughts; Quentin Walesch for the incisive design of this book; Lewin Quehl, Mike Gaughan, Frank Bode and the team at Eidotech, for their commitment and skill in making it present; Hauser & Wirth, Marian Goodman Gallery, Galerie Chantal Crousel, kurimanzutto, for their support; and Rosario Nadal.
I would like to express my deepest gratitude to Liria Bégéja, Patrick Ghiringhelli and Olivier Goinard whose continuous input and contribution has been invaluable in the making of the films in this show.

Serpentine Gallery
Kensington Gardens
London W2 3XA
T +44 (0)20 7402 6075
F +44 (0)20 7402 4103
www.serpentinegallery.org

First published by
Koenig Books London
Koenig Books Ltd
At the Serpentine Gallery
Kensington Gardens
London W2 3XA
www.koenigbooks.co.uk

Distribution:
Buchhandlung Walther König, Köln
Ehrenstr. 4, 50672 Köln
T: +49 (0) 221/20 59 6-53
F: +49 (0) 221/20 59 6-60
verlag@buchhandlung-walther-koenig.de

Switzerland:
AVA Verlagsauslieferungen AG
Centralweg 16
CH-8910 Affoltern a.A.
T: +41 (44) 762 42 60
F: +41 (44) 762 42 10
verlagsservice@ava.ch

UK & Eire:
Cornerhouse Publications
70 Oxford Street
Manchester M1 5NH
T: +44 (0) 161 200 15 03
F: +44 (0) 161 200 15 04
publications@cornerhouse.org

Outside Europe:
D.A.P./Distributed Art Publishers, Inc.
155 6th Avenue, 2nd Floor
New York, NY 10013
T: +1 212-627-1999
F: +1 212-627-9484
www.artbook.com

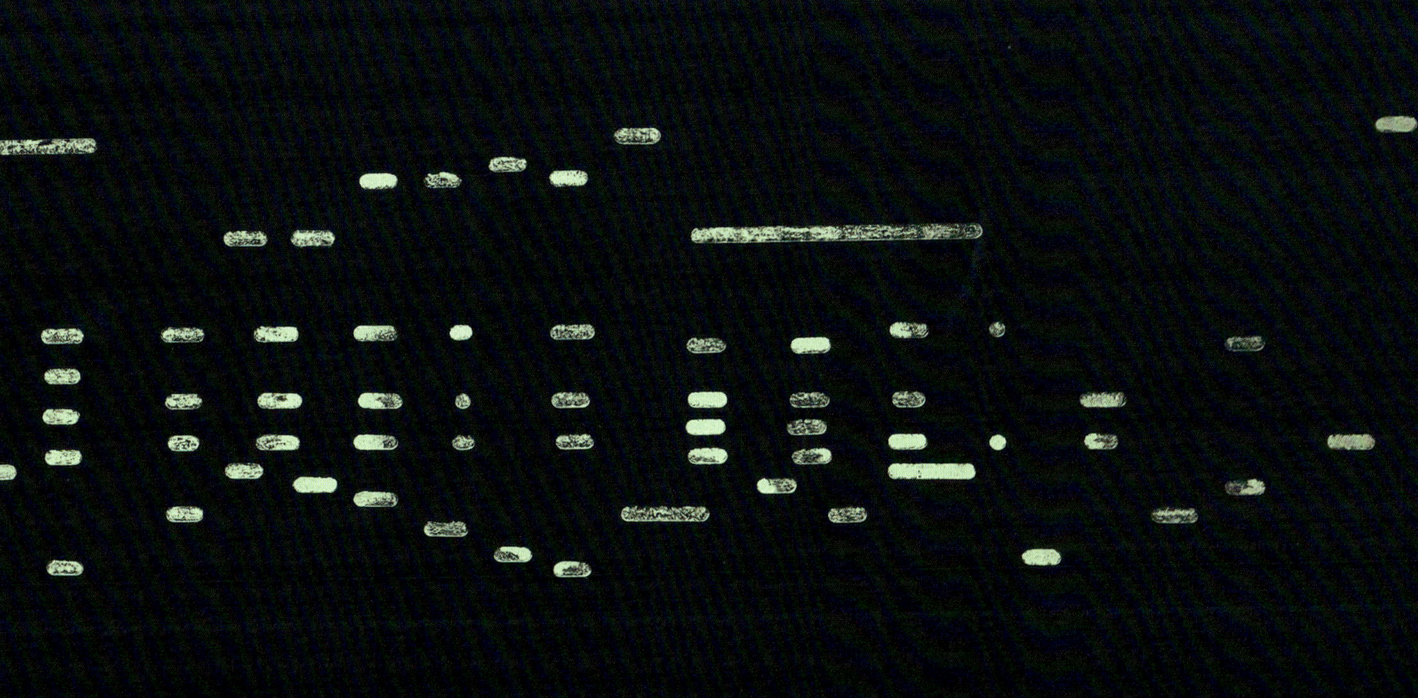